THE MOUNTBATTENS
— AND —
THE MAKING OF MODERN INDIA

K Z ISLAM

THE MOUNTBATTENS
&
THE MAKING OF MODERN INDIA

By

K. Z. ISLAM

Author:

K. Z. Islam

Publisher

Ghostwriting Partner

www.ghostwritingpartner.com

Prologue

The Partition of India in 1947 was one of the most consequential and tragic upheavals of the twentieth century. While a land was torn apart by political chaos, communal carnage and human displacement, there's one man at its centre — Lord Louis Mountbatten, last Viceroy of British India. This book is not just catalogue of the events of those fateful months, but seeks to understand how and, more importantly, why Mountbatten came to be a such a key figure in the subcontinent's destiny.

His appointment was neither a product of democratic deliberation nor colonial precedent. It was, as Clement Attlee claimed, an "inspiration." Yet this assertion is contested by other witnesses and sources, hinting at a deeper network of influence, royal lobbying, and political calculation. Mountbatten's charm, naval distinction, and royal pedigree cloaked an alarming lack of political insight into India's complex realities. He entered the theatre of Partition armed with intuition, not expertise.

This was then followed by a chaos of hurriedly drafted plans; back room deals and a dangerous speeding up of India's division. Mountbatten's political role, however, was not that of a neutral executor, as its partisanship was particularly evident in his personal relationship with Nehru and the Congress leadership. As in official histories, the intimacy between Edwina Mountbatten and Nehru was routinely denied and seldom discussed; but the subliminal effect of it on the emotional temperature of a delicate transition was never considered.

Mountbatten surrounded himself with carefully selected aides, including a Press Attaché — a first for a Viceroy — ensuring that the narrative projected to the world was one of noble exit and orderly transfer. But the documents, testimonies, and post-Partition consequences tell a more troubling story. This was not merely an imperial withdrawal; it was a rushed disengagement, executed with charisma but little foresight, leaving millions in suffering and South Asia permanently scarred.

This book does not aim to glorify or condemn Mountbatten. Instead, it attempts to debunk the myths that have surrounded his viceroyalty and tries to answer the question whether India's Partition was navigated with vision or vagueness, resolve or expedience. This narrative is based on declassified archives, personal correspondence, and divergent accounts in order to bring Murphy's legacy into reevaluation — to neither condemn nor praise, but to understand the train wreck that was imperial withdrawal and the tragic human cost it extracted from, probably, more haste and ambition than understanding.

Acknowledgement

By writing of this book, it explores the complicated and stormy years of the 1947 Partition of India and the decisive leadership of Lord Louis Mountbatten, would be impossible without the efforts of many individuals and organisations whose support, knowledge, and inspiration have been invaluable.

Above all, I would like to thank the librarians and experts from organisations like the Broadlands Trust, the Nehru Memorial Museum and Library, and the National Archives of India and the United Kingdom for their vigilant preservation of declassified files, personal letters, and historical documents that were the starting point for this study. Access to Nehru's letters, Mountbatten's official files, and the Transfer of Power were invaluable in reconstructing a balanced narrative that challenges myths and presents new insights of the time of partition in 1947.

I owe a deep gratitude to the historians and scholars whose earlier research on the Partition, Mountbatten, and South Asian historiography influenced and motivated the initiative to writing this book. The careful analysis and commitment to laying bare the political and human aspects of this era were an inspiration for me. I want in particular to thank those individuals responsible for their unpublished writings or discussions that helped to refine the scope of this book's scriptures, notably on the contentious Power Transfer and decisions of the immediate post-Transfer period and their calamitous outcome.

I also express my sincere gratitude to my research assistants, whose long hours of sorting through vast archives, cross-checking sources, and collating facts were invaluable. Their dedication for fact-checking and their capacity for spotting elusive yet essential details added immeasurably to the account. I further owe gratitude to my editors and peer reviewers, whose feedback improved the manuscript, ensuring clarity and balance in tackling a subject as contentious as Partition.

I want to thank my family and my friends for their enduring support and forbearance through long hours of writing and research. Your encouragement kept me going in moments of doubt and fatigue. I dedicate this book finally to the voiceless millions of victims of the Partition, those who suffered unimaginable displacement and loss of many lives. Their lives, usually neglected in official histories, are the core of this volume, and I hope that for all that is said here, this narrative does support their strength and dignity with justice.

This is a collaborative effort, and any errors or omissions are my responsibility. I extend my heartfelt gratitude to all those who assisted me directly or indirectly.

Dedication

The 20th century will be remembered as the century during which mankind butchered more human beings than any other in history. Even a rough estimation of **200 million** is a staggering figure. During this period disputants harnessed engineering inventions on an unprecedented scale to resolve their differences via force of arms.

The resulting immensely costly wars completed the destruction of empires. The conflicts ushered in new political structures in which populations, instead of being ruled by aristocrats, chose governments that were accountable to their citizens.

This radical transformation relied on efficient military innovations that killed massive numbers of combatants and non-combatants alike. More and more defenceless civilians fell victim to the machinery of battle.

Among the numerous instances of carnage that broke out was the Partition of British India into Pakistan and India. Instead of the planned peaceful division of a sub-continent into two states and the smooth transfer of inhabitants, massacres erupted between two major religious groups, namely Hindus and Muslims.

The wounds and scars of that fateful year, 1947, keep erupting periodically-and therefore remain fresh. Ironically subsequent wars between the successor states have compounded existing misery. Regrettably both sides have failed to learn lessons.

The decision to divide the Indian Subcontinent was made by individuals largely unelected and unaccountable. On the other hand, those who would be profoundly and often tragically affected by the Partition were not consulted nor were their views sought. Their stories remain untold.

Individuals who led the partition movement were offered Solomon's choice. Regrettably, they did not have his wisdom.

Table of Contents

CHAPTER 1: INTRODUCING MOUNTBATTEN

Mountbatten: Whose Choice?

Prince Louis Francis Albert Victor Nicholas of Battenberg, mostly known as Lord Mountbatten (neversuchinnocence.com)

At the outset let it be stated categorically that Louis Francis Albert Victor Nicholas Mountbatten was one of the most outstanding personalities of the twentieth century. As his official biographer Philip Ziegler adulates, "He was glamorous, indecently handsome, married to one of Europe's richest and most beautiful heiresses. He was (in youth) a playboy who counted Douglas Fairbanks and Mary Pickford among his closest friends and who starred with his wife in a movie that Charlie Chaplin made just for them. Everything about him was on gigantic scale: his courage (Noel Coward's World War II Film in Which We Serve was based on Mountbatten's heroism at sea), charismatic charm, energy, generosity; his vanity, arrogance, manipulation of the truth.". His fascinating biography will be presented for the readers to relish. However, our present concern is to ascertain as to how Mountbatten was chosen to be the last Viceroy of India.

Clement Attlee for whom the chroniclers do not seem to have much eulogy has claimed in his autobiography *A Prime Minister Remembers* "I thought very hard and looked all around. And suddenly I had what I now think was an inspiration, I thought of Mountbatten." On the other hand, H.V. Hodson in his *The Great Divide* states, "The story that Sir Stafford Cripps virtually nominated Lord Mountbatten after bringing him and Pandit Nehru together is false, though it is also false to deduce from Lord Attlee's recollection that he alone made the choice in a flash". So, we already see two different versions from two eminent sources Several versions will be quoted. One wonders if an extensive research has been undertaken to determine precisely how the choice of the Viceroyalty fell on Lord Mountbatten.

To begin with let us see what Mountbatten has to say himself as to how he was chosen. Larry Collins and Dominique Lapierre the authors of *Freedom at Midnight*, an inaccurate but thoroughly readable book on his Viceroyalty interviewed Mountbatten over countless hours. *Freedom at Midnight* as Philip Ziegler has stated, "is remarkable chiefly for the faithfulness with which it portrays the history of the period as Lord Mountbatten would have wished it to be seen." A part of the interview of Collins and Lapierre in *Mountbatten and the Partition of India* is given below for the readers to draw their own conclusions.

Q. Why do you suppose the choice to become the last Viceroy fell on you? What ties did you have to India that would have recommended you to Attlee?

The BBC conducted a summary of sorts on India during their series known as All Our Yesterdays, to which they invited a young conceited man by the name of James Cameron. To quote him, 'Mountbatten did an extraordinary job of political manipulation without knowing anything about politics. Very, very, interesting. 'He had this strange intuition that he got the information and somehow or other he computerised it and came up with the right answer. But I don't think he could ever have told how he came to that conclusion. Very, very, very, very interesting. In fact, he's the only (member of a) Royal House who's done a constructive job as far as I know.'

The most intriguing thing for me is that there is a newspaper journalist who reports events for the current affairs and he has travelled the country delivering lectures and interviews and talks. in his opinion, I happened to reach the correct answers purely by 'intuition.' As a royal family member, one simply cannot possess a single brain cell, but lo and behold, I apparently came to the 'intuitive' solution!

Q. Did I ever show you the little farthing I got for a lecture on India?

In 1931, the Postwar Brotherhood of Portsmouth assigned me a lecture, and they required that I charge a fee of at least a farthing. I earned 1 farthing, as well as additional words for my actual speech, "for his brilliant and interesting speech on India." An hour's duration, 1931.

I bring this up because it demonstrates how I have never given up on the topic of India. And that a correspondent of a newspaper who has considered himself the self-proclaimed professional in India for all these years, should up until now have misread me is interesting. I do not think he would dispute this, since it was logged.

Q. Why didn't Stafford Cripps insist on going out as Viceroy himself?

He was well aware that he lacked everything a Viceroy is expected to have. As I said before, I think one requires and, if possible, someone helps incorporate a figure like what I have referred to as a leader. None whatsoever... his sibling Fred - wonderful hunter, polo enthusiast, lavish gentleman - he had ten times the leadership Stafford did. One cannot possess leadership without indulging in drinking, smoking, or eating at least something... I think the same appeal came with Anthony Eden. Did you notice how he was eager to go out with me? He was fully aware that he had everything figured out and all that was needed was strength to mobilise me, what he sorely miscalculated (it seems to me that all of them did) was that I am also fully capable of answering my own questions.

Q. Do you think the Labour Government was looking for a scape-goat in you - in case it all went wrong?

'Not by Attlee - for one very simple reason. Attlee had learnt to respect - not the way I conducted the war, but the way I conducted the post-war liberations, which I did with him. That's what made him choose me.'

Q. While going to India, you brought with you a Press Attache. No Viceroy had one in the past. That seemed to be a misplaced approach. If the Press had to be dealt with, it should have been done by the Private Secretary, not by some Press Attache. Many believed that was a big blunder. You got into a lot of trouble for that and Alan Campbell-Johnson had quite a hard time when he went to India, had he not?

"I'll tell you one thing", the King said to me later, "it's the best thing you ever did, we could not have otherwise got through to the world press". You see, they couldn't see the point of that, and that was one of the first appointments I made. Even in E n g l a n d, Attlee said, "Why do you want a Press Attache?"

None saw the point. God, if I hadn't had Campbell-Johnson to soften up the Press...They were absolutely eating out of our hands in the end. If it had gone wrong, we would have had the most awfully tough time.

Q. You mean a Press Attache not only gives out information but also gets feedback?

Of course. What must be understood is...There was a type of sentiment in the air abroad – I'm not arguing about envy (that there was enormous of), but about a certain disquiet – disbelief, to be precise, that with my history. The job was too good for my background. They would expect that for every situation somebody else had worked for me - and no one has ever been more obstinate at every juncture than I was. Many people, however, still thought I was really the Royal 'front.

Q. You had acquired a reputation in the popular press before as a kind of playboy, hadn't you?

Yes. Yachting and polo... They genuinely believed that I was some arrogant guy who poured his intelligence into collections after the success of a war, when in fact, I was, and always will be, a nerdy bookworm who worked non-stop up until that point. Everything about my life has been fully mapped out in a sequence leading up to what comes next.

Q. What were your own feelings about your appointment?

I was raised with a peculiar longing for the position of Viceroy for as long as I could remember. That came from being out in 1921 and thinking India was the most marvelous country and the Viceroy had the most marvelous job. India, to me, was an incredibly magnificent country; the Viceroy's position was delightful to think about. Much to my dissatisfaction, I was unable to pursue such fantasy. I appreciated my time in the Navy, but with such a job in mind, it was clear there was no possibility of attaining it. But indeed, what a delight it would be to be a Viceroy! Not only would all the hunting, shooting, and ceremonies be an absolute delight to partake in, but my longstanding inclination to assist the Indian populace would be taken care of. There was a distinct allure to that position. I wasn't the only one who wished for such things, I shared some of those thoughts with my wife and eventually it all came together.

This is a new story that Dominique can verify in Paris. A long time ago in 1931, my wife was on a European vacation and heard about a well-known crystal gazer who had some of the wildest predictions. My wife spoke fluent French and went to look for her very carefully. Her visit was not publicised so no one would have known that she wasn't French, let alone a Lady Louis Mountbatten. This is what she said after her crystal session, "You are a peculiar and tricky case. I envision you seated on a sort of throne, which is not exactly regal. You are reigning with contest of your husband." All of them laughed. They thought it was the dumbest forecast she had ever thought of. This was circa 1931-32.

Of course, my viceroyalty was totally different from what I had experienced and admired as a young man. In other words, it was completely different satisfaction. It was not in any way what I was looking forward to.

Q. How was the offer in fact made to you?

On the 18th day of December, in the year 1946, Mr. Attlee, being my Prime Minister, asked to meet me and it left me completely shocked. I had no element of surprise save for the fact that he had always consulted me with concerns pertaining to Burma, or Malaya, or even both. I had grown used to being interrogated on these topics so I suspected that this meeting would deal with Burma, but from a surprise perspective, to the very beginning of which fully captivated me, he commenced with." He was in the chair of the Prime Minister in number ten of Downing Street with Sir Stafford Cripps, the Chancellor of the Exchequer seated by his left in the Chancellor's chair am having always assumed the position of having this discussion in broad amicable, informal manner and how we used to speak about India.

I am certain that you know that there was a lot of talking when Wavell was home, and I believed that they were only trying to get my opinion on the situation. I kept in contact with Wavell and I was aware of what was happening. As we progressed, they began posing increasingly probing questions, including what my plan of action would be and what I thought should be done.

I said, "Good God, Mr. Prime Minister, I have a very, very, very, uneasy, unpleasant feeling that you're trying to suggest - no you can't be - are you trying to suggest that you're going to ask me to relieve Archie Wavell?"

As we shall see there are countless documents to confirm that the above astonishment of Mountbatten was a feigned one - if one is to assume that the interview given by Mountbatten to Collins and Lapiere from memory is even remotely accurate.

CHAPTER 2: NEHRU - EDWINA LETTERS

Nehru - Edwina Letter - 1

'Ten years!' Nehru wrote to Edwina on March, 1957. He had been looking through his papers. 'I came across your letters neatly placed in separate bundles in large envelopes. For each year there was a big and sometimes rather fat envelope. The first one was for 1948 and though this was for six months only it was far the fattest. The next one, for 1949, was also a heavy one but smaller. . . Progressively these annual envelopes became thinner, representing fewer letters. And of course, my letters to you during these years followed the same pattern. Had the poetry turned into prose. But nine years ago there was the novelty of a new and wonderful discovery which moved me to the depths and possessed me. That novelty could not last in that way, for we adapt ourselves even to surprises and wonders. Indeed, it was wonderful enough for us, living far from each other and meeting infrequently, to continue the experience, that deep feeling which itself is so full of wonder and which gives a certain fullness to life. My life has been full enough in many ways and I have been absorbed in and half passionately pursued the love of India and her people and sought to give them such service as I could. But you came to add to it and not to come in its way. And so, I am infinitely thankful. . ."

As has been mentioned earlier Nehru's letters are in the custody of the Broadlands Trust and Edwina's letters are with the Nehru family. When Stanley Wolpert author of *Nehru* met Lord Romsey Edwina's grandson he suggested Wolpert write to his father, Lord Brabourne, who chairs the Broadlands Trust to request permission to read Nehru's letters to Edwina. Lord Brabourne replied: 'We made an agreement with Mrs. (Sonia) Gandhi . . . for copies of Nehru's letters to be sent to Mrs. Gandhi and she arranged for copies of Lady Mountbatten's letters to be sent to us . . . The condition made at that time was that no permission would be given to anybody to read the letters without the agreement of both families.' So early in 1994 Wolpert met Sonia Gandhi in her Jan Path fortress in New Delhi. 'Let me be totally honest with you,' she said after refusing to show Wolpert the letters, 'I don't want you to think we have anything to hide . . .'

The only person who was ever granted permission by both the families to read the love letters was Janet Morgan, Lady Balfour of Burleigh. All the excerpts are quoted from Janet Morgan's *Edwina Mountbatten A Life Of Her Own*. Janet Morgan has quoted only a few letters which gives us only a brief glimpse into the collection which when totaled from both sides would may be run into thousands of pages. Wolpert laments, 'The deepest passions and fears that drove and tortured Nehru throughout his adult life have always remained hidden, first by himself, then by Indira, and now by those who zealously secret documents recording his intimate thoughts and concerns during India's first decade of independence, trying more than three decades after his death to perpetuate myths and hoping to hide the true nature of that great man. Nehru, however, played too important a role in recent Indian history to be kept locked away in closets and trunks in the basements of Broadlands, Jan Path, and Teen Murti, For almost a decade, foolish British bureaucrats kept Jawaharlal Nehru behind bars, and his equally foolish heirs and self-appointed guardians have locked up his mind and heart for three times as long.'

20 June 1948 was the Mountbatten's last night in India. The Cabinet gave a banquet in their honour. When Nehru and Dicke spoke, Edwina could not restrain her tears. Nehru was too upset to take in a word of her farewell speech. Seven thousand people came to the reception. ' To bed 05.00, Dicke noted, ... called again 05.45 Edwina did not sleep. 'Night spent in attempting to round up, write and work'. They said goodbye to the servants and the staff. Dicke inspected the guard of honour, pictures were taken. Rajagopalachari and Nehru drove with them to the airfield at Palam. 'Three guards of honour', Dicke reported afterwards, 'all Cabinet and Corps Diplomatique Fighter Escort, 33 Gun Salute, Tears all round. Left 08.20' It was the most miserable day of Edwina's life.

Lord Mountbatten, Edwina Mountbatten & Jawaharlal Nehru captured on the steps of Delhi's Government House in 1948
(brownhistory.substack.com)

Back home Broadlands was Edwina's consolation. 'It has a character quite of its own', she told Nehru. She loved the view of the river from her bedroom windows, the walk through the trees and across the fields, the smell of new-cut grass. The place needed attention, for only the most urgent repairs and maintenance had been done during the war. 'I have resorted to very hard work as a possible solution to the present situation', she told Nehru at the beginning of July, it has helped although it is really only a drug'. She tried to sort out her papers, but it was not easy to do so at 16 Chester Street, with people constantly coming and going. Compared with the vast spaces of Government House, the place was 'a sardine tin, out of which we and all our belongings are literally bulging! I am sitting on the floor in the bathroom, the only corner.

On holiday near the sea-side in Ireland in August Edwina's letters to Nehru were ecstatic.

'Scrambled over the rocks and dabbled in the pools. Back by the beach of white sand   brilliant sun and sapphire and multi-emerald-colored seas and countryside with its white-washed thatched cottages we shrimped off the rocks and sat about in shorts sunbathing' Edwina ate fried sole, in Dublin she feasted on lobster. 'Bought sweets, sheets, linen and underclothes, all without coupons', Ireland, Edwina told Nehru, was like India, beautiful and pitiable.

'Feeling quite awful', she noted at the beginning of August', general exhaustion and depression, I think'. Small things upset her - 'Domestic dramas which are becoming increasingly boring. Cook versus Charles!' - and she worried about the state of the world. Attlee had given a dinner for the Mountbatten's at Downing Street, ministers and their wives were kind but Edwina thought them insular. 'Life is lonely and empty and unreal', she told Nehru. The Buckingham Palace garden party was 'a waste of time but Dicke insists'. In mid-September the Mountbattens took Pamela to stay with Yola and her sister in the South of France. 'I somehow seem to have grown out of all this', Edwina told Nehru, 'the people, the life, even the scenery'. She was shocked by the black market; the meals, she said sternly, were much too plentiful. People chattered all the time about trivia. It was difficult to find time and a place to concentrate on her daily letter to Nehru: 'nothing to write on anywhere - a peculiarity of all French houses - and I am precariously balanced on the edge of my bed writing on my knee'.

She was homesick for India. Dinner with an Indian students' society in London was more fun than the most splendid party, an evening watching Indian dancing better than the plays or concerts she had once enjoyed. On weekdays Edwina went across the Park to her office, hoping to find letters from India, sent over from the Residence by Krishna Menon, now High Commissioner in London. When they came, her heart was light. On days when there was no letter she was cast down; sometimes, able to wait no longer, she telephoned. The calls were hardly private. Her 'clear exciting voice', Nehru said, had come through with the guidance of half a dozen administrators: 'Delhi, Bombay, Poona ...indeed, once or twice they repeated your words to me.' On paper Nehru and Edwina could speak more intimately; even so, there was a risk that letters might go astray. They were sent to and from London in the diplomatic bag, each letter in a double cover. At first Edwina marked the inner envelope 'For the Prime Minister'; later on, reflection, she changed this to 'For Himself', as she did on envelopes for Dicke, numbering the letters so that Nehru would know if there were gaps. She was anxious in case they might go missing. 'I have awful thoughts of lost letters being read by Communists or stenographers.'

'I write to you in a very restrained manner', Nehru told Edwina. Not so. His letters were all she could desire. He had walked alone through the Mountbattens' former quarters at Government House. Dicke's swords and trophies had been removed from his study and the place was empty. Edwina's things had also been taken away but he still felt her presence, 'a fragrance on the air'. Where was she? Seeking her, he had read her letters a second time and a third: 'I lose myself in dreamland, which is very unbecoming in a PM. But then I am only incidentally a PM.' Work overwhelmed him; he sought refuge in poetry, myths and legends, fairy tales. The French Ambassador had asked him to dine and see Cocteau's film *La Bette et La Bete* 'I liked it and it soothed me.... the cares that infest the day folded their tents like the Arabs and as silently stole away'. Nehru was living his own fairy tale, he said, the story of a battle between convention and chemistry. 'Chemistry won, more or less'.

Nehru - Edwina Letter - III

Six days later, on 21 March 1949, Edwina and Pamela took off from Delhi. From the airport Edwina sent a last letter to Nehru: 'A huge tear just about to drop'. The Prime Minister walked in his garden: 'The house was lighted up, except for one wing ... your rooms down below and mine on the first floor. The darkness stood out, a sign of a light that had gone, of life stealing away and leaving an emptiness behind.' Next day, to console his master, Nehru's cook produced *Poussin Contesse Mountbatten* and *creme brulee*, one of Lady Louis' favourite puddings. Anthony Eden was in Delhi and came to the Prime Minister's House for lunch. Nehru had no appetite.

'Fate or bad fairies always see to it that one does not become too favoured and spoilt and secure', Edwina observed to Nehru, 'A good thing I suppose!' She revived when Nehru came to England in the spring of 1950 for a meeting of Commonwealth Prime Ministers. Two Weekends were kept free for Broadlands. Edwina was intoxicated by the early spring: 'double cherries etc azaleas starting and beeches just about to burst out. Woods a mass of bluebells and primroses and pink ragwort.' For Nehru it was all unreal: the sharp, insistent English April, Edwina's adoration. Another

Jawaharlal Nehru, and Lord and Lady Mountbatten strolling during their holiday (Historiamag)

parting: Nehru left for Switzerland, the Mountbattens for Malta. He was back at the beginning of October, on his way to America with Indira, returning four weeks later on his way home. Three days later he was gone again.

What were they to each other? Edwina thought of Nehru as a poet but he was also a politician, bold and far-seeing, constantly putting his ideas and his person to the test, offering himself to the vast crowds that flocked to hear him. Edwina was his safety-net. Policemen and soldiers guarded him, a reminder of how vulnerable he was. People badgered him all the time, yet he was alone. Millions thought him all-powerful but the problems he faced could not be solved by one man in one lifetime. His countrymen seemed to forget that he was only a human being. Nehru was comforted because Edwina cared for him.

He liked to mesmerise. It pleased him to manage a crowd - how much more difficult to hold one individual in thrall. He was vain: the rose, the spotless linen… He tried to keep trim and fit. 'PS' he wrote, 'I am having a daily swim'. From time to time he thought of giving up smoking; 'I don't want to be smug. But always at the back of my mind is the thought that I am slipping away, getting soft...'

Nehru could not work unceasingly. It was pleasant to have an intelligent woman friend in whom he could confide. It delighted him to be of service as he brought sugar for Edwina from America (There was rationing in Britain). She asked him to send *petits-suisss* from Switzerland; when his hosts warned him that soft cheese would not travel and presented him with Gruyere, he packed that off instead. He brought Edwina mangoes from India, cigarettes from Egypt; he sent her the chocolates he had been given by the Arab League. To Nehru it was an ideal relationship. No great adjustments need be made; this was not a marriage, with its infringements and compromises. He had been a widower for many years and liked his privacy.

The correspondence between Edwina and Nehru was ecstatic but modest, suggesting in general terms only to the physical affection they denied themselves. In the first month of 1949, for instance, Nehru mailed Edwina a new photobook of the seductive sculpture on the "Temple of the Sun" in Orissa. 'I must say they took my breath away for an instant', he told her. 'They were strong meat. And then my mind wandered and tried to picture to itself the society in which these sculptures were made. Obviously, no one could have put them there on the walls of a sacred temple if there was any thought of impiety or of any passion or lust attached to them. It was presumably about a dispassionate and objective rendering of life. There was no sense of shame or of hiding anything ... The old Indians wrote amazingly detailed books about the sex business, treating it quite calmly and dispassionately.

There is no attempt at what is called sex appeal...'

Edwina took up the cue. 'I am so intrigued about the Sun Temple Sculptures', she replied. 'I never feel worried and shocked at something which is natural and frank and factual. It is only vulgarity and subterfuge which disgusts and bores me. That is why I dislike vulgar stories and cheap books and films based on crude sex appeal. I am even rather disgusted by them and I know in consequence am thought sometimes to be rather boringly prudish!' Edwina had indicated that she had once had romantic friendships; Nehru had observed indulgently that he wished he had known 'her other selves'. She was at pains to explain that her attitude was 'primarily mystical'. 'I think I am not interested in sex as sex', she continued. 'There must be so much more to it, beauty of spirit and form and in its conception. But I think you and I are in the minority! Yet another treasured bond.'

'I feel you understand as no one else has ever done', Edwina wrote gratefully to Nehru. They were fellow-creatures. She had always felt herself to be a foreigner; indeed, she assured him, she was hardly English at all. Edwina had found her identity: she belonged to India. He sent her his photograph; she exclaimed that they were beginning to look alike. This was absured.

Edwina's devotion was not surprising. Edwina saw a man in Nehru who she could love and trust. Her grandfather had been too remote, her father too weak. Dicke was an enthusiastic boy, Bunny too tame. Nehru's love was worth having, for he was wise, subtle and clever. He treated her as an equal, unlike Garter, who believed that he did so, but failed to get the balance right, either deferring too much or being inadvertently patronising. Edwina wanted her opinions to be taken seriously; she liked to feel that she was contributing to a discussion. She could discuss everything with Nehru - Berlin, Malaya, Korea, China, the expected result of an election. She spoke about these things to Dicke, to Peter Murphy and, for that matter, to the Prime Minister and the Chancellor of the Treasurer, but, although they knew she was intelligent and experienced, she sensed that they considered her an amateur. The men she met in London and Malta were always giving women the benefit of their views: Nehru did not condescend.

He was gallant and graceful, never trampling on her feelings, able to express the finest shades of emotion with delicacy. Edwina had been afraid of love. She could accept it from strangers - refugees, prisoners of war, sick adults, starving children - but she withdrew from the embrace of her family and friends. Nehru changed her. She learnt not just how to give but to receive. He respected, stimulated and needed her, he taught her that she needed him.

You have given me everything I ever wanted, She flew back to London, in May 1949, 'happiness, balance, misery even! but we know the reason (and we would not change it) and there is infinitely more power and purpose to life ... 'She was bound to Dicke and he to the Navy: Edwina squared up to her duty and made the best of it. This was not always easy.

Edwina was irritated by the parochialism of British society, by the insularity of its leaders. In July 1951 she flew back to London from Cornwall in a small aeroplane: the country looked heavenly, she told Nehru, 'serene and peaceful and solid .. I suddenly felt *exasperated* at it'. Britain was so small compared with India's vast deserts, towering mountain ranges and endless plains. Nehru was struggling to bring his people into the twentieth century; at home, Edwina said, things were going backwards to the nineteenth. In October 1951 the Conservatives were returned to office; Edwina was not impressed. 'The new Cabinet all with vast fortunes and incomes and fleets of private cars and chauffeurs have patriotically cut their salaries and their transport. We have all swallowed hard and tried to clap!' She considered that important jobs had gone to the wrong people: 'Poor Walter Monckton went in to Winston hoping he was going to be offered the Attorney General and came out with Labour! Oliver Lyttelton's appointment to Colonies I don't like at all ... Still no Minister for Education or health. So, it appears that Health, Education and Social Services do not interest the new Government. But the people feel differently! At all Lord Mayor's Banquet, where Churchill was to make his first public statement since the Election, Edwina sat between Lord Woolton, the new Lord President, and the Speaker or the House of Commons, 'Shakes' Morrison. She was horrified by the Prime Minister's speech, 'extolling the virtues of the USA', she told Nehru disbelievingly, 'linking them all with that most valuable asset the Atom Bomb!!' Her neighbours agreed. 'A most unfortunate reference', they whispered consolingly. 'But no one can control him!'

Nehru- Edwina Letter - IV

Nehru wondered whether eventually politicians made much difference. 'There is a sense of unreality about it all', he told Edwina, in a letter from a Conference of Commonwealth Foreign Ministers in Colombo in January 1950: 'a vast mass of human beings, impelled by elemental urges ... people seem to be unaware of this and imagine that they can deal with them in some superior governmental way.' Speculative, fatalistic, conscious of the limits of his own power - it was not surprising that Nehru took this view. Edwina was not so sure. She had spent years trying to deal with the misery and confusion caused by political and military leaders who were misguided, deluded, in some cases plainly wicked. In her eyes, the fact that people believed in promoting a particular cause or ideology did not make them any less responsible for the consequences.

'Why does it always seem easier for the leaders of Communist and Fascist movements to get released and carry on their dangerous and insidious activities than any other category of offender?', she wrote desperately to Nehru in late 1949, after listening to discussions about the Amnesty Bill in France. 'It is the same in every country and it terrifies me. I am always haunted by the endless war memorials in every town and village of the British Isles and a sense of horrible guilt creeps over me, because one feels so powerless and so apprehensive that all these sacrifices seem to have been in vain.'

Edwina was sickened by British and American Cold War rhetoric. Nehru had given her his views: 'The problem is not Communism,' he told her in January 1950. 'The problem is there in varying degrees all over the world. Communism offers a solution. That solution, though partly right, is not adequate and in some respects, is very wrong, that is, in so far as it is based on hatred and violence and the suppression of the individual ... Merely to shout and curse at Communism in not to find a solution.' People Edwina knew accused her of being 'pink'; at a party in June 1950 she was seated next to Hewlett Johnson, 'the Red Dean of Canterbury'. 'Riveting, I thought, charming and extremely balanced! Perhaps Protocol and Precedence etc. thought I was the best person to put next to such a 'hideous Communist" ... Very progressive views and says so... Wasted in the Church!'

In 1951 she went to West and East Africa. Edwina thought Britain's post-war colonial policy was all wrong. The British Army officers who entertained her in Nigeria tried to please by asking how they could obtain *Polo* by Marco for their clubs in Lagos and Kaduna. Edwina was not impressed. Kenya was no better. 'Some unbelievably boring British who should be firmly removed', she told Nehru, 'and sent to Cheltenham to retire painlessly.' Here., of all places, Britain needed enlightened representatives. When Edwina came home, she arranged to see the Prime Minister and the Secretary of State of Commonwealth Relations. 'There will be some plain speaking!!' she said bravely. Nehru did not hold out much hope. 'You might have produced some slight effect on Clem Attlee', he observed, 'but it is sheer optimism to believe that Gordon-Walker can be influenced in this way.'

Edwina did not give up. In March 1952, on her way to look at relief work in Japan, South Korea and North Borneo, she returned to Malaya. There she saw General Sir Gerald Templer, who had been sent out as High Commissioner .... 'Amazed me with his ignorance of the problem and his completely mad approach to it', she reported to Nehru. 'I told him quite plainly that, if those were his intentions, in a few months he would be packing his bags for the UK as what structure there was would entirely collapse.' On her return Edwina went to see the Foreign Secretary. She also told him what she thought about Korea. 'He was *furious,* rather like Oliver Lyttelton and Kenya!' For she had also expressed her disapproval of British policy there. 'I despair of what they are doing .'.. , she lamented to Nehru. 'Most of my African colleagues - even reactionary ones - appear to be in gaol ...'

'My watch still keeps India time', Edwina told Nehru, in a letter written on the flight from Bombay to London in April 1951. In Cairo, where the aircraft stopped to refuel, she found one of Nehru's handkerchiefs in her grey wool overcoat pocket: 'that cheered me'. Edwina clung to every reminder of the country she loved and the man she adored. India and Nehru, Nehru and India: in her mind and her heart they were intertwined. His letters were her lifeline; his gifts fragments of another world: pressed flowers from Kashmir, dried ferns from Sikkim, saffron, tea, orchids, mangoes, a sandalwood box, a crocodile skin (shot by a Maharajah). In return Edwina sent heather from Classiebawn Castle and 'gentians and alpenstocks' (she meant 'edelweiss') gathered in the Swiss Alps. Nehru was enchanted. Overworked, lonely, often uncertain, he looked to Edwina for companionship and support. In the summer of 1954 he talked of giving up the premiership, of retiring to the mountains. He was tired, bored with politics and politicians, afraid, he said, of losing his grip:'... I would probably come back in a better mood some time later'. If only he could discuss it all with Edwina. She had become as indispensable to Nehru as he was to her.

Nehru did not resign. Instead, he took himself to Mashobra for a rest: 'Six years ago, almost to the day ... the air and the rooms and the corridors are full of whispers of the past. I have lived here for five days in this atmosphere, getting rather mixed up with what has been and what is.' Whenever he could, he came to England, eight times between 1950 and 1957. His visits were short, for he was either tied up in meetings at Downing Street or Chequers or hurrying on to official engagements in Europe or America. But he always left at least one weekend for Broadlands. It was there, one summer evening, that Mrs. Travis, the Mountabttens' archivist, saw them across the fields as she made her way home - Pandit Nehru and Lady Louis, silhouetted against the sky. They seemed so much at ease that she felt it right to wish them well. Mrs. Travis waved, together, they returned her salute. No two people could have looked more in harmony.

In the early summer, there was a major row. On 1 June, the day before the Coronation, Prime Ministers were received for lunch at Buckingham Palace. The Mountbattens were there, and Nehru, who had come to London for the celebrations. At the reception Edwina found herself standing next to Oliver Lyttelton, the Colonial Secretary. After making what Edwina considered disparaging remarks about Malta, India and Malaya, Lyttelton asked to be introduced to Nehru. The conversation was disastrous. Somehow, they found themselves discussing terrorism in Kenya, a topic on which the Colonial Secretary was feeling touchy. Allegations of brutality by British police and military officers had just been brought to his attention and an investigation was under way. Edwina did not know this. When she murmured something about 'the perpetuation of violence, bitterness and hatred', Lyttelton exploded. Edwina managed to change the subject but she was horrified. She was so angry and upset that, unusually, she wrote a memorandum of the conversation when she got home.

Dicke next heard, 'through a more than reliable source', Edwina told Nehru, that Lyttelton had reported the whole matter to the Prime Minister and the Cabinet, saying that Lady Louis had declared that British police and troops were worse than Mau Mau terrorists, that she had a reputation for being anti- British ('not Anti-American', she observed to Nehru, 'You will smile!) and left-wing. Dicke's informant also told him that, for these reasons, it had been thought unwise for Lady Louis to accompany her husband in *Surprise* on his forthcoming official visit to Turkey. Sure enough, a letter then came to Mountatten from the First Lord, saying that *Surprise* should stay behind. The danger of press criticism was given as an excuse. The Mountbattens were taken aback. The President of Turkey had invited them both as his guests and Edwina was to carry out an official programmeme of visits to hospitals, universities and other insitutions, as well as attending formal naval functions.

Edwina wrote a blistering letter to Lyttelton, attaching the relevant part of her memorandum of the Buckingham Palace conversation. She was disgusted, she told Nehru. Turkey is serious but not the end of the world. My reputation and the campaign against me are not all-important. Dicke's is!' If her support for the National Health Service meant that she was left-wing, she declared, 'Who isn't!' If she was considered anti-British because she believed in racial equality, she was certainly guilty and proud of it. 'But it's pretty disillusioning that Individuals are persecuted and penalised because of their views - and that through the back door!' She might as well be living in a police state, she said bitterly, 'in fact one might be behind the Iron Curtain!!' How could she fight something like this, she asked, 'especially where most of the Campaign is carried on behind Closed Doors and underground? Not by exchanging letters with the Colonial Secretary, that was clear. Edwina did some sapping and mining. She showed the correspondence, including Nehru's recollections of the incident, not just to the First Lord but also to the Foreign Secretary. Five days later Dicke received a signal from the Admiralty saying that there were no objections to Lady Louis accompanying him to Turkey in Surprise.

The literary output of Nehru is prodigious. Had Nehru not been in politics he would certainly have been remembered as a literary figure. His lengthy incarcerations were a blessing in disguise. Most of his writings were compiled during his confinements. The writer had often wondered why Nehru had not written after the assumption of Prime Minister ship. The fact is he has probably written just as much, if not more, during his days in power. The writings were in the shape of his letters to Edwina. The brief account that has been given of Nehru's letters to Edwina indicate that they were voluminous. It is indeed lamentable that till now the world has been deprived access to his writings which must surely be of high literary quality. If these were ever to be published, as indeed was the wish of Edwina, then combined with his earlier writings would may have even qualified him for the Nobel Prize for literature. The reader can form his own judgement by a glance at the list of his writings which the writer has come across:

Glimpses of World History: An Autobiography, India and The World, Letters From a Father to a Daughter, Eighteen Months in India, China, Spain and The War, Towards Freedom, The Discovery of India, The Collected Writings The Unification of India, Independence and After: A Bunch of Old Letters, India: Today and Tomorrow, India's Foreign Policy, Selected Speeches September 1946 - April 1961, Nehru's Letters to His Sister, Selected Writings of Jawaharlal Nehru (First Series), Selected Writings of Jawaharlal Nehru (Second Series), Social Revolution and Independence of India, and Letters to Chief Ministers 1947-64.

At first Nehru and Edwina had written to each other every day. A year later they were writing once a week, by 1954 once a fortnight. Now, ten years on, Edwina's letters came at three-week intervals. The falling-off was greater on Nehru's side. He tried but the volume of his work made correspondence difficult. 'You tell me that you waited day after day ... and there was no letter', he wrote contritely in February 1955, 'except the brief and rather formal one from the office of Air India International from Geneva ... I am so sorry ... I shall now try to send a letter once a week, writing on Sunday usually or perhaps Monday. So long as I am in Delhi this can be done more or less regularly, but when I travel it might be more difficult to keep to this timetable...' A week later: 'This is my Sunday letter! Then: 'I have missed Sunday and am writing to you on Tuesday.' Edwina did not reproach him. In mid-March 1955 a madman had hurled himself at the Prime Minister's car and tried to stab him. When Edwina heard the news, her heart stood still. Nehru thrust the man away: 'There was no danger ...', he assured her. Intermittent letters were better than an everlasting silence. 'Ten years ...', Edwina wrote in March 1957, '... monumental in their history and so powerful in the effects on our personal lives. All the incidents you mention and the strange course of events ... I seem steeped in them.' His letter had touched her deeply.

In 1958 Nehru again began to talk of resignation. Edwina instructed him to have a holiday and in late May he set off with Indira for a month's trek in the Kulu Valley. His doctors had forbidden him to climb higher than seven or eight thousand feet. He ignored them, he told Edwina triumphantly, '... up to thirteen thousand five hundred!' He had spoken of getting away from everything. 'Tell me whether I should continue to write to you or *not*?' Edwina asked. 'I shall well understand if you say "not a note for the next months".' 'Her question took his breath away. 'What have I said, written or done to deserve this?' Nehru replied. 'I am hurt at the suggestion. And how do you think I would fare if months passed without a letter from you? ... Have you realised what your letters mean to me?' Edwina was relieved. Never ceasing to marvel at what had happened, she could not believe that her letters were so important.

Dicke could not fail to see the attachment between Nehru and Edwina. He asked no questions. Whatever the situation was, tact and understanding would see them through. Until the denouement Dicke was determined to behave naturally. He sent Nehru encouraging letters, full of political tips; when Edwina went to Delhi, he wrote ahead, begging her host to see she got some rest. Nehru replied in a kindly way, never failing to take an interest in his friend's enthusiasms; flying saucers, cosmology, computers. 'Dicke once spoke to me about a memory machine', Nehru told Edwina, 'and I have been recently reading about it ... I confess I disliked the look and the thought of it.'

Dicke did not expect Edwina to confide in him. He only wished he knew how to make her happy. Their relations were harmonious for ninety-nine per cent of the time but then there would be an explosion over some trivial incident: a row when Edwina's canaries were alarmed by a gun salute on *Surprise*, an argument over the merits of a certain journalist. Depression and loneliness impelled Edwina to lash out; she then looked for evidence to justify her outburst. These battles generally ended with an announcement from Edwina that she intended to leave Dicke; in the early and middle nineteen-fifties she spoke constantly of divorce. 'I've never attempted to stop you or hold you and I never shall', Dicke declared. 'I don't want you to stay against your will. I'm not that selfish ...' This was true. Dicke had told Patricia and Pamela that the great advantage of his having the mews flat was that he would have somewhere to go if Edwina asked him to leave Wilton Crescent and Broadlands.

Edwina and Dicke did not part. They were inextricably bound together, not just by their children and grandchildren, their friends, shared history and possessions, but by ties that were harder to break than these. Knowing people suggested that the Mountbattens stayed together because Edwina valued her husband's royal connections and because he needed her money. This showed how ignorant they were. From the beginning Dicke had been bewitched by his 'divine Edwina', beautiful, vivacious, intelligent and forthright. That magic remained. He could not cure her tormented heart but he could help and comfort her; he believed she needed him as much as he needed her. Adoration, excitement and a sense of responsibility held Dicke to Edwina; affection, duty and gratitude tied her to him.

Once and once only Edwina revealed her feelings. This was in February 1952, just after her haemorrhage. She thought she might be dying and before she was taken into the operating theatre she handed Dicke an envelope. He took it away to open when he was alone. 'I have been thinking about all those letters I have from Jawaha', Edwina wrote, 'and what should be done with them ...' 'I would like you to have them for your life time', she told Dicke that You will understand that they constitute an ensemble of average Jawaha letters, which are interesting, full of facts, and true historical documents. Some of them do not contain any "personal" comments. Other letters are of a loving nature, but you yourself will appreciate the strange bond – much of it metaphysical – which we share. Jawaha has without question meant a great deal in my life in these years and I think I in his. Our part meetings have been few and always hasty, but I think I grasp him and perhaps he me as well as any of us can ever grasp one another. Especially when two such as us, for the most part, are thousands of miles apart and in such different lives and conditions. She told Dicke where the letters were and asked him to read them. He might want to publish some excerpts: as having been addressed to you and me, or better yet, perhaps as though addressed to no one, merely as a sort of journal. It seems selfish otherwise for this treasure of material, a wealth of his thoughts and actions, never to be made public at all.

So far Edwina's letter had been chiefly about herself and Nehru, but it was written as a tribute to Dicke, a testament to her feelings for him. At the end Edwina said so, if obliquely. 'It was rather wonderful that my affection and respect and gratitude and *love* for you are really so great that I feel that you would understand and not in any way be hurt, rather the contrary. We understand each other so well although so often we seem to differ and to be miles apart ... My admiration and my devotion to you are very great. I think you know that. I have had a very full and a very happy life on the whole — all thanks to you! Bless you and with my lasting love ...'

Dicke said little. He was too dazed with happiness at hearing, later that day, that Edwina was going to be all right. It was a year before he gave her considered reaction, in a letter to Delhi, where she was resting after another illness. This was in February 1953. Whatever were to happen to either of them, he told Edwina, he would treasure her letter. 'I am glad you realise that I know and have always understood the very special relationship between Jawaha and you — made the easier by my fondness and admiration for him and by remarkably lucky fact that among my defects God did not add jealousy in any degree or form ... Only my desire for your happiness exists, This is why I've always made your visits to each other easy and been faintly hurt when at times (such as in 1951) you didn't take me into your confidence right away.' He had been reading her letter and thinking over the history of their marriage. 'Considering how deeply fond we are of each other and how proud and admiring I certainly I am of all your achievements, I cannot but be sad and worried that we should have had so many differences.' He could not understand it. She had no need to feel envious or injured. 'I know I am selfish and difficult but that doesn't change my deep and profound love for you ... You have been my mainstay, my inspiration and my true companion for far more than half my life ...'

Nehru - Edwina Letter - VI

Edwina could not speak to Dicke about her feelings for him but no wife worked harder to help her husband succeed, in small and in large. When Lord Selkirk, the new First Lord of the Admiralty, visited Delhi in September 1958, Edwina asked Nehru to put in a good word. 'He is pleasant and intelligent . . . Please give D. a pat on the back.' The new Minister of Defence, Duncan Sandys, was invited to dine at Walton Crescent and to shoot at Broadlands. Within weeks he had been won round to Dicke's idea of what a post-Suez Navy should look like. In May 1958 the Prime Minister offered Mountbatten the post of Chief of the Defence Staff, the head of the new and powerful central organisation, directly responsible to the Minister of Defence and independent of the three Chiefs of Staff. Edwina was delighted. 'I think at heart Dicke loved Politics', she told Nehru, 'though he would *never* admit it!!' To help things along, the Macmillans and Sandys were asked to Broadlands for a weekend in November. 'Can't you see our little party', Edwina asked Nehru, '... Dicke trying (very unsubtly !!) to get what he can out of the PM and Minister of Defence!! And I chatting madly about nonsense as though I knew nothing about all the machinations!! And watching Lady Dorothy doing her embroidery! What extraordinary things one does . . .'

These days, Edwina did not complain. She was calm and sweet-tempered, smiling through ministerial dinners, official visits, and State occasions. The storms seemed to be over. Yola (Dicke's girlfriend) came to stay at Broadlands and, although Edwina watched every move she and Dicke made, there were no scenes. She was kind and considerate, even meek. Dicke was astonished to find her sitting in the hall waiting quietly until he was ready. This was a new Edwina. When she was abroad, he

Pandit Jawaharlal Nehru with Lady Mountbatten in New Delhi, February 1959
(Mathrubhumi.com)

missed her more than ever. His life was incomplete without her. 'The house is very lonely without you', he wrote in 1959, when she had set off on some tour of inspection. 'I shall hate passing your door in a few minutes when I go to bed, without looking in.' His birthday present that year – she was 58 – was a handsome wrought-iron gate for Broadlands, her monogram on one side, his on the other. It closed an epoch and opened another; the years of difficulty were over and journey ahead promised to be peaceful and companionable.

The family flourished. Patricia, with four children now, was happily established in Kent, John was making a name for himself as a film producer. In mid-November 1959 Pamela became engaged to David Hicks, an interior designer. 'He is very charming and I like him so much', Edwina told Nehru in an excited letter, '. . . just older than she, works hard and seriously, is artistic and gifted . . .' They were married in Romsey on 13 January 1960. 'Snowed hard all day and dislocated traffic', Dicke noted in his diary, but the staff struggled in Broadlands and, although some of the family missed the lunch party, everyone reached the Abbey in time.

In the autumn of 1958, a swelling appeared on her face, a growth in the parotid gland which was surgically removed. For a time, Edwina's face sagged at one side, as if she had had a stroke, an educative experience, she told Nehru afterwards (she said nothing about her operation at the time), for people stared at her lopsided cheek and drooping eye. To prove to herself that she did not mind, she flew to Paris to display her face to Yola, who was aghast. Getting over the operation took weeks. Then in January 1959 Edwina caught chickenpox from a grandchild. To convalesce, she went off to Delhi, coming back apparently restored. At the end of June, however, Edwina told Nehru that 'she was not so good.'

Edwina admitted that she was doing too much. In October she went with Dicke on a twelve-day tour of defence establishments in the United States, 'a killer', she confessed to Nehru; on the day after her return, she had five major engagements, the next day four. 'Quite happy, though rather breathless', she reported at the end of 1959. After Pamela's wedding, she promised to come to India for a rest, before beginning a tour of Malaya and Borneo that even she thought daunting. Before she left, she saw Dr Wilkes Harvey and Dr McManus. They warned her not to overtax herself, for her angina was worse. Without care, she was told, she had only months to live.

Six non-stop days in Cyprus, a difficult flight to Bombay, on to Delhi: 'Of *course* my arrival coincided with President Voroshilov's official State Visit and of course I was photographed being introduced to him', Edwina told Dicke,'... So, the *Express* etc. will have great fun ...'Edwina left India on 5 February, scribbling a long letter to Dicke before her departure, full of news about his sister Alice, who was in Delhi, and instructions for the packing and storage of Pamela's wedding dress and veil. 'I am off at 5.30 am . . .'

On 18 February, after a fortnight in Malaya, Edwina arrived in North Borneo. She was met at Jesselton Airport by the Acting Governor, Mr. Turner and his wife, and by the local Commissioner General of the St John Ambulance Brigade, Dr. Blaauw, and his headquarters officer, Miss Checkley, who was stationed in North Borneo for a year. It was hot and humid; Edwina changed into a fresh uniform before alighting from the aircraft but, by the time she got out of the car at the Turners' residence, her skirt was saturated. The next day, the 19th, was a rest day; Edwina asked if she could spend it at Kota Belud, a jungle training area for the Army. On the way home, she was in good spirits and, although she said she felt a little unwell, she would not allow Miss Checkley to call doctor. That night, on the way back from a dinner in her honour, she stumbled, steadying herself by catching a railing. She slept little and, when she woke, she had splitting neuralgia.

Edwina agreed to see Dr Blaauw in the morning. He thought she might be starting 'flu or malaria' but she insisted on carrying out her programmeme. At midday Mrs Turner persuaded her to rest in her room; when Edwina heard that her hosts had cancelled a luncheon that had been arranged for her, she observed that 'this seemed rather drastic'. In the late afternoon, after inspecting a St John Parade, shaking hands with everyone (except the Police Band, who were encumbered with their instruments), presenting certificates and watching first- aid demonstrations, Edwina's head was bursting. She decided to return to the Residence, skipping a tea party. Dr Blaauw came again. In the evening a reception was being held at the Residence; the Turners suggested that Edwina take things gently. Miss Checkley and a maid supported her downstairs but she insisted on entering the drawing-room unaided. At nine she withdrew, apologising for not having taken a more active part, and collapsed. In the morning, Edwina was due to leave for Singapore.

At half past seven Irene Checkley went to Edwina's room to call her. There was no reply. She had died in her sleep. The doctors said her heart had given out at about at about half past two in the morning. That evening, Sunday 21 February, her coffin, covered with a St John Ambulance flag, was placed in the aircraft to begin the long journey home. With it, among the wreaths, were the orchids that had been sent to the Jesselton Show. Mr. Turner had opened the boxes himself: 'I intended to ask her to do so', he said sadly in his report to Dicke, 'as she so clearly knew much more about flowers than I did.' Miss Checkley brought Edwina's possessions. Besides the bed she had seen a pile of papers and, thinking that Lady Louis' correspondence was not for other eyes, she put them in her own suitcase. Once home, she consulted Marjorie Brecknock, who had come to the airport to receive the coffin. They were Nehru's letters, Edwina's nightly reading. Marjorie told Miss Checkley that she should not be shy about handing them over to Lord Louis. Dicke gave them to Pamela to look through.

Stanley Wolpert records in *Nehru*: her body was flown to Singapore the next day and then on to London, reaching Heathrow Airport on February 24, 1960, taken directly to Broadlands, and kept for half a day at Romsey Abbey, where the family and friends could pay respects. Dicke had hoped she would agree to be buried in the family crypt in Romsey, but Edwina's will requested that her remains be set free in open sea, so her coffin was taken to Portsmouth on February 25, the tiny body released from British navy's *Wakeful* into the wind- whipped waters onto which the Indian frigate *Trishul* dropped its prime minister's farewell garland of marigolds, sent to adorn her body, as every good Hindu garlands his goddess.

Nehru shed no tears and showed no emotions. His face was "expressionless and self-contained," Marie Seton recalled, watching him enter Delhi's Sapru House to introduce Arnold Toynbee, who lectured there that Sunday evening, when a mournful Indian capital learned of Edwina's death. Four days later, Kingsley Martin's wife, Dorothy Woodman, dined with Nehru alone and told Marie how 'surprised' she was to note with what "detachment" Nehru spoke to "Lord Mountbatten on the phone to England" that evening, the first time they had talked since Edwina's death. He had risen to his feet in silence at Sapru House with all the rest of them, as he did next day in Lok Sabha, but he canceled none of his appointments, having known in his heart and head long ago that she was lost to him, their love affair no more than a fragrant memory.

CHAPTER 3: THE MOUNTBATTEN FILES

The Rise and Rise of Mountbatten

Even his severest critics would have to admit that Mountbatten was one of the most outstanding personalities of the twentieth century. He seems to have had a totally charmed life. Anyone studying his biography would only wonder in amazement at the continuous run of successes throughout his life. His career appears to be a saga of the rise and rise of Mountbatten. Anyone achieving even one-fifth of his accomplishments would have left his mark in the history books. On 25 June 1900 Louis Francis Albert Victor Nicholas was born and was the second born of Prince of Louis of Battenberg and Princess Victoria of Hesse to the Queen of Hampshire. His great-grandmother was Queen Victoria, who attended his christening, and who, at the time of his birth, had been on the British throne since 1837 and Empress of India since 1876. Just a year after Mountbatten was born, Queen Victoria died and an Empire mourned.

Battenberg family in 1902, the future lord Mountbatten on his mother's lap. On his left are his sisters, Alice, later the mother of Prince Philip, and Louise, the future Queen of Sweden
(wordpress.com)

At the time of Mountbatten's death, nearly eight years later, there was no Empire left to mourn and five more sovereigns had occupied the throne. The young Prince Louis would achieve heights of which his great-grandmother would surely have been proud. After having his royal titles stripped from him when he was seventeen, along with those of all his German relations who were resident in Britain during the First World War, Mountbatten would go on to amass a multitude of new honours and decorations far in excess of the titles of which he was deprived. He became the first Earl Mountbatten of Burma; Knight of the proud Garter, Privy Counsellor; holder of Order of Merit; Knight Grand Cross of the Bath; Knight Grand Commander of the Star of India; Knight Grand Cross of the Royal Victorian Order; Knight Grand Commander of the Indian Empire; Companion of the Distinguished Service Order and Fellow of the Royal Society. Most mortals would consider their life fulfilled to have acquired even one of the honours listed above. Readers please note that Mountbatten was not only a

Fellow of the Royal Society, usually the domain of intellectuals, he was also awarded the Order of Merit, an exclusive decoration for the most distinguished. As we shall see later quite a number of the distinctions were obtained after active lobbying.

In the Second World War, he commanded HMS *Kell;* became Commander of the Combined Operations 1941; Chief of Combined Operations in 1942 and Supreme Allied Commander, South-East Asia, in 1943. In 1947, Mountbatten was appointed to be the last Viceroy of India and subsequently its first Governor-General. Resuming his interrupted naval career in 1948 he became, successively Fourth Sea Lord, then Commander-in-Chief, Mediterranean in 1952 and in 1955 he achieved his life time ambition when he became First Sea Lord. Four years later, he completed an extraordinary service record when he was appointed Chief of the Defence Staff. In a career spanning fifty-six years he had a reason from being a humble cadet to his final rank as Admiral of the Fleet.

A study of Mountbatten's career and biography should be a must for every ambitious young man. It is indeed a lesson in planning and executing cautiously one's career using all possible methods for advancement in life. His official biography by Philip Ziegler is a marvelously compiled book which takes a balanced look at the life of this great man. Even if his father, Prince Louis of Battenberg, had not been chosen as First Sea Lord by Winston Churchill, then First Lord of the Admiralty, the Royal Navy would have been a natural choice of career for his son. Before joining the Navy, young Dicke -- the name by which he would be known to family and close friends for the rest of his life -- grew up near the centre of the gigantic family tree that united Europe's royal houses. He spent much of the year 1908 in Russia staying with his relations in Moscow and St. Petersburg. The splendours of the Tsarist Court appealed immediately to the young Prince and imbued in him a life long love of ceremonial and royal pageantry.

Louis Mountbatten and Edwina Ashley

Mountbatten's affection for Britain and all things British stemmed from his parents. His father had been promoted to command the Atlantic Fleet in 1907 and, as a naturalised British subject from the age of fourteen, his loyalty never wavered.

Throughout his life Mountbatten would claim that he inherited his determination to succeed both sides from his family. Mountbatten's father passed on to his son a characteristic that they would both deny at first, but which, at least as far as Mountbatten was concerned was cheerfully admitted in later life. This quality was a burning desire to be noticed. If he achieved something, he wanted to know the world to know about it and recognise that he was the person who had done it. He used to say, 'If I don't blow my trumpet, no one else will.' As will be detailed later, Mountbatten's first shock in his life came at the age of fourteen when he learned that his beloved father had been forced to resign to his position as First Sea Lord after forty-six years' distinguished service in the Royal Naval Force. Within twelve weeks of the World War-I the scandal mongers became active in destroying a brilliant career. They claimed that the First Sea Lord could not possibly be loyal to Britain with so many of his closest relations fighting on the other side. A cousin was Admiral of the German Fleet. His German name (Battenberg) and title were constantly held against him and newspapers blamed him because in those first few weeks of the war, Britain's naval superiority was being challenged with some success by the Kaiser's fleet. Finally, Prince Louis could take no more and offered his resignation to Winston Churchill, the First Lord. His letter was a brief masterpiece in his understanding of the situation and typical of the dignity with which he had always conducted himself. He wrote:

Dear Mr. Churchill

"I have lately been driven to the painful conclusion that at this juncture my birth and parentage have the effect of impairing in some respects my usefulness on the Board of the Admiralty. In these circumstances I feel it to be my duty, as a loyal subject of His Majesty, to resign the office of First Sea Lord, hoping therefore to facilitate the task of the administration of the great Service to which I have devoted my life, and to ease the burden laid on HM's Ministers."

I am, Yours very truly!

Louis Battenberg, Admiral.

Churchill and Battenberg had worked brilliantly together for some years before the war and a close friendship had developed between the two men. It was from this stage that Churchill had developed deep affection for Dicke, Battenberg's son. It will be seen later that the most crucial breaks in Mountbatten's distinguished career were given by none other than Churchill a quarter of a century later, perhaps to make amends for the wrongs and the injustices that were done to his father.

Prince Louis's family knew that on the day he left the Admiralty his life was virtually over. His heart was broken and though he lived for seven more years, he never recovered his spirits or his health, and it would be left to his younger son to restore the family's reputation. It would be forty-one years before the final act was to be played out when the selfsame politician Winston Churchill would appoint Mountbatten as the Chief of the Naval Staff. This was the greatest triumph in the career of Mountbatten to have redeemed the family honour.

Other side of the story of a royal lobbyist

Mountbatten's leisure reading was restricted to study of genealogy, specially relating to his own family. During his Viceroyalty, when his predecessors might have occupied their spare time writing poetry (Wavell) or reading the latest detective story of Agatha Christie, Mountbatten would relax over the complex web of his ancestry delving into the generations that divided him from the Emperor Charlemagne and deriving pleasure at the intricate lattice of cousinship which bound him to all the royal families of Europe. He derived great satisfaction from his regal ancestry and pride in his family background was Mountbatten's most prominent characteristic. It will take far too much space to endeavour to unravel his family tree, suffice it to say that Mountbatten's heritage was truly royal.

Mountbatten was born in the Home Park of Windsor Castle and in Queen Victoria's words 'born under the shadow as it were of the castle', and urged that it should 'bear my name of whatever sex it may be'. Among his names, therefore was Victor in deference to the Queen's wishes. A nickname was a must and the Queen suggested Nicky. There were, however, so many Nickies at the Russian Court that Mountbatten's name was changed to Dicke – a name that remained for the rest of his life. For Mountbatten to join the Navy was just to continue the family tradition. The usual practice for budding naval officers was to go to the "Royal Naval College at Osborne" and then to continue to Dartmouth. After having graduated as a naval officer and served a brief period in battleships, Mountbatten went as an undergraduate to Cambridge. The Admiralty had reluctantly permitted Mountbatten to complete his university education.

It is worth recalling his university career to get some idea of some of the extraordinary contemporaries that Mountbatten had which assisted him throughout his life. It may be recalled that Mountbatten was already a serving officer in the Royal Navy when he went to Cambridge. At the beginning, he was quite indignant, as he records: 'Oh, it's unbearable. After over three years actually at sea in this Blessed War, having been Executive Officer of my own ship responsible for the discipline of her sixty men, I come to this place during the B.....y Peace and get treated worse than a sniveling school kid.' Such outbursts were rare, however, as Mountbatten immensely enjoyed his university life. Work did not figure prominently among his preoccupations, although his interests were varied. Mountbatten was more likely to be found dining with his cousins Bertie – future Duke of York and King George VI – and Harry – future Duke of Gloucester – who were his fellow students in Cambridge. It certainly helped Mountbatten in his career to have had King George VI not only as a cousin but also a close friend.

It was as a debater that he entered most vigorously into the university life, eventually being elected to the Cambridge Union. Once Mountbatten got Churchill down to speak. Churchill being a close friend of his father was to feature prominently in furthering Mountbatten's career in future. In Cambridge Mountbatten be   came an active debater and although he was never a politician he was an accomplished public speaker. He experienced the intoxication of feeling an audience stirred by his words: 'It's one of the most wonderful sensation in the world, and I can quite understand people going mad on it. Mountbatten also had an extremely active social life and during his stay at Cambridge had lost his heart to half a dozen girls, often two at once.

At the end of December 1919, Mountbatten was in London for a dance. Prince of Wales came up to him and asked whether he would like to accompany him in the *Renown* (the Royal Ship) on a tour of Australia and New Zealand. 'Of course', wrote Mountbatten to his mother, 'I nearly jumped out of my skin for joy and to be quite candid Audrey (his latest heartthrob) slid completely out of my mind.'

From the moment he had heard that in March 1920 the Prince of Wales was to visit Australia and New Zealand, Mountbatten had been dreaming that he   might go too. Indeed, he did more than dream, and pulled every string at his disposal, successfully involving his fellow undergraduate Prince Albert (the future King George VI) as an ally. We shall see that throughout Mountbatten's career, he lobbied very actively for every advantage, promotion and honour that he received. And to have had King George VI as a classmate put Mountbatten miles ahead of others. To be in the Prince of Wales' entourage, Mountbatten's role was that of flag-lieutenant to the head of the royal party Rear-Admiral Holsey, but in practice he was to serve as A.D.C., companion and nanny to the Prince.

Up to that time Mountbatten had not known his cousin David, the Prince of Wales very well. The Prince was six years older and exuded the aura of a future king. In the social circles the princes' charm was overwhelming. Less well known was the lighter side of him, the frivolity and the selfishness that was to destroy him as King Edward VIII. Suspicious of any courtier put about him by his father, the Prince of Wales responded warmly to the presence of the hero-worshipping Mountbatten. The *Renown* sailed for Australia on 15 March 1920 and returned to Portsmouth in October. Even before they had reached Australia the Prince had decided that he must have Mountbatten's companionship on the next long journey to India and Japan. This was certainly the most crucial episode of Mountbatten's career.

The Prince of Wales' visit to India was undertaken against all advice. Coming at the end of 1921 against the backdrop of constitutional reforms which introduced trial without jury for those accused of political crimes coupled with the Jalianwalah Bagh massacre more than undid any possible advantage. The Prince would certainly encounter hostility and possibly his life would be in danger. But such thoughts did little to dampen Mountbatten's enthusiasm. 'Tomorrow we arrive in India,' wrote Mountbatten in his diary for 16 November; 'I am not by nature incurably romantic but there is something rather wonderful, rather thrilling at the idea of setting foot for the first time in a country which genuinely belongs to the Far East. India is a country one has heard about, read about, even dreamt about but upto the present I have found it hopeless to conceive what it is like in real life. The next four months ought to show me. We are going to traverse India from East to West, and then from South to North, with a trip to Burma wedged in between these two tours. Finally, we double on our tracks and return to the West – Karachi.'

This tour of India was to change Mountbatten's life and set him up for his meteoric rise of his career. This was the trip when he became engaged to Edwina. Edwina was the child of Wilfred Ashley, a "Conservative Member of Parliament". And granddaughter of Sir Ernest Cassel who made a fortune as private banker and financial adviser to the future Edward VII. His wife had died in 1880 and his beloved only child, Edwina's mother, followed her in 1911 leaving Cassel totally dejected with life. Edwina became his main interest in life and when she was only seventeen, came to live with him in Brook House, his massive house in Park Lane.

Edwina was highly intelligent, elegant and blazed in the London society with her fierce brilliance that dazzled almost all. Her love for dancing, her pursuit of hectic pleasure, was indeed extravagant, if not absurd and she rejoiced in the attention earned by her talents and her position as Cassel's favourite grandchild. She was one of the most sought-after girls in London. When Mountbatten first met her at Claridge's at a ball in October 1920 she was being vigorously wooed by the Duke of Sutherland and Mountbatten himself was still embroiled with 'heavenly' Audrey James. They met occasionally that winter but it not until they were in the same party at Cowles in August 1921 that they really took notice of each other. From that moment the pace was furious. Mountbatten quickly decided that this was the girl for him; Edwina was little slower in responding. It is possible to view their mutual attraction as royalty meeting wealth.

Mountbatten's Wiles and Windfall and Wealth

Dicke Mountbatten was only nineteen when he heard that his cousin David was to set out on an extended visit to Australia, New Zealand and the West Indies, and he determined that he too would go on the trip. Months before the date of the departure he started his campaign to be included in the party. He used anyone and everyone he thought might be able to pull a few strings. The Prince of Wales, who had first been approached by Mountbatten, was agreeable, but he did not do anything about it himself. He always preferred to leave the logistics to others and he thought that Mountbatten could handle that part of the negotiations without his help. Mountbatten then tried to persuade Bertie (later King George VI) and Henry (later Duke of Glouchaster) to use their influence, but as the time for departure drew nearer and he heard nothing, he decided to take the matter into his own hands.

He could not make a formal application to join the tour; he had to wait to be invited, and the only person who could do that was the Prince of Wales. As anxious as he was, Mountbatten did not like being forced into a corner. Mountbatten then discovered that his cousin was going to attend an important dance in London given by Lady Ribblesdale, to which he, Mountbatten, had not been invited. This mere oversight was not a serious obstacle to the enterprising young officer and he persuaded another friend, who he knew had been invited, to ask the hostess if Dicke might also be included in the invitation list. It was a ploy he would use over and over throughout his life. He was never above asking to be invited somewhere if he felt it was important and useful for him to be there.

He was successful, as usual, and managed to find a quiet moment to remind the Prince of Wales that he had earlier agreed that Dicke should accompany him on the tour. The Prince there and then invited him to go along and, as Mountbatten afterwards wrote in his diary, 'Of course, I nearly jumped out of my skin for joy.' When the formal invitation arrived, it wasn't quite what Mountbatten had expected. Instead of being attached directly to the Duke of Wales's suite, as he had wished, he was appointed as the Flag Lieutenant for the Rear-Admiral Sir Lionel Halsey, His Royal Highness's Chief of Staff. In theory this meant that he was supposed to be working as a junior officer looking after the administrative details the Admiral could not be bothered with. In practice, it meant that for seven months he was 'minder' to the Prince of Wales; keeping him constantly amused, occupied and in a happy frame of mind. It was a role he relished as it gave him access to the Prince at all times, and not for the first time or last time in his life, he would use the connection to go over the heads of colleagues who were senior to him both in years and rank.

Mountbatten's natural enthusiasm and self-confidence, coupled with his tender years, ensured that in the early days of the tour he made several enemies among those closest to the Prince of Wales. Most of them had accompanied him on his earlier tour of the United States and Canada, and they had formed themselves into a small clique that resented the interloper who was so familiar with their royal master and even called him by his Christian name. They knew that he had forced himself on the Prince and, in the first instance, most of them felt he was not going to be of much practical use. However, it didn't take long for Mountbatten to establish himself as an integral and indispensable part of the team, and the others quickly realised that in him they had an ally to whom they could entrust all sorts of delicate tasks which protocol prevented them from carrying out themselves. He was also a useful sounding board about the Prince's moods and, from time to time, a buffer between them and his explosive and unpredictable temper.

Mountbatten used to say that it was in India that he met the three great loves of his life: India itself, Edwina and the game of polo. He was first taught to play the game by his Indian host and it became his life-long recreation. Later in life, he even wrote a book called *Introduction to Polo* under a pseudonym Marco. This book remains till today the standard guide for this game and has been reprinted several times. Within a few weeks of Mountbatten's departure for India accompanying the Prince of Wales Edwina decided that a visit to India to stay with the Viceroy, Lord Reading, would be in order. One can marvel at the level of the contacts of both Dicke and Edwina as Lord Reading happened to be a close family friend of Edwina's. King Edward VII was the godfather of Edwina. Be that as it may, Edwina had to borrow £100 from a friend to pay the fare because she did not have enough money in her bank account at that time. And this was after her grandfather had died and left her millions in his will. It had simply not entered her head that her bank would have been delighted to offer her any advance she needed until the will matured.

It was in the midst of a magnificient ball in the Vicerigal residence on Valentine's Day, 14th February 1922, that Dicke popped the question to Edwina. Everybody appeared to have been delighted at the engagement with only the Vicereine Lady Reading striking a discordant note.

Cautiously she wrote to Edwina's father 'I hoped she would have cared for someone older, with more of a career before him'. The wedding took place less than a month after Mountbatten's return, on 18th July 1922. It was suitably magnificent with fourteen hundred guests gracing the occasion. For the public the wedding provided a glorious opportunity for celebrations and the press had a field day. Whether one believed with the *Star* that labeled it as the "Wedding of the Century" or preferred the more sobre judgement from the

Lord and Lady Mountbatten on their wedding day
(townandcountrymag.com)

Daily Telegraph that it was merely the wedding of the year, it was a considerable occasion.

Getting back to Edwina, there is no doubt that Mountbatten's spectacular career was largely due to the enormous wealth that Edwina had inherited from her grandfather Sir Ernest Cassel. When Sir Ernest Cassel died he left £7.5 million, which at today's prices would be worth several billions. Edwina, Sir Cassel's favourite granddaughter, was to inherit the lion's share of his legacy when she got married, which would make her one of the richest women in the world. Mountbatten's pay at the same period was £310 per year and his income from dividends provided an additional £300. The reason for giving these figures is to illustrate the style and grandeur of Mountbatten's life once he had married, and the changes to his lifestyle that access to virtually unlimited money made.

Some idea of opulence which he believed for his whole life can be gauged from getting a few glimpses of his residences. Mountbatten, when he was 24, was posted to train as a specialist signal's officer at Portsmouth and the Naval College at Greenwich. The Mountbattens settled at Adsdean, a large Victorian house about twelve miles from Portsmouth, which was taken initially for nine months but was to remain their base until Edwina inherited Broadlands just before 1939. Edwina furnished Adsdean with style, there was a polo practice ground, a golf course, three tennis courts, eight hundred acres of shooting, room for twenty guests – an establishment certainly ampler than any of his naval colleagues including Admirals of the Fleet. Mountbatten also had the use of the palatial Brook House in Park Lane. From Adsdean and Brook House, Mountbatten conducted a furious pursuit of pleasure in which every moment that was not dedicated to work seemed to have been spent at meals, on the dance floor or in one of the sporting activities. Mountbatten would rush to London at the end of a day in Portsmouth, dine and dance away the night, then be driven back in his Rolls Royce which had been fitted with a collapsible seat to allow him to sleep in transit, often arriving at Adsdean only just in time to change and drive on to the signal's school. It was a regimen made possible only by the prodigal expenditure of wealth.

Edwina's Indiscretions

The main players in the episode of the partition of India are Mountbatten, Edwina, Nehru, Jinnah, Patel, V.P. Menon, and Krishna Menon. Any analysis of the events of 1947 in the Indian sub-continent requires an insight into the characters of the main actors. In the best of circumstances looking back over half a century in hindsight one wonders how in a matter of few months dramatic events have left serious consequences for millions and has kept South Asia in a political tangle which might take centuries to correct. It is being endeavoured to gain insights into the behaviour patterns of the prime participants to find some rationale and logic to explain the events.

We have seen that by design or accident Mountbatten married the richest heiress in the world. In spite of never having to work again if he chose not to, once he had married, Mountbatten decided to continue his naval career, with the full agreement of his wife. His new-found fortune made life as a peace time officer in the twenties and thirties very pleasant indeed. He was able to indulge in a variety of expensive pastimes without having to rely solely on his service pay. However, in spite of his wealth, social position and royal connections, Mountbatten took his career seriously and worked as hard as he played. He made himself into an expert in radio communications at a time when the subject was not fashionable and with his natural aptitude for languages he qualified easily as an interpreter in both French and German.

On the domestic front the Mountbattens' life appeared harmonious enough in the early years. Two children were born, Patricia in 1924 and her sister Pamela in 1929. Already cracks in the marriage were beginning to show, with both partners indulging in extra marital affairs that would litter the remainder of their lives together. A large part of the British Navy was based in the Mediterranean during the interwar period, and Mountbatten spent a considerable amount of his life in this part of the world; years in which he was able to polish his talents as a polo player, scuba diver and water-skier. In 1932 he put his newly acquired technical skills to excellent use when, as Mediterranean Fleet Wireless Officer, he invented a system by which the whole fleet was able to listen to the first of King George V's historic Christmas broadcasts to the Empire. By 1934, Mountbatten had been advanced and appointed as a Full Commander and taken over his first ship, "*The Destroyer HMS Daring*". It was an appropriate name. Some would say Mountbatten was reckless to the point of danger.

The Mountbattens lived lavishly. Brook House their palatial residence in Park Lane was maintained in the grandest style with Mountbatten relishing every item of their conspicuous expenditure and Edwina more amused than irritated with his obsessive love of detail. At considerable expense his bedroom was remodeled to resemble an officer's cabin. Similarly, Adsdean their Portsmuth manor house was run with similar splendor. House-parties were large and usually glamorous; film stars and members of the royal family, admirals and politicians mingled freely. It seemed that life could hardly hold more, yet the idyll proved more apparent than real. Once the first delights of matrimony had worn off it became evident to both of them that, though they complemented each other admirably in many, perhaps most, respects, in others they were woefully incompatible. Restless, dissatisfied, rapacious for new experience, it is unlikely that any one man could have given Edwina all she needed. Certainly, her husband proved inadequate. His failure was not solely, or even primarily, physical. Edwina rebelled fiercely the fetters of domesticity. Mountbatten's vision of an ideal marriage was a relationship so close that every confidence was shared, no private fancies pursued. He longed to possess and to be possessed. The vision filled his wife with horror. She valued above all her independence and her privacy: independence to do what she wanted when she wanted; privacy in which to pursue her own development unobserved.

The clumsiness and tactlessness that once had seemed so charming now became irritants; sharply alive to every nuance of her own sensitivity, Edwina rarely stopped to reflect that he might have feelings too. His affection sometimes moved her but too often it provided a new cause for irritation. A proud spirit, she was doomed to live alone in a fortress whose walls Mountbatten could never breach, whose existence, indeed, he never more than dimly suspected. Mountbatten's letters were expressed in affectionate, sometimes cloyingly sentimental terms. Edwina's responses were more brittle and less heartfelt, catalogues for the most part of weekends and dances. Increasingly they fretted each other's' nerves, Edwina withdrawing ever more in angry isolation, Mountbatten baffled and reproachful. To be alone together, once a source of delight, became a peril to be avoided. Peter Murphy was enlisted as something close to a third member of the marriage: an essential emollient, good-humored, tactful, fond of both parties, too intelligent to become involved in the ever more frequent rows. References to him in both their diaries are so frequent that it seems he almost took up residence in their houses. To the children, indeed, he appeared part of the family. Yet even Murphy could not be everywhere.

In September 1924 the couple went to New York. Minor vexations, tolerable when Mountbatten was occupied with his career, proved more painful when on holiday. Edwina became impatient. On the eve of their return to England she announced bluntly that she would not be coming. It was the first of many temporary desertions. Gossip began to spread and was embroidered busily even after her return. 'Went to see David at St. James's Palace,' noted Mountbatten in his diary. 'He had a queer story about Edwina.' Their lives diverged. When in England, Mountbatten more and more often stayed at Adsdean during the week, working or playing golf, tennis and polo with his naval cronies, while Edwina remained in London, reappearing at weekends with large house- parties. From Malta she would leave on adventurous expeditions around the globe, doing her bit as a naval officer's wife on her return, but rarely doing it for long. 'Lovely to see the old girl again,' Mountbatten would note wistfully, or, 'Divine having the old girl back.'

Early in 1928 a divorce action was threatened in the United States in which Edwina was to be cited as co-respondent. Beaverbook was called in to help. 'If threat is serious it is a matter of utmost importance that suit should be stopped,' he cabled the New York lawyer Paul Cravath. 'Our money resources are sufficient or if money is of no use we will offer immense social influence in support of plaintiff.'

Gossip linked Edwina's name with many men but in the late 1920s she became associated almost exclusively with Laddie Sandford, a rich, polo-playing American of the type for which the word 'cad' seems to have been invented. To the outside world Mountbatten appeared to observe this liason with the same tolerant indifference as he had shown towards her other affairs; only to Edwina did he admit that Sandford had been 'the cause of pretty well all the unhappiness I have known'. Even then, he grasped touchingly at his wife's offer of renewed friendship and shared confidences: 'I offer you all my sympathetic understanding about Laddie, and will really. . . try to feel nicely about him always.' For a man often accused, and with some reason, of arrogant self-confidence, his humility and readiness to admit his own inadequacies in his relationship with his wife are constantly astonishing. He wrote to her from H.M.S. *Warspite* in 1927:

'I wish I could drive a car like Bobby Casa Maury, play the piano and talk culture like Peter, make enthusiastic remarks like Ralph, play golf like Ronnie, shoot like Daddy, play polo like Jack. I wish I knew how to flirt with other women, and especially with my wife. I wish I had sown many more wild oats in my youth, and could excite you more than I fear I do. I wish I wasn't in the Navy and had to drag you out to Malta. I wish I had an equal share of the money so that I could give you far handsomer presents than I can really at present honestly manage. In other words - I would like to feel that I was really worthy of your love.'

Mountbatten's Loyalties?

One aspect of Mountbatten's character can be seen at the time of resignation of King Edward VIII to marry Wallis Simpson. It may be recalled the amount of wheeling and dealing Mountbatten did to get into the entourage of Prince of Wales' tour of India, Japan, and New Zealand and Australia. During that tour although their age difference was six years they had come extremely close and Mountbatten considered Prince of Wales to be a dear friend.

Early in 1936 Mountbatten visited London for the funeral of King George V and the coronation of Edward VIII. In the period since the royal tours the two men had grown apart. Mountbatten's closest ally among the royal princes was George (future King George VI), now Duke of Kent. The new king found his former 'best friend' Mountbatten boringly committed to his career and a little pompous. He complained that Mountbatten always seemed to be asking for some favour. They were still fond of each other, Mountbatten had prepared in the early thirties for his cousin a list of eighteen unmarried European princesses with ages ranging from fifteen to thirty-three.

(L to R): Edward VIII; Mountbatten; Esmond Harmsworth; Mrs Rogers; Wallis Simpson; Gladys Buist; and Edwina Mountbatten (wordpress.com)

Mountbatten had already met Mrs. Simpson several times in the Mediterranean and seemed to have approved of her. In the beginning Mountbatten had approved of the Prince of Wales and Simpson match. As late as 7 December 1936 Mountbatten was still putting himself forward as a loyal supporter of the King. 'I can't bear to be sitting here doing nothing to help you in your terrible trouble'. He wrote to the King:

'If you want me to help you, to do any service for you or even to feel you have a friend of Wallis' to keep you company you have only to telephone. I don't want to be bothersome but there is nothing I can do to help except to bite people's heads off who have the temerity to say anything disloyal about their King - and there are practically none who do so - at any rate in my presence.'

Evidence suggests that although Mountbatten was making strong pronouncements in favour of 'My monarch right or wrong' his actual feelings were at best ambivalent. While on one side he was showing loyalty to the king he was keeping his options open towards the future King George VI. Between 30 September, when they travelled down from Balmoral together - 'Long and interesting talk with David' - and the lunch at Fort Belvedere on 10 December, when all four brothers assembled for the final confrontation. 'Dicke down at the Fort all day where chaos reigns,' Edwina wrote in her diary. 'Everyone completely sunk except the King who remains fairly calm and cheerful.' Mountbatten was called on to provide a destroyer for his cousin's departure; 'Long talk to Bertie,' he noted that evening. In the interval he was, as he told the King, 'sitting here doing nothing', excluded from his cousin's innermost councils, half relieved and half resentful at his exclusion.

His own view of King Edward VIII was less rosy than might have been deduced from his protestations of devotion. He still liked to think of the King as his best friend, but had been quite upset by the King's abandonment of his former girlfriend Freda Dudley Ward. Mrs. Simpson, he liked, and was amused by, but he had concluded that she would never sit happily on a throne. Wallis had got off to a bad start when she had first gone to stay with the Mountbattens and brought with her a cold chicken from Fortnum and Masons. Edwina who flattered herself having the best chef in Europe was not amused. 'I can't understand why he wants to *marry* the woman,' was Mountbatten's mother's comment and her son saw no reason to dissent.

But as important Mountbatten's disillusionment with Edward VIII was he acquired a new respect for the future King George VI. In the past he had seen the 'Duke of York' through the eyes of the 'Prince of Wales' – 'Dear old Bertie' (King George VI), honest, loyal, a little stupid. Only as the crisis deepened and the abdication became more likely did he begin to appreciate the integrity and radiant decency which were to make the unfashionable younger brother so much better a monarch than the more glamorous Prince of Wales would ever have been. Mountbatten and the future King George VI were together at Fort Belvedere as Edward VIII was preparing for his final departure. George was agonised arguing his inadequacy for his new role: 'I've never even seen a State Paper. I'm only a Naval Officer, it's the only thing I know about'. Mountbatten's reply was to encourage his cousin Bertie to become the King. 'This is a very curious coincidence,' he said. 'My father once told me that, when the Duke of Clarence died your father came to him and said almost said the same things that you have said to me now and my father answered: 'George, you are wrong, there is no more preparation for a King than to have been trained in the Navy'.

A day after the King's departure Mountbatten wrote to the new King on December 11:

'My dear Bertie,

Heartbroken as I am at David's departure and all the terrible trouble he has brought on us all I feel I must tell you how deeply I feel for Elizabeth and you having to shoulder his responsibilities in such trying circumstances.

Luckily both you and your children have precisely those qualities needed to pull this country through this ghastly crisis. You will have the sympathy of all except a few extremists (be they Communists or Fascists) who may use this opportunity to stir up trouble.

On all hands in the Admiralty one hears the profound satisfaction of the Navy expressed at having once more a Sailor King - as the 1st Sea Lord remarked today, the first King to have fought in a naval battle.'

Readers may compare the supportive letter which Mountbatten had written on December 7 to Edward VIII with the letter he wrote to King George VI On December 11.

Mountbatten has been accused of abandoning King Edward VIII and switching allegiance to his brother with indecorous haste. Certainly, he was never one to hitch his wagon to a star unless he was first satisfied that it was unlikely to sputter out into eternity. He did however volunteer to act as best man at the Duke of Windsor's wedding. It is claimed the offer was refused as the Duke had already invited his equerry to do the job. In fact, the Duke was distressed that he was not able to have his two brothers as supporters had announced that he would not invite anybody connected with the royal family. An extract survives from a letter written to the Duke by Mountbatten on 5 May, 1937:

'You will have heard that although I succeeded in fixing a date for your wedding that suited Bertie, George, etc, other people stepped in and have produced a situation that has made all your friends very unhappy. I have made several attempts to get matters put right, but at present, I cannot even accept your kind invitation myself. I haven't quite given up all hope yet, though my chances don't look good. I'll write again when I know finally.'

One can infer from the above letter that Mountbatten decided not to break ranks in his own interests. His long-standing friendship with King Edward VIII was forgotten and also forgotten were the countless favours that he had received from the Prince of Wales. No doubt an embargo had been placed on the members of the royal family to attend the Duke of Windsor's wedding. Mountbatten who was then serving as the Naval A.D.C. to the new King thought discretion to be the better part of valour fell in line with the other royals. What would have happened if the Duke of Windsor had accepted his offer to be best man and the ban on attendance had subsequently been imposed is a matter for conjecture. It was fortunate for Mountbatten that his cousin's truculence spared him a painful struggle with his conscience.

Mountbatten: Whose Choice? - II

It may be recalled that when Mountbatten had visited India with the Prince of Wales there was widespread boycott of the tour which had resulted in countrywide riots. Gandhi had organised the boycott as an act of civil disobedience. The non-violent movement had resulted in violence and the Viceroy Lord Reading ordered leading Indians to be arrested all over the country though Gandhi himself escaped the order. Wherever the 'Prince of Wales' party rode through elaborately decorated streets, the local people remained at home and left the streets empty of onlookers. In Allahabad the young Jawaharlal Nehru and his father were both locked up when the royal party came through. The royal party who were really keen to meet the Indian leaders were quite disturbed at the state of affairs. Mountbatten had suggested to the prince 'Why don't we go talk to Gandhi? It would show that we understood and sympathised. Between us we could convince him that we should be friends' (*Edwina* by Richard Hough). Officialdom was outraged at this radical suggestion. Undismayed Dicke had asked if, instead, he could go alone. This idea was sharply rejected.

One of Edwina's friends in London before the war was 'Vengalil Krishnan Krishna Menon' who was a Middle Temple lawyer and a politician but he described himself as an educator and a publicist. His main goal as a publicist was the freedom of Indian. His second goal was to spread socialism, and in this capacity, he was a borough councilor for St. Pancras from 1934 and a one-time parliamentary candidate. Moreover, he was one of the originators of the paperback book concept which he had presented to 'Allen Lane' in the May of 1932 and which became Penguin Books and he became the very first editor of Pelican Books. Edwina was a fan of his critical thinking, his intellectualism, his intense socialism and antimilitarist. It was because of Menon that Edwina had learned about his disciple, Jawaharlal Nehru, and in 1936, she came across Nehru's autobiography which was published by the Bodley Head, for whom Menon was editor. According to Krishna Menon, Nehru who was the former pupil of Harrow School, former pupil of Trinity College, Cambridge, Temple barrister, would be the first Prime Minister of a free India. He joined non-cooperation movement which was started by Gandhi in 1920, and after 19 years, succeeded his father as Chairperson of All India National Congress (*Edwina* by Richard Hough).

Edwina's time spent in India in 1945 made her even more eager to meet this man who dedicated his life fighting for the freedom of his people – and in prison, to which he had been confined in 1942. Her heart was fixated on him ever since she had first visited India in 1922, and Dicke was not given permission to see him at that time and he had been confined later. The journey in January 1945 included a trip to Dacca by ambulance train, where she spent three days. On the first night Edwina watched a show in an officers' ward, on the next she was at a dance for the men. At Chittagong Edwina dutifully took a rest day at an army holiday camp, before moving on to Cox's Bazar and Akyab.

Mountbatten was not allowed to see Nehru for a second time in the first month of 1944 when Nehru was in Ahmednagar Fort. The permission was denied by the governor of Bombay despite Dicke being cousin of the King. No Englishman in the Indian Service imagined at the time that Mountbatten would be the next Viceroy of India. Mountbatten wanted to meet him as badly as Edwina now, but not only because he was curious. He felt a great connection with India, which he thought he had adapted from the Japanese. He also felt a bit patriotic for the country. Just as Edwina, he also believed that it was only a short while before control was taken from Britain by the people of India, and he already recognised that he might be involved in the process in one thing or another. Some people thought, he had his eyes set on the Viceroyship at the end of the war. 'All this business about being surprised when he was offered the job of giving away India as Viceroy – and then at first refusing it – is all my eye,' one of the officers in his crew at the time said. 'Dicke was steering towards the Delhi job in 1945, maybe while the war was still on. It was all part of The Great Plan.'

Some have commented that Sir Stafford Cripps, a member of the Cabinet Mission to India, wanted Mountbatten to become the last Viceroy and put the idea to the 'Prime Minister' on his return to London. Or was it Attlee himself who planned the meeting between Nehru and Mountbatten in Singapore as an overture to the replacement of Archibald Wavell by Mountbatten as the Viceroy? Nehru himself stated to his biographer, Marie Seton, that 'Agatha Harrison, the Singapore Quaker who was the representative of Gandhi in London, and Krishna Menon, also in London, set up the Singapore meeting and reception in cahoots with the British authorities'.

The facts cannot be changed. Mountbatten was in Delhi in the second month of 1946 at the time when Nehru, who just got out of jail, wanted to visit the Indian communities and troops in Malaya and Burma. Wavell talked about this issue with Mountbatten, still Supreme Commander, who approved without any questions. Wavell then sent an official telegram to the Governor of Burma, Colonel Sir Reginald Dorman-Smith, who rejected the idea of the visit. He was at once overruled by Mountbatten, who deputed two officers, 'Choudhury Mohammed Ali, future Prime Minister of Pakistan, and Major Sawhney', to handle the situation so that there won't be any clashes. The ongoing situation in Singapore was at that time quite unstable. There were a lot of Bose's INA (Indian National Army) troops loose on the streets. They had fought with the Japanese against the Indian and Allied armies, and their leaders were still being sought by the British military administration. It was a surer thing that Nehru would receive a thunderous reception from his own people, and the military arranged an open route from the airport to the Government House with tight security.

Mountbatten accompanied by Edwina, arrived in Singapore precisely 24 hours before Nehru, and found out that the British had refused to provide him with transport to openly show that they had no respect for him. As soon as, Mountbatten found out about this disrespectful act, he sent a car for Nehru himself, and added a bonus to Nehru's welcome by providing tickets to any Indian who wanted to see their national hero at the airport, and he also offered them free bus transport. Thousands of Indians accepted his offer. Nehru's landed right after noon on the 18 of March in 1946, and he was welcomed

Jawaharlal Nehru with Lord Mountbatten in Singapore, 1946
(commons.wikimedia.org)

by a great uproar when the passed through the door at the Airport. Mountbatten's man met him at the staircase and took him to his car in which they went to Government House for tea. He saw his supporters cheering for him throughout the way from Airport to Government House. There Mountbatten met him and, an hour later, escorted him into his own open limousine.

Marie Seton wrote:

'Side by side, with aplomb, the future Viceroy of India and Prime Minister were driven out of the tall wrought-iron gates into the street packed with Indians craning their necks to see Panditji. A cameraman caught the expression of surprise at the unexpected sight of Indian and British soldiers saluting side by side. As Mountbatten later told one of his staff, he was gratified and not a little amused to find himself included in the cheering.'

Nehru wanted to go to his hotel as he was tired from plane ride, but Mountbatten had another plan. 'My wife is very anxious to meet you. She is inspecting the welfare services in Singapore and is at the YMCA (Young Men's Christian Association) with a number of her workers,' he said. Nehru agreed to Mountbatten's plan without any problems. He also wanted to meet the honourable wife of the Commander-in-Chief of the Armed Forces who gave so much for his countrymen, as she would have wanted to see him. He noticed that there was a change in their route but he had no time to ask any questions and he entered the wooden building with Mountbatten before Indians people rushed in through the other entrances. Indira, the daughter of Nehru, recalled 'Lady Mountbatten was flat on the floor when my father and she met in Singapore. When my father went in everyone rushed and they just knocked her down. So, the first thing they had to do, Lord Mountbatten and my father, was to rescue her and put her back on her feet.'

What the Butler Saw!

Charles Smith was Mountbatten's butler and valet for nearly fifty years. He has left a fascinating account of the personal lives of the Mountbattens in his Fifty Years with Mountbatten. Charles Smith lived in Mountbatten's silhouette for nearly half a century sharing his fortunes, his triumphs and his agonies. He was with him during historic times: In Singapore, where he saw Mountbatten, as Supreme Allied Commander, accept the surrender of the Japanese; in Delhi, when he was proclaimed Viceroy of India; in Malta, where he was Commander-in-Chief, Mediterranean; and in many other parts of the world. Charles Smith was with Mountbatten during two British coronations; he drove him to Fort Belvedere in Sunningdale when Mountbatten was summoned there to be privately informed of King Edward's decision to abdicate; and on many other eventful occasions. In 1947, when the Mountbattens had to return to India, Charles Smith was responsible for the running of Broadlands during Princess Elizabeth and Prince Phillip's honeymoon.

The Mountbattens were lavish entertainers and a constant stream of the rich and famous visited them. All the monarchs of Europe, Queen Mary, George VI, Gandhi, Nehru, Noel Coward, Charlie Chaplin, Elizabeth Taylor, and many others. The Prince of Wales and Mrs. Wallis Simpson were frequent visitors, as were the royal family. Princess Elizabeth and Princes Margaret were playmates of the Mountbattens' two daughters, Patricia and Pamela. Prince Philip often stayed with them as a child, as in later years did Prince Charles. Charles Smith has a fund of anecdotes about them. It is good fun reading his *Fifty Years With Mountbatten*.

Lord Mountbatten kissing Queen Mary's hand at the prize-giving ceremony after the Duke of York's Cup polo match (wordpress.com)

A few of the episodes are related which the readers might find amusing. Mountbatten liked to be fashionably dressed, there was a period in the thirties when he fell behind modern-day style which became transparently clear on a visit to America where he was to inspect a U.S. Naval Base. The Mountbattens were in Miami changing planes where a U.S. Naval Officer who had come to receive them mistook Charles Smith for Mountbatten as the valet appeared more distinctly better dressed! Imagine Mountbatten's

Chaplin with Edwina and Louis Mountbatten in Hollywood (wordpress.com)

outrage when the Naval Officer nudged him and asked 'Where do you think the old man wants his luggage put in?' Mountbatten looked daggers at the Officer and sternly directed him towards his valet.

Poor Mountbatten, dressed in an unflattering grey flannel suit that he insisted on wearing, could not get over the shock of being mistaken for the valet. Disgusted by the mistaken identity Dicke told Edwina about it. Edwina seeing Mountbatten's suit said that she was not surprised looking at Mountbatten's suit. Mountbatten, then feeling conscious about his dress ordered his valet in the transit lounge to unpack his case and to locate another suit for him. Mountbatten then proceeded to change his suit in record time in the rest room. When he reappeared in a dark, pinstriped suit Edwina gave her approval. There was one snag, however, while Mountbatten was changing, their luggage had been loaded on the plane and the poor valet was left holding the grey flannel suit. The Naval Aide who had come to receive Mountbatten looked coveted at the suit. Charles Smith not knowing what to do with the suit promptly presented it to the Naval Aide.

That might well have been the end of the episode except, that a few months later, back in England when Charles Smith inquired of Mountbatten what he would like to wear that day he wished to wear the self-same grey flannel suit. When his valet confessed what he had done to the grey flannel suit Mountbatten slapped a hand to his forehead in disbelief and cried out, 'Edwina come quickly!' Edwina came rushing anticipating some disaster and immediately inquired from Dicke the cause of his consternation. 'It's my grey flannel suit. You know the one. What do you think? Charles gave it away in Miami!' Edwina's face lit up. She turned to Charles and said, 'Congratulations, Charles! That's the best day's work you've ever done!'

There was another incident when Charles and Mountbatten found themselves buying a Panama Hat in Jamaica. Dicke liked the hat but thought the price was too high. Charles who went to the shop later bought the same hat after severe bargaining for a fraction of the price the shopkeeper had demanded from Mountbatten. Seeing his valet wearing the hat that Mountbatten had wanted to buy he was most distressed and immediately informed his valet that he was being paid too much. Anyway, after some hilarious incidents relating to the hat Mountbatten surreptitiously pinched the hat from Charles. This hat had a long innings and Mountbatten wore it during his Viceroyalty in India.

There was another incident in a very fashionable ball in Miami when much to Mountbatten's despair an American millionaire asked him, 'You don't mind Dicke if I borrow your valet now, do you?' Charles and the millionaires danced away all night. Obviously, Charles must have been a very handsome, well groomed, and an attractive personality as the biography is full of incidents of this nature involving the royalty, the rich and the famous. When Charles reported for duty the next morning, Mountbatten noticed that his valet was still dressed in evening clothes. 'Good heavens, Charles, the way you are carrying on you will be in the gossip columns if you are not careful' quipped Mountbatten. Feeling exhausted after a sleepless night Charles crept into a bunk at the rear of the fuselage in the twin-engine sea plane that was to take them on to Jamaica that day. The valet thought he would have a short nap during the flight. When Mountbatten noticed an empty seat earmarked for Charles he thought his valet had not boarded the flight at Miami. He instructed the pilot to return to Miami to collect the valet! Luckily Charles was discovered as the plane was making its approach to land back in Miami. With exasperation ringing in his voice Mountbatten barked, 'The next time we are in Miami remind me not to let you go dancing!'

Charles' love for the good life landed him into trouble many a time. Once while staying at Darmstadt Palace in Germany as a guest of Mountbatten's uncle, the Grand Duke Ernest Louis of

Hesse. Charles ventured out for a night. He had been invited to a beer garden party and when he got back to the palace in the middle of the night it was locked, and despite incessant ringing of the night bell he could not arouse anyone. Then he spotted a magnolia tree close to the open window of his bedroom in the palace. He clambered up the branches only to be hauled down by his ankles by the palace guards, who suddenly appeared out of the darkness. The guards didn't speak English and Charles did not know German. He was promptly arrested and confined to the cell. When ultimately the valet's identity was established profuse apologies followed and he was released at 7:30 a.m. which delayed giving the wake-up call to his master by half-an-hour.

Over breakfast Mountbatten was treated to the tale of the valet's adventures and at a palace banquet that evening Charles was summoned before the guests. Mountbatten announced, 'Here is our prisoner…' to the delight of those present. Charles stood shame-faced muttering something incoherent with Mountbatten savoring every moment of his valet's discomfort.

Butler Knows All

At the outbreak of World War II Mountbatten's butler had to join military service. Much to Mountbatten's annoyance Charles informed him that he would not be joining the navy but the air force. Mountbatten not to be outdone said, 'I don't want to injure your feelings, but I don't honestly think you've got the legs – or the stomach – for the sea.' 'Actually' replied the butler, 'You can't have two Admirals in one house, can you?' The remark brought a twinkle to Dicke's eyes. Obviously, Charles was never overawed by Mountbatten.

Unfortunately, Charles' war career was totally uneventful although he kept on trying to get some action. All the action he saw was in the Officers' Mess as a steward. He was transferred to various stations ultimately ending up in Secundrabad in India where he spent the entire war in peace. By this time Mountbatten was appointed Supreme Commander of the Southeast Asia Command. Charles wrote a letter directly to Mountbatten as Dicke had told him, 'If you ever come out East, then please let me know Charles'. Charles posted his letter and was promptly arrested two hours later for breaking military regulations by writing direct to the Supreme Commander. He was hauled up before the C.O. who wanted to know how he had dared to break service rules. Very meekly Charles informed the C.O. that in civilian life he was Mountbatten's valet and that he was writing to him on personal matters. Learning about this the C.O. relented and let the letter be sent. Mountbatten replied within a fortnight but the letter was confiscated by the C.O. who sent for Charles once more and ordered him to open the letter in front of the C.O. Charles quickly sped through the contents and gave it to the C.O. to read. It was a typically chatty letter from Mountbatten telling of a week leave he had spent in England, but the most interesting part was the postscript, 'I may want to borrow you to open up Government House Singapore for me' (The letter is reproduced). The fact that the Supreme Commander SEAC found time to write to his old valet shows favourably about his character. In fact, in Charles Smith's biography at least twenty letters have been reproduced which show the kindliness and consideration with which Mountbatten treated Charles.

Prince Charles and Lord Mountbatten, wearing full naval uniform
(express.co.uk)

The Commanding Officer was visibly shaken to see such an intimate letter from the Supreme Commander to the lowly Sergeant. As luck would have it that very moment the telephone rang and he practically stood up talking on the phone. It was Mountbatten himself requesting the immediate release of Charles and his prompt dispatch to Kandy in Ceylon where Dicke had his headquarters. Within the next couple of hours Charles was air-lifted to Kandy where he was hurriedly produced before Mountbatten. 'Charles, how good to see you' said Mountbatten shaking his hand. 'First, let me hear what you've been doing during the war. I want to hear all about it.' The enquiry caused extreme embarrassment as probably the only exciting event for Charles during the entire war was spilling some drinks in the Officers' Mess. Mountbatten on the other hand was hallowed throughout Southeast Asia and had won all the coveted decorations.

Mountbatten rose from his desk and picked up a green leather-faced wooden box that Charles instantly recognised. It was Dicke's decoration box which Charles had bought for him in London before the outbreak of the war. Mountbatten brought the box over from the other side of the room and placed it on the desk. Charles remembered the severe scolding that he had got from his master when he had bought it. It was far too big and he was told that no one could have possibly filled the box with decoration. As Mountbatten was opening the box, Charles thought he was in for another castigation. But, no. Mountbatten smiled and reflected, 'Charles, do you remember, when I tore you up a strip for buying this box to put my medals in? I thought it was too massive at the time and I think I told you so. Well Charles, I take back everything I said. Just have a peep at it. There isn't room to put another medal or ribbon in.'

Charles then moved on to Singapore to take charge of the Government House. Seven days later, the formal surrender ceremony was arranged in the Council Chamber of Singapore Town Hall where Mountbatten accepted the surrender of 680,879 Japanese in Southeast Asia in the presence of military representatives of the United States, India, Australia, China, France and Holland. Mountbatten insisted that the Japanese Supreme Commanders should not only sign the surrender treaty, but hand over their ceremonial swords, thus stripping them of their last vestments of honour and dignity. Charles was present throughout the ceremony. We now skip to the period of the Viceroyalty of Mountbatten in India. His butler records that Mountbatten's 'swearing-in' ceremony as Viceroy was an occasion marked with almost as much pomp and pageantry as a coronation. To all intents and purposes, it was a coronation for Mountbatten had become the emperor of India. Mountbatten's love of pomp and pageantry was well known. The way Mountbatten was dressed for the occasion has been elaborately described in Freedom at Midnight and an extract is given below. With meticulous eagle-eyed attention to detail he had developed during twenty-five years in Mountbatten's service, he threaded the silk cornflower blue sash of the Order of the Garter as it is called, the company of the world's most exclusive gentry, through the right epaulette and drew it even tighter across the breast of the uniform. He placed the gold aiguillettes which marked the owner as a personal A.D.C. to King George VI over the right epaulette.

Smith removes from their violet boxes his employer's medal bar and the four major stars which he will don for the day. Order of the Garter, Order of the Star of India, Order of the Indian Empire, Grand Cross of Victorian Order were gleaming in their gold and silver enamel, waiting for the last touch of polish. It is said that the butler knows all. Charles Smith has left a brief description of the goings on of the Viceregal Lodge. Charles says Gandhi

Lord and Lady Mountbatten with Indian lawyer and anti-colonial campaigner, Mahatma Gandhi
(andmeetings.com)

visited the Mountbattens three times. Nehru was a more frequent visitor and so too was another of the politicians, Sardar Patel. Their conferences would be conducted in Mountbatten's office, the picture rails of which were hung with his wartime regimental plaques. The punch-line in the entire book is 'It was Mr. Nehru who had recommended Lord Louis for the post of Viceroy'. This is a most significant observation made by Charles Smith. He certainly had some firm basis for making these remarks. He would have done history a monumental service had he elaborated even a little bit as to how he came to this conclusion. The interested reader can only take this as the Gospel truth as the butler knows all. It may be mentioned that Charles' book does not refer to a single League leader. We shall leave Charles Smith in Delhi. His book is full of anecdotes and he stayed on with Mountbatten till his last days. In Smith's own words 'No man is a hero to his valet? What mockery Lord Louis made of that saying. In my eyes he will forever remain a hero.'

CHAPTER 4: THE MAKING OF A VICEROY

Appointment: Mountbatten's Version

The lesson of history is that facts, figures and events are handed down to us for generations in many cases based on conjectures, inferences and downright guesswork. Which historian knows what goes on behind the scenes of great events. For example, the reader may study several sources of the travel route of Marco Polo to China. Each chronicle records substantially different route followed by this great traveler. As the well-read reader knows the travels of Marco Polo were related to people and different versions arose from the perceptions of each of the chroniclers. A dramatic version also states that Marco Polo never travelled at all and the whole episode was the figment of his imagination.

Lord Mountbatten, appointed as the Viceroy of India

A few pertinent facts should be glossed over to delve into the appointment of Mountbatten as a Viceroy of India. One of Mountbatten's favourite stories about his Viceroyalty was that he had nearly been appointed four years earlier instead of being given the South East Asia Command. Churchill had asked Leo Amery, the Secretary of State for India for a list names for a successor to Lord Linlithgow, shortly to retire. Four names were suggested, those of Anthony Eden, Rab Butler, Lord Salisbury and Mountbatten. Churchill favoured Eden, but the King turned him down because, for safety reasons, he had to have Churchill's successor at home. Butler was out because as Minister of Education he was too busy and his work too important. Salisbury was considered ineligible.

According to Mountbatten's story, that brought his own name to the top of the list. According to Leo Amery, he had put his name in as an outsider, and at the bottom of the list. Churchill laughed at the suggestion. 'No, no, much too young!' he said. But Mountbatten maintained that he had not been given the job, and that had been given SEAC instead, because Churchill feared that he might be too swift and too successful in India. There's a note that Churchill was worried four years later in the Mountbatten's debate in the Commons during his exit as the final Vice-Roy. 'The fourteen months' deadline is lethal to any systematic transfer of power,' explained Churchill. 'And I am forced to comment that the entire affair gives the impression of an attempt by the government to utilise brilliant war figures to mask a sad and disastrous deal.' It was illuminating how foretelling was Churchill's remarks. The writer has endeavored to make extensive study from the sources available of the circumstances leading upto the appointment of Mountbatten and the picture that emerges is that a lot of effort has been made to distort the truth. At this juncture, it may be pertinent to return to *The Viceroy's Journal* of Wavell. The entry on March 27, immediately after he had relinquished his Viceroyalty and returned to London, reads:

'The only thing I have to record from the India angle in the next few days is a talk with one of my staff. He said that there had been a leak from P.S.V.'s office; that George Abell's Indian stenographer, whom he trusted absolutely though I had once or twice questioned the advisability of trusting any Indian with really secret stuff, had been passing copies of George's letters out to Congress; that Nehru had brought some home and showed them to Cripps as evidence that my staff at heart biased against Congress; and that this was largely responsible for my dismissal. In case there exists some level of truth, it does illustrate a jaw-dropping mentality on the part of Cabinet Ministers. Instead of alerting

the P.S.V. or myself of the leak, if one considers that the letters which were put out took the disloyalty to P.S.V. or myself towards H.M.G.'s policy, then rather than ask us for explanations, they permit the leak of confidential documents to take place. Or at a minimum, they do not warn us and plan to try and replace me more or less at the suggestion of Nehru. 'Politics is a corrupt game', R. A. B. Butler said to me in 1943. It certainly does alter the morality of men who would, I suspect, consider themselves ordinarily as men of integrity and character. I feel glad that I have given up politics.

Portrait of Richard Stafford Cripps
(londonremembers.com)

It is also pertinent to note the comments of Collins and Lapierre in *Freedom at Midnight*. This book is practically the autobiography of Mountbatten as he spent endless hours with the authors and fully cleared the draft. Though Mountbatten was unaware, the idea of sending him to India had already been floated to Attlee by the Chancellor of the Exchequer, Sir Stafford Cripps. The idea had emerged out of a clandestine meeting that took place in London in December (1946) between Cripps and an exceedingly leftist Indian, Krishna Menon, who happened to also be a close associate of the Congress leader Jawaharlal Nehru. Menon had advanced the suggestion to both Cripps and Nehru of the possibility that Congress did not see any chances of progress in the country so long as Wavell remained Viceroy. In response to a question from the British leader he proffered an equally highly respected name, that of Nehru, Louis Mountbatten. The two men knew that Mountbatten's usefulness would be completely obliterated if the Muslim leaders of India were to know how his appointment came about. He withdrew the details of the conversation to reveal. In a series of conversations with one of the authors, Menon told me about his discussions with Cripps in New Delhi in February 1973, a year before he died. There is another noteworthy piece of information to consider. On the 29th of November in the year of 1946, the notes were made by Ian Scott who was Wavell's Deputy Private Secretary, and Lord Wavell himself. This minute was done in advance of the scheduled visit of Indian politicians to London for the last stage of talks. An extract is given:

'I should like to suggest that it would be a good thing if Nehru and perhaps Tarlok Singh (probably meaning Baldev Singh) with him, could stay in a private home in London. At his hotel he will inevitably have crowds of Indian callers and journalists on his return each evening; and he will not so easily have an opportunity of meeting the kind of people with whom contact is very desirable. Lord Louis Mountbatten might be his host.'

Wavell had noted after the above report, 'I am afraid we can hardly ask Lord L. to put up N. and I doubt whether N. would accept'

Nevertheless, Nehru remained at the Dorchester Hotel, where Edwina maintained a permanent suite with views of Hyde Park. Jinnah was comfortably lodged in Claridge's.

Now here is the writer's point that people really don't know what goes on behind the scenes surrounding great events. One suggestion that pops into mind is why did Ian Scott think it appropriate to propose to Wavell that "Nehru must stay on with Mountbatten"? It can be presumed that the one intention of Nehru's trip to London in December 1946 was to see Mountbatten who had been earmarked to take over from Wavell as Viceroy. Looking at the records pertaining to Nehru's time in London, one assumes that his participation in the discussions was next to nothing. It is safe to guess that the meetings with Mountbatten had to have occurred at the Dorchester in Edwina's suite.

In his Journal, Wavell had lamented on 20 December 1946: 'I saw the P.M. at 9 a.m. and told him that I thought I had been very discourteously treated. It was a fortnight since the discussions with the Indian leaders, and in that time there had been only three conferences held. To enable Nehru to get back for the Constituent Assembly, three or four meetings a day had been for three days, but the Viceroy was kept hanging about without any consideration for his convenience.'

As per the records, the first time Mountbatten met with the Prime Minister Attlee in connection with his appointment, was on the 18th of December, 1946. Attendant seems to remember meetings very precisely such as in this example when he attended meetings during his diary entry, 'Attlee's engagement diary'-however he Has cabinent meeting arranged with Mountbatten for 5.30pm for 18 December is one such example. And then there is an entry in Mountbatten's diary for that day, "PM sent established order me and staggered me." indicates that the meeting was held. After this, Mountbatten wrote to Attlee on December 20, 1946, saying: 'I am deeply honoured by the offer you have made to me, to succeed Wavell.' Therefore, the letter

British prime minister Clement Attlee
(britannica.com)

proceeds, and remarks in the end: 'Under these circumstances, I feel that I can be useful to you only if I am on an open invitation from Indian parties, in a role which will be set out by them.' It is clear that this was a suggestion that was utterly nonsensical and so it was cast aside without delay.

Mountbatten next met Attlee on 1 January 1947 at 5.30 p.m. The writer has failed to locate any official minutes of this meeting in the *Transfer of Power* documents. The chronicles and biographies, however, contain accounts of lengthy conversations between Mountbatten and the P.M. Most of it, and one may safely say all of it is Mountbatten's version. The records of the meeting were first described in *Mission with Mountbatten* by Alan Campbell-Johnson, Mountbatten's Press Secretary and then *Freedom at Midnight* elaborated. Numerous biographies have repeated Mountbatten's version. Even the other party to the conversations Clement Attlee's *A Prime Minister Remembers* gives a different version and is not recorded in a conversational form. Throughout his life Mountbatten was extremely conscious and cautious about records relating to his life and endeavoured always to ensure that history would see him in a favourable light.

Appointment: Mountbatten's Version - II

It is said that there are no historical truths: there is evidence and there is interpretation. It is quite extraordinary the effort Mountbatten has made to interpret evidence to show his entire career in a favourable light. The book *The Great Divide* by H.V. Hodson is generally acknowledged to be a classic and undoubtedly it is a well written and is an incisive analysis of the partition period. This is particularly significant because it was written before the publication of the official British Government documents *Transfer of Power*. It is wondered how many readers have noticed Hodson's remarks in the introduction.

Hodson says:

'First and foremost my thanks, therefore, are offered to Admiral of the Fleet, Mountbatten of Burma, who entrusted to me all the papers that he brought back from India, encouraged me, was patient with me, talked with me in complete frankness, answering my questions or volunteering recollections, and finally read my manuscript and made many valuable comments, yet without attempting to alter my conclusions or to press any amendments, save on verifiable facts.' An enterprise initiated and developed by Mountbatten is hardly likely to contain any interpretation of events derogatory to the benefactor. The writer cannot bring to mind the name of any individual who stood behind so many classics eulogising him.

All the conversations of the initial meetings with Prime Minister Attlee and the King are recollections of Mountbatten. These are frequently quoted in numerous chronicles written about his appointment, so all accounts of events related are really Mountbatten's version. All the official records, and Mountbatten's own records in the Broadlands Archives, add little to the story of the transfer of power in India to what has already been written, in *Freedom at Midnight* by Larry Collins and Dominique Lapierre (1975), for which Mountbatten provided considerable documentation and as much of his time and as many of his memories as the author desired.

In late 1946, Mountbatten could see the progression of his service life clearly. He wanted to return to the Mediterranean, to command the 1st Cruiser Squadron, the closest parallel to his father's appointment as Rear-Admiral Commanding the 2nd Cruiser Squadron in 1905. Then he would be appointed Commander-in-Chief Mediterranean, the 1919 appointment of which his father had been robbed. Next, he would come to the Admiralty as his father had done, and work his way up to First Sea Lord. Then, and only then, would his naval and family ambitions be fulfilled, and pride and order restored in the annals of the Battenberg-Mountbatten achievement and duty.

As a start, and a refresher after his years of absence from the common round of naval practice, he went on a Senior Officers' Technical Course at Portsmouth. His attendance was brief. One morning, he was interrupted with a message from Downing Street. Please come and see me – signed Clement Attlee. It was not the first of its kind. Recently, his advice had been sought over Burma and about 'the mess caused there by the Governor', as Mountbatten himself expressed it. 'I recommended General Rance as Military Administrator.'

This time India was the main item on the agenda. With Attlee was Sir Stafford Cripps, an expert on the subject, who had recently led a mission to Delhi which had very nearly pulled off an agreement for the transfer of power. 'I had kept in touch with what was going on,' said Mountbatten, 'and I was able to produce reasonably intelligent answers. Suddenly I began to have suspicions. We were talking about Wavell, who was having a very difficult time. I said, "You're not by chance talking about me relieving him?" Attlee said, "Yes", and I said, "Not on your life. And I'll give you my reasons. First, Wavell is a very honourable man. He may be taciturn but he's first class and if he can't succeed, no one can."

'This, and all other reasons were swept away, so I started making conditions. I must choose my own staff, and there'd be a lot of them, and I'd want Wavell's too, and everyone must be allowed cars and to bring their wives. I wanted "Pug" Ismay. I wanted complete control of the Honours List at the end, with no queries. I wanted my old York aircraft back, fitted out just as I liked it. I wanted . . .'

Was Mountbatten teasing them? Did he know that all the conditions that he was likely to ask would be met? We can assume that he did. Then he tried two rough ones. First, he demanded that he could have his present appointment to the 1st Cruiser Squadron back again when he had finished in India as Viceroy, the highest appointment any British citizen could hold. Attlee said yes. But Mountbatten insisted on Admiralty approval, now. So, the First Lord (Lord Hall) and the First Sea Lord (Admiral Sir John Cunningham) were called to Number 10.

Hall agreed at once. 'Hey, not so fast!' said the Admiral. 'We had the gravest doubts about Dicke coming back after running SEAC, where he commanded fleets. It was only allowed after a lot of hesitation. But to come back after being Viceroy of India – absolutely out of question.'

There was a brief pause. Then Attlee spoke in his dry, sharp, even-toned voice. 'I am not asking for your comments,' he said to Cunningham. 'I am giving you an order.'

After they left, there was another pause before Cripps said that he would gladly go as Mountbatten's Chief of Staff if that would help. Mountbatten thought this a terrible idea, and that it would be read by Indians as confirmation that Mountbatten was a mere regal figurehead. 'It's very good of you, sir. But this is too great an honour,' said Mountbatten. Years later, Mountbatten insisted that he was being relentlessly cornered. 'I went on fighting.' Next, he brought up the King's name. He would have to discuss it with him. Attlee said he had already squared George VI, and that he thought it was a marvellous idea. But, argued Mountbatten, the King had not yet heard his argument against his appointment. The meeting broke up with nothing decided except that Mountbatten would see the King at once.

Prince Albert (later King George VI) and Lord Mountbatten (later Viceroy of India), during their time at Cambridge. (tumblr.com)

Mountbatten reminded George VI that there were hundreds of princely and native states. The Government had treaty relations with them, the King had a special responsibility towards them. Then, if there was civil war, terrible massacres, the royal family would be directly associated, perhaps even held responsible for them, through himself, even if he was only a minor member of the royal family. Mountbatten reported George VI as saying that it was precisely because of his rank that he approved, that the royal family still had a cachet in India, that Mountbatten should take personal message from him to the princes.

Mountbatten: 'You do know that the job is almost impossible?' George VI: 'It *can* be done.'

Mountbatten: 'Only by a miracle. And look how bad it will be for you and the family if I fail.'

George VI: 'Ah, but look how good if you succeed!'

'And that was that!' said Mountbatten. 'I went back to Attlee and said I thought the King was quite wrong, and produced my trump card. I asked innocently if the Secretary of State for India was above the Viceroy, and was told yes, but that he was only a spokesman for the Cabinet.

'You mean I am going to have Cabinet sitting on top of me all the time? This is ridiculous. The decision must be mine and mine alone, on the spot.'

Attlee replied, aghast, 'But anything else would mean giving you plenipotentiary powers. We cannot possibly consider that.'

Mountbatten claimed that at this point he rose from the chair. 'For this relief much thanks,' he said, smiling.

'You don't mean you're going, Dicke?'

'I am going all right. I am going back to the Navy.'

With hardly a second's pause, Attlee said, 'All right, you can have plenipotentiary powers.'

Appointment: Various Impressions

Mountbatten wrote his own history. As we have seen, the major sources relating to the partition period were largely influenced by him. The *Transfer of Power* documents which formed the official record of events of Mountbatten's Viceroyalty are largely minutes dictated by him. The descriptions of Mountbatten's meetings with the political leaders and his account of the staff meetings are entirely his. For example, we do not have any other version of his meetings with Nehru, Gandhi, Patel or Liaquat. Historians have merely repeated the proceedings as seen by Mountbatten.

Nehru, Gandhi and Sardar Vallabhbhai Patel
(scroll.in)

Mountbatten claimed that he had been granted 'plenipotentiary powers' by Prime Minister Attlee. No official record exists to substantiate this claim. In 1968, Vice-Admiral Brockman (Brockman was Mountbatten's personal secretary in 1947) questioned Mountbatten's use of this phrase, and said that he had never heard it referred to during Mountbatten's time as Viceroy. 'It is quite true that I only mentioned this to Pug Ismay and he strongly advised that I should not mention it to anybody else at all,' replied Mountbatten. 'The only person who tumbled to the situation was Panditji (Nehru) himself, who realised what had happened within a week.' When Brockman was still politely sceptical, Mountbatten retorted, 'it is a pity that Attlee, Cripps, Ismay and Nehru are all dead.' The discussion was engraved on his memory, 'and I am quite prepared to put in a signed statement, if necessary going to a Commissioner of Oaths. I do not personally believe it will be any use searching the Cabinet records because there was no secretary in the room to make any notes.'

Neither in Cabinet records nor in Attlee's correspondence is there any mention of special powers. It seems probable that the words were used in the course of discussion between Attlee and Mountbatten but unlikely that they held any precise legal implications. Undoubtedly, Mountbatten enjoyed a discretion far wider than any Viceroy had known since the invention of the telegraph had brought Whitehall to within a few minutes of New Delhi. Mountbatten also insisted the replacement of Pethick-Lawrence as Secretary of State by someone with whom he could work more easily. Attlee immediately acceded by putting young Lord Listowel as suggested by Mountbatten.

Mountbatten later explained 'because I already knew him and knew that he was deeply seeped in India and I thought would be an easy person to deal with.' Stafford Cripps had caught Mountbatten off-guard by suggesting that he should accompany him as Chief of Staff. He recovered quickly and ingeniously suggested that the most useful thing Cripps could do would be to go to the India Office and act as a rear-link in London. 'You certainly had a brainwave in asking Cripps to take on the I.O.' wrote the King approvingly. 'I should never relish the idea of having him either on my staff or stay in my house.'

Mountbatten insisted on, and was granted without argument the right not merely to pick his own staff but to superimpose it on the existing administration in Delhi. His most important acquisition was Churchill's former Chief of Staff General Ismay who was appointed Chief of the Viceroy's Staff. This choice was surprising as during the war as Churchill's Chief of Staff Ismay never hesitated to hit Mountbatten over the head, hard and often, whenever he deserved it. Sir Eric Mieville, for long a Private Secretary to the Viceroy was also recruited to serve as Principal Secretary. Various old India hands were to come along; Brockman as Personal Secretary; Alan Campbell-Johnson as Press Attache; Peter Murphy as Peter Murphy. Cripps, prompted by Nehru and Krishna Menon, recommended that the present Private Secretary George Abell should be replaced as soon as possible. The Congress leaders referred to Abell as Moulana Abell. Mountbatten, however, approved what he had heard of Abell, and insisted he should stay.

Nehru found one pleasant aspect in the appointment of Mountbatten as the new Viceroy. Somebody had recounted to him the tale of how, during 1945 elections, a Labour Party canvasser came to interrogate Lord and Lady Mountbatten. "We do not need to be convinced," said Mountbatten, "But you are going to have a hell of a job in the kitchen. The butler along with the staff are all full-blown Conservatives."

"After all these Hindus," remarked Nehru with a condescending gesture towards his fellow Congressmen, "It will indeed be refreshing to encounter a candid English Socialist once more."

When it was said that Mountbatten was to be the new Viceroy, Patel had me summon a brief on him from my contacts in London. He told me that Mountbatten was a liberal aristocrat who had some revolutionary tendencies. Upon hearing this news Patel quipped "He will be a toy for Jawaharlalji to play with, while we arrange the revolution."

Liaquat Ali Khan commented upon Mountbatten's appointment admitting I have heard he is coming to India most unwillingly and his primary goal is to be Admiral of the Fleet. Settle down, grant us Pakistan and we will whole heartedly devote our first budget to constructing and manning a battleship for you - Azad would be the laundryman, the steerman would be nobody else but Nehru, Gandhi would be in charge of breathing hot air in to the boilers.

For a day to day recollection of the events from the appointment of Mountbatten, his arrival in India on 22 March 1947, the transfer of power on 14/15 August 1947, his Governor-Generalship of independent India and his final departure, we have to turn to Alan Campbell-Johnson's *Mission with Mountbatten*. Needless to say, this publication is heavily pro-Mountbatten and contains in later editions a foreword by him. As the author recollects in the preface to the edition published in 1985, 'Against this background of an ever-growing

Nehru and Jinnah signing Mountbatten plan
(Partition of India)
(Indianarrative.com)

volume of commentaries and re-evaluations, *Mission with Mountbatten* still is and remains inevitably a primary source. Indeed, I have collected over the years more than fifty books the authors of which have drawn on and quoted from it as such. Accordingly, I have avoided any temptation or to abridge or amend the text of the diary or to seek to be wiser after the events than I was at the time.'

The only other day to day account we have is from *Diasastrous Twighlight*, the diary of Shahid Hamid, Private Secretary to Field Marshall Sir Claude Auchinleck, the C-in-C of the Indian Army. This book had a scathing foreword written by Philip Ziegler, the official biographer of Mountbatten. The contents of the book are rarely quoted but as Ziegler has noted in his foreword, 'His book deserves to be widely read. Any student of the period who accepted it as the whole truth would be gravely misled, but if you were to ignore it altogether he would be missing a statement of real importance.' Quotations given from the book may be judged by the readers as they deem fit.

Hamid's entry on 24 March 1947 reads:

"Mountbatten said that he was forced to accept the Viceroyalty of India by His Majesty the King. There can be no bigger untruth. It is common knowledge that he wanted it badly to enhance his political standing and he worked towards it. he established close contact with Nehru knowing that he would one day become the Prime Minister of India. It was the efforts of Krishna Menon which further cemented their friendship. It is reported that Cripps wanted to come out as Mountbatten's Chief-of Staff but Mountbatten refused and said that he was a 'cheeky, doddering old man, who has stupid and ludicrous ideas.' He, Cripps, considered himself an authority on India and wanted the Governor-Generalship".

According to common gossip Mountbatten has come to partition India as quickly as possible, irrespective of consequences – sort out the Princes; take all possible measures to keep the two countries in the Commonwealth; ensure that Britain's strategic and mercantile interests in South Asia are not jeopardised and, finally, keep the Indian leaders under pressure and give them no time to think. It is also said that the unitary form of the Government and the Cabinet Mission Plan is out of date. The Congress is jubilant over Mountbatten's appointment. He is using Krishna Menon as his contact man with Nehru, V.P. Menon with Patel and Sudhir Ghosh with Gandhi. Delhi is a beehive of rumours and conjectures. Everyone has a story to tell. each story is supposed to be coming from the horse's mouth.'

Pre-Assignment Briefings

As we have seen earlier there are so many publications relating to Mountbatten's life influenced by him that it is very difficult to find an objective account of his life. Any biographer has to make a really serious study of the events of his life to endeavour to give a detached interpretation. When the distinguished biographer, Philip Ziegler, wrote his authorised Life of Mountbatten in 1985, he brought out what one reviewer called Mountbatten's 'combination of gargantuan vanity with cockily unlimited self-assurance and conceit.' He also revealed the lengths to which Mountbatten went to exaggerate his achievements and exonerate himself from blame. In the end the author resignedly put a sign on his desk which read: 'Remember. In Spite of Everything, He Was a Great Man.'

It is to be noted that on 8 March, 1947 the Congress Working Committee passed some resolutions with the full support of Nehru and Patel. The message in the long-winded resolution was that Congress were willing to accept the principle of Pakistan provided only a few small pieces in the northwest and the northeast were acceded to Pakistan and the rest of India could then be built up into a strong and consolidated India. This entire message was conveyed to Mountbatten *prior* to his departure from London to take up his Viceroyalty in India.

It is curious not many authors have elaborated on the discussions which Krishna Menon had with

Mountbatten *before* he left London. The writer feels certain that many a meeting took place clandestinely between Menon and Mountbatten. Had it not been for the publication of the *Transfer of Power* documents this fact would never have been known. Krishna Menon gave an elaborate note to Mountbatten. We do not know what must have transpired between the two in their secret meetings. The fact that the meetings took place comes to light in the letter which Krishna Menon wrote to Mountbatten on 13 March, 1947:

My dear Lord Louis Mountbatten,

"I enclose the last page of my notes, which was inadvertently left out of the copy I gave you. As I told you, there are a number of matters to be included in it if the basic idea appears to be of any use. If you need me, I shall be glad to see you again before I leave. Your A.D.C. apparently knows how to get in touch with me. I recognise the importance of hastening slowly, but it appears that in India things will not rest as they are. There is a grave threat of famine also, which may add to complications, but at the same time makes effective central authority essential. I was glad to see you and to have had our talk. Perhaps you will let me know sometime what you think of what I've said."

Yours sincerely,
V.K. Krishna Menon

Now, is it not a demonstration of bad faith in the extreme for Mountbatten to be hobnobbing closely with one party to the dispute to the total exclusion of the other? Let us examine the elaborate brief of Krishna Menon which is contained in the *Transfer of Power* documents. No such brief appears from the British side. Some extracts are given below:

Section I.

'The problems are: -

(1) The crisis in the Interim Government.

(2) The machinery for taking over.

(3) The Princes.

(4) Indo-British relations.

(1) and (2) are obviously closely inter-connected, and (4) is closely connected with (1) and (2), both severally and jointly.'

Section II.

(1) 'The decision of the Congress to force the issue of a genuine coalition or the dismissal of the League members is in suspense *for the moment*, pending

(a) the arrival of the new Viceroy

(b) the slight hopes of response from the League to a further approach.

(2) The resolving of the crisis, in my view, rests basically on the relation of the Ministry to the Viceroy - that is, British power.

The assumption of a new role by the Viceroy quite obviously (not merely willy nilly) is essential to a change for the better in the present situation.

(3) The Attlee declaration, apart from all other causes, makes it both logical and incumbent on the British side that its power (as distinct from its influence) should not only rapidly diminish (to vanishing point in 1948) but that immediately there should be a change in this relationship whereby the entire onus of administration is in the hands of the Interim Government.'

With regard to Lord Wavell's willingness to accept this position, it is his failure to do so and his most unfortunate journey in the opposite direction from the middle of last September that accounts for a large portion of the current crisis.

Another part of the note of Krishna Menon is virtually the Partition Award. It appears distinctly apparent that Mountbatten carried with him the full brief of the Congress Party. The relevant extract reads:

'Therefore, I propose the following: -

(a) A Western Pakistan in the North-West, to include the Moslem majority districts of the Punjab together with the Moslem districts of Sind, with an approach to the sea at Karachi, irrespective of the composition of the population on this boundary. Any attempt to provide a homeland which is boxed in on all four sides is an unfair offer from the League point of view.

The port of Karachi, irrespective of its predominant non-Moslem population and all-India importance, to be included in Western Pakistan, thus giving the League a first-class sea and air port and a great city.

The remainder of the Punjab to be constituted into a separate province of all- India. The question of the remainder of Sind has to be thought out.

(b) Eastern Pakistan in the North-East, to include the districts of Eastern Bengal which are predominantly Moslem, and certain areas of Assam, thus partitioning Bengal (shades of Curzon!).

The problems here are (i) the comparatively strong opposition in Bengal to partition and (ii) Calcutta.

I believe that partition is the price that will have to be paid for any stability in Bengal. With regard to Calcutta, any solution which hands over Calcutta to Pakistan will be unstable and impractical. The reasons are well known. On the other hand, the League has to be given a port on the East, and the solution is that as part of the compromise settlement India should build a large- sized city and port in Chittagong, that is, provide the money for it however many millions it may cost.

c) *Question of powers and status*. The Pakistans shall be styled as autonomous states, and not provinces. They should all have all the attributes of statehood except foreign relations and defence. The two cannot in any event, before 1948, be made available to any Pakistan, because any new state created would have no foreign relations by that time even if it succeeds in getting recognition, except with the co-operation of the rest of India. This is therefore a problem of the future, and is dealt with further below.

Defence is equally not capable of being vested in any Pakistan at the time of its creation. Even if it were, it would confer little power on Pakistans, as the heavier defence of all-India would reduce the defence power of the Pakistan's to impotence.'

Does not the above prove that right from the beginning Mountbatten's Viceroyalty was a tale of duplicity and deceit. Abundant evidence will be produced to establish this. Krishna Menon's note ends as follows:

Section V (VI).

'The creation of Pakistan and the conferring on it of rights and functions far in excess of the Cabinet plan will evoke protests and opposition from Congress and other groups. Mr. Jinnah would regard it, on the other hand, as a truncated Pakistan. But for either side the alternatives are far worse, and for the British it would involve a repudiation of the solemn pledges of the Attlee declaration and the prospect of having to deal with anarchy or the termination of relationships in such ways as are injurious to both sides.

It may be further pointed out that the proposals here are not based upon theoretical considerations, and are largely, in fact, a planned approach to what would willy nilly be the position if in July 1948 no constitution has emerged.

Finally, even if a constitution emerges, the approach in these proposals would *at present* be called for, but it would have to be made clear that this is no substitute for constitution making which is untouched by them.

It may also be added that these proposals concede to Mr. Jinnah his demand for two Constituent Assemblies.'

CHAPTER 5: POLITICS OF PERSONALITY

The Two Menons - I

Two Menons played a most extra ordinary role in the prelude to partition. Although their role was behind the scenes their effects were far reaching and have left an indelible stamp on the saga of the sub-continent. The two Menons as every reader knows are V. P. Menon and Krishna Menon. No study of the partition period can be complete without a look at their backgrounds.

Let us consider V. P. Menon first.

V. P. Menon has the happy distinction of having played a major role – some would say the all-important role in the drama of India's independence without having been

(a) to school in England, (b) to university anywhere and (c) without being (d) a lawyer.

He was for some time the Reforms Commissioner and Constitutional Adviser to Linlithgow, Wavell and Mountbatten, the most senior post in the Indian government Service ever to have been held by an Indian which, considering his background, is even more astounding. He was born in Malabar in 1889, being a member of one of those Jain family clans which cultivate the golden hills of this beautiful part of India. He became extremely sick with typhoid fever at 15 years old, which meant months away from school. But he did take his matric and

VP Menon working on his desk
(bbc.com)

passed as well; the trouble was that due to his illness, he had not spent the required time in school which meant that he could not pick up his certificate without attending for another year. The situation was that his family was undergoing one of the worst financial meltdowns; his father, the clan head, had passed away and there were endless brothers and cousins still needing schooling. Menon decided that he had no choice. Pack up, get a job, support yourself and your family back home.

With no credentials on hand, he trekked in a direction where education could make the difference between living luxuriously and dying of hunger. He often proved to Hindu business owners that he was proficient in English, could read and write, was good with numbers; and they in turn repeatedly kicked him out because he didn't possess the ever so vital diploma. While he was still working at the railway workshops, he was all but starving until an Englishman helped him out. Menon found an ad in the Madras Mail looking for a clerk to hire in the Kolar Goldfields in Mysore; he also saw another ad looking for a contractor overseer to work in the mines. He figured he might as well apply to both and was invited for an interview.

The English manager took a liking to the young Menon and dismissed the fact that he did not hold a certificate. He suggested to Menon to accept the easy, reliable offer of the clerk position in the office and guaranteed good opportunities in the future if he tried hard, but Menon knew of the legends of the enormous wealth that could be earned by contract overseers and was fiercely determined, despite being warned about the risks, to give it a shot. The manager had given him some money, instructed him to hire a group of coolies, and set out to work in the mine. He would receive a percentage of all the gold his group was able to procure. "The harder you work them," the manager claimed, "the more you will make. But don't overdo it; you'll kill them."

Menon wasn't that kind of man. For the first couple of weeks, his 'coolies' worked hard for him. He earned close to a thousand rupees a week, which he was sending most of home. After that, he made the mistake of increasing his coolies' rations and giving them sick leave at full pay. From that point on, the coolies thought he was a soft touch. He and his wife would go down to the second or third levels of the mine where it was cool, and

VP Menon working on his desk (bbc.com)

they would sleep instead of work. For weeks on end, Menon's quota of gold reduced, until at the end of three months he had accumulated a substantial amount of debt. He was constantly waiting for the day when he would be working full-time as a coalface miner until he could pay off his debt. Instead, the Englishman summoned him into his office.

'I told you not to be a damned fool' he said. 'Too bloody nice, that's your trouble, Well, it's all up, my lad. Here, take this-and get out and don't come back'.

He handed Menon an envelope. Inside were two 100-rupee notes, and a letter to a tobacco firm manager in Bangalore, He was never asked to repay his debt.

The Englishman assisted V.P. Menon's entry into Government Service. Menon was nearly starving years later when he borrowed enough money to take the train to Malabar. On his way to the train station, he encountered an Englishman he had met in Bombay. The man was head of the Home Department in Delhi and offered Menon a job to study in night school.

Menon had become a specialist in Indian matters and virtually invaluable to the government by the year 1940. In 1941, he proposed a plan for the Federation of the Princely States with the rest of India which would have allowed the State to join British India on a Guaranty basis where they would manage their own internal affairs while Defence, Foreign Affairs and Communications would be managed by the Centre. The plan would have been a first step towards a Unified India. The Viceroy, Lord Linlithgow, kept the plan in his infamous Little Black Box that he was said to always take with him to the bathroom, jokingly, in case anyone tried to open it. He indeed never paid any attention to the plan.

'It's all very well for you to hang around, Menon' he said on one occasion. 'You expect me to make you Reforms Commissioner when the job comes up, don't you? You had better get it out of your mind. It is not a job for an Indian'.

When the office went unoccupied, H.V. Hodson was eagerly appointed to the post, seemingly over Menon's objection. Menon was never resentful towards him, and they subsequently became close friends. This, however, did not lessen Menon's appreciation and admiration towards the brits, even though he found it impossible to love Lord Linlitgow. But he was a patient man. In 1943, H.V. Hodson had a falling out with the Vice Roy and went back to Britain, earning distinction for writing with the London Sunday Times, and Linlithgow began the search for a replacement. His advisors already told him that there wasn't an Englishman in India who had even an ounce of the knowledge of Indian affairs, law, civil administration and relations with the Princely States as V.P. Menon did. Linlithgow remedied the previous wrongs and called Menon. He was an outstanding Reforms Commissioner and men of his stature and the Indian government appeared like his shadow and this started from that very moment. Most of them, however, did not understand the extent to which he contributed for their success, just like most people failed to see how crucial his role was in attaining independence.

One thing can be established from the onset. V.P. Menon stands out as one of the most peculiar Indians to top the Government Services. He did not possess a college education in any form, and entered civil service almost as a fluke. Unlike most men, he was candid and devoid of any sophisticated conceit, and regardless of a person's status, he did not bow down to authority blindly. "You have been kind enough to attribute this recovery of your balance to my" Mountbatten claimed that in his opinion, you have 'your only weakness,' which is shared by so many of the greatest in India, is that you lose your sense of balance in emotional periods, with many arguing this shareable quality is 'over-Indian-ness'. He could 'over-Indian' wrongs (though never over his own work) himself into quite a state, one of the few characteristics he shared with Nehru. Fortunately, unlike many others, you yourself recover your balance long before any hasty decisions have emerged. Unless you were ti re-stated yourself, I could not have been able to help without any influence from your inherent stability. Were you under severe emotional pressure, all I would kindly suggest is stopping to consider what a Mountbatten would assume after disengaging the word?

The position of Reforms Commissioner was a role V.P. Menon had always dreamed of achieving. The only other thing he wished to see was India's independence while he was still alive. He met Sardar Vallabhbhai Patel in 1946 and became his close friend which also meant he became his collaborator (to the extent that Menon's job allowed). The connection was one which greatly contributed to the development of Indian history than the people from that period understood.

VP Menon and Sardar Vallabhbhai Patel
(thebetterindia.com)

The Two Menons – II

There is no doubt that V.P. Menon played a role far more important than any other Indian official did for the British Government in the transfer of power in India. Menon has left two most important publications. *The Transfer of Power in India* is a remarkably calm and impartial review of the events leading to the partition and independence. *The Integration of the Indian States* is a colourful tragi-comic story of the end of the princely system in India. Both these books were written virtually as text-books and indeed they are included presently prescribed in the reading of history in the Indian Universities. It is doubtful if any Indian official or non-official saw the workings of the British Indian Government more closely than V.P. Menon. V.P. attended the Round Table conferences in 1932-33. He was one of the two Secretaries of the Simla Conference called by Wavell in August 1945. Among the Indian Officials who assisted the Cabinet Mission Delegation in 1946 was V.P. Menon. And the grand finale was his single-handed drafting of the Partition Plan as directed by Mountbatten.

Whilst serving as a Viceroy, Mountbatten chose to retain certain members of Wavell's staff in diwans. Indeed, V.P. Menon stayed on as the Reforms Commissioner. It was common knowledge by

Menon's closeness to Patel. Mountbatten had been forewarned of Menon's prejudice too. Every day, Mountbatten's aides, with the exception of Menon, gathered in the post prandial hours for a talk session during which plans for the day were formulated. It was very much a Mountbatten speciality, modelled on his wartime conferences in Burma, during which one was obliged to participate in a verbal free for all, with a good measure of verbal counter-blasts to the issues surrounding Indian independence, while he remained to witness and function as a kind of friendly referee. It was a snug, British haven, away from exuberant spirits and exuberant expression of all sorts, which would have shocked anyone outside the region. Over some issues, one was required to provide superficial answers.

Indians were called 'the bods', while Gandhi was known as 'His Nibs' and Jinnah as 'Gimlet'. Initially, V. P. Menon did not get an invitation to these meetings based on Abell's recommendation because, as he put it, 'The constant meeting with him would, a Hindu, will lead to Muslims believing that we are overly sympathetic to Congress.' Menon did fume and grumble back in the ante room saying that his Abell must be very convincing to people that his train of thought suggests will is pro-Muslim League so then why must there be a Hindu to counterbalance it? Much later is when he was called in at infrequent intervals to which the proceedings were serious and formal. It did not take long, however, for V.P. Menon to get close to Mountbatten. V.P. writes of Mountbatten on 28 March, 1947:

'Even that early, only four days after his arrival, I got the feeling that he had decided which way he was going, what solution he had in mind. I told him on this occasion that in my view, Jinnah and the Muslim League would be willing to accept even a truncated Pakistan rather than go into a central Government. He seized upon the point right away. I left him feeling that he had come to India armed with plenipotentiary powers and if the parties were not able to come together, the decision would ultimately have to be given by His Excellency. I think the decision will not be palatable to either party.'

V. P. Menon did his best from his corner in the ante-room, where he sat on a virtual dunce's stool, to rescue his British colleagues from their own blunders while simultaneously trying to salvage his own reputation. To George Abell her letter was written because she wanted to voice her discontent.

Dear Abell,

'I have been thinking of writing to you about the difficult position in which I am placed as Reforms Commissioner. I would not have raised this issue but for important practical reasons of great urgency. Since power has to be transferred not later than June 1948, it is essential that there should be some organisation to evolve a plan of operation then implement it. I have so far assumed that the Reforms Office acting under HE's orders would be that organisation. However, if the Reforms Office is to do this work it is essential that I should be kept in touch with all the relevant developments. Unless I am able to view all issues in their true mutual relationship and have sufficient background information, I cannot advice HE with full knowledge… Surely our general approach has to be settled before we start settling the details. There is very little time and a great many problems to solve. There is a grave danger of lack of coordination if departments work in water-tight compartments…. It is essential that there should be an automatic procedure by which I am kept informed of developments.'

In all fairness, one ought to acknowledge that Menon's curiosity about the events transpiring within the Viceregal parlour was not completely impartial. He was a meticulous civil servant and a staunch British sympathiser. But he was also, of course, an ardent supporter of Indian nationalism and, more significantly, a near associate and awe-inspirer of Sardar Patel, the Congress Party's hard man. No doubt he was not the first civil servant, however, to have kaleidoscopic opinions and preconceived notions, and there certainly seems to be no suggestion that he allowed them to influence his service in the Government of India.

As we shall see undoubtedly V.P. Menon was far superior intellectually to his British colleagues and it did not take him long to become the master of the situation behind the scenes. Mountbatten's sinister plan was already taking shape. From all evidence it is apparent that he had come to India with pre- conditioned ideas which was to convince the various leaders to accept Pakistan with as small an area as possible, and he worked to this end relentlessly immediately after his arrival and within a month had convinced all the Congress and League leaders. By 11 April, 1947 Mountbatten had a plan ready and Lord Ismay wrote to V.P. Menon:

'My dear Menon, - I send you herewith the bare bones of a possible plan for the transfer of power. The Viceroy would be glad if you would *a.* amend the draft in any way you think right and put some flesh on it; *b.* consider what the procedure would be immediately after HMG had made their announcement. For example, would a general election throughout India be necessary? How would we set about the partition of the Punjab, Bengal and Assam? Presumably, the decision will be left to HE and will not be open to argument. What will be the machinery for those groups who wish to get together to frame their constitution and so on and so forth? *c.* Work out a rough timetable. I ought to explain that nothing very precise is required at this stage but only to give HE an idea of how this plan would be implemented if adopted, and how long it would take.'

Yours very sincerely,

Ismay.

Just think that the freedom that is being offered to V.P. It was up to Menon to slash and hack the Plan as he pleased. Menon's draft was forwarded to the Governors of India's eleven provinces a few days later who had been called to Delhi for a meeting with the Viceroy. The moment those gentlemen scanned through it, they understood time was no longer on their side. 'The blighter's pulled it off,' one of them said. 'What is he, a swami or something?'

Lord Mountbatten, Gopalaswami Aiyangar and V.P. Menon at party in 1948 (Indianexpress.com)

Even Sir Evan Jenkins, Governor of the Punjab, who against all logic was an ardent opponent to partitioning that province did not object. Only Sir Frederick Burrows, the Governor of Bengal, who on account of sickness was absent, showed some opposition and suggested he was supporting the campaign in Calcutta for a separate State of Bengal to be carved out free from Pakistan and Hindustan. Vimla Pradhan lettered and handed over systematic analyses of every State's national and armed forces in Europe.

They, in any case, were bold enough to offer the Viceroy forward with no concern to what might be other order did the Governments. It is truly astonishing how many of them actually did care not what the future for India was still for most of them were from British's divisions. They seemed to lift a massacre of the sahibs to save the people notion that the do what would slaughterer of.

The way V.P. Menon puts it in his book The Transfer of Power in India, in a chapter titled, "Lord Mountbatten's Draft Plan," the Viceroy had changed his working plan 'after having talked to the Governors and party leaders, and sent this plan to London with Lord Ismay and George Abell on 2 May... Nowadays, however, while talking to party leaders and others, even with the disparate opinions they have tried to balance and merge, none had sought to call into question in any way his personal neutrality or the good faith of His Majesty's Government.'"

But Menon added: 'I had always been opposed to the plan which Lord Ismay and George Abell had taken to London. The theory that the provinces should become initially independent successor States was particularly abhorrent to me. But my protests and my views in the discussion with the Viceroy's advisers went in vain.'

The Two Menons – III

V.K. Krishna Menon
(starofmysore.com)

Having seen the profound role played by V.P. Menon in influencing the decisions leading up to the Partition of India let us now turn to Vengalil Krishnan Menon or Krishna Menon as he was generally known. Before we delve into his background the writer would recall an incident relating to this person. Way back in the 1950's there used to be a magazine programme on the BBC TV conducted by Cliff Michelmore. This programme was telecast every evening at seven. It went on for many years during which innumerable celebrities round the world were interviewed by Michelmore. Many years later Michelmore was himself interviewed and asked about the most attractive and amiable personalities he had interviewed and he gave his answers. After this, Michelmore was asked if he had interviewed persons he disliked. His spontaneous reply was that the most objectionable character that he had ever interviewed was Krishna Menon.

For a candid and probably authentic assessment of Krishna Menon's character and career it may be interesting to look at the chapters on Krishna Menon written by M.O. Mathai. Mathai was Nehru's private secretary from February 1946 till the end of 1959. No individual was closer to Nehru than Mathai who was himself quite an extraordinary personality. Since he has pulled no punches in his evaluations and assessments of various personalities he is not the most popular of authors. In fact, it is quite difficult to get hold of his two publications: *My Days with Nehru* & *Reminiscences of The Nehru Age*. Mathai was so close to Nehru that even Indira was jealous of him. One can fairly confidently give considerable credibility to the contents of his books.

After Patel's death, Ministers, M.P's and senior civil servants came to call Mathai, 'Deputy P.M' or the 'Power behind the throne'. In his The Story of My Life, C.D. Deshmukh spoke of Mathai as, 'The most powerful acolyte of the P.M.' No document or any paper containing a particular recommendation was put to the P.M. without Mathai's observations being on a slip or a routine note. Such notes never formed part of the files as they were taken off when the documents went down from the P.M. Krishna Menon was born in 1896. While he was doing his college studies in Madras he met Annie Besant, who in 1924 sent him to England to teach at a theosophical school in Letchworth. He taught in this school for one year and in 1925 obtained a diploma in teaching in London. From 1925 he studied political science under Harold Laski in the London School of Economics and got a B.Sc. He was joint secretary of Annie Besant's Commonwealth of India League.

In 1934, at the age of 38, he was called to the bar at the Middle Temple, when all one had to do was eat a few dinners in dinner jackets. He in fact never studied law, nor did he have any legal practice in London that was worth listing. A great deal of attention has been placed on his "editing" books in London. Editing, in this case, meant to condense. He edited only the first batch of the Pelican Books series. He had a partnership with Allen Lane from the Bodley Head who in turn quickly found Menon as a burden on his nerves, and a bottleneck. This effectively brought the partnership to an end. Menon resided in the slum neighborhoods of London in abject poverty. He lived for many years on endless cups of tea, biscuits, and occasionally, lentil cutlets which, over time, took a toll on his health.

Following the breakup of the Commonwealth of India League, Krishna Menon transformed the league into the India League, taking on the role of Secretary. Most of the funding towards the India League came from wealthy Indian doctors living in England. With little to no checks and balances in place, they granted him complete control of the finances which went through the India League and later poured money into his other personal investments. It's said he lacked the basic necessities to sustain himself, but one can only say this with generous assumptions of his character. What changes few appreciate is the degree to which he convinced people to see him as the centrepiece of a phenomenon; you couldn't want Indian independence without wanting Krishna Menon, and wanting any other figure meant you were anti-patriot.

Mathai records: 'I first met Krishna Menon in New Delhi in 1946. He came about the time the interim government was formed on 22 September, 1946. I did not like his lean and hungry look, nor his nose which resembled a vulture's beak. He had unkempt hair, perpetually reminding people that he needed a haircut. He wore cheap and badly cut English clothes. Fortunately, he did not wear a hat – otherwise he would have looked like a tramp. He had all the characteristics of a man who had lived in the slum areas of London for long.' Krishna Menon was soon appointed Nehru's personal representative in Europe in September 1946 to carry out all the public relations in favour of Congress.

Mountbatten's arrival as Viceroy activated Krishna Menon, who interspersed himself as a middleman between Nehru and the Viceroy. This annoyed Patel and Azad greatly. Patel, at least, was unwilling to grant big interviews. His house's response was, "He can join him on his morning walk at 5 AM." Menon found this the most inconvenient, but had no other options.

Azad writes in his *India Wins Freedom* (In the parts that were published ten years after his death).

'When war broke out, Krishna Menon suggested that he should be provided with funds so that he could carry on propaganda in London on behalf of India. When Hitler attacked Russia, he came in touch with the Soviet Embassy in London. He sent us many messages that he was meeting the Soviet Ambassador as Nehru's personal representative. He sent all kinds of proposals for securing the help of interests friendly to India. He also prepared schemes asking for funds from the Congress. Jawaharlal was impressed by him and requested me to grant some money. I did so and placed the matter before the Working Committee. Gandhiji and Sardar Patel told me frankly that they did not like my action but they would say nothing since I had paid the money in good faith. They however asked me not to make any further payment. They pointed out that Indians in London were sharply divided in their judgement about Krishna Menon. He had some supporters but there was a strong body of opponents who brought all kinds of charges against him. The general impression I got was that his conduct was not above reproach. I could not therefore trust him fully. Later events proved that Gandhiji and Sardar were right in their suspicion of Krishna Menon. He was, to take a charitable view, unreliable and had little concern for the way public funds were spent. Most people took an even worse view and regarded him as downright dishonest.'

Mathai has recorded: 'One day Nehru told me that Mountbatten had mentioned about Krishna Menon being closely related to the royal family of Cochin and that, according to the matriarchal system obtaining in Cochin, Krishna Menon would succeed then present incumbent as the Maharaja of Cochin. Nehru asked me if I knew anything about it. I laughed and said that obviously Krishna Menon had managed through someone to take Mountbatten for a ride. I told Nehru that, much to my amusement, Krishna Menon had told me sometime before about his relationship with royal families. Living in the London slums in abject proverty for long, Krishna Menon developed a type of inferiority complex which prompted him to invest himself with imaginary royalty.'

With the formation of the dominion government on 15 August 1947, Nehru hoped to add Krishna Menon to the Cabinet, but Gandhiji was unwaveringly opposed to the notion which prompted Nehru to let it go. Even Sardar Patel was in the dark. Of course, neither was Menon aware about this too. In fact, for a long time, Nehru did not  envision appointing Menon as the High Commissioner in London. Krishna Menon became restless and thereupon solicited help from Mountbatten. Eventually, Mountbatten recommended the appointment of Menon as High Commissioner. Mountbatten spoke with Gandhiji also on this issue privately. So, it happened. We have seen the minute which Krishna Menon had given Mountbatten prior to the latter's departure for India as Viceroy. In Mountbatten's own words as poured to Collins and Lapierre, let us see what he had to say about Krishna Menon.

'My unofficial link with Nehru was Krishna Menon, whom I made friends with in England (*Readers to note Mountbatten's confession*). We've remained friends. A very curious creature. I must tell you – you won't want this for your book, but it'll help you to understand – Menon did the most frightful thing to Nehru: because Krishna Menon, who was Minister of Defence, actually got this invasion of Goa linked up without Nehru understanding or knowing about it, and

Jawaharlal Nehru and Krishna Menon,
London, 1949
(Openthemagazine.com)

then faced him almost with a *fait accompli*, and he had to approve or else be held up as the man who was going against popular clamour. And so, they had the invasion of Goa, and in doing so, he destroyed Nehru. Nehru was the great idealist, who had always said that force must never, never be used. If the people of Goa wanted to stay with the Portuguese, they couldn't be forced, and in forcing Nehru to bless the invasion of Goa he destroyed him, not only his credibility, his prestige, his reputation, but he destroyed his faith in himself, for he felt that he had been betrayed. And he later killed him with the disastrous Chinese war.'

The Two Menons – IV

Krishna Menon was a political operator like few others even in the eyes of Indian and British leaders. It must be said that the way he tackled political problems during the diplomatical years he served as High Commissioner (1947-1949) was singularly impressive. However, he created a mess in the management of India House. With each passing day, a new scandal came to light which only drove Menon more and more into his delusions of persecution. He began abusing very strong drugs, particularly as his many imbecilic deals came under fire in the Indian parliament. Menon was completely broken down, both mentally and physically, by 1950.

With the growing unrest in the Parliament after mid-1949, furor in the parliamentary became rampant. In 1950, the Prime Minister directed the Secretary-General of the Ministry of External Affairs, N.R. Pillai, to London to make some unofficial vis-a-vis inquiries that could help him. Pillai performed the round trip in a manner similar to that of S. Dutt in an earlier instance. Pillai refused to give me a report in writing. However, he suggested to the PM that large scale payments changed hands in the circumventions of the various arrangements of deals undertaken by Krishna Menon. He would not state it went into the pockets of Krisha Menon, although it could very likely have been received by the India League whose funds Krishna Menon had a penchant for not giving out. Pillai stated that the lack of Krishna Menon's salary payments only worsened the speculation.

Londoners started to wonder, "How did he get the funds out of nowhere to establish a huge closet full of expensive garments?" Their suspicion was exacerbated when one took into consideration the utter lack of justification for the considerable amount of money he claimed to spend on entertaining other people. No one entertained in India House other than Krishna Menon who did so in its subsidised canteen. Pillai told the PM that all scandals relating to different transactions had been laid out before the Public Accounts Committee and Parliament and that the government would have to cope with them in whatever manner possible. Pillai remarked that the action taken with regard to Krishna Menon was of a political nature. The PM did not respond to the suggestion and persisted with the policy of indecision.

Amid the outburst in parliament, the government had become fierce since the mid-1949. In 1950, The Prime Minister appointed Secretary- General N.R. Pillai to the Ministry of External Affairs and sent him to London to make inquiries. Pillai, like S. Dutt, did not appear to have been involved in this case in any significant way. Unlike S. Dutt, Pillai refused to submit a report. What he reported to the PM was that there were very strong indications that vast sums of money changed hands with respect to Krishna Menon's several deals. He would not say it went into Krishna Menon's pocket; it was most likely received by the Indian League whose accounts Menon had irrevocably relinquished. Krishna did not draw his salary and his not doing so did not help allay suspicions. Londoners started to say, "Where did he get the money suddenly to build up a very large bulk of expensive clothes?" His refusal to account for a considerable portion of the entertaining money he withdrew from government accounts did not help. What was well-known was that Menon never entertained anybody except at the subsidised Indian House canteen.

Pillai explained to the PM that the deals had several scandals attached to them, which were already under investigation by the Public Accounts Commitee in parliament, thus, the government needed to respond as best as it could. Pillai concluded his argument stating that the decision in the matter of Krishna Menon was political in nature. The Prime Minister did not follow the clue and went on with his policy of drift. Criticism aimed at Krishna Menon escalated relentlessly. In the meantime, visitors returning from London, including Rajkumari Amrit Kaur, reported the virtual breakdown of work at India House; Krishna Menon was propping himself up by powerful drugs and some sex scandals. During 1951 October, the PM asked me to go to London to discuss with Krishna Menon and also look into all the recent reports. He was aware that I did not dislike Krishna Menon and whatever report I made, it wouldn't be biased. I lodged at the cheap Indian Club, which was close enough to India House for me to walk to it.

Upon reaching India House, I was instantly captivated by a code telegraph bearing a message directed towards the Secretary of State for the Commonwealth Relations, Lord Home, anticipating him a week before I had departed from Delhi. It was still resting carelessly on the desk of Krishna Menon. Because Krishna Menon was way too intoxicated on tellurium and was having an extremely difficult time even opening his eyes, I headed towards First Secretary P. N. Haksar, where I whisked away the cable and probed him about the event. He informed me that the High Commissioner was forwarded the pre-prints so long as he didn't clear the orders, and therefore this specific telegram was never viewed. I urged him to clear the message and send it out to the Commonwealth Relations Office. In turn bounded with flimsy assumptions, he could presume the High Commissioner had cleared the order. My travels to see him came to an immediate standstill. I suggested that I would meet him on the condition he was soberer than he currently was. If he chose not to comply, I would take whatever route necessary to get back to Delhi. Reasonably soberer, the rest of my evening was spent at the India Club with Krishna Menon. I explained to him I did not want publicity which included face to face discussions with him and a handful of friends who were truly supportive along with his British psychiatrist. But I made in clear that a meeting with that doctor would require him to escort me to it, notwithstanding the fact that Mountbatten was more than willing to set the meeting up for me.

The first person to meet was Dr. Handoo, a former friend and admirer of Krishna Menon. He acquainted me with Krishna Menon's conditions and claimed that he was both ill and "mad." He was using Luminol and other potent medications clandestinely. With surprised undertone, he said that it was astonishing that the PM continued to keep him in office. Mountbatten stated that Atlee along with the other primary ministers of the Labour government thought that Krishna Menon ought to have been substituted at least one year prior. Mountbatten thought the same.

P. N. Haksar was, even if fairly young civil servant, one of those who said without mincing words the truth, that it was time to replace Menon. He indicated that the change should have occurred long ago. He gave me a bareheaded note at my particular request which contained his evaluation and which

I could leave with the PM.

I met with the doctor from Britain who informed me that Krishna Menon was receiving electric shock treatment and so was one of his female staff members. He claimed that it was his nursing care, which did not even begin to allow for serious office work, that Menon required. He further asserted that Menon was a lunatic with a severe persecution delusion, but the central difficulty was that he was so supercharged with libido that he was completely impotent. That produced a lot of unexpladjusted behavior which he called normal, and which his mind was indeed very simple. That, plus some of the more overt acts of violence and self-injury, is how he became so agitated. He provided me with a blank letter, which I was to keep confidential and address personally to the Primer.

One evening, Krishna Menon took Cleminson to my room in the Indian Club and he left him with me. Cleminson was one of the more daring of the many adventures who was associated with some of Krishna Menon's deals. He expected Cleminson to tell me the facts which had led to the deal and the reasoning behind it. The first thing Cleminson told me was what happened in his flat the night before. He came with one of his Indian lady secretaries at one o clock along with electric shock therapy minutes of her in good spirit, she removed her clothes and started to dance. He told me that had some fun with this lady and the poor girl emotionally got stuck. Because of not receiving the best from Krishna Menon, she too turned into a head case. He told me that the girls in the office also attended. He told about some other things and at the end he did not add anything about V.K Menon's dealings.

Menon had a number of conversations with me, and almost all of them pertained to the various arrangements he had made through undesirable middlemen which resulted in great loss to the government. Most of the conversations Menon had with me in the past few months included ministers and civil servants and in one of them, he mentioned bluntly that he did not trust any of them. The most recent conversation I had with him left me believing that he was either daft or exceedingly too simple. He told me to ensure that the government understood that the office of High Commissioner in London came second to the Prime Minister's office and that the President of the country should bestow the title of Deputy Prime Minister on him for the period of time he would be serving in London as the High Commissioner. He spoke as if he was about to become High Commissioner for life and that his only condition was remaining the Deputy Prime Minister. Given that Menon was already highly subjective, even on the most flexible circumstances, had he been the Indian Ambassador to Peru, he would have argued for the Deputy Prime Minister position with the same unyielding conviction.

Jinnah – The "Mediocre Lawyer"

Mohammad Ali Jinnah, a lawyer
(Dawn.com)

Amongst those on Mountbatten's staff was Alan Campbell-Johnson, his Press Adviser, who became the first and only Press Attaché to a Viceroy. Campbell- Johnson had joined Mountbatten as War Diarist at Combined Operations, aged twenty-nine, and had performed an invaluable function as public relations officer to the Supreme at SEAC. There he had received memoranda from Mountbatten asking him to emphasise 'my personal intervention' in various engagements, and to play down the roles of commanders such as Somerville, Figgard and Peirse, who were about to be sacked. One of the founders of the modern PR industry, Campbell-Johnson was a talented and tireless aide. He attended almost all staff meetings and travelled constantly with the Viceroy. His diaries of the period, entitled *Mission With Mountbatten*, constitute an invaluable record.

The propaganda Campbell-Johnson put out a SEAC was considered some of the best in any theatre of the war and helped ensure that the Fourteenth Army was never really the 'Forgotten Army' and that Mountbatten was certainly never the forgotten Supremo. Writing in the PR industry's house journal, *Persuasion*, in 1949, Campbell-Johnson recorded how he gave 'press guidance' to the 100 correspondents resident in Delhi. Sitting in on staff meetings also meant 'the field was clear for me to ensure that the PR implications of any proposed action were considered promptly and at the highest level. As such, he can lay claim to have been the first political 'spin- doctor'.

Mountbatten started off in India as he meant to go on. At the second staff meeting he declared himself 'very much in favour of Honours on a considerable scale being granted to members of Princely families'. He instructed Campbell- Johnson 'to ensure that all issues of the Court Circular were in future rendered to him, through the Personal Secretary, for approval'. He also wanted it stated that he 'received' people at audiences. Top of the agenda for the fifth staff meeting on 29 March 1947 was a directive to Campbell-Johnson 'to find out and inform him whether the complete lack of publicity given by *The Statesman* that morning to the party he had given the previous day… was deliberate, and whether an account of this event had been sent to London'. By the seventh item, the Viceroy was directing his Military Secretary 'to arrange that the actions of only himself, Her Excellency and the Hon. Pamela Mountbatten [their younger daughter] were reported in the Court Circular', as it had come to his attention that news about Ismay had somehow crept in. An inordinate amount of time was later spent by Mountbatten on the ceremonies for the transfer of power. Discussion of them, and 'Flags for the New Dominions', often came far higher on the meetings' agenda than, say, 'Situation in the Punjab', which was usually relegated to the end.

The new Viceroy did notice that the Viceregal Staff had never had a whole-time spokesman and quite some of Wavell's distance from the public can be rationalised by the absence of someone who could 'interpret' or 'project' him to the Press. Mountbatten had no plan of concealing his personality beneath any Indian or other bushels. In this case, it was Campbell-Johnson's role to pound endlessly, in both the Press and public, at the Mountbatten name being a name synonymous to triumph.

Mountbatten made a substantial departure from the normal practice of swearing in ceremonies of Viceroys. He decided to make a brief speech. George Abell, Mountbatten's Private Secretary made the first draft. The speech was short and was to last no more than a couple of minutes. The speech was revised by Mountbatten and handed over to Campbell-Johnson for a final vetting. He suggested certain alterations which were in the first instance turned down by the Viceroy. Campbell-Johnson records "It is just after 1 a.m., an A.D.C. has come through to say that His Excellency has revised his speech and what is he to do about giving to the press? The ambiguous sentence, I am relieved to say, is out."

Now here comes the crunch. In the *Transfer of Power* documents Mountbatten's inaugural speech is published as follows:

"No. 2326. Circular. Following from Principal Information Officer."

"Following is not repeat not for publication before 05.00 hours repeat 05.00 hours G.M.T. on 24th March 1947. Following is text of brief address by H.E. Lord Mountbatten at swearing-in ceremony to-day."

The speech follows and there is a peculiar footnote: "Text not to be released before stipulated time. For Joyce, Information Department."

How Sudhir Ghose Gandhi's close crony qualified to get a copy of this highly secret and classified document before anyone else is left to the reader's imagination. The swearing-in ceremony was a fifteen-minute affair which gave Mountbatten and Edwina an opportunity to look regal and resplendent in all their glittering ceremonial uniforms and to display all their medals. From the very afternoon of the swearing-in Mountbatten got down to business. The first two persons to be interviewed were the Nawab of Bhopal and the Maharajah of Bikaner. In keeping with

Mahatama Gandhi and
Mohammed Ali Jinnah
(Firstpost.com)

Mountbatten's vowed objective of writing his own history in between all interviews he allowed fifteen minutes during which he dedicated his own version of the proceedings of the conversation with the person he was interviewing.

On the afternoon of 24 March, 1947 Mountbatten interviewed Nehru. It was all fraternity and bonhomie. During the course of the interview, Mountbatten asked Nehru to give his assessment of Jinnah. The following is minuted:

"He gave me a remarkable word-picture of Jinnah's character. He described him as one of the most extraordinary men in history. A financially successful though mediocre lawyer, Jinnah had found success late in life. He had not been politically successful until after the age of 60. Nehru explained Jinnah's creed, which he admitted had scored enormous success, as always to avoid taking any positive action which might split his followers; to refuse to hold meetings or to answer questions; never to make a progressive statement because it might lead to internal Muslim dissensions. These negative qualities were ones which had a direct appeal to the Muslims – therefore it was not to be hoped that logic would prevail."

"I said that it was not a question of logic but of the time limit. What if I were to say to Jinnah that he would be granted his Pakistan? Nehru agreed that it might be possible to frighten Jinnah into co-operation on the basis of the short length of time available."

It is interesting to go through the contents of Nehru's assessment of Jinnah. It is hardly within the capability of the writer to comment on the assessment of one great personality of another. But one does wonder if Nehru who never had a legal practice of any significance calling Jinnah a mediocre lawyer appears to be hardly appropriate. Let us examine some of the comments made by M.C. Chagla in *Roses In December*. Chagla, a barrister who ultimately had a distinguished career ending up as a member of the Indian Cabinet, worked for six years as an assistant to Jinnah in the Bombay High Court. Writes Chagla:

'I joined his chamber and remained with him for about six years. I read his briefs, went with him to court, and listened to his arguments. What impressed me most was the lucidity of his thought and expression. There were no obscure spots or ambiguities about what Jinnah had to tell the court. He was straight and forthright, and always left a strong impression whether his case was intrinsically good or bad. I remember sometimes at a conference he would tell the solicitor that his case was hopeless, but when he went to court, he fought like a tiger, and almost made me believe that he had changed his opinion. Whenever I talked to him afterwards about it, he would say that it was the duty of an advocate, however bad the case might be, to do his best for his client.'

Also, among hundreds of lawyers who were practicing in the Bombay High Court why Jinnah was chosen to defend Tilak in a serious case of treason is to be pondered. Jinnah defended Tilak successfully. We have already dwelt at some length about the immensely successful practice which Jinnah had which made him one of the few super tax payers of his era. A book by itself can be written about the successful legal practice of Jinnah therefore Nehru's remark about Jinnah being a mediocre lawyer only reflects on his own judgement. As regards Nehru's remark that Jinnah had not been politically successful until after the age of sixty we can only quote Patrick French in *Liberty or Death*: 'For Nehru to describe the League Leader as a mediocre lawyer and unsuccessful politician demonstrates his own bias by this time, and forgets the fact that Jinnah was a major nationalist politician at a time when Nehru was still a Harrow schoolboy in short trousers.'

We may also have a look at M.C. Chagla's *Roses in December*:

'The question may well be asked why, if I was a nationalist, I ever joined the Muslim League. When I left India in 1919, Jinnah was the uncrowned King of Bombay. He was the idol of the youth. His personality and his sturdy independence attracted and appealed to the best elements in the city. He was the President of the Home Rule League, and had made stirring speeches in Shantaram Chawl, which was then the venue of political meetings. He had opposed the presentation of an address to Lord Willingdon, who was then the Governor of Bombay, because he believed that his policies were anti-Indian. **So great was the enthusiasm of the people for Jinnah in those days that from contributions made by rich and poor alike they had built a Hall, which they named after him.** Even today, Jinnah Hall exists as evidence not only of the past nationalism of Jinnah, but of our own tolerance in that although he later became the architect of partition, we have not changed the name of the Hall.'

It is wondered if any monument honouring a personality has ever been built in the sub-continent by public contributions.

Mountbatten's View of Jinnah

There are plenty of evidences to indicate that Mountbatten was working to a clear blue print even before his swearing-in as the Viceroy. The plan was to partition India and give Pakistan as small a piece of the cake as possible. The Mountbatten Plan will be dealt with at great length but let us start with Mountbatten's assessment of Jinnah. Excerpted below are some of his own pronouncements about Jinnah:

'Jinnah was 60, I think, before he started taking an interest in politics – came to it very late in life and he came in at a very critical moment, because' (I remember his saying this, and I think he was absolutely right) 'in 1938 they had elections after the Government of India Act 1935. In these elections, they put up the popular locally elected governments in various provinces. And in every province, of course the Congress Party won the election. The Muslim League went to the wall.'

Mohammad Ali Jinnah with Lord and Lady Mountbatten
(dailytimes.com.pk)

Instead of employing common sense to create coalition governments by incorporating the Muslim League, or at least attempting to treat the Muslims better than expected, they chose the opposite approach: completely excluding them and then oppressing them. This treatment is what made the Muslim League believe that not seeking independence would result in worse treatment for them.

The Muslim League sought independence and yet there was a vast ocean of Muslims doted all over India. In reality they could only with some right claim to incorporate two provinces. Jawaharlal Nehru's wonderful idea, of course, was to take over whole Punjab, whole Bengal and just take it with countless of Hindus which would have been all fine provided he was going to lead them in the right way. But without trusting him was not what they said.

What a naive and a distorted impression Mountbatten had of the political scene in India. He goes on:

'Gandhi, unfortunately, had nothing to contribute to finding a solution. His only contribution was to tell me, quite early on, that whatever happened, I mustn't *dream* of patitioning India.'

'I said it was the last thing I wanted to do – I mean the one great legacy we can leave to the subcontinent, is this unification. But, I said, if in fact there is no common meeting ground between the Muslim League and the Congress Party, and they won't settle down – and if Jinnah has now reached the point where the Muslim League are prepared to fight – and don't forget Direct Action Day in Calcutta which was a warning of what he could do (August 1946) – I mean he killed 5,000 people and wounded 15,000 people just as demonstration, and I think he has the capacity to cause civil war and if we don't meet him halfway.'

'However, it is clear that Wavell and others knew that Jinnah was seriously ill by the time I reached Delhi. No such rumor meached me, my wife, my staff, my daughter. Nor any of my immediate British staff. The previous British staff if they knew about it, kept it to themselves. This was disastrous because if I had known, things would have been handled quite differently. Liaquat Ali Khan was a man one could deal with, an Indian gentleman. Jinnah was a **lunatic**. He was absolutely, completely impossible. I don't think we would have waited for him to die because that, I don't think… we neither could have afforded the time, nor could we have felt certain of it. But what we could have dome is to argue with him in a very different way. I assumed I was dealing with a man who was there for keeps, and had Pakistan as his object on which I couldn't steer him around. If in fact, we suppose for a moment that Jinnah had died, literally before the transfer of power, I believe the Congress would have been so relieved that their arch enemy was dead – and none of the others were regarded as anything more or less than Jinnah's shadow – we would have been dealing on a basis where Congress would have been prepared to give up much more and the others would have been ready to accept that. It's a horrifying thought that we were never told.'

Mountbatten further states elsewhere:

'Mind you, Jinnah is now forgotten. He was the man who did it. Bangladesh and all that misery which I forecast. Twenty-five years ago Rajagopalachari and I said it would last 25 years. It had to… It couldn't go on. All this misery and trouble was caused by Jinnah and no one else. And he hasn't had one word said against him. He was the **evil genius** in this whole thing.'

And he goes on:

'I then realised that if he had this faculty of closing his mind to the thing – he could see points, he was an able debater, he had a well-trained mind, he was a lawyer, but he gave me the impression of having closed his mind, closed his ears; he didn't want to be persuaded, he didn't want to hear. I mean whatever one said, it passed him absolutely by. In the case of partitioning Punjab and Bengal, he didn't even seem to have been listening to the previous thing at all. His great strength…he got all this by closing his mind and saying, "No." And how anybody could fail to see Jinnah held the whole key to the situation, to the the continent, in his hand, I fail to understand. I was under no illusions. I saw that dear old Gandhi held nothing at all in his hands.'

And Mountbatten goes on:

'Now I can tell you that if he had shaken his head, the whole thing would have been in the bumble pot. To think that I had to say yes for this clot to get his own plan through, it shows you what one was up against. This was probably the most hair-raising moment of my entire life. I've never forgotten that moment, waiting to see it that clot was going to nod or shake his head. He had no expression on his face. He couldn't have made a smaller gesture and still accepted.'

'They disliked it because they thought it was a trick of mine. I knew it was unpopular but I couldn't care less. It was unpopular because they felt they were being put under pressure and they were. The reason they were under pressure was that if I'd let up on them the whole thing would have blown up under my feet.'

'I have no worry about Jinnah being shown up for the **bastard** he was. You know he really was. I actually got on with him, because I can get on with anybody. He made not one single effort at all. The worse thing he did to me was that he kept on saying I mustn't go, that I must stay, that if I didn't stay they wouldn't get their assets transferred so that after the transfer of power I must stay out in over-all charge. When this was analysed by my staff and myself, we realised that we couldn't have two governors-general with a Viceroy over them after independence.'

'You see, I found it very difficult to believe that an educated man, a man of apparent goodwill, with great affection and admiration for the British, a man who'd shown me consideration, although of a rather cold sort, I found it rather difficult to believe that he would accept India becoming a second class power, and destroy everything, and produce what he himself had said would be an unviable Pakistan. I had hoped that he would say, "If you would give me absolute and complete autonomy, if he would the centre's interference to inter- dominion committees which will sit and elaborate a common defence policy, I might go along with keeping India together.'

The above excerpts from Mountbatten's statement to Lapierre and Collins summarises the scorn

Mountbatten had for Jinnah, whom he described as 'evil genius,' 'clot,' 'psychopathic case,' and 'bastard' while maintaining all through public life that he was utterly neutral. An interesting postscript to the episode is that Jinnah was probably the only individual who understood Mountbatten and truly brought the man down to earth. While the Congress leaders were desperately turning on all their charm to please Mountbatten, Jinnah refused to prostrate himself. For this, Jinnah and indeed the whole Muslim populace, paid a very terrible price.

'HAUGHTY' MR. JINNAH

Mountbatten met Jinnah for the first time on the 5 April, 1947 and the following day Mountbatten had Jinnah and his sister Fatima for dinner. Records Mountbatten in the minutes of the meetings:

'When Mr. Jinnah first arrived on Saturday 5th April, he was in a most frigid, haughty, and disdainful frame of mind.'

What, however, Mountbatten did not know was that over the years Jinnah had behaved in a similar manner with some of the previous Viceroys and other senior British officials. Let us cast our minds back to recollect some of Jinnah's interactions with the British officials. Jinnah was never the one to be obsequious or sycophantic to them.

Lord Willingdon, Governor of Bombay (1919-1921): Jinnah's arrogance started early. There is a famous incident relating to Ratanbai, Jinnah's wife. Stanley Wolpert has given a most exquisite description of Jinnah's wife. It is reproduced for the readers to relish. 'Ruttie as she came to be called, was a thoroughly enchanting chilled, precociously bright, gifted in every art, beautiful in every way. As she matured, all of her talents, gifts, and beauty were magnified in so delightful and unaffected a manner that she seemed a "fairy princess" almost too lovely, too fragile to be real. And her mind was so alert, her intellect so lively and probing that she took as much interest in politics as she did in romantic poetry and insisted on attending every public meeting held in Bombay during 1916, always sitting, of course, in "the first row," chaperoned by her "multimillionaire philanthropist" maiden aunt, Miss Mambai Petit.'

In the summer of 1916 when Ruttie was sixteen and Jinnah at least forty, they shared the Petit chateau within view of Mount Everest, perched 7,000 feet high in the idyllic "Town of the Thunderbolt" – Darjeeling – where only the choicest tea plants and the silent snow-clad mountain peaks and isolated trails witnessed the passionate glances of longing and love that passed between these two.

Despite severe family opposition (Ruttie's father Sir Dinshaw Petit even obtained a court injunction against Ruttie marrying Jinnah) Jinnah married Ruttie on 19 April, 1918. And they went off for their honeymoon to Nainital and on their return to Bombay the couple were the toast of the town. 'They were a stunning couple' records Stanley Wolpert. 'Ruttie's long hair was decked in ever-fresh flowers, her lovely lithe body draped in diaphanous silks of flaming red and gold, pale blue, or pink. She wore headbands replete with diamonds, rubies, and emeralds, and smoked English cigarettes in long ivory and silver filters that added a flamboyance to her every graceful gesture, bend and twirl of arm or body, as the musician ring of her uninhibited laughter reminded the world of her beautiful presence. Jinnah, with his bristling black moustache and brilliantly luminous eyes, dressed as smartly as any British lord inside Buckingham, seemed the perfect consort for his bride, and they looked that spring of 1918 as happy and fulfilled as they felt. With a start that perfectly beautiful, surely, they had reason to expect that the future might be one long life of continuing happiness, if not eternal bliss.'

Jinnah's public conflict with Willingdon was reflected in their bitter social relationship. The Jinnahs had been invited to dinner at Bombay's Government House soon after returning from their honeymoon. Ruttie wore one of her lowest-cut Paris evening gowns, and Lady Willingdon was quick to order her servant to bring a "wrap to cover up Mrs. Jinnah – in case she felt cold." Jinnah did not wait for the servant's return, jumping up from his table to inform his hostess, 'When Mrs. Jinnah feels cold, she will say so, and ask for a wrap herself." He escorted his wife from the room. They did not set foot inside the Government House again till the Willingdons had moved out.

Viceroy Lord Chelmsford (1916-21): Jinnah was during Chelmsford's viceroyalty member of the Central Legislative Council. That was the time when a severely repressive legislation was passed known as "The Black" or "Rowlatt Act". Jinnah made a scathing attack against the act with the Viceroy in the chair. His warnings fell on deaf ears. Chelmsford, Rowlatt and the others were determined to go full steam ahead despite the unanimous opposition of all 22 members on the Council. Jinnah wrote a scathing letter to Lord Chelmsford resigning his membership of the Council as a protest against the Black Act.

Viceroy Lord Reading (1921-6): Viceroy Reading had much more in common with fellow barristers like Jinnah than had the Cavalry Captain Chelmsford. Before the end of 1921 Reading enlisted Jinnah's assistance in seeking to reopen lines of communication with political India. In 1926, the final year of Reading's Viceroyalty, he offered to include Jinnah's name on the coveted list those he was recommending for knighthood, if only Jinnah would agree to accept that honour.

'I prefer to be plain Mr. Jinnah," he replied, "I have lived as plain Mr. Jinnah and I hope to die as plain Mr. Jinnah." Ruttie reportedly responded to a query of how she would like being addressed as "Lady Jinnah," by snapping – "If my husband accepts knighthood I will take a separation from him"

Viceroy Lord Irwin (later Halifax) (1926-31): Lord Irwin was much more sympathetic and sensitive to the Indian feelings. It appears Jinnah had a fairly civil relationship with Lord Irwin and Lord Irwin on a number of occasions used Jinnah to communicate with the Indian leaders.

Viceroy Lord Willingdon (1931-36): Jinnah's bête noire as governor of Bombay during World War I returned to take the helm of India's government at New Delhi from 1931-36. it was not entirely coincidental perhaps that for most of Lord Willingdon's term as Viceroy, Jinnah remained out of India, though by then he more closely resembled the formidable Marquis in temperament as well as appearance than he did that radical young nationalist leader of the 1918 anti Willingdon protest. Willingdon's feeling toward Jinnah sufficed to keep the latter out of the joint committee appointed to fashion final Round Table conference proposals into a new government of India bill for Parliament. Jinnah opted to live in London, however, despite Willingdon's presence in India (a "target" who must have temped him sorely at times to return to the legislative assembly), as much as because of it. Jinnah did not hesitate to return, periodically, for visits to Simla, Delhi, and Bombay during his half decade of "permanent" residence in London.

Viceroy Lord Linlithgow (1936-43): The relationship between Jinnah and Linlithgow appeared to have been very close. On 1 November, 1939 Jinnah met Linlithgow, Gandhi, and Rajendraw Prasad at his new house at 10 Aurangzeb Road, and then drove to the Viceroy's house in Jinnah's car. It must have given Jinnah great satisfaction to have the Viceroy, Gandhi, and Congress President Prasad come to *his* sitting room and drive in *his* Packard Eight to the Viceregal Palace. With Churchill and Amery at the Helm in London, Jinnah's stock rose much higher in New Delhi and Simla. Jinnah's influence on the Government appeared to be overwhelming and the attitude appeared to be that no step could be taken, however reasonably, lest Mr. Jinnah should be offended. Linlithgow however considered Jinnah's escalating demands obstructive to the war effort and felt that Jinnah wanted to become in effect the Prime Minister, a goal the Viceroy had no intention whatever of furthering. Jinnah took pains at this time to remind the British of how loyal Muslims had been and how worthy of partnership. To Linlithgow's objections Jinnah was overheard saying on his face, "You have double-crossed me." By then Jinnah considered the Viceroy "wooden and antediluvian" and had concluded that Linlithgow and his official coterie at Simla merely "want our support on the assurance that we shall be remembered as loyal servants after that war and will even be given a *baksheesh!*"

Jinnah's position remained firm throughout the remaining years of World War II and his stock rose to new heights in London as well as in New Delhi. In his frank Assessment of Jinnah, Linlithgow remarked, 'His curse is personal vanity which at his age he is no likely to shake off.'

Viceroy Lord Wavell (1943-1947): In September 1943, Wavell's assessment of Jinnah was that, 'It is hardly too much to say that Jinnah is the Muslim League. He is a vain, shallow and ambitious man who would probably think the present time inopportune for any rapprochement with the Hindus'.

After the Simla Conference in mid-1945 Wavell's assessment of Jinnah's conduct during the conference was 'Narrow and arrogant…actuated mainly by fear and distrust of the Congress…constitutionally incapable of friendly co- operation with the other party.'

Mr. Jinnah with the Viceroy Lord Wavell
and Master Tara Singh
(Flickr.com)

A unique tribute was paid to Jinnah's power of debate during the visit of the Cabinet Mission in April 1946 when Turnbull, Wavell and Cripps each prepared "brief" on how best to tackle Jinnah. A day after Muslim League joined the Interim Government on 29 October 1946, Jinnah spent on hour with Wavell and the Viceroy found him "at his most Jinnahish…. completely unsatisfactory." Wavell's coined epithet "Jinnahish" sums up Jinnah's behaviour.

It is certainly a monumental task to give a detailed account of Jinnah's treatment of and attitude towards the Viceroys. A few instances have been quoted to establish that Jinnah's behaviour towards the British Officials was fairly uniform throughout his life. Therefore, his being 'frigid, haughty and disdainful' towards Mountbatten in his first meeting with him on 5 April, 1947 was no exception. The only difference being that the previous Viceroys did not take Jinnah's attitude as a personal offence and make it a cause for unfair treatment.

Coincidence or Conspiracy?

On 20 February 1947, Prime Minister Clement Attlee declared that the British government planned to transfer power to India no later than June of 1948, as well as stating that Mountbatten would replace Wavell as Viceroy. Was it coincidence or blueprint that on March 8, 1947 the Congress Party should pass a resolution accepting the principles of Pakistan, something they had fiercely resisted for years?

Interalia the Congress Resolution stated:

'These tragic events have demonstrated that there can be no settlement of the problem in the Punjab by violence and coercion, and that no arrangement based on coercion can last. Therefore, it is necessary to find a way out which involves the least amount of compulsion. This would necessitate a division of the Punjab into two Provinces, so that the predominantly Muslim part may be separated from the predominantly non-Muslim part.'

The author of the Resolution was Sardar Patel, and he, perhaps During the course of his career, he made, for some of his colleagues, astonishingly shocking decisions which confused them. Started with them being permitted to vote on their It additionally enables Sikhs the liberty of electing which faction they desire to inhabit and engage with. The importance of such an action was surely clear to any person: If Congress was willing to concede a province, they had one set divided into two, one of which could no longer claim they opposed the division of the rest of the nation. Not in His Eyes, surely. To reiterate, is clear that he had chosen to abandon the defence of certain concepts. So as far as Muslims are concerned, freely accepting movement of their people and resources regardless of which regions they have settled in.

America had made the decision to remain passive in its control over the Congress and positioned itself as a few moves away from implementing the suffice which bordered, worse still incorporate the Muslim League. The steps taken by Liaquat Ali Khan, the deputy leader of the Muslim League, as a Finance Member of the interim Government had scared him hen, because, as it is known, Liaquat's Budget had drenched the millionaire supporters of Congress and exposed the Party's pretense of being Socialist. Not only did Patel work to secure a revision of the Budget (which, thanks to the Viceroy's aid, he was able to accomplish) but he also determined that he would never allow himself to be put in such a position again. Not that Patel explained his attitude to his colleagues with quite such brutal clarity. For them he had another line of reasoning more calculated to appeal to their desire to preserve Indian unity at all costs.

'If the League insists on Pakistan,' he wrote to one of the Working Committee, **'the only alternative is the division of the Punjab and Bengal**... I do not think that the British Government will agree to division. In the end, they will see the wisdom of handing over the reins of Government to the strongest party. Even if they do not, it will not matter. A strong Centre with the whole of India – except E. Bengal and part of the Punjab, Sind and Baluchistan – enjoying full autonomy under the

Centre will be so powerful that the remaining portions will eventually come in.'

It was this argument that was most likely appealing to Pandit Nehru. Everything in the reasoning's structure made little sense; Jinnah and the Muslim League as irrational figures weren't taken seriously. The goal was to undermine their standing decisively, while making it evident to the Muslims of India that their aid could be safely put in the hands of the congress.

In his eyes, Patel's Resolution was a ruse and not an acceptance of anything concerning partition. The meeting of Congress' Working Committee and their endorsement of the Partition of Punjab was accomplished with his support. He believed it was not drastically progressive in nature; it would only serve to demonstrate to the Muslims the consequences they would have to confront should they persist in their struggle for a separate state of Pakistan. Even Mr. Jinnah himself would come to understand that his agitation could only produce a dismembered State whose suffering will make it permanently nonfunctional. The resolution was set to be accepted at a time when Gandhi was occupied with the healing work in Bihar while the only significant Muslim member of the hierarchy of the Congress, Maulana Abul Kalam Azad, was feeble and absent. Patel and Nehru were well aware that both of them will oppose it as they will do everything in their power to prevent it from being implemented. So much so that after the resolution was received, measures were taken to ensure that it was not publicised, and no communication was forwarded to Gandhi to inform him of what had occurred.

'I have long intended to write to you asking you about the Working Committee resolution on the possible partition of the Punjab,' he wrote to Nehru, nearly three weeks later. 'I would like to know the reason for it. I have to speak about it. I have done so in the absence of full facts with the greatest caution. Kripalani (who had now taken the Congress presidency from Nehru) said in answer to a question in Madras that it was possible that the principle might also be applied to Bengal. I was asked by a Muslim Leaguer of note… if it was applicable to the Muslim-majority provinces why it should not be so to Congress-majority provinces like Bihar. I think I did not know the reason behind the Working Committee's resolution. Nor had I the opportunity. I could only give my own view which was against any partition based on communal grounds and the two-nation theory. Anything was possible by compulsion. But willing consent required an appeal to reason and heart. Compulsion or show of it had no place in voluntaries.'

He wrote at the same time to Sardar Patel asking him to explain the 'Punjab resolution'.

Patel was the first to reply, and it was a response disingenuous in the extreme:

'It has been difficult to explain to you in the resolution about the Punjab. It was adopted after the deepest deliberation. Nothing has been done in a hurry or without full thought. *That you had expressed your views against it, we learned only from the papers.* But you are of course entitled to say what you feel right. The situation in the Punjab is far worse than in Bihar. The military has taken over control. As a result, on the surface things seem to have quietened down somewhat. But no one can say when there may be a bust-up again. If that happens, I am afraid even Delhi will not remain unaffected. But here of course we shall be able to deal with it.'

Pandit Nehru's reply, which followed a day later, was much more lame.

Jawaharlal Nehru and Muhammad Ali Jinnah
(Indianhistorycollective.com)

'About our proposals to divide Punjab,' he wrote, 'this flows naturally from our previous decisions. These were negative previously, but now the time for a decision has come and merely passing resolutions giving expressions to our views means little. I feel convinced, and so did most of the members of the Working Committee, that we must press for this immediate division *so that reality might be brought into the picture. Indeed, this is the only answer to partition as demanded by Jinnah.'*

He still could not be convinced that Jinnah would rather have a 'moth-eaten Pakistan', as he was to call it later, than no Pakistan at all.

When forwarding these Congress resolutions to the viceroy the next day, Nehru explained "our intention" to urge the Muslim League to join Congress in the assembly and to work together amicably toward reaching a final settlement. He added with an almost audible sigh of resignation:

'If unfortunately, this is not possible, we… have also suggested the division of the Punjab into two parts. This principle would, of course, apply to Bengal also… not pleasant for us to contemplate, but such a course is preferable to an attempt by either party to impose its will upon the other. Recent events in the Punjab have demonstrated… that it is not possible to coerce the non-Muslim minority in the Province, just as it is not possible or desirable to coerce the others… In the event of the Muslim League not accepting the Cabinet Delegation's scheme and not coming into the Constituent Assembly, the division of Bengal and Punjab becomes inevitable.'

As we shall see as we go on Jinnah fell into the Congress trap hook, line, and sinker.

HAPTER 6: THE IDEA OF INDIA

The Blueprint

Lord Mountbatten with Jawaharlal Nehru and Muhammad Ali Jinnah discussing about the partition (opindia.com)

As we have seen the Congress Working Party passed a resolution on 8 March, 1947 accepting in principle the concept of Pakistan something which they had consistently and continuously opposed. On 13 March 1947, Krishna Menon met Mountbatten and gave him an elaborate note which was virtually the Congress blueprint of the events that followed in the following months during Mountbatten's viceroyalty. Mountbatten in his interview with Lapierre and Collins stated:

'My unofficial link with Nehru was Krishna Menon, whom I made friends with in England. We've remained friends. A very curious creature. I must tell you – you won't want this for you book, but it'll help you to understand – Menon did the most frightful thing to Nehru.......'

As admitted by Mountbatten he had 'made friends' with Krishna Menon. This statement leads one to conclude that they must have had several meetings before Mountbatten headed towards India to take up his viceroyalty. What transpired in the meetings is not recorded. One can only conjecture that those intense discussions must have related to the Congress formula of the division of India. In all probability Menon did not think the document given to Mountbatten would be filed among the Mountbatten papers and would survive and eventually be printed in the *Transfer of Power* documents.

This is a very vital evidence pointing towards a serious Congress influence over Mountbatten's decision making. Any thoughtful student of the partition period should read Krishna Menon's note most attentively. The note is a long one and some parts of it have been quoted before. It is being repeated in the present context to assess Mountbatten's viceroyalty. It is quite curious to note that the letter was written from the India House. How Menon was permitted to use the India House facilities to give pro-Congress advice to Mountbatten is indeed baffling. In March 1947 Menon had no official status except as an envoy of Nehru. Menon wrote a covering letter to his note which is below:

'India House, Aldwych, London, W.C.2,

13 March 1947

My dear Lord Louis Mountbatten,

'I enclose the last page of my notes, which was inadvertently left out of the copy I gave you. As I told you, there are a number of matters to be included in it if the basic idea appears to be of any use. If you need me, I shall be glad to see you again before I leave. Your A.D.C. apparently knows how to get in touch with me. I recognise the importance of hastening slowly, but it appears that in India things will not rest as they are. There is a grave threat of famine also, which may add to complications, but at the same time makes effective central authority essential.

I was glad to see you and to have had our talk. Perhaps you will let me know sometime what you think of what I have said.'

Yours sincerely,

V.K. Krishna Menon

Mountbatten has himself stated that he met Menon more than once before his departure from London to take up his viceroyalty in India. It may be pertinent to note that he did not think it necessary to meet any representative of any other party.

Some relevant extracts from Krishna Menon's note are reproduced below: '*Section I*

The problems are: -

(1) The crisis in the Interim Government.

(2) The machinery for taking over.

(3) The Princes.

(4) Indo-British relations.

(1) and (2) are obviously closely inter-connected, and (4) is closely linked with (1) and (2), both severally and jointly.

Section II. The crisis in the Government

(1) The decision of the Congress to force the issue of a genuine coalition or the dismissal of the League members is in suspense *for the moment*, pending (a) the arrival of the new Viceroy and (b) the slight hopes of response from the League to a further approach.

(2) The resolving of the crisis, in my view, *rests basically* on the relation of the Ministry to the Viceroy – that is, British power.

The assumption of a new role by the Viceroy quite obviously (not merely willy nilly) is essential to a change for the better in the present situation.

(3) The Attlee declaration, apart from all other causes, makes it both logical and incumbent on the British side that its power (as distinct from its influence) should not rapidly diminish (to vanishing point in 1948) but that *immediately there should be a change in this relationship whereby the entire onus of administration is in the hands of the Interim Government.*

(4), (5), (6), (7), (8) …..'

'Section III. Taking over

(1) In July 1948 it is obvious there must be machinery for taking over. This machinery may well be

(a) that which is established under a new constitution by a Constituent Assembly with or without Moslem League participation; or

(b) the Interim Government (under Dominion conditions) or

(c) the de facto repositories of power and power relationships: or

(d) some machinery arbitrarily decided by the outgoing authority.

I do not propose to deal with the question of what constitution may emerge by one process or another.

The immediate problem is what has to be done for obtaining comparatively stable conditions for (a), (b), (c) and (d) above, or some combination of these.

In hard reality this poses the question, *what about the Moslem League* and, in a lesser way, the Princes, and what solution or way out can be found by the Viceroy using his great influence as contemplated in II above?

(2) What I propose here is intended as a realistic approach rather than a crystallised formula, and I think aloud in this way.

Recognise, if the League so desires it, its claim for "Moslem homelands"- Pakistanis.

This recognition is possible only on the basis that the homelands are to be limited to those areas where at present the Moslem population is predominant, and where the League holds an appreciable majority of elected seats.

In other words, it is impossible to think in terms of homeland on the basis of British Provinces. This is not a question of whittling down Pakistan or driving a bargain on it, but of seeking the only method which would enable a Pakistan to be created at all.

Therefore, I propose the following: -

(a) A Western Pakistan in the North-West, to include the Moslem majority districts of the Punjab together with the Moslem districts of Sind, with an approach to the sea at Karachi, irrespective of the composition of the population on this boundary. Any attempt to provide a homeland which is boxed in on all four sides is an unfair offer from the League point of view.

The port of Karachi, irrespective of its predominant non-Moslem population and all-India importance, to be included in Western Pakistan, thus giving the League a first-class sea and air port and a great city.

The remainder of the Punjab to be constituted into a separate province of all-India.

The question of the remainder of Sind has to be thought out.

(b) Eastern Pakistan in the North-East, to include the districts of Eastern Bengal which are predominantly Moslem, and certain areas of Assam, thus partitioning Bengal (shades of Curzon!). The problems here are (i) the comparatively strong opposition in Bengal and partition and (ii) Calcutta.

I believe that partition is the price that will have to be paid for any stability in Bengal.

With regard to Calcutta, any solution which hands over Calcutta to Pakistan will be unstable and impractical. The reasons are well-known. On the other hand, the League has to be given a port on the East, and the solution is that as part of the compromise settlement India should build a large-sized city and port in Chittagong, that is, provide the money for it however many millions in may cost.

(The rest of Krishna Menon's note will be given in the next installment.)

The Blueprint - II

We continue with the note which Krishna Menon gave to Mountbatten before his departure to India:

'(c) *Questions of powers and status.* The Pakistanis shall be styled as autonomous states, and not provinces. They should have all the attributes of statehood except foreign relations and defence. These two cannot in any event, before 1948, be made available to any Pakistan, because any new state created would have no foreign relations by that time even if it succeeds in getting recognition, except with the cooperation of the rest of India. This is therefore a problem of the future, and is dealt with further below. Defence is equally not capable of being vested in any Pakistan at the time of its creation. Even if it were, it would confer little power on Pakistanis, as the heavier defence of all-India would reduce the defence power of the Pakistan to impotence.

On the other hand, it is proposed that the Pakistanis as here contemplated should have vaster powers than for the groups under the Cabinet plan. Therefore, they should be given not merely the title of autonomous states, but all the competence except the two mentioned above, that is to say all tariffs, currency, control of communications, including posts and railways, flag, external trade, control of resources and independent heads of states. They should also be accorded the right to secede from India and establish themselves as independent states when they are in a position to obtain foreign recognition and to build up their defences sufficiently effective(ly) for the independent

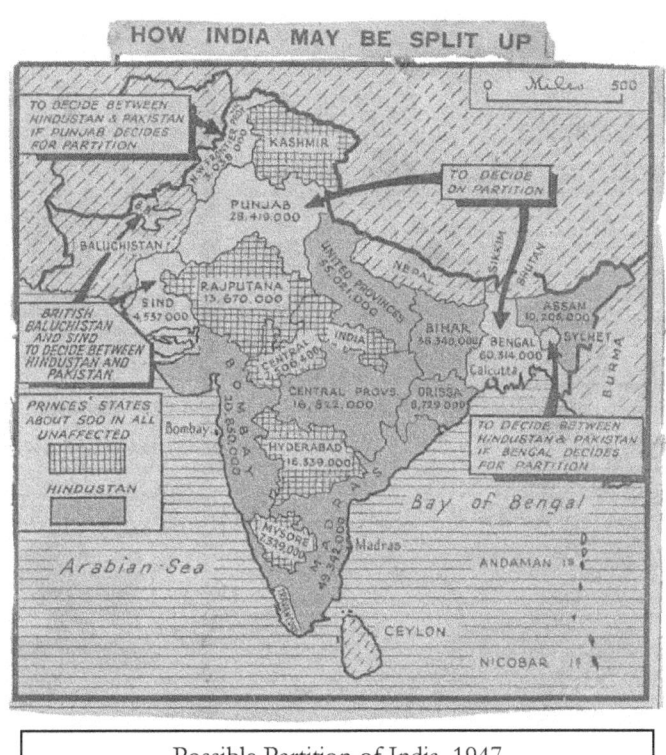

Possible Partition of India, 1947
(Nationalarchives.gov.uk)

protection of their homelands. This right of secession must be genuinely conceded, irrespective of whether it will be used. All these rights and functions can obviously be made amenable to any agreements of give and take with India.

(d) The Pakistan would, as different from the provinces, maintain a High Commissioner or Agent General, or some such functionary of the semi- ambassadorial level at New Delhi, who would be the link on the problems of defence and foreign relations and be a general liaison in the neighborly relations contemplated. Obviously, no taxation will be levied in the Pakistans, except by their own Governments. They would make an agreed contribution annualy to the Government of India in respect of defence and foreign policy, which shall not be varied except with consent.

(e) The inclusion of areas other than those mentioned here need not in principle be ruled out. For example, if the League is able to make terms with the rest of Punjab and bring such areas into its Pakistan, it should be permitted, but such consent must be a matter of plebiscite in which at least 75 per cent of the population votes in favour of such incorporation.

(f) It should be pointed out here that in this arrangement the Pakistanis receive a far higher status of independence and considerably more powers and functions than the present provinces claimed for Pakistan would receive if power were handed over in July 1948 on the basis then likely to exist in the absence of any agreement of this kind. For provinces, in spite of autonomy, have much less power than contemplated for the Pakistans as herein.

Section III. (IV). The Princes...

Section IV (V) Indo-British Relations... Section V (VI).

The creation of Pakistan and the conferring on it of rights and functions far in excess of the Cabinet Plan will evoke protests and opposition from Congress and other groups. Mr. Jinnah would regard it, on the other hand, as a truncated Pakistan. But for either side the alternatives are far worse, and for the British it would involve a repudiation of the solemn pledges of the Attlee declaration and the prospect of having to deal with anarchy or the termination of relationships in such ways as are injurious to both sides.

It may be further pointed out that the proposals here are not based upon theoretical considerations, and are largely, in fact, a planned approach to what would willy nilly be the position if in July 1948 no constitution has emerged.

Finally, even if a constitution emerges, the approach in these proposals would *at present* be called for, but it would have to be made clear that this is no substitute for constitution making which is untouched by them.

It may also be added that these proposals concede to Mr. Jinnah his demand for two Constituent Assemblies.'

The theory of the blueprint is further reinforced by the fact that five days after Krishna Menon handed his scheme to Mountbatten, Attlee thought it fit to write to Mountbatten giving him directions about his actions in India. A few extracts are given below:

'**18 March 1947**

My dear Mountbatten,

The statement which was issued at the time of the announcement of your appointment sets out the policy of the Government and the principles in accordance with which the transfer of power to Indian hands should be affected.

My colleagues of the Cabinet Mission and I have discussed with you the general lines of your approach to the problems which will confront you in India. It will, I think be useful to you to have on record the salient points which you should have in mind in dealing with the situation. I have, therefore, set them down here.

It is the definite objective of His Majesty's Government to obtain a unitary Government for British India and the Indian States, if possible within the British Commonwealth, through the medium of a Constituent Assembly, set up and run in accordance with the Cabinet Mission's plan, and you should do the utmost in your powers to persuade all Parties to work together to this end, and advise His Majesty's Government, in the light of developments, as to the steps that will have to be taken.

Since, however, this plan can only become operative in respect of British India by agreement between the major Parties, there can be no question of compelling either major Party to accept it.

Since, however, this plan can only become operative in respect of British India by agreement between the major Parties, there can be no question of compelling either major Party to accept it.

If by October 1 you consider that there is no prospect of reaching a settlement on the basis of a unitary government for British India, either with or without the cooperation of the Indian States, you should report to His Majesty's Government on the steps which you consider should be taken for the handing over of power on the due date…'

It is a long letter and for the first time a Prime Minister was acknowledging that a solution other than a unitary India was possible. It was left to Mountbatten to suggest a solution for any possible impasse.

In the words of Nicholas Mansergh: 'political bias, its belief in centralisation and planning, its concept of a socialist State, all predisposed its leaders in favour of the aspirations of the left wing of the Congress, and made them if not antipathetic, at least allergic, to Muslim League demands for partition and a separate Muslim State.'

The three major events came in quick succession:

(1) Congress' Working Party Resolution of 8 March, 1947 accepting in principle for the first time the concept of Pakistan.

(2) Krishna Menon's note to Mountbatten of 13 March, 1947 outlining the Congress' blueprint for partition of India.

(3) Attlee's letter to Mountbatten of 18 March, 1947 accepting the idea of a solution other than

unified India is one to assume that they were un-connected or was there a well-laid scheme for events to come.

Gandhi Sidetracked

Mohandas Karamchand Gandhi
(History.com)

Mountbatten arrived in India with a clear-cut blueprint. As we have seen earlier the idea was to banish the Muslims once and for all to their own – very small and unworkable country. The plan was already there, Mountbatten merely had to go through the motion. A close study of the minutes of Mountbatten's daily meetings since his arrival reveals that with the Congress leaders he was all good cheer and bonhomie. The first major Indian Political Leader Mountbatten met after taking up his Viceroyalty was Nehru. They had met once before, in Malaya in March 1946 and the attraction between the two men was mutual. They had much in common. Both were proud men. Both were aristocrats who had espoused popular cause. The deeper thought and sensitivity belonged to Nehru; he was a man, even in triumph, who was often consumed by doubt and self-accusation. It was therefore natural, perhaps, that he should be enormously attracted to the personality of the new Viceroy, so serenely self-confident, so utterly devoid of doubt, so completely in control of himself and all who came into his orbit. Nehru found it easy to talk to Mountbatten, and he talked without stint or reservation. The Viceroy was shrewd enough to spot from the start one of Nehru's weaknesses; he cannot help, when encouraged, being gossipy and malicious about his friends and colleagues. It was from Nehru that Mountbatten obtained much of the ammunition which he subsequently used upon other Congress leaders and when he led Nehru on to talk about Jinnah, He found him no less frank.

The very first sentence of the minute reads: 'Pandit Nehru struck me as most sincere.' Thereafter a cordial discussion followed in which Nehru gave Mountbatten his opinion on the economic problem facing India, his assessment of Jinnah, and his evaluation of the workings of the Interim Government. An interesting addendum to the minutes reinforces how close Mountbatten had become to Nehru in such a short time 'I think that it was evidence of Nehru's fairness of mind that he said he would look for someone other than his previous nominee to be Trade Agent in Malaya, since Lord Wavell had objected to him on the ground that he took part in an anti-British movement during the war.' By the end of their three-hour talk, Nehru was completely won over

Jawaharlal Nehru with Gandhiji and Abul Kalam Azad, Wardha, August 1935 (governancenow.com)

and Mountbatten had the measure of his man. He could be flattered. He could be persuaded. 'Mr. Nehru,' he said as they parted, 'I want you to regard me not as the last Viceroy winding up the British Raj, but as the first to lead the way to the new India.'

Nehru was intensely moved. 'Now I know,' he said, 'what they mean about your charm being so dangerous.' But he was Mountbatten's man from that moment on, and his attachment to the Mountbatten menage was much increased by his subsequent contact with Lady Mountbatten. Later in the day on 24 March, 1947 Mountbatten met Liaqat. Liaqat also gave Mountbatten his version of the workings of the Coalition Government which Mountbatten recorded 'He gave me his version of how the Coalition Government has been formed – a totally different version to that rendered by Nehru – and quite untrue. In a matter of hours how Mountbatten concluded that Nehru gave him the

correct version and Liaqat told him lies is to be pondered. Somehow, Mountbatten knew the detailed functioning of the Interim Government. The following day Mountbatten met Patel. The record starts, 'Sardar Patel was most charming for the first hour of this interview, evincing a considerable sense of humor. He is apparently very fond of Sir Stafford Cripps. The next day he met Azad. The meeting was of little consequence as Azad was

Gandhi with Lord and Lady Mountbatten (picryl.com)

- 108

no longer a major player in the Congress.

One of the objectives of the Blueprint Mountbatten was following was to neutralise Gandhi. Gandhi had been consistently and persistently opposed to any partition of India. Therefore, Congress was forced to pass the partition resolution on 8 March, 1947 keeping the matter quite secret from Gandhi. Now it was Mountbatten's turn to play along with the Congress formula and to eliminate Gandhi from the decision-making forum. This was done in a masterly fashion. Mountbatten met Gandhi for the first time on 31st March, 1947. For this meeting, which Mountbatten considered all important, he was prepared to give all the time Gandhi desired. In fact, they met on two consecutive days. On the first day, Gandhi talked for almost three hours, but it was almost entirely about his early life and struggles. For Mountbatten, who believed that no man needed more than an hour in which to explain himself, it must have been something of a strain to give it his whole attention as he thought of the wreckage of his timetable. On the following day, Gandhi became (for him) more practical. He produced a plan – but it was just the kind of plan which was apt to make Wavell writhe in agony and call him an 'obscurantist'. He proposed that the Congress-Muslim League deadlock might be solved by a simple solution: The Viceroy should call upon Jinnah to set up a Government immediately, leaving him to decide whether it should be all Muslims or contain both Muslims and Hindus; and this Government should be allowed absolutely free hand, with the exception of a Viceregal power of veto, to rule India.

The Viceroy replied at once that he found the plan 'attractive', and promised to regard it sympathetically if Congress, too, agreed to its feasibility. He posed for smiling portraits with Gandhi and Lady Mountbatten, and introduced his daughter, Pamela. 'I shall be sending her to your prayer meeting tomorrow', he said. Gandhi returned from the meeting, in the words of his biographer, Pyarelal, 'greatly impressed by the Viceroy's sincerity, gentlemanliness and nobility of character.' He was not so impressed a little later. He found his plan rudely rebuffed by Congress, and the Viceroy wrote to him to point out that there had been a 'misunderstanding' about his own reception of it. What happened, in fact, was that immediately after the meeting Mountbatten and his staff set to work to sabotage the plan, which they (and many Congress leaders) considered unworkable.

The sabotage was so effective that Gandhi shortly afterwards informed Congress that he would take no further part in the discussions with the Viceroy or play anything other than a minor advisory role in Congress affairs, and he departed once more for his healing mission in Bihar. Within a fortnight of his arrival, the Viceroy had eliminated him from the negotiations for Indian independence. It was an elimination of enormous importance and gravity for India. For Gandhi was one of the only two members of the Congress Party who, despite all the propaganda and pressure, remained unshakably against the partition of India into Pakistan and Hindustan. The *Transfer of Power* documents contains an exchange of correspondence between Gandhi and Lord Ismay Mountbatten's Chief of Staff with Gandhi giving details of his plans. Mountbatten's total lack of sincerity to Gandhi is reflected in the letter which he wrote to Gandhi on 7 April, 1947 extracted below:

'Ismay has shown me your letter to him of 6th April, and we both are most upset to think that any act, or omission, on our part should in any way increase the great burden you are bearing. I therefore think it right to send you the following personal explanation.

As we were parting last Friday afternoon, I said that your plan had many attractions for me and I asked you if you would be so good as to explain it to Ismay, who had not been present when you first propounded it. On your agreeing to do so, I asked Ismay to make a note of its salient features, and I authorised him to talk it over in confidence with the Reforms Commissioner. I am extremely sorry if by these observations I gave you the impression that I wished your plan reduced to the terms of a formal agreement.

As I explained to you during the many talks that we have enjoyed, my aim has been and is to keep a perfectly open mind until I have had the advantages of discussions with important Indian political leaders with the object of seeking an agreement between all parties so that peace can be restored in the country and an acceptable basis for the transfer of power be worked out. When these preliminary conversations have been completed, I shall then have to make up my mind as to what I am going to recommend to His Majesty's Government and, before I do so, I shall most certainly take advantage of your kind offer of further discussion with you.'

What a lot of jugglery of words and verbiage to eliminate Gandhi from the scene!

P.S.: In his interview with Lapierre and Collins Mountbatten made the following statement about Gandhi's plan. 'It was absolute moonshine – I mean, this is the level of his political advice, absolutely nonsensical – but he had enormous charm and enormous influence.'

Rough Encounters

When Mountbatten first met Jinnah on 5 April, 1947, *The Statesman* of Calcutta reported the fact with the cryptic comment, 'Other riot news on page 4.' The Viceroy was never to gain any pleasure from his meetings with Mr. Jinnah – a form of address that he continued to use in his most private and informal engagement diary when every other Indian was given a first name or bare surname. The hostile relationship between Mountbatten and Jinnah stood in stark contrast with the Viceroy's relationship with Nehru. After the Mountbattens' first garden party on March 28, 1947, to which all members of India's Constituent Assembly were invited, Nehru took Edwina and her daughter back to his own house at 17, York Road for a nightcap in that more modest and intimate setting. Thus Nehru, India's Prime Minister-in-waiting was to become virtually a member of the Viceregal family.

When Jinnah first arrived for a meeting a number of photographs were taken of him standing between the Viceroy and the Vicereine. He was recorded in the newspapers as describing himself on this occasion as 'A thorn between two roses.' Mountbatten however records, 'Later I challenged him on this and told him I thought he had said, 'A rose between two thorns.' He said, 'Yes, but in my mind, I was expecting Her Excellency to between you and me.' There appears to be no comment from Jinnah's side of the subsequent correction by Mountbatten. This leaves a lot of room for conjecture. Either according to Jinnah's alleged original statement the description was correct or if we are to take Mountbatten's version one may assume Jinnah had seen something beyond what appeared in the picture. Excerpts from Mountbatten's record of the interview:

'Mr. Jinnah claimed that there was only one solution – a "surgical operation" on India, otherwise India would perish altogether. I replied by reiterating that I had not yet made up my mind, and pointed out that an "anesthetic" must precede any "surgical operation." He gave me an account (which worries me a great deal) about his previous negotiations with Mr. Gandhi…. He emphasised, and tried to prove from this account, that on the Muslim side there was only one man to deal with, namely himself…. But the same was not true of the representatives of Congress-there was no one man to deal with on their side. Mr. Gandhi had openly confessed that he represented nobody… had enormous authority with no responsibility. Nehru and Patel represented different points of view within Congress-neither could give a categorical answer on behalf of the party as a whole…. He also spoke of the emotionalism of the Congress leaders…. He accused Congress leaders of constantly shifting their front…. They would stoop to anything…. At the end of our interview, after he had told me a succession of long stories about how appallingly the Muslims had been treated, I informed him that what fascinated me was the way that all the Indian leaders spoke with such conviction.'

They met again on April 7, with Lord Ismay joining the discussion that afternoon. Mountbatten "tried by every means" to get Jinnah to say he "would accept the Cabinet Mission plan and enter the Constituent Assembly." Jinnah remained adamant, however.

'I then asked him what, if he were in my place, his solution would be; and he repeated once more the demand for Pakistan.... I invited Mr. Jinnah to put forward his arguments for partition. He recited the classic ones. I then pointed out that his remarks applied also to the partition of the Punjab and Bengal, and that by sheer logic if I accepted his arguments in the case of India as a whole, I had also to apply them in the case of these two Provinces.... He expressed himself most upset at my trying to give him a "moth eaten" Pakistan.

He said that this demand for partitioning the Punjab and Bengal was a bluff on the part of Congress to try and frighten him off Pakistan. He was not to be frightened off so easily; and he would be sorry if I were taken in by the Congress bluff.'

'I told him that I regarded it as a very great tragedy that he should be trying to force me to give up the idea of a united India. I painted a picture of the greatness that India could achieve.... I finally said that I found that the present Interim Coalition Government was everyday working better and in a more co- operative spirit; and that it was a day-dream of mine to be able to put the Central Government under the Prime Ministership of Mr. Jinnah himself.... Some 35 minutes later, Mr. Jinnah, who had not referred previously to my personal remark about him, suddenly made a reference out of the blue to the fact that I had wanted him to be the Prime Minister. There is no doubt that it had greatly tickled his vanity, and that he had kept turning over the proposition in his mind.'

'Mr. Gandhi's famous scheme may yet go through on the pure vanity of Mr. Jinnah! Nevertheless he gives me the impression of a man who has not thought out one single piece of the mechanics of his own great scheme, and he will have the shock of his life when he really has to come down to earth and make his vague idealistic proposals work on a concrete basis.'

And after three more hours alone with Jinnah on April 10, Mountbatten reported to his staff that he considered "Mr. Jinnah was a psychopathic case."

'The viceroy had brought all possible arguments to bear on Mr. Jinnah but it seemed that appeals to his reason did not prevail.... Mr. Jinnah had not been able in his presence to adduce one single feasible argument in favour of Pakistan. In fact, he had offered no counter arguments. He gave the impression that he was not listening. He was impossible to argue with.... He was, whatever was said, intent on his Pakistan-which would could surely only result in doing the Muslims irreparable damage... until he had met Mr. Jinnah he (Mountbatten) had not thought it possible that a man with such a complete lack of sense of responsibility could hold the power which he did.'

Mountbatten found Liaquat Ali Khan much easier to deal with than Jinnah in that he was more like Nehru in his urbanity and relative reasonableness. He met with Liaquat for two hours on the evening of April 10, taking him into confidence, as to 'how my mind was beginning to work towards a solution.... I started off with Pakistan and complete partition of the Punjab of Bengal and Assam.

I told him that I had no doubt that the Indian leaders, and their peoples were in such an hysterical condition they would all gladly agree to my arranging their suicide in this way. He nodded his head, and said "I am afraid everybody will agree to such a plan; we are all in such a state." I told him that the worst service I could do to India, if I were her enemy or completely indifferent to her fate, would be to take advantage of this extraordinary mental condition to force the completest partition possible upon them, before going off in June 1948 and leaving the whole country in the most hopeful chaos.'

As we shall see later Mountbatten's pronouncements to Liaquat were quite hypocritical and that night Mountbatten sought some consolation in hope, writing 'I have an impression that Mr. Liaquat Ali Khan intends to help me find a more reasonable solution than this mad Pakistan.'

Mountbatten's meeting on 10 April, 1947 appears to be the most crucial for the attaining of Mountbatten's objectives. The final paragraph of the minutes of the meeting summarises the substance of the discussion.

'I pointed out that so far as I could see the only difference between the scheme I was prepared to give him and that which he could get under the Cabinet Mission plan was that under the Cabinet Mission plan he was obliged to accept a small weak Centre at Delhi controlling Defence, Communications, and External Affairs. I pointed out that these three might really be lumped together under the heading of General Defence, and that I did not see how under the new scheme he could possibly avoid joining some organisation at the Centre to take care of General Defence.

In fact I prophesied that he would find that he had thrown away the substance for the shadow and that he was going to get an almost unworkable truncated Pakistan which would still be obliged to share a common organisation at the Centre to arrange over-all defence. Whereas if only he would come back to the Cabinet Mission plan, he could have the whole of the Pakistan he wanted, without really having any tighter organisation over him at the Centre than he would sooner or later be bound to accept under the truncated scheme; added to which, I pointed out, he was ruining the position of India as a great Power, and forever pulling her down to something below a second class Power.'

Kautilya and Machiavelli

Sir Francis Tuker, GOC Eastern command Indian Army in his *While Memory Serves* writes:

The attitude of the Congress in early 1947 was:

'Well, if the Muslims want Pakistan, let them damned well have it and with a vengeance. We shall shear every possible inch off their territory so as to make it look silly and to ensure that it is not a viable country and when they have got what's left we'll ensure that it can't be worked with economically.'

A speech that Sardar Patel delivered in the Constituent Assembly in November, 1949, fully bears out Tuker's impression. Although delivered more than two years after these events, it still breathed a spirit of vengeance. In the course of this speech, Patel said: "I agreed to partition as a last resort, when we should have lost all…. Mr. Jinnah did not want a truncated Pakistan, but he had to swallow it. I made a further condition that in two months' time power should be transferred."

The acceptance by Congress of partition was a tactical move, but the strategic goal – to rule over entire subcontinent – remained unaltered. To ensure the success of this goal it was necessary that:

1. Hindustan or the Indian Union should be recognised as the only successor to the British government in India; Pakistan would be treated as certain territories that had seceded.

2. The areas to be included in Pakistan should be as small as possible and confined to East Bengal, West Punjab, Sind, and Baluchistan and should exclude the North-West Frontier Province. Pakistan should, if possible, be encircled strategically.

3. Pakistan should be subjected to the maximum handicaps by being denied time and resources – civil and military, manpower and material – to establish and consolidate itself.

4. Whatever could be done to make Pakistan unviable should be done. (The Congress leaders were convinced that Pakistan could not last for long; their aim and endeavour was to hasten the collapse of its economy).

5. The Indian states should be incorporated in the Indian Union.

To achieve these objectives, the Congress leaders needed the help of the British who still had control over the civil administration and the armed forces. What the Congress wanted, above all, was an immediate transfer of power to itself. Attlee's government had been willing enough to do what the Congress wanted, but it was felt that the British government's representative in India, Lord Wavell, had not quite played the game by bringing the Muslim League into the interim government. Now a new Viceroy had come and it remained to be seen how he would behave. As things turned out, he exceeded the expectations of Congress leaders and won an everlasting name for himself in the annals of the new India. He was too enamoured of success to risk annoying the powerful men who had his predecessor virtually dismissed. And in subtlety of intellect he was no match for the Hindu leaders who were so imbued with the spirit of Kautilya, the author of the famed book on statecraft, *Arthashastra*, that Machiavelli appears a crude and clumsy blusterer in comparison.

It has always been a mystery as to why there was never a harsh word from Jinnah about Mountbatten. In fact a man with the cold dignity and reserve of Jinnah spoke in unusually warm terms about Mountbatten. We have seen earlier about the most vile language used by Mountbatten in his reference to Jinnah. The vile language is in print. One can only surmise the language that he actually used about Jinnah that has not been printed. How did this come about?

All the opinions of Mountbatten about Jinnah has come to light after the publication of *The Transfer of Power* documents and the three books by Collins and Lapierre. We now see from a very credible source i.e. *The Emergence of Pakistan* by Chaudhri Muhammad Ali the reason why Jinnah spoke of Mountbatten with respect. Muhammad Ali was witness to events first- hand at the highest level. In 1946 he was working as financial adviser, War and Supply, in the Government of India. When the Muslim League representatives joined the Interim Government of India and Liaquat Ali Khan became Finance Minister, his association with the Muslim League leaders became even closer. During the crucial days of partition, Muhammad Ali was one of the two members of the Steering Committee which was responsible to the Partition Council for the immense administrative tasks involved in partition. After formation of Pakistan Muhammad Ali became Secretary General and ultimately the Prime Minister of Pakistan. One would attach some credibility to his pronouncements. A crucial commentary on the dialogue between Mountbatten and the Indian leaders is excerpted below. The writer has not come across this very significant and probably true analysis of the discussions in any other literature:

'In the well-founded belief that political opponents of such long standing as the leaders of the Congress and the Muslim League would not exchange notes, he won the confidence of both by denouncing the one to the other. At the very time when he was wooing Congress leaders day and night, he was portraying them to Jinnah as unreasonable men whom it was exceedingly difficult to persuade into accepting any fair term. These words naturally found a sympathetic response in Jinnah's mind. It is not difficult to imagine the terms in which Mountbatten must have described Jinnah to the Congress leaders; even his staff were told that a dinner engagement with Jinnah was put off by a day because "Mountbatten felt that he could not sustain another session with him today." Nevertheless, the technique worked. Both the Congress and the Muslim League leaders felt that here was a man who had political and psychological insight, understood human character and motives, was frank enough to point out difficulties in the way, and made a sincere effort to remove them. In any case this voluble man of keen perception and quick understanding was a welcome contrast to his predecessor with his awkward silences and stony reticence.'

Mountbatten's discussion with Jinnah, which followed those with Gandhi, were remarkable for the way in which he succeeded in winning Jinnah's confidence. At the end of the second interview on April 7, Mountbatten remarked to his staff, "Jinnah can negotiate with me but my decision goes." The main reason for Jinnah's trust in Mountbatten was the belief he had at this time that Mountbatten would endeavour to carry out partition in a fair and impartial manner. Mountbatten himself was constantly emphasising that "his mandate was impartiality." Jinnah knew that even though the Congress had accepted partition, it would do its utmost to mutilate and injure Pakistan. He realised that the Punjab and Bengal would have to be partitioned – note his remark that "a moth-eaten Pakistan would be better than no Pakistan at all." But that made the manner and method of partition all the more important. The British had a vital role to play in the execution of the partition plan. If they held the scales even between the Congress and the Muslim League, Pakistan might be saved from the worst depredations of the Congress.

The directive given to Mountbatten by the British government required him to make efforts for a unitary government in accordance with the Cabinet Mission plan. But the Cabinet Mission plan had been mangled by the Congress months before, and was unacceptable to the Muslim League in that form. Mountbatten knew that his predecessor had broken himself by his well-intentioned endeavours to make the Congress accept the plan in conformity with the intentions of the Cabinet Mission and the British government. The discussions with Congress and Muslim League leaders during the first fortnight convinced Mountbatten of the futility of insisting on the Cabinet Mission Plan. Although he toyed with the idea that he might "get Congress to accept the Cabinet Mission Plan in full and then confront Jinnah with coming in or accepting a truncated Pakistan," he never actually made such an attempt. An alternative to which he gave some thought was that the representatives of Pakistan and Hindustan should come together on a basis of parity in a central government that would deal with external affairs, defence, and communications. This alternative also never got beyond the stage of discussions at his staff meetings. What he was really groping for was a solution that would enable both Pakistan and the Indian Union to remain within the Commonwealth.

Plan "Union" vs Plan "Balkan"

The fast-paced developments of April 1947 should be followed meticulously by any serious student of the partition because it was in this very month that the fate of India was decided and sealed. It is proposed to focus on the day to day development of April 1947. Within a pace of a fortnight Mountbatten had succeeded in preparing the outline of his plan. On 11 April he directed Ismay to work out plans for a possible partition. Ismay's initial draft of the partition plan was as follows:

'ONE OF THE POSSIBLE PLANS FOR THE TRANSFER OF POWER WHICH ARE RECEIVING EXAMINATION.

1. Since it has been impossible to reach agreement on the Cabinet Mission plan for a unified India, H.M.G. have decided, with effect from June 1948, to demit authority to Provinces, or to such confederations of Provinces as may decide to group themselves together in the intervening period.

2. The Indian States will become independent from the date of the transfer of power and are, of course, at liberty to negotiate with any confederation to join them (?).

3. In order to create Provinces to which authority can be demitted, it will be necessary, unless stable Ministries can otherwise be established by a certain date, to –

    (a) Partition the Punjab

    (b) Partition Bengal and Assam: and

    (c) Arrange for a general election in the N.W.F.P.

4. In order that Provinces or such groups of Provinces and States as may be formed may be in a position to receive authority on the due date –

    (a) Those Provinces and States which wish to be grouped together should arrange forthwith to work out their respective constitutions: and

    (b) Provinces may from hence forward take over from the centre all subjects, except the union subjects, for which they can make suitable administrative arrangements. This take over will clearly be progressive as time passes.

5. Therefore, the Central Government will be left only with the union subjects, and such other subjects as the Provinces themselves desire them to retain, e.g. perhaps food.

6. When the date for transfer arrives, the Central Government, as it at present exists, will disappear. Consequently, in the period between now and then it will be necessary to create machinery to co-ordinate the policy governing the union subjects for all India, or alternatively to arrange for a standstill period during which the existing machinery functions, pending the completion of arrangements to take its place.'

Who should now appear on the scene but of course V.P. Menon. From April to August 1947 and even afterwards, it is Menon who appears to be the king-pin. No policy paper was usually transmitted without him; nor any scheme was formulated without prior discussion with him. Thus Menon had a rare opportunity to play the Congress card and lead the British official hierarchy, pied-piper fashion, down the Congress path.

It can be seen that the initial outline plan which Ismay had prepared envisaged the demission of British authority by June 1948 to Provinces or to "confederations of Provinces"; independence for the Indian Princely States with freedom to join any confederation; partition of Assam, Bengal and the Punjab; a general election in the NWFP; progressive transfer from the Centre to the Provinces of all subjects except Defence, Foreign Affairs and Communications which were to be administered by the Centre until the date of the transfer. Ismay then gave a blank cheque to V.P. Menon to chop and change the plan as he deemed fit. Ismay's letter to Menon is reproduced:

11 April 1947

TOP SECRET

My dear Menon,

'I send you herewith the bare bones of a possible plan for the transfer of power. The Viceroy would be glad if (you) would:-

(a) Amend the draft in any way you think right and put some flesh upon it.

(b) Consider what the procedure would be immediately after H.M.G. have made their announcement. For example, will a general election throughout India be necessary? How will we set about the partition of the Punjab, Bengal and Assam? Presumably the decision will rest with H.E. and will not be open to argument. What will be the machinery for those groups who wish to confederate to get together and to frame their constitution? And so on and so forth.

(c) Work out a rough timetable.

I ought to explain that nothing very precise is required at this stage. The object is to give H.E. a general line on how this plan would be implemented *if* it were adopted, and approximately how long the various process would take.

Yours Sincerely,

ISMAY

PS. Would it be convenient for you to come to a Staff Conference on the above at my office at 3.0 p.m. tomorrow, 12th April? I much hope so.'

It is quite amusing to read the minutes of Jinnah's meeting with Sir Eric Miéville, Principal Secretary to the Viceroy whom Jinnah met on 11 April, 1947.

'I saw Jinnah for half an hour this afternoon. He was at his very best. He started by recalling the luncheon party at which we were both present at Buckingham Palace last December and told me how much he had enjoyed it. He said that his enjoyment was enhanced by the fact that on talking to the King he found that His Majesty was pro Pakistan. On talking to the Queen after luncheon he found that Her Majesty was even more pro Pakistan, and finally when he had a conversation with Queen Mary he found that her Majesty was 100% Pakistan! I replied that I was sorry that Their Majesties had acted in such an unconstitutional way as to express their opinions on political matters connected with their Indian Empire, at which he laughed quite a lot.'

As intense negotiations and discussions with the Indian leaders continued Mountbatten and his staff were of the opinion that of the many possible plans which were still under consideration, the two receiving most thought at that moment were:-

i. Plan "Union", which was the Cabinet Mission's plan possibly modified in some respects; and

ii. Plan "Balkan", which contemplated leaving to each Province the choice of its own future and would almost certainly result in a form of truncated Pakistan and the eventual abolition of a Centre, although it would be necessary to retain a Centre for some time after June, 1948, at least to deal with Defence until the Armed Forces were divided.

It is worth recalling Azad's comments to Mountbatten. These minutes reflects the sagacity of Azad and his impartiality in the League Congress Divide. Mountbatten writes:

'I gave Maulana Azad the broad outline of my conversations with Mr. Jinnah. In conclusion he told me that whereas the full Pakistan, such as proposed by the Cabinet Mission, could be made to work, a truncated Pakistan would spell disaster for the Mussulmans, and that if Mr. Jinnah were now prepared to accept such a decision he would be committing suicide.'

'He failed to see why Mr. Jinnah could not accept the Cabinet Mission plan, since after all it gave them the right to secede from the rest of India at the end of ten years if they wished.'

'He said that I had handled the negotiations on absolutely correct lines, but advised me to find out the precise points on which Mr. Jinnah had decided to withdraw his acceptance of the Cabinet Mission plan, and that I should then try and meet these points.'

'He understood that Mr. Jinnah's objections were twofold: -

i.   The way that the Sections would function in Group C. The main worry was Bengal and Assam, but this appeared to have been solved by H.M.G.'s statement of the 6th or 7th December.

ii. This was a minor point about the constitution of the Cabinet. Mr. Jinnah had been most insistent that if any vacancy among the minority seats in the Cabinet occurred, he should have a voice in filling the vacancy. Maulana Azad felt that the Congress could well agree to this League request if it were put up for action.'

Krishna Menon – Not Again!

The Transfer of Power documents are so voluminous one wonders if the countless scholars and writers who have written books on the partition period have meticulously studied the contents of the volumes. One must give due credit to the Viceroy and the bureaucrats who surrounded him to have left such detailed day to day accounts of the events and developments of the period. Mountbatten's style was that immediately after interviewing any Indian leader or senior British official to dictate the minutes immediately afterwards. Detailed minutes of the staff meetings, letters to various officials in London or elsewhere have been meticulously preserved. The masses of words are like a jigsaw puzzle and it would take endless hours of very close scrutiny and serious study to unravel the pattern of events in that crucial period. These papers cannot tell the whole story. They are merely minutes, carefully written, of meetings, or records of notes, or copies of letters and telegrams. They do not cover the secret negotiations going on, and the understanding reached between Mountbatten and the Congress. They do, however, help in piecing together the story with whatever other information is available from other sources.

It takes quite an effort to piece together Mountbatten's maneuvers to bring independent India in the Commonwealth. Today this may appear to be ridiculous: the organisation itself may seem to be a strange creature of no consequence, neither fish nor fowl, defying description. But in those days it had great prestige as an association of free nations, with common citizenship and the common link of the Crown. The Government instructions to Mountbatten were to try to keep India in the Commonwealth, and he himself was deeply attached to the idea and thought that it would add to the prestige of the Crown, to which he felt personal and family loyalty. From the time he came as Viceroy, he was as much concerned with the way to transfer power as with making the subcontinent retain its link with the Crown. The main hurdle in achieving this aim was the attitude of the Congress. Nehru, it may be re-called, had vehemently opposed his father's proposal to accept Dominion Status and since 1929 the Congress had become committed to 'Complete Independence'. The Constituent Assembly had adopted a resolution moved by Nehru himself that India would be an 'Independent Sovereign Republic'.

Mountbatten had been looking for a formula which would make it possible for India to stay in the Commonwealth despite that resolution, when he received a telegram from the Nawab Bhopal on 27 March, saying that he had had a talk with Jinnah and his impression was that Jinnah could be persuaded to stay in the Commonwealth. This piece of information should have made Mountbatten very happy, but it did not. He told his Staff meeting on 28 March that 'he was not prepared to discuss this question with different parts of India.' On 9 April when Jinnah, at a meeting with him, indicated that Pakistan would stay in the Commonwealth, surprisingly Mountbatten showed no enthusiasm at all. Mountbatten did not even mention this in his record of the interview but brought it up at a Staff meeting two days later. He told Liaquat on 11 April, that he 'was not prepared even to discuss the suggestion of any part of India remaining in the Empire unless the suggestion came from all parts together.'

To be forced to divide India was bad enough for Mountbatten, but to have Pakistan, and not Hindustan, inside the Commonwealth would be a double defeat. He was at first distressed at this development, but before long decided that it gave him an opportunity to persuade Hindustan. Hindustan should be told of the enormous advantages that Pakistan would enjoy – Pakistan would get, *inter alia*, the services of experienced civil and military officers which would be so badly needed in the initial years, but which would not be available to country outside the Commonwealth. The British officers would organise Pakistan's armed forces into a magnificent fighting machine, and see to it that it got all the required military equipment and stores; this would turn the military balance in favour of

Pakistan. While casting this bait, Mountbatten would pretend that he himself and the British Government had no interest in the matter and that it was for the Congress itself to think over and decide.

Enter Krishna Menon. While Mountbatten was having stern dialogues with Jinnah his conversations with Krishna Menon were decidedly chummy. It is interesting to study the minutes of the very cosy chat which Mountbatten had with Krishna Menon on 17 April, 1947. Some extracts given below:

'Mr. Krishna Menon reminded me that he was staying out here specially in the hope of being of use to me personally as a friend (or acquaintance) of some four years standing, to help to give me the background of what was going on in Congress circles, and to help me put over any points that I found too delicate to handle directly myself. He offered to stay as long as he was of use, and I have asked him to stay at all events till next week.'

'He asked me how I had got on with Jinnah, and I told him that I might have to yield to a truncated Pakistan. Krishna Menon said that although Congress would regret this, he did not think they would resist it any longer if I made a point of it; and he offered to help me put this idea over with Nehru if required. I told him of the demand to split the army, and how over-rapid nationalisation would render it so weak that it could not be split until well after June 1948.'

'After some discussion about the origin of India wishing to shake the dust of the British Empire off her feet, he admitted that he himself had been responsible for inventing the term "Independent Sovereign Republic" for the Resolution in the Constituent Assembly; and he said that he now regretted choosing such drastic terminology so early on in the final stage. He asked what he could do to try and make amends.'

'I told him that it was up to Congress to make the first move if they wanted a move to be made. I had no intention of making one, because I had received the strictest instructions not to make any attempt to keep India within the Commonwealth; indeed, I was not sure if H.M.G. would even approve any move at all, since a meeting which was taking place at Whitehall at the time of my departure had come to the conclusion that we could get all the commercial benefits we wanted out of India through the sterling balances and a friendly treaty, without having to go to the extent of including such a very weak nation in our defence organisation.' (*Writers comments – A bluff typical of Mountbatten!*)

'Finally, he said to me: "Unless you take the first step and approach us, nothing will be done". I replied: "Then nothing will be done, because it is entirely your loss, and I am not going to allow any sentimental reasons make me pull your chestnuts out of the fire. If you do not take the first step, you will have a rotten army; you will lose all the benefits of the Commonwealth; and you will save the other nations of the Commonwealth the expense, anxiety and responsibility of your defence.'"

'I then asked him what he proposed. He said: "If the British were voluntarily to give us now Dominion Status, well ahead of June 1948, we should be so grateful that not a voice would he heard in June 1948 suggesting any change, except possibly to the world dominion if that had been actually used up to that date."'

As we shall see later a hasty grant of independence and partition was part of the grand design of the Congress and that Krishna Menon kept a constant liaison with Mountbatten and aided and abetted the plan. The two met again after five days, when they 'properly let down our hair together and discussed every aspect of the plan now being worked on.' Mountbatten said that although he would advise the Government against admitting Pakistan into the Commonwealth, yet if the demand was made over their heads to the British people, it might be too strong to be resisted, and he listed the advantages that it would have against India. 'In fact,' said Mountbatten, 'backed by British and American arms and technique, Pakistan would in no while have armed forces superior to those of Hindustan,' and that 'places like Karachi would become big naval and air bases.' 'How can we prevent this?' asked Krishna Menon. 'By the simple expedient of being in the Commonwealth yourself,' said Mountbatten.

It was at this meeting that Krishna Menon suggested that Mountbatten should take Nehru away for two or three days on holiday, 'for,' he said 'between you, you can solve the problems of India.'

It is proposed to reproduce the minutes of Mountbatten's meeting with Krishna Menon on 22nd April and to let the readers conclude about Mountbatten's India.

Chummy Chats with Krishna

It is to be noted that in the series of interviews which the Viceroy was granting to the prominent Indian leaders the duration would be between half an hour and hour and a half but on 22 April, 1947, Mountbatten 'let down our hair' for two hours with Krishna Menon who held no official position either in the government or the political parties. Extracts from the meeting will show how seriously Mountbatten was being influenced by the Congress functionaries. No such meeting is recorded with any League leaders. Extracts below:

'I had a long and friendly talk with Mr. Menon over a cup of tea. We properly let down our hair together and discussed every aspect of the plan now being worked on, and in particular of its relation to the world situation. I found that he had very shrewd views on the future trend of governments in the U.K. and America, and on world-wide politics.'

'I discussed with him the announcement in the Press that if Pakistan were formed it would undoubtedly wish to remain within the British Commonwealth. I told him that I had made clear to those Muslim Leaders, who had spoken to me about it that I had no authority whatever to deal with the question of Pakistan remaining within the British Empire, and that in fact I should probably advise against it, since we could not wish to back one side of India against another if it came to civil war. The only way of avoiding the risk of this would be, of course, be not to concede the Pakistan demand to remain within the Empire. But I pointed out that if the demand went over our heads to the peoples of the British Commonwealth, the demand might be too strong to be resisted, and that in fact he must now reckon with the extreme likelihood of Pakistan being a British dominion.'

'If that happened they would of course have a complete call on British officers, and all the Services, who wished to remain in India, since they could so remain whilst retaining the King's Commission. Not only would they be able to get the same equipment as Hindustan, but could do a great deal better, since they could obviously get secret equipment not available to anybody not within the Commonwealth, and they could go to our schools and make use of our experimental establishments, and keep up-to-date. In fact, backed by British and American arms and technique, Pakistan would in no while have armed forces immensely superior to those of Hindustan, and in spite of the obvious disadvantages from which they would at first suffer, there was no reason why they should not be able to rise above these with British and American help; and I presumed that places like Karachi would become big naval and air bases within the British Commonwealth.'

'I asked him how he would like to see that happen; and he absolutely shuddered, and said "How can we prevent it"? I said "By the simple expedient of being in the common wealth yourselves; and then there can be no question of Pakistan getting ahead of you, nor could there be any question of the unilateral use of bases without full consultation."'

'He said "I see that, but how in the world can it be achieved?" (He pointed out that they had pretty well burnt their boats by the statements about leaving the Empire and that it would be extremely difficult for him to get it over, even with Nehru, who would be the only person who would immediately understand it, and even more difficult with Patel; and that even if the three of them got together, he did not see how they could get it across to Congress or to the peoples of Hindustan).'

'I pointed out that this was entirely a matter for themselves to decide. But I suggested to him a solution along the lines he himself had raised last time, namely Dominion Status before June 1948, so as to avoid the necessity of having to make any declaration when we left, and thus leave India within the common wealth. My proposal was that if we could possibly get the scheme working in time, Pakistan and Hindustan should be declared independent dominions, with a Central Defence Council, a single army (pending partition) and with myself at the head of the Central Defence Council and as Governor- General of both dominions on a constitution basis. I pointed out that the British Army would come directly under my command, and that that would be my personal contribution to the Defence Council. I suggested that in order not to imperil the sovereignty of dominion status, each dominion could voluntarily accord me the right of a casting vote as Chairman of the Defence Council.'

'He seemed rather smitten with this idea, but said immediately, that it would be far better to declare India a single dominion which would consist of two parts – Pakistan and Hindustan, since he still harped on the fact that to give each side dominion status was advertising the complete separation of Pakistan.'

'I urged him to open his eyes and see things clearly. If Pakistan were given independent status, then they were cutting themselves adrift from the British Commonwealth.'

'He said that the furthest he thought it would be possible to go would be to call themselves an Independent Nation in relation with the British Commonwealth.'

'I reminded him that the crux of the matter was that they should not sever their connection with the Crown, since on this depended the ability of British officers holding the King's Commission to serve in India. Once more I said to him "You cannot have your cake and eat it; make up your mind which you want to do."'

'Finally, he told me that Pandit Nehru was over-working to the point of a breakdown; that he had relays of shorthand typists in and out all during the day and night. Not only was he dealing with the big problems, but he was always going down and attending to every little item; personally, attending small meetings, and even trying to interfere in street scenes. He asked me if I could not take him away for two or three days on a holiday; and said laughingly "to avoid both of you breaking down from over work". I said "Where shall I take him, Simla?" He said "No, that is too official; you would neither of you stop working". I said "Where else"? He said "Why not try Kashmir"? I said "What would happen? I thought he wanted to make the Maharajah lick his boots, or alternatively that the Maharajah was likely to throw him into jail." He said that that was all nonsense; it would be an opportunity for the Maharajah and Nehru to get together again, and he believed that I might possibly heal the breach.'

'He asked me if I could persuade the Maharajah to release political prisoners from the jails in Kashmir in the same way as I had persuaded Dr. Khan Sahib to release his; after this the way would be open to restore friendly relations between Nehru and the Maharajah. I said I thought this was a bit difficult to arrange at long distance, and I should probably have to go and see the Maharajah personally at first. He admitted that this was a more reasonable way of setting about it.'

'But he still wished me to take Nehru away for two or three days, anywhere restful, so that we could get to know each other – "For", he said, "between you, you can solve all the problems of India".'

'He told me that Nehru was becoming unpopular with the Hindus through his international and unbiased outlook. 'I told him I was expecting to see the President of the Hindu Mahasabha soon; and he then urged me, in that case, to see the Secretary of the Shia Conference, Mr. Ali Zaheer, who had been in the first Interim Government and had made way when Mr. Liaquat Ali Khan joined. He said he was at Lucknow, but would come up if sent for. He claimed that the Shias were a fairly numerous sections of the Muslim community, all of whom were opposed to the Muslim League.'

A Plan A Day

Lord Ismay records in his memoirs 'A new version of the plan was drafted almost daily.' It might be interesting to examine the various wheeling and dealing of Mountbatten before the evolution of the final plan. The severe political problem which had baffled countless minds for several years was hastily solved by Mountbatten. He presented his plan within six weeks of his arrival. Or was he perhaps working with a preconceived blueprint? It may be recalled that on 11 April, 1947 Ismay had asked V.P. Menon to put "some flesh upon" a draft plan which he had prepared. V.P. Menon very quickly prepared the first draft based on the Plan Balkan.

The broad basis of which was the demission of authority to the provinces, or to such confederations of provinces as might decide to group themselves in the intervening period before the actual transfer or power. The plan provided that the members of the Legislative Assemblies of Bengal and the Punjab should meet separately in two parts, i.e. representatives of the predominantly Muslim areas, and representatives of the predominantly non-Muslim areas; and if both sections of each of these Assemblies voted for partition, then that province would be partitioned. Under the plan, in the event of the partition of Bengal, the predominantly Muslim district of Sylhet in Assam would have the option of joining the Muslim province. The plan also envisaged the holding of an election in the North-West Frontier Province to ascertain the wishes of the people of that province. Thus, the responsibility for the division of the country was to be placed on the shoulders of the Indian people themselves.

Mountbatten put this plan before a conference of governors on 15 and 16 April, 1947. When considering this item on the agenda the Viceroy opened the discussion by stressing that this was only one of the many plans which were at present being considered. He also emphasised that, if it was not possible to obtain a united India, it was of utmost importance that, in the eyes of the world, it should be Indian opinion rather than a British decision which made the choice as to the future. Mountbatten had already started trying to put the onus of the decision on Indian shoulders rather than take responsibility himself. Mountbatten also said that the partition of India would be a most serious potential source of war. This was certainly an accurate prophecy.

Mountbatten's was manifestly revealed as the minutes recorded "His Excellency the Viceroy pointed out that a quick decision would also give Pakistan a greater chance to fail on its demerits. The great problem was to reveal the limits of Pakistan so that the Muslim League could revert to a unified India with honour."

Mountbatten turned to Sir Evan Jenkins and asked his opinion about the partition of the Punjab. Jenkins gave a full explanation of the difficulties inherent in the partitioning ot the Punjab, describing particularly the demands of the Sikhs and the Jutts. He said that, if, in the present situation, attempts a partition were made without having obtained the prior agreement of all interested parties, there would be fighting on a large scale. Partition could then only be imposed by force, and a large number of troops would be required.

Mountbatten then asked Tyson Chief Secretary of Bengal (Standing in for Governor Sir Frederick Burrows) about the partition of Bengal. Tyson said that, when the Cabinet Mission's plan had first been published, it would be true to say that there was a feeling of relief in all the parties in Bengal that that Province was not to be partitioned. When H.M.G.'s statement of 20th February had been shown to the Chief Minister, the latter had declared that it looked as if his Government would inherit Bengal. He had evidently been thinking of an independent Bengal, preferably as a Dominion within the British Commonwealth. The Hindus had also evidently read into the statement of 20th February a danger that Bengal would be handed over to what was, in effect, a Muslim League Government.

Tyson explained that there was no alternative Ministry to that at present in power. Bengal (unlike the Punjab) was only really concerned with two communities- 33 million Muslims, and 25 million Hindus of whom 9 million were members of the scheduled castes. It was very difficult to say whether the scheduled castes representatives in the Assembly really did represent the opinions of the scheduled castes. But it could be taken that, in general, all the Hindus were opposed to the idea of Pakistan.

Tyson went on to explain in detail the distribution of Muslims and Hindus in the different divisions and districts of Bengal. He said that a partition of Bengal on the basis of majorities in districts could be carried out. He believed that the Hindus would prefer that to an independent Bengal. And he believed that Western Bengal would be economically possible – so long as it included Calcutta. All the heavy industries were in Western Bengal In Eastern Bengal jute was grown and baled but not manufactured. In Northern Bengal tea was grown and manufactured – but there was very little tea in the predominantly Muslim areas. Eastern Bengal alone was not a going concern and never would be. It could not feed itself and never would be able to do so even if the jute- growing there was topped in favour of crops. It would become, in Sir Frederick Burrows' words, a "rural slum." Tyson said that the Muslims knew all this as well as the Hindus – so they felt that the object of the cry to partition Bengal was to "torpedo" Pakistan. He could not think of any way in which it would be possible to "sell" Eastern Bengal as a feasible proposition.

Mountbatten said that there was no question of trying to "sell" it. Mr. Jinnah had already virtually accepted the proposition. Anything that resulted in "torpedoing' Pakistan was of advantage in that it led the way back to a more common-sense solution. He asked what the Bengal Chief Minister's reactions were likely to be when he heard that Mr. Jinnah had accepted a truncated Pakistan.

Tyson said that he thought that the Suhrawardy would be very frightened and would go a long way to keep Bengal a separate unit. He was not, he believed, very keen to link up with the North-West Muslim Provinces. He wanted to run Bengal as an independent Province with a Muslim majority. Mountbatten then directed his Private Secretary to arrange for him to see the Chief Minister of the Bengal Government when he next came to Delhi. While concluding the Governor's conference Mountbatten said that it appeared possible that the Muslims in Bengal would not follow Jinnah's lead; that there was a chance of a Congress Ministry being returned again in the N.W.F.P.; and that Jinnah's Pakistan would, in the end, consist of Sindh and part of the Punjab. We added he wished to make it quite clear that he was in no way opposed to the Muslim League and pro-Congress. His one object was to hand over India in the best interest of her people. Anyone reading the *Transfer of Power* documents would certainly that Mountbatten was constantly professing that he was neutral whereas his India bias is conspicuously evident. His statements and contentions of impartiality were perhaps a sign of his guilty conscience.

The Governor's conference resumed the following day 16 April, 1947. In a parrot fashion Mountbatten preambled the meeting with his stock gambit by repeating his honest assurance that he maintained complete impartiality towards both the Muslim League and the Congress. He felt that as a matter of principle it would be preferable to hand over to a unified India, but that equally it would be wrong to force the Muslims to give up Pakistan if sufficient safeguards for their minority position in a united India could not be provided. He reiterated that, if a former Pakistan was eventually decided on, he would under no circumstances agree to a split in the Indian Armed Forces before June 1948.

Dialogue Status – Mid April 1947

After the numerous meetings Mountbatten had with Jinnah the situation in mid-April 1947 was that Jinnah had made it abundantly clear that the League would not under any circumstances reconsider the Cabinet Mission Plan and was completely intent on having Pakistan. Mountbatten got Jinnah to see Ismay and give him his idea of Pakistan. But when Ismay produced the notes he had made, Jinnah said, "This is your scheme, not mine." When pressed for details of his scheme and how it would be carried out Jinnah said, "You must carry out a surgical operation; cut India and its army firmly in half and give me the half that belongs to the Muslim League". Mountbatten then told him that if he accepted Jinnah's arguments on the need for partition of India, then he could not resist the argument that Congress were putting forward for the partition of the Punjab and Bengal. Jinnah was quite horrified and argued at great length on the need to preserve the unity of the Punjab and Bengal, pointing out that the Punjabis and Bengalis regarded their provinces as unified territories which they would hate to see split up.

Mountbatten told Jinnah he was so impressed by his arguments that he was prepared to accept them. Jinnah was delighted, but only until Mountbatten pointed out that Jinnah's arguments had also convinced him that the partition of India itself would be criminal. Both of them, "Started going around the mulberry bush again."

Mountbatten told Jinnah that he had conclude that the best solution for India would be a complete union with the strongest possible central government. In fact, Mountbatten insisted that he would like to see the Interim Government strengthen by Jinnah joining it himself so that he could turn over power to the Interim Government in toto by June 1948. Mountbatten records, "If I had invited the Pope to take part in the Black Mass he could not have been more horrified. I hastened to assure him that I should not allow my personal feelings on what was good for India to interfere with working out a solution which would be acceptable to the people of India in their present frame of mind."

Mountbatten warned Jinnah categorically that if he finally decided to recommend to HMG that there should be partition, then that principle would be applied right through to the provinces and that partition would follow the boundaries of the communal majorities. Mountbatten records, 'Although Jinnah did not lose his friendly attitude his arguments became more and more futile. And he ended by saying, "If you persist in chasing me with your ruthless logic we shall get nowhere." I regard Jinnah as a psychopathic case; in fact, until I had met him I would not have thought it possible that a man with such a complete lack of administrative knowledge or sense of responsibility could achieve or hold down so powerful a position.'

Mountbatten summed up by pointing out the choices before Jinnah were likely to be: -

1) The Cabinet Mission Plan which gave Jinnah all five provinces of Pakistan with complete autonomy and with only a very weak centre to which they would allegiance which might be covered by the general term Defence.

2) A very moth-eaten Pakistan, the eastern and north-west frontier parts of which were unlikely to be economic propositions, and which would still have to come to some centre for general defence subjects for a long while after the British had left.

Jinnah said, "I do not care how little you give me as long as you give it to me completely. I do not wish to make any improper suggestions to you, but you must realise that the new Pakistan is almost certain to ask for dominion status within the Empire." Mountbatten hardly showed any interest in Jinnah wanting dominion status although he was desperately cajoling and coaxing the Congress for accepting similar status.

Mountbatten states in his report, 'My first conclusion therefore is that our decision must be announced before the end of May at latest. Secondly, I have very slender hopes of getting acceptance of the Cabinet Mission Plan, and I am very much afraid that partition may prove to be the only alternative. Thirdly I feel strongly that the scheme of partition should be such as will not debar the two sides from getting together, even before the transfer of power, if saner council prevails when the bewildering complications of partition are more clearly realised .

Mountbatten reported to London that he would not send even a first draft of the plan at that stage, as it was all so tentative, but what was optimistic that he would be able to send the plan to London with Ismay by the end of April 1947.

Once Mountbatten had sent the plan he was hoping to get Jinnah, Nehru, Patel, Liaquat, Bal Dev Singh and possibly Nawab of Bhopal and Maharajah of Patiala, to come and stay with him in Simla. Mountbatten had aimed for 15th of May for this Assembly. It will be seen later that the trip to Simla became a cosy get together for Mountbatten and the Congress and became the venue where Mountbatten's final plot was hatched.

Alternatively, Mountbatten thought he might aim at a rather bigger "round table conference." and make one final determined effort to secure some compromise on the basis of the Cabinet Mission plan. If that failed, then he would fire his last shot in the shape of the announcement of partition. Mountbatten asked both Nehru and Jinnah to have their working committee in Simla, so that they may refer to them before pronouncing a definite view.

Mountbatten thought that whatever the decision may be, he felt that the central Government should be as strong as possible until the hand over. In this connection he was thinking of trying to get Jinnah to join the Cabinet. One of the difficulties would be the question of an appropriate and acceptable portfolio. He doubtd whether Congress would surrender either External Affairs or Home Affairs, and he doubted whether Jinnah would look at anything else. Perhaps he might be Leader of the House? The talks in Simla would then be in the nature of a discussion of a Cabinet Committee, which would, he thought, be all to the good.

The Governors had expressed their unanimous support of the line Mountbatten had taken with the various Indian leaders; and all of them urged the greatest possible speed in making a decision and an announcement; for even the quieter Provinces felt that they were sitting on the edge of a volcano and that an eruption might take place through any of the three main craters – Bengal, Punjab and N.W.F.P. – at any moment; with the risk of sporadic eruptions in Assam, Bombay and Bihar.

The Mountbattens had two garden parties and about three luncheon parties of 30, and larger dinners each week, at which Mountbatten made it a rule that not less than 50 per cent of those present must be Indians. There was the greatest spate of Indian names in the Visitors Book ever known at Viceroy's House, and the atmosphere appeared to be remarkably friendly. Mountbatten had three full time Indian A.D.C.s, a sailor, soldier and airman from the major communities. Unfortunately, Mountbatten records "that my young daughter sitting with two English ladies to whom she had not been introduced heard one say to the other "It makes me absolutely sick to see this house full of dirty Indians." I had recounted this story to the Governors, and have invited their co- operation in sending home anybody who expresses sentiments of this type'.

Meanwhile on 17 April, 1947 Mountbatten received a message from Prime Minister Attlee which read we shall, "In the very near future be announcing the resignation Lord Pethick-Lawrence and the appointment of Lord Listowel as Secretary of State for India. I thought you would like to have this information, which is of course for yourself alone, in advance." This change as we shall see was most significant and brought about at the behest of Mountbatten to facilitate the implementation of his blueprint.

CHAPTER 7: THE SIMLA SCHEME

The Simla House Party

Within a week of Mountbatten's arrival in India on 23 March, 1947 in his Fourth Staff Meeting on 28 March, 1947 it was decided that the Viceroy would invite at the appropriate moment, certain important leaders to stay with him at Simla. Those invited would be:

1) Mr. Gandhi

2) Mr. Jinnah

3) Pandit Nehru

4) Mr. Liaquat Ali Khan

5) Sardar Patel

6) The Nawab of Bhopal

Viceregal Lodge, Simla, India
(Medium.com)

This represented the minimum number. There would be no representatives of minorities. There would be no formal meetings, no agenda, no secretariat in evidence – just an informal exchange of ideas. It was possible, in such an atmosphere, that a measure of agreement would be obtained. There would be no press statements, and the Viceroy would ask his guests to give an undertaking not to issue information to the press. He would also ask them to refrain from making bitter remarks on this occasion. The Viceroy agreed with Lord Ismay's suggestion that no advisors, only those with executive responsibility, should be present at these informal meetings.

After discussion Mountbatten decided provisionally on the week beginning 21 April as the best time for this House-Party. He said that he considered it of great importance that the Nawab of Bhopal should be persuaded not to resign meanwhile. George Abell expressed the opinion that there was a risk that the Congress representatives would refuse to attend. The Viceroy then said that he hoped very much to be able to persuade Nehru. He added that he did not believe that the Indian political leaders yet realised the full extent of his powers. Mountbatten then directed his Private Secretary to ask Sir Conrad Corfield to do all in his power to persuade the Nawab of Bhopal not to resign from the Chancellorship of the Chamber of Princes until after these meetings.

In the *Transfer of Power* documents throughout the month of April 1947 there are several references to the Simla House Party. For instance, in the staff meeting in 16 April Mountbatten said that he would, before sending out the invitations for the Simla House Party, asked Sir Conrad Corfield's advice as to which Princes to invite. He said that he thought the date of 7 May was optimistic for this party. Mid-May would be nearer the mark. Evan Jenkins said, as he saw it the Simla Talks were likely to be a turning point. The Congress and the Muslim League would either agree to revert to the Cabinet Mission's statement or refuse to do so. If they agreed, the position of the Sikhs still constituted a difficult problem as the Sikhs were demanding partition in any event. The Muslim League would not agree to such partition as they would say that they had accepted the Cabinet Mission's Plan on the basis of a unified Punjab.

Sir Conrad Corfield said that the Maharajah of Patiala could probably help in this matter and suggested that he should be invited to attend the Simla Talks in his capacity as pro-Chancellor.

In the Viceroy's personal report sent to London on 17 April Mountbatten records:

'I will not send you even a first draft of the plan at this stage, as it is all so tentative, but I have discussed it with the Governors and hope to let you have a further report next week. The chances are that I will send Ismay home with the draft announcement towards the end of this month to discuss it with you, and try to reach the earliest possible agreement on the precise terms.'

'Once this is done, I plan to try to get Jinnah, Nehru, Patel, Liaquat, and Baldev Singh and possibly Bhopal and Patiala, to come and stay with me in Simla. The date at which I ma aiming is the 15ᵗʰ May. Alternatively, I might aim at a rather bigger "round table conference". I will then make one final determined effort to secure some compromise on the basis of the Cabinet Mission plan. If I fail, I shall have to fire my last shot in the shape of our announcement of partition. I shall ask both Nehru and Jinnah to have their working committees in Simla, so that they may refer to them before pronouncing a definite view.'

On April 20 Erskine Crum Conference Secretary of Mountbatten prepared a detailed paper for the meeting of the Indian leaders with Mountbatten. The venue suggested in the paper was Delhi rather than Simla as Delhi would probably be more convenient to all concerned. This paper dealt at length with the venue, date, composition, and purpose of the conference. The paper had draft invitation letters, draft telegram to London, draft announcement and draft timetable of events. The paper involved the Viceroy to approach the Congress and ask them to agree that the League should have one more seat in the Cabinet, provided this is taken by Jinnah himself. If the Congress agree, Mountbatten would speak to Jinnah. Jinnah should be told that if no agreement *on the basis of the Cabinet*

Mission's Plan is reached in a very short time HMG will announce a decision on the basis of the small Pakistan. It will be a great advantage to be able to discuss plans for the transfer of power in a small committee inside the Government.

The note goes on to state whether Jinnah agrees or not he and the other principal leaders (Nehru, Patel, Liaquat and Baldev Singh) should be invited to take part in discussions at Delhi started on about 5th May. Nehru and Jinnah should arrange that their Working Committees are in Delhi.

On 24 April in Mountbatten's report to London "At the moment I favour a final meeting to consist only of Nehru, Patel, Jinnah, Liaquat Ali Khan and Baldev Singh (with Gandhi hovering about in the background as usual) and with the Working Committees at their disposal. I aim at getting this meeting together about the middle of next month and may hold it at Delhi rather than Simla.

Erskine Crum the Conference Secretary redrafted his proposal for the meeting on 30 April, 1947. The note contained arrangements for the demission of power. The fact is despite repeated mention and arrangement for the informal meeting with the Indian leaders it never took place. When Mountbatten went to Simla in the first week of May, 1947 the only Indian leader who was invited for the private meeting was Nehru and his associate Krishna Menon who held no official post. The Viceroy was completely in the confidence of V.P. Menon the Reforms Commissioner a confidante of Sardar Patel. The meeting in Simla which we shall examine at length later decided the fate of the sub-continent. The records of events in Simla are extremely suspect and quite questionable. One has, therefore, to endeavour to piece together the events with whatever corroborative evidence there exists.

No less a person than Philip Ziegler Mountbatten's official biographer has commented on this meeting. Ziegler is generally acknowledged as a neutral and fair chronicler and his comments carry some credibility:

'Mountbatten was accused of injustice in that he consulted Nehru while the first plan for the transfer of power was still in draft, but gave Jinnah no similar opportunity. He could reply that he was confident Jinnah would accept the draft but had doubts about Nehru. To this the Muslims would retort that the complaisance of the Lague was no reason for giving Congress an advantage denied to their rivals. But the decision to show the plan to Nehru, it could be pleaded, was taken at the last moment, and only because he happened to be staying at Simla. Precisely, the Muslims would reply. And why was he staying at Simla, and Jinnah not? To this the only honest answer was that Jinnah would probably have refused even if invited and that his presence would anyway have ruined what was intended to be a few days of pleasant relaxation. The fact remained, however, that Nehru had been unfairly privileged for little reason except that Mountbatten found him sympathetic; the fault perhaps was Jinnah's but the Muslim League had some reason to think themselves hardly used.'

Mountbatten's Offer

Lord Mountbatten, his wife Edwina, daughter Pamela in Viceroy's Lodge in Shimla (theindosphere.com)

Mountbatten gave detailed account of his discussions and events in April 1947 eighteen years later to Lapierre and Collins when they were researching for the book *Freedom at Midnight*. Mountbatten had also meticulously preserved the documents relating to the period which somewhat ensures the authenticity of his statement. It was just not from memory alone that he gave verbatim account of his conversation with the Indian leaders. In fact, a sizable number of the *Transfer of Power* documents of the partition period have been obtained from the Mountbatten archives. Let us see what Mountbatten himself had to say about conversations and events retrospectively – particularly relating to Jinnah and Pakistan. Assuming Mountbatten's version is credible the readers may assess its reliability. Mountbatten records:

All I could do was just to negotiate. For instance, he wanted to have the whole of the Punjab, the whole of Bengal, and I told him this was not on. And then of course there followed that amusing and rather tragic game of around and around the mulberry bush which I shall describe.

When I told Jinnah I don't want you to have a partitioned India, I gave him all my reasons, and he said, "Well, I am afraid we must. We can't trust them. Look what they did to us in 1938-39. When you go, we'll permanently be at the mercy of the elected Hindu majority and we shall have no place, we shall be oppressed and it will be quite terrible."

I told him I was quite certain that people like Nehru, and there were many of his colleagues like him, had no intention whatever of oppressing them.

He said, "Well, that's what you say, but Nehru was still the most important figure when they did, in fact, oppress us in 1938-39. And he failed to stop it. But," he said, "you must give me a viable Pakistan. You must give me the whole of the Punjab as well as Sind and NWFP and Bengal and Assam, and I shall want a corridor to unite them."

I said, "Look, Mr. Jinnah, you have said that you won't agree to having a minority population ruled by a majority population."

"Absolutely."

"Alright. I happen to know that in the Punjab and Bengal there are wide areas where the opposite community is in the majority. It happens also that they just about divide east and west. So I'm afraid that if you want Pakistan, I shall have to arrange for the partitioning of both the Punjab and Bengal. You cannot take into Pakistan the Hindus of Punjab and Bengal."

"Your Excellency doesn't understand that the Punjab is a nation. Bengal is a nation. A man is a Punjabi or a Bengali first before he is a Hindu or a Muslim. If you give us those provinces you must. Under no condition, partition them. You will destroy their viability and cause endless bloodshed and trouble."

"Mr. Jinnah, I entirely agree." "Oh, you do."

"Yes, of course. A man is not only a Punjabi or a Bengali before he is a Muslim or Hindu, but he is an Indian before all else. What you're saying is the perfect, absolute answer I've been looking for. You've presented me the arguments to keep India united."

"Oh, you don't understand. If you do that…" and so we'd start all over again. "Look, Mr. Jinnah, it is a fact you want partition?"

"Yes, of course."

"Well, if you want partition then you must have partition of Punjab and Bengal."

You know, not only did this go on for hours, it went over several discussions. He simply was caught in his own trap. He finally gave up and said, 'So you insist on giving me a moth-eaten Pakistan."

I said, "You call it a moth-eaten Pakistan. I don't even want you to take it at all if it's as moth-eaten as that. I'd really like you to leave India unified."

But he was absolutely set on his great cry of no – he was the de Gaulle of his day – and when after about three or four of these sessions I realised the man was quite unshakeably immovable and quite impervious to any quarrel or logical argument and not even prepared to look at any safeguards which I might be able to devise, I told him, "Mr. Jinnah, if only you would believe me, if only you would accept some organisation like the Cabinet Mission Plan you would find that you could have great autonomy, the Punjab and Bengal could rule themselves, it would be even more autonomous than the USA. It would be quite independent. What is more, you could have the great pleasure of oppressing the minorities in any way you wanted to, because you'd be able to prevent the centre from interfering. Doesn't that appeal to you?"

"No, I don't want to be a part of India. I'd sooner lose everything than be under a Hindu raj."

He went on and on. Very early I realised what I was up against, I never would have believed, I had never visualised that an intelligent man, well-educated, trained in England, was capable of closing his mind – it wasn't that he didn't see it – he closed his mind. A kind of shutter came down. Then I realised that while he was alive, nothing could be done. The others could be persuaded, but not Jinnah. He was a one – man band, and the one man did it like that.

Mind you, Jinnah is now forgotten. He was the man who did it. Bangladesh and all that misery which I forecast. Twenty-five years ago Rajagopalachari and I said it would last 25 years. It had to… It couldn't go on. **All this misery and trouble was caused by Jinnah and no one else. And he hasn't had one word said against him. He was the evil genius in this whole thing**. He presented a peaceful solution. He wouldn't play along at all. He was perfectly friendly and courteous and polite, at the end, emotionally pleased when I took him around and prevented him from blowing up. But with him there, you couldn't move him. You could move all the others. When Jinnah came to see me, he always sat there (relaxes, sits back easily). Ali Khan, when he came in with Jinnah sat right on the edge of his chair. He'd keep saying, "Yes, Qaidi." He would not even sit back.

The only difference between the scheme I was prepared to give Jinnah and that which he would have got under the Cabinet Mission Plan was that under the Cabinet Mission Plan he was obliged to accept a small, weak centre at Delhi controlling the defence, communications and external affairs. The tree might really be lumped together under the general heading of defence.

That speech was absolutely the last plea for a united India. Please remember, every one of these interviews lasted one-hour. They were reduced in my notes to three or four pages. They represented, each page, 15 minutes of talking. Therefore, one eighth of what was said was compressed into this.

I then realised that he had this faculty of closing his mind to the thing he could see points, he was an able debater, he had a well-trained mind, he was a lawyer, but **he gave the impression of having closed his mind, closed his ears; he didn't want to be persuaded, he didn't want to hear. I mean whatever one said, it passed him absolutely by**. In case of partitioning Punjab and Bengal, he didn't even seem to have been listening to the previous thing at all.

His great strength… he got all this by closing his mind and saying, "No." And how anybody could fail to see Jinnah held the whole key to the situation, to the continent, in his hand, I fail to understand. I was under no illusions, I saw that dear old Gandhi held nothing at all in his hands.

You see, I found it very difficult to believe that an educated man, a man of apparent goodwill, with great affection and admiration for the British, a man who'd shown me consideration, although of a rather cold sort, I found it rather difficult to believe that he would accept India becoming a second class power, and destroy everything and produce what he himself had said would be an unviable Pakistan. I had hoped that he would say, **"If you give me absolute and complete autonomy, if you limit the centre's interference to inter- dominion committees which will sit and elaborate a common defence policy, I might go along with keeping India together."**

One can conjecture as to why Jinnah did not opt for Mountbatten's suggestion to accept the Cabinet Mission Plan with all sorts of safeguards against Nehru's threats to dismantle the grouping system of the Plan. This will be focused at length.

Fate of Calcutta

It is interesting to examine the thoughts and conclusions of Mountbatten and his staff about Calcutta on the eve of the final plan that was carried by Lord Ismay to London. In a meeting on May 1, 1947, where the Governor of Bengal Frederick Burrows was present the deliberations were as follows.

Mountbatten said that it was his conviction that the only sensible solution for the future of India was one which produced the greatest degree of unity that the people would be persuaded to accept. In fact, he still backed the Cabinet Mission Plan. However, Jinnah had repeatedly stated that he would not consider accepting it on the grounds that Congress did not intend to carry it out fairly. Mountbatten stated that he was beginning to think that Jinnah might be right in this belief, especially in view of recent pronouncements of Patel. Viceroy said that he had explained to Patel that the thing that most frightened Jinnah was the prospect of a Centre permanently dominated by the Hindus. He had asked Patel whether he could think of any way to reduce this fear and the latter had replied that he would never consider parity in the Central Government. Mountbatten also said that although he considered Jinnah about the most difficult and unreasonable man with whom he had ever had to deal, he, and the senior members of his staff did feel Jinnah's fears had some foundation. Therefore, it was to be considered that the Cabinet Mission Plan was dead. Burrows also felt that there was then no chance of getting the Cabinet Mission's Plan accepted.

Mountbatten went on to explain that following Jinnah's demand for Pakistan, Congress had demanded the partition of certain provinces. Jinnah had produced arguments against the partition of provinces. Logically, however, the partition of provinces should follow the partition of India. Jinnah had stated that he would insist on the partition of Assam if Bengal was partitioned.

Burrows said that he would not put the case for the partition of Assam very high. Jinnah had no more right to assume that the tribal areas wanted Pakistan than Congress had to assume that they did not. If the tribes were excluded and the scheduled castes were taken as neutral than the population of Hindus and Muslims in Assam was about equal. Burrows also said that he was not sure that there was a general demand among the Bengali Hindus as a whole for the partition of Bengal. The idea, however, was being sold rather well. There was a definite attempt, because of the feeling of frustration among the Hindus in Bengal, to get command of at least part of the province. Shyama Prasad was a clever and unscrupulous politician. The Mahasabha had failed completely to gain representation in the Legislative Assembly, except for Shyama's own seat. The Mahassabhites were good propagandists.

Mountbatten said that he agreed that Jinnah was right in claiming that the demands for the partition of Bengal were maneuvers; nevertheless, these maneuvers were well-founded in logic. Burrows said that he agreed that the agitation for the partition of Bengal must indeed be taken seriously. Mountbatten went on to explain that the present plan for leaving the choice of their own future to the provinces themselves. He stated that he was unwilling to put his name to any partition plan on behalf of the British, because the British would then be blamed for the results of the partition. He was proposing to make a broadcast explaining this position.

Burrows stated that he had, the previous weekend had a long conversation with Christie who had been sent down to see him as the Viceroy's representative. He had considered the draft announcement which was to be put up for the approval of HMG. He noticed in the present form of this announcement it was intended to include Calcutta in Western Bengal. Calcutta, in his opinion, was peculiar and deserved independent consideration. It had grown up simply because of European trade interest and had reached its status dependent on both East and West Bengal. It had been the capital of India for many years. There was no doubt that the Hindus were a majority of the population. However, for the future prosperity of Calcutta, if it was not to perish, the city should if possible, be given the chance to serve both halves of Bengal, if the Province was partitioned. It would be unfair for all the revenues to go to one half of the Province when the other half had done so much for the prosperity of the city. Nearly all the jute was grown in Eastern Bengal and that half should therefore have a share of the excise duties on jute. Burrows went on to say that he did not believe that Eastern Bengal could live in partition.

Burrows went on to say that he had kept off all questions of partition in discussion with Suhrawardy, except on the latter's return from Delhi after an interview with Mountbatten. Suhrawardy declared that he would be prepared to accept Calcutta as an international city. If Calcutta was excluded from East Bengal the latter would not accept the decision, but there would be a tremendous row. Burrows explained that he was in favour of a joint control of the city of Calcutta. The city should, he thought be administered by five Muslims and five Hindus, elected from each half of Bengal. These persons would form an independent administrative council or cabinet. The chairman would be elected from amongst them. They could make informative reports to the assemblies of both halves of the Province but would have full control themselves. They would work out the proportion of customs duties, etc. to go to either half of the Province.

Mountbatten asked his staff to put the case *against* declaring Calcutta a free city. Abell explained that the crux of the problem was the question of relationship with the centre. The Muslims would insist on practically complete freedom but the Hindus would not enter into the administration of any free unit. On this basis it was most difficult to obtain agreement between the communities in the Provinces. Abell explained that the problem in Calcutta was similar to that in the Lahore Division of the Punjab which contained both Lahore city and Amritsar, which was the most holy Sikh city. There had been suggestions that the Lahore Division would present too great difficulties to divide. However, it seemed to him that the present situation was that the communities would not share anything. If Calcutta were excluded from the general plan, it would become a bone of contention in the same way as the Lahore Division. The only hope of getting a more reasonable attitude was to let each party – especially the Muslim League – know what they were to get. Mountbatten pointed out it was evident from Abell's remarks that anything but a clean partition would produce enmity on the part of Congress. If he fell foul of Congress it would be impossible to continue to run the country.

Mountbatten said that he entirely saw Burrows' reasons for wanting to make Calcutta a free city, and he considered it essential to meet Burrows' views as far as possible while not compromising his position in India as a whole. He then put forward a suggestion which would increase the chances of Bengal remaining an independent unit. Briefly this suggestion was that members of the Constituent Assembly in Bengal should vote on the future, as between independence or joining Hindustan or Pakistan, before deciding the issue of partition. They would then clearly know the alternatives when they came to vote for partition. Mountbatten said that he wanted a clause which would make possible this change of procedure included in the draft announcement.

Burrows said that he considered that such an amendment to the voting procedure would give only a very limited chance of Bengal remaining unified and independent. He believed that the only hope was that a strong Coalition Government should be formed immediately. He did not know, however, whether the Hindus would agree to coalition without a link with the centre. He believed that they would want assurance that there would be some such link. Mountbatten said that Burrows should renew his efforts to persuade Suhrawardy to create a Coalition Government, and explain to him the outline of the changes which were being made in the plan. Mountbatten also suggested that Burrows should try to persuade Suhrawardy to make a promise of joint electorates in the future if a decision on a unified independent Bengal was reached. Burrows said that Suhrawardy had already accepted this principle but was opposed to reservation of seats. Burrows also said that Suhrawardy's position in the Muslim league was not at all secure. Though clever, he was not popular and would have been got rid of if an alternative leader could have been found. He discounted a great deal of Suhrawardy's claim of being able to put across any particular course of action.

The Plan Taken by Ismay to London

Now the vital question arises did Nehru and Jinnah actually see the Partition Plan which Lord Ismay carried with him to London on 3 May, 1947. This is an extremely important matter as we shall see later despite the approval of this plan by the British Government it was totally denied by Nehru. The events in Simla from the 7 to 10 May, 1947, are the most baffling in the entire partition episode.

We have already seen that on 22 April, 1947, Nehru participated in a meeting with Mountbatten and his staff and was fully in the knowledge of the Partition Plan that was being forwarded by Mountbatten to London. On the following day Jinnah participated in a meeting with Mountbatten and his staff. The minutes of the meeting reads:

'His Excellency the Viceroy explained to Mr. Jinnah the outlines of a plan then under consideration, whereby the provinces would be given the choice of their own future.

Mr. Jinnah asked for this plan in writing, and His Excellency the Viceroy said that a copy would be sent to him as soon as possible. Mr. Jinnah gave his word of honour not to show the document to anybody except Mr. Liaquat Ali Khan. Mr. Jinnah also said that he would be prepared to consider any plan which Congress might let him have for the partition of Bengal and the Punjab. His Excellency the Viceroy invited Prin. Sec. To take a copy of the plan at present under consideration to Mr. Jinnah when practicable.'

It is abundantly clear from the *Transfer of Power* records that both Nehru and Jinnah had seen the plan that was taken to London by Lord Ismay.

General Hastings 'Pug' Ismay
(ccw.ox.ac.uk)

The plan which Ismay presented in London on 3 May provided for partition, with Bengal and the Punjab having the option of being split between India and Pakistan, joining in entirety with either state, or going it alone. The position of the Princely States was left obscure, the implication being that it would be for them to decide their own future. It was inherent in such a scheme that India and Pakistan might in the end prove to be only the two largest units in a patchwork of more or less viable independent states.

To British Ministers, committed to the precepts of self-determination, this seemed eminently proper. Mountbatten had urged the Cabinet to consider and approve the plan within ten days at the most. They took only a week. Such amendments as they made were mainly at the behest of the parliamentary draftsmen who wished to clarify a few obscurities. Their changes certainly made more evident the right of the different parts of India to decide their own future, but no fresh element was introduced. The only new point that appeared likely to cause disturbance was the proposal that the North-West Frontier should also be allowed to opt for independence – and to Mountbatten and his advisers it seemed that this was as likely to distress the Muslim League as Congress. 'Everything is going well at home,' reported Miéville. 'Our proposals have been generally accepted and indeed improved in many ways by the draftsmen at home.'

Just for the record the actual text of the Partition Plan that was taken by Lord Ismay to London on 3 May, 1947, is reproduced below.

ARRANGEMENTS FOR THE DEMISSION OF POWER

Procedure for Bengal, Punjab, Assam, NWFP, and Sind: 7. For the other Provinces, in some of which there have been insistent demands for Partition, the following preliminary arrangements will be necessary.

Preliminary Steps: (a) In Bengal, the Legislative Assembly (excluding European members) will be asked to sit in two parts, one representing the Muslim majority districts and the other the rest of the Province.

(b) In the Punjab, where the position of the Sikhs presents particular difficulty, the Legislative Assembly (excluding European members) will be divided as in Bengal, into two parts representing Muslim majority districts and other districts respectively.

(c) In Assam, the members of the Legislative Assembly, (excluding European members), elected from territorial constituencies included in the Sylhet District will be asked to sit separately.

(d) In the N.W.F.P. a general election will be held under Section 93 Government. In determining the population of districts the 1941 census figures will be taken as authoritative.

(e) Thereafter the Legislative Assembly of Sind (excluding the European members), the newly-elected Legislative Assembly of the N.W.F.P., and the two parts of the Legislative assemblies of Bengal, the Punjab and Assam will elect representatives on the principle laid down in the Cabinet Mission's statement of the 16th May, 1946.

(f) Not reproduced.

(g) The representatives so elected of West Bengal and East Bengal, sitting separately, will vote as to whether or not their Province should be divided. A majority vote of either body in favour of Partition will decide the issue. A similar procedure will be followed in regard to the Punjab and Assam.

Note:- There may be a demand for a preliminary joint meeting of the representatives of both halves of the Punjab or Bengal to consider whether, if the Province remains united, it should enter a joint Constituent Assembly with other Provinces or remain independent. It will be open to either Governor to summon such a joint meeting if he considers it advisable.

(h) Immediately thereafter the representatives of the Provinces or half Provinces (dependent on the decision in paragraph 10 above) of the Punjab and Bengal will decide whether, on behalf of the areas which they represent, they wish:-

(a) to join the existing Constituent Assembly or

(b) to group together in one or more Constituent Assemblies, or

(c) to stand out independently and act as their own Constituent Assembly.

If, as a result of these votes, Bengal is partitioned, the representatives of Sylhet will sit separately and decide whether

(d) Sylhet should remain part of Assam, or they should join the Constituent Assembly of East Bengal with a view to Sylhet being incorporated in that half Province.

The representatives of Assam (with or without Sylhet, depending on the decision in paragraph 12 above) and of Sind and the N.W.F.P. will decide whether, on behalf of the areas which they represent, they wish

(e) to join the existing Constituent Assembly, or

(f) they should join the Constituent Assembly of East Bengal with a view to Sylhet being incorporated in that half Province.

(g) to stand out independently and act as their own Constituent Assembly.

In order that the successor authority or authorities may have as much time as possible to prepare themselves to receive power, it is essential that all the above processes should be completed without undue delay.

Baluchistan not reproduced.

Framing of constitutions: 16. The Constituent Assembly or Assemblies will then proceed to frame Constitutions for their respective territories, and will in due course, elect Executives to whom power will be demitted when the time comes.

Joint consultation on common subjects: 17. The administrative consequences of partition are complex and considerable. Accordingly, the Constituent Assemblies, if more than one, should also create machinery for joint consultation among themselves on matters of common concern, particularly Defence, and for the negotiation of agreements in respect of these matters.

Part III – The Tribes of the North West Frontier

As soon as the successor Authorities have been determined, it will be for them to negotiate fresh agreements with the tribes of the North West Frontier of India.

Part IV – The States

His Majesty's Government wish to make it clear that the decisions announced above relate only to British India and that their policy towards the Indian States remain unchanged. When paramountcy lapses, all the rights surrendered by the States to the paramount power will return to the States. They are free to arrange by negotiation with those parts of British India to which power will be demitted whatever measure of association they consider to be in the best interests of their people.

Part V – Further Announcements By The Governor-General

The Governor-General will, from time to time, make such further announcements as may be necessary, in regard to procedure or any other matter, for the carrying out of the above arrangements.

The Partition Plan London

The fact that that the Partition Plan which Lord Ismay took to London was seen by the top Indian leaders is amply evident from the fact that it was reproduced almost completely by the *Hindu* of 2 May 1947. The following day the *Hindustan Times* commented on the assumption that this plan would be the one to be adopted.

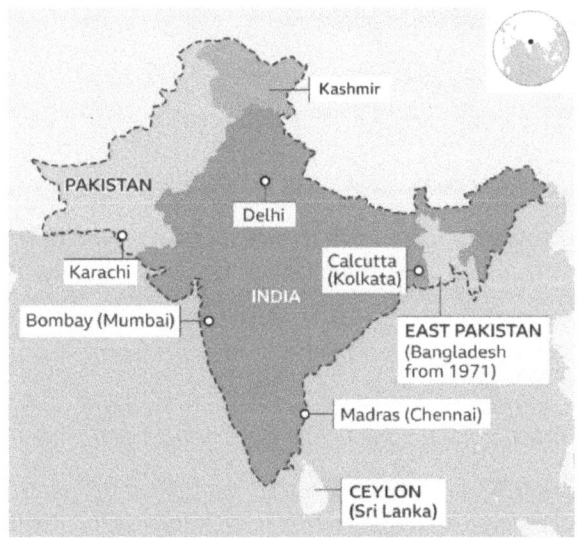

Partition of India, 1947
(bbc.com)

Mountbatten was quite disturbed by the leakage as he knew that the only leaders who had seen the full draft were Jinnah and Nehru – and they had not been allowed to retain any documents. Apart from them the outline of the Plan had been discussed with Liaquat, Patel and Baldev Singh. The only persons who knew of it besides them were members of the staff, including VP Menon. Mountbatten thought it was surely inconceivable to think that there had been a leakage from a member of the staff. Since nothing had appeared in the League newspapers and disclosure of the Plan would be against League interests, the field was narrowed to Nehru, Patel and Baldev Singh.

Mountbatten believed that Nehru had discussed the outline of the Plan with the Congress Working Committee. He felt that the article which had appeared in *Hindustan Times* was a deliberate blackmail which led him to believe that Congress feared that Mountbatten was going to give a decision which was inimical to Congress interests. That, he felt, must either be fear of an unfair decision which they would contest, or a fair one which they could not face up to.

Lord Ismay, who left for London on 2 May, 1947, carried with him a communication sent by the Congress Working Committee to the Viceroy containing its reactions to the tentative conclusions which the Viceroy had reached on the Indian Situation.

The Viceroy's conclusions were on the following lines:

(1) Both the Congress and the League consider division of India inevitable.

(2) The division will involve district-wise partition of the Punjab and Bengal and the appointment of a boundary commission. In the alternative Bengal should have a constitution on a fifty-fifty basis, the status of Bengal corresponding roughly to the position of Quebec in the Canadian constitution.

(3) Before division is carried out the M.L.A.s of the districts concerned should be given the opportunity to decide whether they would prefer to remain in the Indian Union or have a separate State for their areas.

(4) If the M.L.A.s decide in favour of partition then they will be asked to elect new representatives to a constituent assembly or constituent assemblies for their joint or separate areas on the basis of one representative for each million. The present Constituent Assembly for the Indian Union will remain intact. Only the members representing the partitioned areas will cease to be its members.

(5) If partition to take place the N.W.F.P. should have fresh elections to decide whether its people would desire to remain in the Indian Union or join Pakistan or become an independent territory. Since there was a tug-of war in the province for political power the present Governor will be replaced by another and Section 93 administration will be set up to conduct elections.

The Congress Working Committee's reactions to the above proposals were stated to be on the following lines:

(1) The Congress would have favoured a strong united India but considered that the division of the country was the best solution in the circumstances. But the division should be absolute and complete since that alone would give the majority of the people of India the opportunity of building up a powerful State with a strong Centre.

(2) There must be partition of the Punjab and Bengal giving chance to the non-Muslim areas to join the Indian Union. Since the Punjab was the homeland of the Sikhs its partition should not rest merely on the basis of Sikh and Hindu population but also other considerations such as the need for bringing in a large number of Sikhs within one territory, the considerations of property and natural geographical boundary. As regards Bengal division of the Western districts and Calcutta from the rest of the province was clearly indicated.

(3) The method of violence used in the North-West Frontier Province, the Punjab and Assam to

settle political issues must be put an end to. The Congress would resist to the utmost any attempt to force issues by methods of intimidation and violence.

(4) The Congress had no objection to a separate constituent assembly or assemblies being summoned for those areas that choose to stand out of the Indian Union but hopes that such areas will have the opportunity to decide for themselves whether they would remain independent or form union with other parts

(5) There was no occasion for any change in the Frontier. The last election was fought on the issue of Pakistan and the verdict having been given by the electorate the present M.L.A.s of the Frontier Assembly are competent to decide the future of the province.

The Congress Working Committee was expected to draw up a resolution embodying the points covered in the letter sent to the Viceroy. The Committee would meet for another two days and will then re-assemble about May 15 or 16. It was said that Jinnah has been asked to summon his working committee about that date so that the British Government's proposals which will be ready by then may be considered by the two committees. Mountbatten's Partition Plan was placed before the India Committee of the British Cabinet. The meeting was chaired by Prime Minister Attlee.

Lord Ismay said that the Viceroy had found that communal feeling in India was far more bitter than he had expected: it had become an obsession with both Hindus and Moslems and had been much intensified by the statement of 20th February. Since his arrival, the Viceroy had made every effort to persuade the Indian political leaders to accept the Cabinet Mission's plan. Jinnah had, however, shown himself inflexibly opposed to acceptance, and the Viceroy had reached the conclusion that the prospects of agreement were negligible. The proposals set out in his telegram No. 955-S were therefore designed to place the responsibility for dividing India conspicuously on the Indians themselves. He had discussed it with Nehru, Jinnah, Patel, Liaquat, and Baldev Singh, who had at least acquiesced in it. Congress, indeed, seemed to be reconciled to some form of partition. The plan had, however, leaked in the papers, and the political parties were now trying to stir up opposition to it.

Lord Ismay said that the Viceroy's plan might have to be modified in certain respects in view of developments since it had been drawn up. The Governor of Bengal was anxious that that Province should have the opportunity of electing for independence and thus remaining unified, and Mr. Jinnah had agreed to this course. The Governor had been consulted about the possibility of holding a referendum but had advised against this course on account of the practical difficulties involved: in any case it could only produce the same result as the plan proposed by the Viceroy. The Governor of the

Punjab had also advised against the holding of a referendum, and, according to a telegram just received, was no longer in favour of the Viceroy's plan for that Province. Congress had no objection to an election being held in the North West Frontier Province, provided that this was not conceded under threat of violence. On further investigation, the Viceroy had reached the conclusion that there were at present no legal grounds for resort to Section 93 in the Province; Congress would greatly resent such action. He was, therefore, now suggesting a referendum instead of an election, and thought that this course might secure Congress support.

The Viceroy hoped to meet Indian leaders, not later than 20th May, with the object of bringing matters to a head. He wished to make them admit openly that there was no possibility of securing agreement on a unified India; he would then place before them the plan set out in his telegram No. 995-S. The Viceroy did not propose to allow any alterations of substance to be made unless both sides asked for them, but he would be ready to meet the parties on points of detail. He would tell them that the plan was to be announced both in London and India within 24 hours. If the announcement was not made very shortly after the presentation of the plan to the leaders' leakage was inevitable. Lord Ismay said that the Viceroy was most anxious that a decision on his proposal should be taken without delay. It was essential that a very early announcement should be made of the conclusions reached by His Majesty's Government on the matters which were generally known to have been referred to them. The Prime Minister informed the Committee that Field Marshal Auchinleck had told him that morning that the situation in India was dangerous, and had greatly emphasised the necessity for an early decision.

Menon's Machinations

As we have seen, the partition plan taken by Lord Ismay to London was thoroughly examined by the India Committee of the British Cabinet. Apart from Attlee in the chair other cabinet members present were Hugh Dalton, Sir Stafford Cripps, A.V. Alexander, Viscount Addison, the Earl of Listowel, Lord Chorley, and A.G. Bottomley. It can be seen that the most influential members of the British Cabinet had reviewed Mountbatten's plan.

The Cabinet Committee made only a few minor amendments as follows: -

i)   The Committee took great care to suitably amend a paragraph to avoid any suggestion that the plan had been prepared without reference to the will of the Indian people. Greater emphasis was also laid on the fact that the plan would not involve any final demarcation of the boundaries of those provinces which have special minority problems.

ii) In relation to NWFP the Committee feet that the unavoidable delay involved in the election in this Province should not be allowed to retard the progress of the plan in the other Provinces.

iii) The Committee thought that it would be advisable to increase the numbers of the representatives to be elected. In their view, the members proposed were in many cases too small to afford adequate representation of the views of the people of the areas concerned. They recognised that the figures proposed in the draft were put forward on the basis adopted by the Cabinet Mission for the Constituent Assembly. It was agreed, therefore, that representation should be on the basis of 1 for every 250,000 of the population, instead of 1 for every million.

iv) The Committee were informed that careful consideration had been given to the question whether the division of a Province should be decided by majority vote or by a $2/3$ vote; they saw no reason to differ from the recommendations that a majority vote should decide the issue.

v) The Committee considered that, in view of the limited membership of some of the bodies set up to make the decision on partition, it would be inadvisable also to give them right to form the Constituent Assemblies for independent areas.

vi) The Committee thought that careful consideration should be given to the wording of some paragraphs.

vii) The Committee were informed that measures to meet the situation which might arise in Bengal and the Punjab when the proposed announcement was made public were under consideration by the C-in-C.

The Plan was further refined and finalised by Ismay and other officials in the light of the discussions of the India Committee. It can be clearly seen from the above deliberations of the India Committee that Mountbatten's Partition Plan was accepted by the British Government in its totality barring a few minor changes of phraseology here and there. This point is extremely relevant as Congress accusations arose later to the effect that London had substantially altered the plan which had been seen both by the Congress and League leaders. There was actually hardly any objection by the League whereas the Congress had accepted it with a few reservations.

Now let us turn to the dramatic events that were taking place in Simla between the 7th and 10th of May 1947. These events were to change the course of history. But before that we have to cast our minds back a little bit and review the activities of the ubiquitous V.P. Menon. Menon states in his *The Transfer of Powr in India.*

'I had always been opposed to the plan which Lord Ismay and George Abell had taken to London. The theory that the provinces should become initially independent successor States was particularly abhorrent to me. But my protests and my views in the discussions with the Viceroy's advisers went in vain. The main consideration which influenced me was this, that if the transfer took place unilaterally without the willing consent of the party leaders and there was no strong central Government to which that power could be transferred, the whole country would inevitably drift into chaos and civil war.'

'It was at Simla that, for the first time, I had an opportunity of explaining my point of view to the Viceroy in person. As a matter of fact, it was while Lord Wavell was still conducting negotiations with the party leaders, but when agreement between the Congress and the Muslim League on the Cabinet Mission plan seemed – to me at least – to be impossible of achievement, that I had attempted to devise a fresh approach to the problem.'

It was late December 1946, or early January 1947, that V.P. had a lengthy discussion with Vallabhbhai Patel. A united India under the Cabinet Mission plan was, he suggested, an illusion; the three-tier constitutional set-up envisaged was unwieldy and difficult to work; he saw no future for the country under this plan. Besides, Jinnah showed no sign of resiling from his demand for a separate, independent sovereign State for the Muslims – a demand in which the League had the sympathy, if not the support, of a large section of British opinion and, what was even more important from our point of view, the sympathy of most of the British element in the Services. V.P.'s view was that it was better that the country should be divided, rather than that it should gravitate towards civil war.

If they agreed to partition, Jinnah obviously could not ask for those portions of the Punjab, Bengal and Assam which were predominantly non-Muslim. The crucial problem was the basis on which power could be transferred. In a divided India this could best be to two central government on the basis – a point on which V.P. laid particular stress – of Dominion Status. By consenting to accept Dominion Status, the Congress would be gaining three great advantages. Firstly, it would ensure a peaceful transfer of power. Secondly, such acceptance would be warmly welcomed by Britain, and the Congress would by this single act have gained its friendship and goodwill. The third concerned the future administration of the country.

The civil services at the higher levels were manned largely by Britishers, and if India insisted on independence there was no question but that the British element had it in their power to create endless trouble at the time of the transfer of power. It might be possible to carry on the civil administration somehow; but certainly, India could not, during the transitional period, do without some help on the defence side. The Indian Army was largely officered by the Britishers, almost entirely so in the higher ranks, while the Navy and Air Force had to be built up virtually from scratch. After all, the test of sovereignty was the power to amend one's constitution, which remained unaffected by the acceptance of Dominion Status. India could at any time, if she so desired, walk out of the Commonwealth. Moreover, the Princes, with their past associations with the British Crown, would be reassured and be more willing to negotiate. V.P. pointed out that if the transfer of power took place on the basis of Dominion Staus, it would enable the Congress to have at one and the same time a strong central Government, able to withstand the centrifugal tendencies all too apparent at that moment, and to frame a truly democratic constitution unhampered by any communal considerations. Nobody could have been better aware of the situation in the country than Vallabhbhai Patel; he had already been in charge of the Home portfolio for some months.

Patel assured V.P. that if power could be transferred at once on the basis of Dominion Status, he for one would use his influence to see that the Congress accepted it. In his presence V.P. dictated the outline of a plan, which he later sent by special messenger to London to be handed over to the Secretary of State. (With Lord Wavell's concurrence, V.P. had been conducting some correspondence with the India Office on the issue of the transfer of power on this basis). V.P. could not very well convey to the Secretary of State that Patel had agreed, as that might have compromised his position, but V.P. did say that he had reason to believe that the Congress would accept Dominion Status. It might well be that the Secretary of State was feeling that in view of the unequivocal demand of the Congress for complete independence there was no ground for assuming that the Congress would accept a transfer of power on the basis of Dominion Status. In any case, no action was taken on V.P.'s proposals – which, incidentally, Lord Mountbatten mentioned having seen in London before coming out to India. So, we see once again V.P. Menon's overwhelming influence in the finalisation and drastic amendments to the Plan that followed.

The Plot Begins in Simla

To recapitulate we have already seen that within a week of Mountbatten's arrival in India on 23 March, 1947, he decided to invite at an appropriate time certain important leader to stay with him at Simla.

Those invited would be: Gandhi, Jinnah, Nehru, Liaquat, Patel, and the Nawab of Bhopal. There would be no formal meetings, no agenda, no secretariat in evidence – just an informal exchange of ideas. It was possible, in such an atmosphere, that a measure of agreement would be obtained. There would be no press statements, and the Viceroy would ask his guests to give an undertaking not to issue information to the press. In the *Transfer of Power* documents throughout the month of April 1947, there are several references to the Simla House Party.

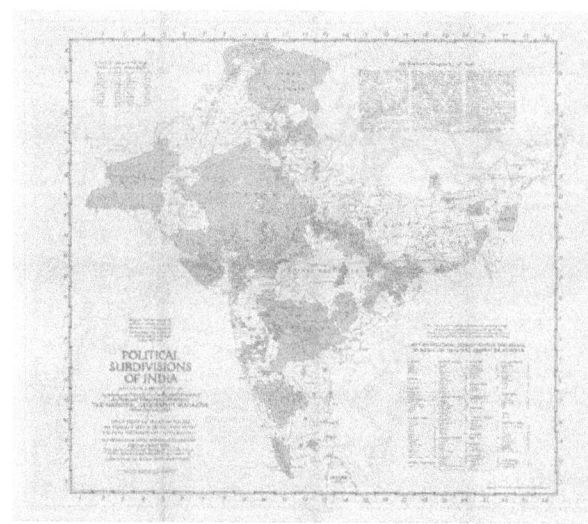

Political Subdivisions of India
(indianhistorycollective.com)

On 20 April Erskine Crum Conference Secretary to Mountbatten prepared a detailed paper for the meeting of the Indian leaders. The venue suggested in the paper was Delhi rather than Simla as Delhi would probably be more convenient to all concerned. This paper dealt at length with the venue, date, composition, and purpose of the conference. The paper had draft invitation letters, draft telegram to London, draft announcement, and draft timetable of events.

What happened in fact was completely different to what had been planned. Despite repeated mention and arrangement for the informal meeting with the Indian leaders it never took place. Let us see Mountbatten's own version of his own move to Simla:

'The way the Simla meeting built up was this. **Remember that the plan I sent home on May 2nd, 1947, had never been seen in writing by any of the Indian leaders at all.** But I had personally created the plan by constantly talking about it, clause by clause, with every leader and getting his reactions, to the point at which I felt reasonably confident that I had not included anything to which they would object. Lord Ismay flew home with it – with Sir George Abell if I remember right – and I thought I'd go to Simla.'

'I sent for Colonel Currie, the Military Secretary, and said to him that I wished to move to Simla. It was very hot, you see, at the end of May. I wanted to get up into the cool hills, the Himalayas, I wanted to have a rest. I had no more meetings, I couldn't have any more. And I had several days to spend there. I said, "We want to move up in eight days' time, the same day that Lord Ismay leaves."

"Oh," he said, "I'm afraid I can't possibly open Viceregal Lodge in eight days. I require three weeks' notice."

"I'm sorry, you haven't got three weeks' notice, you've got a week." "All right," I said, "book me into the local hotel."

"Absolutely out of the question!"

I said, "Well, my dear Currie you've got to make up your mind, whether you're going to put me in a hotel, or in Viceregal Lodge, but I'm going to Simla, eight days from now. And I'm not taking anybody up – just her Ex (the Viceroy's wife was always called Her Ex; the Viceroy was called His Ex) and I'm taking Pammy. That's us three. I am going to ask Nehru and Krishna Menon to come up, just to keep us company, because I'm very fond of them. That's five." Then I said, "The Secretariat will continue to function in Delhi but I'll take up one private secretary (I think it was Admiral Brockman). I think I'll also take up Alan Campbell-Johnson to keep in touch with the Press, and I'll take about three of four of the staff."

And he said, "This is out of the question. I can never get the house open, get everything ready. I can't move all the servants up."

I said, "Think it over, because just remember this. I'm going to Simla in eight days' time; it's up to you to decide where you're going to put us up, and if you can't do it in the house, of course, I am going to a hotel."

He came back and said, "Well, I've had an emergency meeting and we can just do it in eight days provided you assure me that you are going to rest privately, that you won't want to have any luncheon parties."

"No." "Dinner parties?" "No." "Garden parties?" "No." "Cocktail parties?" "No." "Balls?" "No." "Then we can do it."

'When we got up there I sent a note saying. "Please let me know exactly how many people we've brought from Delhi" – knowing that they had quite a big staff in the place. I remember – never got over it – it was 333.'

'There were two ways of getting up into the hills, you could either go by a very delightful little narrow-gauge train which took all the luggage and staff, and which I had been up in, it was rather fun, or you could drive up in a car, more dramatic really, climbing right up into the Himalayas. You could either drive up to Amballa, or you could take the train up, or you could fly there. I actually used to fly.'

'While we were at Simla, London started telegraphing amendments to the plan. They couldn't resist not picking and altering, exactly like the old days. So, by the time they'd finished, the plan did not look the same as it had when I started, although in retrospect I am bound to agree that they had not made any changes of substance. Because it no longer had the same presentation that I had worked out with the leaders, I was worried. I said, "I have an uneasy feeling that this may not acceptable." They'd never seen the old plan, but at least they'd known the words I'd used, and now the words had changes, the presentation was different.'

No sooner had Mountbatten reached Simla the Partition Plan started taking an entirely different turn. We have already seen V.P. Menon's machinations in this matter. All *Transfer of Power* records and Mountbatten's own admission indicate that the Plan (taken by Ismay to London) had been seen and more or less approved both by the Congress and the League. Now in between an Alternate Plan had been prepared (Summarised below). Why an Alternative Plan had been prepared remains a mystery. It will be seen that the Alternate Plan went totally against the interest of the Muslims. In this self-same meeting the Viceroy "invited" his Principal Secretary further to consider what were the best tactics for threatening Mr. Jinnah with the Alternate Plan; and to put forward.

In a telegram Mountbatten informed Ismay (who was still in London awaiting final approval of the plan sent to London) that there was always the chance that Jinnah may spring a surprise by rejecting plan at last moment, although so far there had been clear indications that Jinnah would accepted. It would be out of the question to carry on with the plan in such circumstance and should contingency arise Mountbatten intended to tell Jinnah that the only alternative open was for H.M. Government to demit power on the basis of existing Government of India Act with modifications as necessary.

Mountbatten on the same day i.e., 8 May 1947 indicated in a telegram to London that in his recent conversations with Mieville and himself Jinnah did not appear to contest the idea of a truncated Pakistan. In fact, the general impression which Jinnah had given Mountbatten that he did not intend to reject the Plan contained in the draft announcement. In Mountbatten's interview with Jinnah and Liaquat Mountbatten had always watched them carefully for any indication of an intention to reject the Plan and had never seen such an indication. In fact, every test which, Mountbatten had applied had passed off successfully and led Mountbatten to believe that they were likely to accept the Plan. If Jinnah intended to spring a surprise on him by rejecting the Plan at the last moment Jinnah could not have played his part towards making this surprise complete.

Mountbatten wrote that clearly Jinnah's only reason for rejection of the Plan would be that he would hope thereby to get more than the truncated Pakistan offered. Jinnah would hope to continue negotiations endlessly, and withhold agreement at the last moment, from any other plan put up, hoping that such tactics would result in compelling the British to act as arbitrators beyond June 1948 so as to ensure that he gets a long-term settlement to the greatest possible advantage for the League. Mountbatten contended that Jinnah could make the Plan unworkable in a similar way to that by which he had made the Cabinet Mission Plan unworkable. How absurd were Mountbatten's pronouncement as we have already seen at great length that the Cabinet Mission Plan failed due to the duplicity and intransigence of the Congress.

In the event of Jinnah rejecting the draft announcement it would be out of question to carry with the Plan. Mountbatten felt that he must have an alternative plan against this contingency. **It must be such an alternative as can be imposed if necessary without agreement from the Indian Leaders.** This statement is Mountbatten'sis revealed in its most naked form. Because, Mountbatten's alternate plan was to demit power on the basis of the existing Government of India Act with modification in necessary that is to demit provincial subjects to the existing Provincial Governments and central subjects to the existing Central Government. The Alternative Plan meant simply handing over power to the Congress. It will be seen that it was not Jinnah who rejected the Plan but Nehru. There was no alternative ready for this development!

The Plot Continues in Simla

Mountbatten had brought up with him to Simla V.P. Menon, who was closely involved in all the 1945 Simla and the 1946 Cabinet Mission Plan negotiations. Although V.P. had suffered a period of eclipse, he was still the trusted confidant of Vallabhbhai Patel. The Viceregal Lodge was an ideal venue for quiet, calm deliberation, and the Viceroy's workroom there was in refreshing contrast to his air-cooled and somber teak-lined study in Delhi. The pale green of the former had decided him to have a similar colour scheme in the latter. Mountbatten believed that the darkness of his Delhi room itself induced an atmosphere of depression. He could not understand how past Viceroy's could have endured it, and thought it was monstrous that he should be needing electric light throughout the day during an Indian summer.

Alan Campbell-Johnson records in his *Mission with Mountbatten*

"On arrival I was plunged into two successive Staff Meetings, the first without Mountbatten and the second with him. At both we considered fully the desirability of an alternative plan based on the assumption, which V.P. held was more than possible, that Jinnah would not accept the Plan in the draft announcement. Mountbatten said he had always borne in mind the possibility of rejection by Jinnah, and in all the interviews he had had both with him and Liaquat he had watched carefully for any sign pointing to such an intention, but none had been given. Every test he had applied led him to the belief that they intended to accept, and he could see only two possible suppositions for Jinnah not doing so – the first, if his real aim was to keep the British in India, and by prolonging the bargaining to make it more difficult for the British to leave, in the hope of obtaining thereby a more favourable award; the second, if he had reached the conclusion that Pakistan was not practicable."

But, Mountbatten seriously doubted whether either of these considerations was in Jinnah's mind. None-the-less Mountbatten agreed with V.P.'s thesis on the advisability of having available a clear alternative in his dealings with Jinnah. The second-line plan would involve demission of power under the present constitution. It would not in the last resort require the agreement of the Indian leaders. Provincial subjects would be demitted to existing Provincial Governments, and Central subjects to the existing Central Government; but it would put the Moslems under the Hindu majority.

A telegram was drafted for dispatch to London, giving them the background and asking for approval to hold such a plan in reserve. Mountbatten also went further into the possibilities of retaining India in the Commonwealth, and V.P. confirmed both Patel's and Nehru's positive approach to the subject and the need for dropping the terms "King-Emperor" and "Empire", to which so many Indians objected. V.P. was finally asked to prepare a paper setting out clearly the procedure whereby a form of Dominion Status could be granted to India under the alternative Plans of Partition and Demission. The Dominion Status question was discussed at great length. Mountbatten began by saying he thought it most desirable that if Dominion Status was to be granted to India before June 1948 the grant should in fact take place during 1947. He went so far as to say that he would like to see Dominion Status by 31st December, 1947 – giving as his reason the startlingly apt precedent of a plenary session of the Quebec Conference during the war. The meeting had been asked to approve a directive that war with Japan must be ended by 1948. To this President Roosevelt had said he would never agree. Hopkins intervened, "Well, make it 31st December, 1947." – President Roosevelt, "Agreed."

Nehru and Krishna Menon have arrived in Simla on 9th May 1947. This was obviously a preferential treatment for the Congress. The actual discussions with them the world will never know. What was recorded was that much would depend on Mountbatten's powers of persuasion with them if the

Dominion Status concept was to come to light. Already Krishna indicated resistance to any splitting of the Army if early Dominion Status was accepted. Miéville was inclined to think that there would be more advantage to India than to the Commonwealth from India remaining in, but Mountbatten considered that the value to the United Kingdom both in terms of world prestige and strategy would be enormous; for India as a whole the immense asset of constitutional continuity. He appreciated the many administrative difficulties, particularly those facing Pakistan, but these were inherent in the situation anyhow. "What are we doing?" he asked. "Administratively it is the difference between putting up a permanent building, a nissen hut or a tent. **As far as Pakistan is concerned we are putting up a tent. We can do no more**." What a confession by Mountbatten!

That afternoon there was a brief respite from the intensive discussions. The Mountbatten's brought Nehru out to tea at "The Retreat" at Mashobra, which was located about 10 miles away from Viceregal Lodge. We shall see later the exclusive meeting of Nehru and Edwina at Mashobra. But for the mountains surrounding us, it might have been a typical English garden tea-party. To begin with there was a certain tension which stifled small talk. Fay, Campbell- Johnson's wife, sitting next to Nehru, managed to elicit from him his views on the sugar shortage (Nehru had actually brought their own sugar with them) and his antipathy to Simla. This characteristically was derived from his aversion to the spectacle of the rickshaw coolies, whose labours he thought were an affront to human dignity.

Mountbatten asked Nehru if his responsibilities as Minister for External Affairs covered communications with Burma, and if so, what had become of the great road and airfield projects which had been built during his S.E.A.C. days at immense cost. There had been clamour for years for a land link with Burma – were these being kept up? Nehru showed some interest, but he felt that the cost of maintenance would be very heavy. The Mountbattens fell in love with the place, and are quite determined to come back again. During their walk up and down the orchard terraces Nehru was very agile, and confessed to a liking for hill-climbing. He gave a demonstration of a new technique by walking uphill backwards. This, he said, made breathing easier at high altitudes, and rested the calf-muscles. At the Staff Meeting on the following day Mountbatten reported on a breakfast conversation he had had with Krishna, while V.P. spoke of contact he had made with Patel. The impression was growing that the Dominion Status formula increasingly appealed to both the Congress leaders. Krishna Menon took credit as the first to have suggested an early transfer of power to India on this basis. He thought Nehru was attracted to the concept, if only because it may give Mountbatten opportunity to bring his influence to bear on the more recalcitrant Princes. V.P. suspected that likely delay in completing the Indian constitution could also encourage Nehru to look towards Dominion

Status as an interim device to fill up the time. The main difficulty on the Congress side seems to be the fear of the left-wing exploiting Dominion Status as a "sell out" to Britain.

Simla - The Edwina Factor

Edwina having tea with Jawaharlal Nehru
(theweek.in)

There is no doubt that Edwina played a very key role behind the scenes in Simla through the crucial negotiations in May 1947 when the fate of the subcontinent was sealed. 'Discussions went on all day' writes Janet Morgan in her Edwina Mountbatten. 'Edwina was not present at the meetings but, at meals and during walks in the garden between sessions, she heard how the negotiations were getting on. V.P. Menon told his daughter afterwards that Lady Louis' conversations with Nehru played a significant part in helping him to make up his mind to go for Commonwealth membership. By the time Nehru left on the Sunday evening a new formula had been agreed.' The foregoing quotation from Janet Morgan is just the tip of the iceberg. What really went on the world will never know.

Stanley Wolpert in his Nehru writes, 'In early May, Dicke, decided to take Jawaharlal and Krishna Menon up to Simla's mile-high retreat. His staff all came along, of course, as did Edwina. Campbell-Johnson and his wife had flown up a bit earlier to open the Viceroy's old weekend lodge in Mashobra, a lovely isolated garden spot surrounded by lush orchards, 'Quite glorious and completely remote,' as Edwina remembered it. There she and Nehru strolled and climbed together, alone at last, there rarest luxury - privacy together. She was very much like him, a lonely heart introspectively passionate, a soul long seeking its other half. Each of them had mystic insights and saw in the other the ideal mate that each had always longed to find yet never had before. Cheerful, handsome young Dicke had proved almost as much of a disappointment to Edwina as Kamala had to Jawahar, though not in the same ways, of course. Each of them long looked elsewhere for that friend their much-publicised marriages had failed to provide. Yet here in the viceroy's retreat beyond Simla, strolling arm in arm around those lush and glorious floral paths, they finally found each other, while India lay smoldering far below.'

For Nehru that week's retreat in May 1947 was much more than a holiday or a break in the furious pace of his work. It was his homecoming. Home to Harrow. Home to Trinity and the Cam. Home to London parties and every stroll through Hyde Park. Edwina was all those early joys and pleasures he had loved, now at last, miraculously at his side.

About Edwina's stay at Simla Patrick French writes in his Liberty or Death 'Meanwhile the Viceroy and his retinue had travelled to Simla to escape the heat. He was joined at the hill-station by Jawaharlal Nehru, with his daughter Indira, his confidant Krishna Menon, and his South Indian secretary M.O. 'Mac' Mathai. They stayed at Viceregal Lodge, and spent much of their time at 'The Retreat', a resting place at Mashobra. There was a side of Nehru that sought the approbation of the British Establishment, and the reverence of Dicke and Edwina came as more than a political boon: it was an affirmation of his own identity. Two years earlier he had been languishing in prison, and now here he was as the personal house-guest of the King's cousin. As Mathai wrote: 'One thing that I could not fail to notice was that whenever Nehru stood by the side of Lady Mountbatten, he had a sense of trimph.'

There is a story quoted by M.J. Akbar in his Nehru. 'The nearest this author has come to an answer to the Great Question is this lovely story from Russi Mody (son of Sir Homi Mody, governor of Uttar Pradesh from 1949 to 1952), who has capped a brilliant executive career as the powerful chief executive of the mammoth business empire, Tata Steel. He had met, said Russi Mody, Jawaharlal thrice - and each time Nehru did not speak a word to him. The first occasion was during a visit Nehru made to the steel factory at Jamshedpur. As a junior executive, Russi Mody stood at the bottom of the receiving line and got a silent handshake before the great man continued to the next person. The second time was during the meal that day. Nehru was sitting at the VIP table, and Russi was, along with other juniors, serving. He went up to Nehru and asked if he would like more chicken. His mouth full, Nehru nodded a silent thank-you and returned to his food. The third occasion was at Nainital, where Sir Homi Mody was governor of UP between 1949 and 1952. The Prime Ninister had come to the hills for a short holiday and was staying with the governor. Sir Homi was very pukka, and when the gong sounded at eight he instructed his son to go to the Prime Minister's bedroom and tell him dinner was ready. Russi Mody marched up, opened the door and saw Jawaharlal and Edwina in a clinch. Jawaharlal Nehru looked at Russi Mody and grimaced. Russi quickly shut the door and walked out. Once again, not a word was exchanged.'

'Be it on record that the first Prime Minister of India and the last Vicereine of India came promptly to dinner.'

In Simla after a lot of wheeling and dealing the Partition Plan was completely altered to the satisfaction of Nehru. The new draft was prepared by V.P. Menon

At 6 p.m. V. P. Menon finished the last sentence of the Draft Plan and had it snatched from his hands by Sir Eric Mieville, who was leaning over him.

Menon who now had a splitting headache, took four aspirins and went to bed. It was not until nine o'clock that evening, at a banquet at the Viceregal Lodge, that he got the first hint of the result of his labours. His wife was at one end of the receiving line when the Viceroy and Vicereine came in and he was at the other. He watched the Mountbattens make a bee-line for Mrs. Menon and warmly greet her. Then he had to wait for another five minutes, until Lady Mountbatten came up to him, gave him an affectionate peck on the cheek while she whispered in his ear:

'He accepted it, V.P.'

It had taken one man exactly four hours to draw up the Plan which was to change the face of India, and the world. So the fate of the subcontinent was SWAK (SWAK means sealed with a kiss).

The Simla Plot Summarised

According to the version given by Mountbatten and his friends, he had gone to Simla for a short rest, and had invited Nehru and Krishna Menon as his house guests for the weekend. There, on a 'hunch', he gave an advance copy of the draft of the plan to Nehru. When Nehru read it he was furious, and sent a strongly worded letter to Mountbatten. Mountbatten was stunned by the 'Nehru bombshell'. He asked V.P. Menon to draft another plan. This new plan was shown to, and approved by Nehru: it formed the basis on which India was actually partitioned.

There are far too many gaps in the story. Even so, why, one may ask, was the plan shown to Nehru, when it had not been shown to Jinnah? Was this the act of an impartial umpire? Again, where was the need to do it when Nehru had himself conveyed the Congress approval of the plan in a letter to Mountbatten on 1 May, and the Viceroy had so informed his Government? Jinnah, it was feared, might not accept the plan; and if Mountbatten feared rejection, he should have shown it to Jinnah, not Nehru. What then inspired the 'hunch' that Nehru would not like it And, if Nehru had been aware of the plan, even if he had not known all the details, why was his reaction at Simla so violent? And, if Nehru had gone back on his word, should he have been placated by withdrawal of the original plan arid substitution of another, according to his wishes? Finally, how was it that V.P. Menon was able to propose another scheme, work out its details, and write it down in legal and constitutional form and language, and hand it over, complete in all respects, in 'only two or three hours', as he claimed?

The transfer of Power documents shows that while Ismay was in London with the Mountbatten Plan, those in Simla were discussing alternative plans. Mountbatten arrived on the evening of the 6th, and on the 7th the staff meeting discussed a suggestion by Menon that, in the event of Jinnah rejecting the Mountbatten Plan, they should be ready to produce an alternative. Mountbatten agreed and ordered preparation of an alternative plan based on demission of power to the provinces, the central subjects being given to the existing Central Government.

The next day, 8 May, Nehru arrived and was present at a Staff meeting, where he unfolded a plan of his own. He proposed that power be demitted in *June* 1947 to a Central Government responsible to the Constituent Assembly; that creation of Pakistan straightaway be ruled out; that provinces may form groups, and this power may be extended to leaving the Union, but only after the principles of the Constitution had been worked out. In addition, Menon had a plan, which was officially discussed at. the Staff meeting on 10 May, when Nehru was present. This was the plan, which after 'a lengthy discussion with Vallabhbhai Patel' in 'December 1946, or early in January 1947', Menon had dictated 'in his presence.

Menon's plan had been placed before the Viceroy by Ismay on 25 April, and Mountbatten had ordered that it form an Appendix to the papers that Ismay was taking to London. Is it not extraordinary that, while pressing the British Government to quickly approve the plan that the Viceroy had drawn up after due thought and had sent to London through his Chief of Staff personally, and expecting that approval to come in a day or two, he and his staff should still be discussing that Plan, as well as considering three alternative plans?

It is interesting at this stage to compare Mountbatten's attitude towards Nehru with that towards Jinnah. Nehru, sitting in the inner circle of the Viceroy's staff, explained his own plan and commented on Menon's plan. He was shown the plan that was being examined in London, and when he objected, the plan was substituted by another, which was shown to him for approval. Jinnah, on the contrary, was not only not consulted, the Demission Plan was drawn up to threaten and blackmail him. This plan was based essentially on the long-standing Congress demand to transfer power to the majority community. Mountbatten told Nehru about it and Nehru said that 'Congress would prefer this alternative plan.' Discussing it in the Staff meeting, Mountbatten said that, in case of a boycott by

Jinnah, he would 'go ahead with the plan and allow the Congress minority to supply the voters and form the Constituent Assemblies and Ministries in the Provinces and half-Provinces in which the Muslim League boycotted the proceedings.' This would not require the agreement of the Indian leaders, and 'his present intention was to confront Mr. Jinnah with this alternative the day before the proposed meeting with Indian leaders.'

He had no alternative plan to threaten Nehru with. Jinnah was, of course, unaware of the conspiracy that was being worked out at Simla. Nor do we know all the details from the documents in *The transfer of Power*. These papers cannot tell the whole story. They are merely minutes, carefully written, of meetings, or records of notes, or copies of letters and telegrams. They do not cover the secret negotiations going on, and the understanding reached between Mountbatten and the Congress. They do, however, help in piecing together the story with whatever other information is available from other sources.

Mountbatten's great desire was to bring independent India in the Commonwealth. Today this may appear to be ridiculous: the organisation itself may seem to be a strange creature of no consequence, neither fish nor fowl, defying description. But in those days it had great prestige as an association of free nations, with common citizenship and the common link of the Crown. The Government instructions to Mountbatten were to try to keep India in the Commonwealth, and he himself was deeply attached to the idea and thought that it **would** add to the prestige of the Crown; to which he felt personal and family loyalty. From the time he came as Viceroy, he was as much concerned with the way to transfer power as with making the subcontinent retain its link with the Crown. The main hurdle in achieving this aim was the attitude of the Congress. Nehru, it may be re-called, had vehemently opposed his father's proposal to accept Dominion Status and since 1929 the Congress had become committed to 'Complete Independence'. The Constituent Assembly had adopted a resolution moved by Nehni himself that India would be an 'Independent Sovereign Republic'.

Mountbatten had been looking for a formula which would make it possible for India to stay in the Commonwealth despite that resolution, when he received a telegram from the Nawab of Bhopal on 27 March, saying that he had had a talk with Jinnah and his impression was that Jinnah could be persuaded to stay in the Commonwealth. This piece of information should have made Mountbatten very happy, but it did not. He told his Staff meeting on 28 March that 'he was not prepared to discuss this question with different parts of India.' On 9 April when Jinnah, at a meeting with him, indicated that Pakistan would stay in the Commonwealth, Mountbatten showed no enthusiasm at all. He told

Liaquat on 11 April, that he 'was not prepared even to discuss the suggestion of any part of India remaining hi the Empire unless the suggestion came from all parts together.'

To be forced to divide India was bad enough for Mountbatten, but to have Pakistan, and not India, inside the Commonwealth would be a double defeat. He was at first distressed at this development, but before long decided that it gave him an opportunity to persuade India. India should be told of the enormous advantages that Pakistan would enjoy - Pakistan would get, *inter alia*, the services of experienced civil and military officers which would be so badly needed in the initial years, but which will not be available to a country outside the Commonwealth. The British officers would organise Pakistan's armed forces into a magnificent fighting machine, and see to it that it got all the military equipment and stores; this would turn the military balance in favour of Pakistan. While casting this bait, Mountbatten would pretend that he himself and the British Government had no interest in the matter and that it was for the Congress itself to think over and decide.

Nehru dominates Simla talks

We have seen the very exclusive privilege granted to Nehru and Krishna Menon to join Mountbatten and his staff in Simla in early May 1947. Even the carefully doctored minutes of the meetings and the correspondences as available in the *Transfer of Power* documents do not really add up to the recorded history of that crucial period. The writer has not come across a single book wherein the author has bothered to meticulously sift through the records of the period. To get a clear picture of the events and to endeavour to evaluate the truth one must go through the records line by line and word by word and also to read between the lines. Nehru arrived sometime around noon on 8 May, 1947 and at 3:15 p.m. he was closeted with Mountbatten and his staff in an official meeting. Nehru dominated that meeting. It started with the question of a referendum in the

N.W.F.P. Nehru felt that there was no need for a referendum as elections had taken place only a year ago and a Congress Government returned. A referendum in the N.W.F.P. Nehru felt would result in demands for referenda from hundreds of places in India. V.P. pointed out that since Bengal and the Punjab were to be given the option of partition and then of which Constituent Assembly they would join, the latter choice would surely apply in the all-India context also to the N.W.F.P. After protracted discussions, however, Nehru conceded that a referendum would settle matters-but only if held in a peaceful atmosphere with a clear understanding on the part of the voters of the issues. As a result of the discussion, two telegrams were sent to Ismay in London. The first contained a general description of the conversation and a recommendation that HMG should insist on a referendum; **the second contained a draft which was dictated to V.P. Menon by Nehru after the meeting.** Readers should note the growing Nehru influence in the official correspondence.

Nehru then gave the outline of a plan which he considered preferable to the plan contained in the Draft Announcement. This is clear evidence that Nehru was fully aware of the contents of the Draft Plan. He called his plan "The Cabinet Mission's Plan With Modifications" and explained that it was on the following lines:

1. Power should be demitted to the Central Government in June 1947.

2. The Central Government should then be responsible to either the Constituent Assembly or the Central Legislative Assembly. He would prefer the former but realised that he latter might be easier.

3. Any suggestion that Pakistan should be created straight away should be ruled out.

4. Provinces should be given the option, as in the Cabinet Mission's Plan, of forming groups.

5. This option would later be extended to freedom to leave the Union of India altogether; but this stage would not be reached until after the principles of a new Constitution had been worked out. This would take about three months.

6. At, but not before, this stage the question of the partition of the Provinces should arise .

Wavell asked whether the League would ever enter the Constituent Assembly. Nehru replied that he had no doubt that they would if power was demitted to Central Government responsible to the Constituent Assembly. It was possible that inter-party cooperation therein would break down, but that contingency was possible at any time. Nehru, however, thought that once the principle of partition was recognised anywhere, there would be no limit. Jinnah had claimed there should be a Muslim enclave in every Province in India. Mountbatten felt he considered it essential to meet Nehru's views as far as possible.

A telegram would be sent to London expressing the hope that sufficient emphasis would be laid on the Draft Announcement of the 'Union of India'. Provinces adhering to the existing Constituent Assembly should be referred to as 'constituting the Union of India' and those which did not should be referred to as 'contracting out of the Union.' This was blatant partisanship. Mountbatten then said that it was necessary for him to emphasise that HMG were most unlikely to consent to power being transferred to any organisation in which Congress had a permanent majority, until those parts of India which did not wish to join the Union had been separated.

Nehru declared that he could say with some assurance that the Congress- majority part of India would be able to take over power almost immediately. He could not answer for the Pakistan Provinces. V.P. Menon then contended that it would be possible if Pakistan was not ready to receive power as soon as the Union of India, and if Mountbatten to continued to act as Viceroy for Pakistan and as a Constitutional governor-general for the Union. If Pakistan was not properly constituted by June 1948, full power could then be demitted to an executive by their Constituent Assembly.

That evening on 8 May, 1947, Mountbatten sent the following telegram to Ismay in London.

1. 'I would like you to distribute copies of V.C.P. 40 to the Cabinet Committee and inform them that Patel and Nehru have now themselves indicated through V.P. Menon a desire for a form of early Dominion Status (but under a more suitable name) at least until a new Constitution has been fully framed which it is unlikely to be for some considerable time after June 1948.

2. We shall spend the week-end working out details with Nehru and obtaining Patel's concurrences. A further telegram will be sent to you on Sunday.

3. If this comes off it will not only produce a sporting chance of the main Union of India remaining indefinitely in the Commonwealth; but will also get over the difficulty of Jinnah having already indicated Pakistan's insistence on not being kicked out of the Empire. It will also largely solve the problem of those Indian States which refuse to join a Constituent Assembly.

4. I know that at the time that you and Abell left it did not seem that this scheme could be pulled off but the situation has been completely changed by Patel and Nehru coming forward themselves. This is the greatest opportunity ever offered to the Empire and we must not let a administrative or other difficulties stand in the way. I rely on you both to give this your full backing.'

The above proceedings were totally conspiratorial and partisan. In the next staff meeting held on the following i.e. 9 May, 1947, Mountbatten started by saying that he considered it most desirable that if Dominion Status was to be granted to India before 1948, the grant should take place during 1947. Mountbatten also said that Krishna Menon had told him that Congress would never agree, if India was given early Dominion Status, to the splitting of the army. Krishna Menon had put forward the view that if Pakistan wanted an army it would have to be built up from nothing. Muslims would be released from the Union of the Indian army for this purpose. Mountbatten thought there would be tremendous advantage to the United Kingdom if the succeeding dominions remained in the Commonwealth. The advantages would be:

(i)   'An early transfer of power would gain her tremendous credit.

(ii)   Such a transfer would involve the termination of the present responsibilities.

(iii)   A request by India to remain in the Commonwealth would enhance British prestige enormously in the eyes of the world. This factor alone was of overriding importance.

(iv)   Such a request would be of the greatest advantage to the prestige of the present British Government in the eyes of the country.

(v)   From the point of view of Empire defence an India within the Commonwealth filled in the whole framework of world strategy; a neutral India would leave a gap which would complicate the problem enormously; a hostile India would mean that Australia and New Zealand were virtually cut off.'

Scott said that he considered it possible that Jinnah, if told of Nehru's and Patel's latest reactions, might give up his idea of a completely separate Pakistan. Scott also said that he felt that, if Jinnah was told how things were going, he might well start to think on different lines. Menon interjected by saying that if Jinnah was told at the present time, he might publish a statement which would wreck negotiations. Mountbatten said that he was considering the desirability of Sir Eric Mieville and V.P. Menon going down to Delhi to seek Patel's views at first hand. No consultations were heeded, however, with Jinnah.

Congress Conspiracy Continues

Nehru, in May 1947, as a member of the Interim Government was virtually the Prime Minister of the whole of India. Congress took full advantage of it. Mountbatten in a very exclusive meeting with Nehru in Simla on 9 May, 1947, raised the question of the appointment of ambassadors, governors, etc. He told Nehru that Nehru should not continue to make these appointments, as was being done on an *ad hoc* basis, but should make out a full list of the posts to be filled and the names of those to be appointed. Nehru agreed to do this. They also agreed that Nehru should go ahead with appointing representatives to foreign countries without consulting the Muslim League; Pakistan, when formed could either appoint their own, share his, or share the British representatives. This was obviously a very partisan advice.

Mountbatten asked Nehru what he thought of the plan for transferring power on a Dominion Status basis in 1947. Mountbatten pointed out that it was entirely up to Nehru whether or not he wanted to go ahead with this plan; the advantages were almost entirely on Nehru's side. Nehru said he was most interested in the plan but pointed out that he could not rush his supporters on any suggestion of long-term Dominion Status. Everything depended on the interim period and the way the British behaved.

Nehru thought that V.P. Menon had the timing of this scheme absolutely wrong. In Nehru's opinion the constitution would be finished by September; the new government would be ready to take office by October; elections would be held by then too; and the whole process would be over by the end of the year. In view of the fact that Nehru thought that it was such a simple problem and as his views on the time factor was so very different to Menon's Mountbatten decided to have a meeting with them both the following day. The conspiracy continued. While Nehru was busy wooing Edwina and Mountbatten in Simla, Patel was busy using pressure tactics in Delhi:

Patel, Home Member in the Interim Government, in an interview with the Associated Press of America at New Delhi on May 9th, declared that the current British policy of "remaining neutral, but holding power is a way of propagating civil war," and asserted that India's political impasse would be broken at once if power were transferred to the Central Government "as it now stands," and with "the Viceroy standing out." The functioning of India's Interim Government as a dominion government "with the Viceroy standing out", he added, would have two immediate results.

'Firstly, there would be peace in the country within a week. Those who commit acts of violence do so because they feel there is no strong central power to check them. With dominion functions, the central Government would form a strong centre and would have the necessary power to put down disorder.'

'Secondly, lacking interference by a third party to whom either side could appeal, Congress and the Muslim League would settle their differences at once. If there were conflicts in the Cabinet on any question, the majority would rule.'

Patel characterised the present situation in India as serious and said one of the grave problems was of the private armies now being raised and equipped. As an alternative in the event that the British decided that India must be divided, Patel suggested that power should be transferred to the Constituent Assemblies, saying that the Muslim League already had separate Constituent Assembly in the members elected to the Assembly they have consistently boycotted.

"The other way is much easier," he added, "transfer power to the Central Government, let the Viceroy stand out and not interfere. Then you have a strong centre which would be capable of dealing with the problems facing the country, particularly in such places as the Punjab and the North-West Frontier Province. Immediately there would be peace in the country.

Patel reiterated that Congress stood by the Statement of May 16th "*in toto*" and "in spite of its weakness." Congress would like to have a strong centre. Apart from external troubles, it was absolutely essential that there should be a strong army, and for defence a strong central government. This was a reference to the Cabinet Mission Plan which the Congress had actually rejected giving rise to Jinnah's Direct Action.

'The Congress position has always been that it will not coerce any group or area which does not want to remain. At the same time, it will not be coerced by any group or community. Therefore, if the Muslim League insists it wants separation, then Congress will not compel them to remain by force. But it will result in dividing Bengal and the Punjab. Otherwise coercion would come in. Non-Muslims would be forced into Pakistan and there would be civil war.'

Patel remarked: "It is a dangerous game which Mr. Jinnah is playing." He said except for the League's temporary acceptance of the Cabinet Mission's plan, Jinnah's position has remained the same. "We asked him to refer the question to the United Nations Organisation; he said 'No'. We asked him to arbitrate; he said 'No'."

Obviously, Patel was giving Congress interpretation of event.

Let us, at this stage, turn our attention to the position of the Princely States in May 1947. It may be noted that the Cabinet Mission Plan had made a statement on 12 May, 1946, on the States' Treaties and Paramountcy with the prospect of partition in mind and that its terms still held good. In particular, it was up to the States to negotiate with British India for the future regulation of matters of common concern. The States had however made little or no progress in this direction because they had been waiting to know to whom power would be demitted in British India. The Draft Announcement (Mountbatten Plan) for handing over power, however, contained the guidance they required. Sir Conrad Corfield, the Crown's representative dealing with the States' affairs felt that the existing policy of withdrawing first Political Agents and then Residents, leaving by about March 1948 no more than a nucleus at department headquarters.

In early May 1947 the British government agreed that this procedure was right and in accordance with Prime Minister Attlee's statement of 20 February, 1947.

Nehru disliked this procedure of retraction and argued that since the structure of Paramountcy was built up between the States and the Governor-General in Council, successor Indian governments should inherit the whole nexus of agreements with the States. The British government, however, at that time did not agree with this policy as it thought the agreements were between the Crown and the States. Up to the 1935 act, the Crown used the Viceroy as agent. That

act created the Crown representative as the Crown's agent. The government of British India did not come into the picture. Nehru was in fact anxious for

H.M.G. to do what they had categorically refused to do, viz. transfer Paramountcy to a successor government. Since the 635 States were strewn all over India, arrangements in regard to e.g. posts, telegraphs, railways, etc. should exist between the States and the rest of India.

H.M.G's thinking at this stage was that there could be no question of legislating to transfer the Crown representative's powers to a successor government. Legislation would do no more than abolish the Crown representative, and his abolition would automatically result in the voiding of Paramountcy and of any agreements between the Crown and the States. New arrangements would have to be made between the new parties.

At that time most of the Princely States were under the impression that with the lapse of Paramountcy power will vest in the States thereby becoming independent. The Chamber of Princes which was a sort of a trade union of the Princes, was split. Many were under the influence of Congress and subject to agitational movements in their States. H.M.G. had no clear-cut policy about the future of the States. It was a very complex situation. It will be seen however when we look at the fate of the Princely States that they got a very raw deal from Mountbatten. States like Hyderabad and Travancore had openly declared their intention to be independent of an Indian Union or Union, and desired to negotiate a special relationship with the U.K. after the transfer of power.

The Moment of Betrayal

Early morning on 10th May, 1947, Mountbatten received the finally approved Partition Plan. We have already seen the main features of the Plan. It will be recalled that Mountbatten had already issued invitation letters to the Congress and League leaders to assemble in Delhi on 17 May, 1947 to approve the Plan. Let us now look at Mountbatten's own version as to how he showed the Plan to Nehru.

'While we were at Simla, London started telegraphing amendments to the plan. They couldn't resist not picking and altering, exactly like the old days. So by the time they'd finished, the plan did not look the same as it had when I started, although in retrospect I am bound to agree that they had not made any changes of substance. Because it no longer had the same presentation that I had worked out with the leaders, I was worried. I said, "I have an uneasy feeling that this may not be acceptable." They'd never seen the old plan, but at least they'd known the words I'd used, and now the words had changes, the presentation was different.'

'And I had a meeting with the staff. Now, the staff I'd brought up were V.P. Menon, whom I always took everywhere, Alan Campbell-Johnson and Ronnie Brockman. Anyway, I had quite a high-powered staff of five or six, and I said, "I'm worried about this. I don't like the way the plan is presented now, I don't like to table this without having tried it over. Now time doesn't admit of suddenly having all the leaders up here, or going down and having a formal meeting, and I don't want a formal meeting. I think I'll try it on Nehru and Krishna Menon."'

'"Oh," they said, "this is absolutely out of the question. This would be a breach of faith. If it were known that you'd shown it to them, and it leaked, this would be sufficient for Jinnah to say no, for Baldev to say no; even the Congress Party might go back on Nehru. This undermines the whole principle, it comes back to secret diplomacy instead of honest, open candour."'

'And so we sat for a long while, and I said, "I'm very sorry, I think you're absolutely right. But I have a hunch that I must show it to Nehru and that he's not going to like it."'

They said, "That's even worse, then it wouldn't matter so much if he just liked it, but this... How are you going to handle that?"'

'I said, "I'll handle that when I get to it. I'm going to show it to him."'

'And if I remember right, I told Nehru and Krishna Menon that I had now had a copy amended from Whitehall – though they'd never seen the original they had known its general contents – I now wanted them to see how it had been presented. Nehru took it away to read that night, and the next day I thought he was going to explode; he was white with rage.'

'From memory, I think it happened in the room in which I'd had my meetings. He just came in and I gave him the report and gave a bit of an explanation. He left and went into his room to study it. When I next saw him, he was white with rage. You know, he used to get these tantrums, having been in prison. He took a long while to control himself. I spent hours trying to help him to collect himself together. By the time I left him he had absolutely recovered.'

'He said, "This is absolutely unacceptable, this is the Balkanisation of India, this is exactly what we don't want to present." He went on and on and on, and Krishna Menon apparently went along with him.'

'In my recollection, I then brought the staff in, whose reaction was not, how lucky that it worked. This is the fruit of not taking our advice, you see, you've now got yourself into a jam because, now, he's rejected it, and what are we going to do? Are we now going to call all the leaders together?'

Just for record the letter which Nehru wrote to Mountbatten on 11 My, 1947 after reading the Plan is reproduced:

Dear Lord Mountbatten,

'You were good enough to speak to me frankly and in a very friendly manner last night and to give me an opportunity to see the tentative proposals. I need hardly tell you how much I appreciate you confidence in me or that I am convinced of your earnest desire to help India to achieve her freedom as early as possible. It has been a privilege to get to know you better and I hope that our understanding of each other will be helpful to both and to the wider causes we have at heart.'

'I read the draft proposals you gave me with care they deserved and with every desire to absorb them and accept them in so far as I could. But with all the goodwill in the world I reacted to them very strongly. Indeed they produced a devastating effect upon me. The relatively simple proposals that we had previously discussed now appeared, in the garb that H.M.G. had provided for them, in an entirely new context which gave them an ominous meaning. The whole approach was completely different from what ours had been and the picture of India that emerged frightened me. In fact much that we had done so far was undermined and the Cabinet Mission's scheme and subsequent developments were set aside, and an entirely new picture presented – a picture of fragmentation and conflict and disorder, and, unhappily also, of a worsening of relations between India and Britain. That, I am wholly convinced, was not and is not your intention; nor can I believe that this is H.M.G.'s intention, But H.M.G. seems to function in an ivory tower of their own isolated from realities in India. They proceed apparently on certain assumptions which have little relevance and ignore the basic factors of the situation in India.'

'If my reactions were so powerful, you can well imagine what my colleagues and others will think and feel. I think it will be a disaster if something is done now which will dam up the river of progressively friendly relations between Britain and India and reverse its current.'

'I have written rather hastily a note on the tentative proposals. This is necessarily rather crude as I am in a hurry to let you know how I feel about it all. I tried to make the note brief but it lengthened itself. As soon as it is ready I shall send it to you. Meanwhile I am sending this letter to you to give you some indication of how upset I have been by these proposals which, I am convinced, will be resented and bitterly disliked all over the country.'

Yours Sincerely, 'Jawaharlal Nehru

Records Don't Add Up

The only records that exists which give a first-hand account of events of early May 1947 in Simla are the *Transfer of Power* documents published by the British Government, *Mission With Mountbatten* by Mountbatten's Press Secretary Alan Campbell-Johnson and *Transfer of Power in India* by V.P. Menon. Any analysis of the happenings of that crucial week in May 1947 will inevitably depend on an in depth study of these documents. It is interesting to note that the accounts are quite conflicting even in the limited sources that are available leaving considerable room for conjecture. One therefore has to piece together the story.

On the night of 10 May Lord Mountbatten showed Nehru the plan as he had received it from London. Nehru tuned it down most vehemently and made it clear that the Congress would in no circumstances accept it. V.P. Menon states in his *Transfer of Power*: 'When I saw Nehru on the morning of the 11th, I found that his usual charm and smile had deserted him and that he was obviously upset. I was not aware that Lord Mountbatten had actually shown him the plan but Nehru told me that he had seen it and that its whole approach was wrong. He said that up to the time of the Statement of 20 February the approach had been on the basis of a Union of India. But the draft plan was from the wrong end, that is to say, it encouraged units to cut adrift from the Union and the States to stand out. He did not like the provision as to Baluchistan, nor did he like the paragraph relating to the North-West Frontier Province. I told him that I myself did not like the plan, but that I was sure we could find a new approach. He was too agitated however to listen to me.' The following accounts, however, do not corroborate Nehru's observations.

In the Staff Meeting early morning on 11 May, 1947, Mountbatten informed his team that he had received a most disturbing letter that morning from Nehru who reacted very strongly against the Draft

Announcement of the Plan which he had shown him the previous night. Jenkins, Governor of Punjab, said that he considered that Nehru was reacting to the pressure of Hindu opinion to which all the Congress leaders were very sensitive.

They were all, according to Jenkins, no more than revolutionary agitators in different ways. Jenkins further stated that if the leaders of all parties agreed to carry out the Plan as envisaged in the Draft Announcement, he would summon all the Punjab Party leaders and try to induce them to form a coalition government. Alternatively, separate governments would have to be formed on a zonal basis, but this would be much more complicated. He emphasised that if the Plan in the Draft Announcement was agreed to by the Indian leaders and the partition of the Punjab resulted, it would be a great disaster for the Punjab.

In a later Staff Meeting the same day, where Nehru was present, Mountbatten recalled that Jinnah had originally claimed the whole of Punjab in which there was a slight overall Muslim majority for Pakistan. Sikhs had then started a demand for partition and Congress had agreed to support this demand. Mountbatten contended this support was based on the principle that no districts in which non-Muslims predominated should go to Pakistan. Nehru agreed that this was the rough basis of Congress' support.

Mountbatten explained that he had spoken to Nehru before the meeting concerning the possible rejection of the Plan in the Draft Announcement. He had told Nehru that if the Muslim League did not accept it, the alternative to be put before them would be the demission of power to an united India on a Dominion status basis, and on the understanding that there would be safeguards which would allow Jinnah to form his Pakistan later. Mountbatten stated that Nehru had told him that Congress would prefer this alternative plan. But he (Mountbatten) very much doubted that H.M.G. would allow him to impose it if Jinnah accepted the plan in the Draft Announcement.

The Muslims would feel that they would be out-voted on every count. The great attraction to him was that it would enable the Indians to settle their own problems among themselves. But he was bound to ensure that the Muslim League were given at least a fair chance. Jinnah was reportedly saying that he did not trust Congress but Mountbatten felt that the Congress leaders would be much more inclined to make concessions themselves in order to avoid war than to see him make them.

Nehru agreed with this last point. He said that it was only human nature that it should be so. He pointed out that giving in to Jinnah in the past had not led to agreement but to further demands. The alternatives were settlement and conflict. So far there had not been an element of compulsion one way or the other. If the Indian leaders were left to deal with each other without outside interference, there would be a strong compulsion to come to terms.

Mountbatten said that Nehru had stated that if power was demitted to the Interim Government on a Dominion status basis, Congress would publicly announce safeguards for the Muslim League. Assistance would be given to those areas which did not want to stay in the Union of India to get out. Assistance would be given towards the setting up of Pakistan if this was wanted. But these safeguards were based on Congress' stated word. Jinnah would surely not accept this.

Nehru said that he believed that once these safeguards were publicly announced, it would be physically impossible to go against them.

In a later meeting the same day Mountbatten said that he had that morning received a letter from Nehru containing very considerable objections to the Plan as contained in the Draft Announcement, a copy of which he had shown to Nehru the previous night. He explained that he had been under the impression that there had been a large measure of agreement by both sides to this Plan. Jinnah had never actually accepted it but had implied acceptance. The views of Nehru and Patel, Jinnah and Liaquat had been obtained at a series of meetings with the Viceroy, Lord Ismay, Sir Eric Mieville and Abell. Sir Eric Mieville had then taken the draft of the Plan round to Nehru and to Jinnah. The present draft did not differ in essentials from that.

Nehru claimed that the draft which Sir Eric Mieville had shown him had been rough; that it had dealt mainly with the Partition of Bengal and the Punjab; and that it had consisted of only one-and-a-half pages. He stated that he had at that time criticised certain parts of the draft, particularly in connection with Baluchistan and the N.W.F.P.

Sir Eric Mieville agreed with this latter point; but he made it absolutely clear that the draft which he had shown Nehru was the full draft of the whole Plan.

Mountbatten went on to say that, after Nehru and Jinnah had seen the draft announcement, Lord Ismay had gone to London with instructions to say that nothing had been agreed to in writing by the Indian leaders, but that the draft represented in Mountbatten's considered opinion what the leaders had implied that they would accept. Therefore, he had been extremely surprised at receiving Nehru's letter that morning.

V.P. Menon records in *his Transfer of Power*: 'While I was still with Nehru an urgent summons came for me from Lord Mountbatten, and I went across immediately to see him. He told me that he had shown the draft plan to Nehru and he was not sorry that he had done so. The consequences would have been disastrous if he had followed up his programmeme for a conference of party leaders. In doing so he would have completely misled His Majesty's Government, which had been under the impression till then that Nehru would accept the plan. The problem was how best to retrieve the situation. I told the Viceroy what had taken place at my further meeting with Nehru and suggested that the most promising line of action was to proceed on the basis of my plan. The transfer of power to two central Governments on the basis of Dominion Status was a proposition that was likely to be accepted by the Congress as it would ensure an early demission of power. The only question was whether Jinnah Would accept a truncated Pakistan. But Jinnah knew that Gandhiji was opposed to any division of the country and that the Congress would not possibly agree to let him have areas in which non-Muslims were in a majority. I reminded Lord Mountbatten that he himself had gained the impression that Jinnah was reconciled to the idea of the partition of the Punjab and Bengal; whereas the plan approved by His Majesty's Government would break up the country into several units, my plan would retain the essential unity of India while allowing those areas to secede which did not choose to remain part of it.'

Accounts of Mountbatten's discussions with his staff and V.P. Menon's narration do not really add up. It is obvious from record that other behind the scenes discussions have gone unrecorded.

V.P. Completes the Plan in Two Hours?

In all the chronicles it is usually stated that V.P. Menon had drafted the Partition Plan in two hours after Nehru had rejected Mountbatten's Draft Plan. As Menon states in his *Transfer of Power in India*:

'After the meeting with Nehru I returned to my hotel. I had only two or three hours in which to prepare an alternative draft plan and I set to work on it at once. The Viceroy was anxious to show the draft to Nehru and to ascertain his reactions before he left Simla that evening, and I had barely got the draft into shape when Sir Eric Miéville came and took it away.'

Collins & Lapierre are much more lyrical in their description of V.P. Menon's feat:

'Mountbatten informed Menon that, by that evening, he would have to redraft the charter that would give India her independence. Its essential option, partition, had to remain and it must above all continue to place the responsibility for making the choice upon the Indians themselves through the vote of their provincial assemblies.'

'Menon finished his task in accordance with Mountbatten's instructions. Between lunch and dinner, he had performed a *tour de force*. The man who had begun his career as a two-finger typist culminated it by redrafting, in barely six hours on an office porch looking out on the Himalayas, a plan which was going to re-order the sub-continent and alter the map of the world.'

The facts, however, of V.P. Menon finishing the job in two hours are contradictory. V.P. being the Reforms Commissioner was deeply involved in day-to-day assignment with all constitutional, political, and geographical issues relating to the transfer of power. He had been polishing up a plan with the full concurrence of Patel from the end of 1946. The plan on the basis of which power was actually transferred in India is only marginally different from the plan which has been referred to as the 'Menon Plan' in the *Transfer of Power* documents. So as we shall see V.P. bringing out a plan out of the hat like magic seems hardly credible.

As we have seen before V.P. had been working on a Plan in collusion with Patel since late 1946. In fact, with Wavell's concurrence V.P. had been conducting some correspondence with the India Office on the issue of the transfer of power on the basis dominion status. V.P. Menon believed that if the transfer of power took place on the basis of dominion status, it would enable the Congress to have at one and at the same time a strong central government, able to withstand the centrifugal tendencies. No action, however, was taken on V.P.'s proposals which incidentally Mountbatten mentioned having seen in London before coming out to India.

Even after the arrival of Mountbatten, V.P. gave a note to Mountbatten sometime in the middle of April 1947 outlining his views (With Patel's concurrence of course) on the Partition Plan. On seeing the Plan Ismay had put it forward to Mountbatten with the following remarks:

1) 'In accordance with your instructions, I send you herewith a note on what we generally refer to as the "V.P. Menon Plan".

2) As you will see, it is a long-term plan, which cannot be put into effect until both Hindustan and Pakistan have the necessary machinery to operate it. This is not likely to be until the end of this year, even if everything goes swimmingly.'

3) We think it important that, when the time comes, the suggestion for a plan of this kind or anything like it should come from the Indian leaders themselves and should not appear to originate with us.'

Mountbatten, after seeing the Plan had noted, 'I should like the plan (amended as desired) to be typed out as an Appendix to the papers you are taking home, so that the Cabinet may be aware of its existence.'

'I take it V.P. can get Congress to put this request forward when the time comes – but if they don't we can still pin it to their existing request for interim dominion status.'

Menon's Plan had been given a proper shape and in a Top Secret memo presented to Mountbatten on 1 May, 1947.

'A METHOD OF TRANSFERRING POWER TO SUCCESSOR AUTHORITIES IN INDIA WHICH WOULD RESULT IN A FORM OF TRANSITIONAL CONSTITUTION ANALOGOUS TO THAT OF A DOMINION'

'The attached paper prepared by J.P.S.V., on the basis of a paper prepared by Rao Bahadur Menon, is circulated for information. It should be considered in conjunction with and as an Appendix to the plan contained in the draft announcement which is being sent to His Majesty's Government for approval.

V.F. ERSKINE CRUM'

'1) This note proposes for consideration a method of transferring power to successor authorities in India which would result in a form of transitional Constitution analogous to that of a Dominion.

'2) It is assumed that, initially, partition is inevitable, and that June 1948 is too early a date for the successor authorities to have completed their Constitution- making, and to have set up administrations adequate to discharge their new responsibilities in an orderly manner.'

'3) The object is, by transferring power immediately, and preserving at the same time the constitutional leadership and arbitral position of the Governor- General, to introduce a measure of gradualness and continuity during the process of transfer, to provide a breathing space for the orderly development of the necessary institutions, and to avoid too sharp a constitutional and administrative break. It is not an alternative to the plan for the exercise of a free choice by the people of India between Union and Partition, but a corollary to that plan.'

'4) The following are the main features of the proposal. H.M.G. would announce that provinces, and parts of certain provinces, should choose between Union and Partition. If the choice is for partition, one or more Constituent Assemblies, in addition to the existing Constituent Assembly, would be set up. Each Constituent Assembly would be asked to elect an *Executive Council*, responsible to the

Constituent Assembly. To these Executive Councils H.M.G. would transfer authority in their respective areas, pending the adoption of new constitution.'

'5) This would involve *amendment of the Govt. of India Act*, and its re- enactment, as amended, for as many areas as there are Constituent Assemblies. The amendments should provide for the withdrawal of the control of the Secretary of State for India, and the special powers of the Governors and of the Governor-General. There would be one Governor-General appointed by the Crown. The Governors of Provinces would be appointed by the Governor- General on the recommendation of the appropriate Executive council. The existing Indian Legislature would be abolished and its place taken by the several Constituent Assemblies, which would have power of future amendment of the Constitution Act, of issuing Orders in Council, etc.'

'6) For matters of common concern e.g. Defence, External Affairs, Communications, a *Joint Council* would be set up with an equal number of representatives nominated by each Executive Council. This Council would be presided over by the Governor-General and would decide joint policy on those subjects which would be implemented by the respective governments. But the Governor-General would have absolute discretion in all matters affecting British troops in India.'

'7) Until such time as the executive governments are ready to assume complete control over other subjects and services which are now common, or to negotiate permanent agreements in regard to them, there should be a 'standstill' agreement whereby existing administrative arrangements continued in each area with responsibility to the executive government of that area.'

'8) Similar 'standstill' agreements between Indian States and other parts of India for the continuance of existing economic and other relations should be negotiate pending more permanent agreements and definition of the relationship of States *inter se* and with the rest of India.'

'9) The transitional 'Dominion Status' would continue until and unless brought to an end by the terms of the Treaties to be concluded between Great Britain on the one hand, and the successor governments in India on the other.'

Going back to Nehru's elaborate purportedly handwritten note giving his reaction to the Cabinet approved Draft Partition Plan which runs into five pages in the *Transfer of Power* documents leaves one wondering whether it may have been pre-prepared. Some excerpts however reads 'Although I have had no opportunity of consulting my colleagues…This has become a very long note hastily prepared and yet it has not dealt fully with all the aspects of the problem.' Anyone reading it closely will surely conclude that hardly any aspect of the problem has been left out and the note appears to be well thought out, in logical order and giving a full analysis of the issues. It will be most interesting to follow the subsequent developments in the finalisation of the Partition Plan. The entire text of the note was telegraphed to London the same day it was received for circulation to the India & Burma Committee of the British government.

Mountbatten's Blatant India

The Plan which Ismay presented in London on 3 May, 1947, provided for partition, with Bengal and the Punjab having the option of being split between India and Pakistan, joining in entirety with either state, or going it alone. The position of the Princely States was left obscure, the implication being that it would be for them to decide their own future. It was inherent in such a scheme that India and Pakistan might in the end prove to be only the two largest units in a collection of more or less viable independent states. To British Ministers, committed to the precepts of self-determination, this seemed eminently proper.

Mountbatten had urged the Cabinet to consider and approve the Plan within ten days at the most. They took only a week. Such amendments as they made were mainly at the behest of the Parliamentary draftsmen who wished to clarify a few obscurities. There changes certainly made more evident the right of the different parts of India to decide their own future, but no fresh element was introduced. The only new point that appeared likely to cause disturbance was the proposal that the North-West Frontier should also be allowed to opt for independence – and to Mountbatten and his advisers it seemed that this was as likely to distress the Muslim League as Congress. 'Everything is going well at home,' reported Mieville. 'Our proposals have been generally accepted and indeed improved in many ways by the draftsmen at home.'

Philip Ziegler in his *Biography of Mountbatten* (which incidentally is a masterpiece) states:

'Nehru had "more or less accepted" the plan, said Mieville; it had been "cleared in principle", said Mountbatten. Such phrases cover limitless possibilities for misunderstanding. Mieville had seen Nehru on the afternoon of 30 April "and went through the draft statement with him", but it is not clear exactly what the statement contained, nor whether Nehru was given a chance to study a draft at leisure. It does not seem that anything on paper was left with the Congress leader and H.M. Patel, Indian representative on the Partition Council, is confident that Nehru was vouchsafed only the haziest sketch of what was in the wind. Nehru himself subsequently maintained that he had only been shown a short note dealing mainly with the partition of Bengal and Punjab.

The full truth is unlikely ever to be known, but it is painfully obvious that, given Nehru's propensity for believing what he wanted to believe and Mountbatten's for hearing what he wanted to hear, a genuine misunderstanding could easily have arisen between them. It is hard otherwise to explain V.P. Menon's conviction that Nehru would find the plan unacceptable as soon as he had been given a chance to consider it properly. Nor does Nehru's outburst to Krishna Menon suggest that he was even in part prepared for the proposals. Too much had been assumed on both sides. "It is clear the whole of this sorry postponement has been due to over-trustfulness and impatience," wrote Christie in his diary on 14 May. "The Lord needs George (Abell) or Ismay to steady him.'

On 10 May, 1947, Mountbatten's Press Secretary, Alan Campbell-Johnson, had put out the momentous communiqué announcing that the Viceroy had invited the five leaders to meet him at 10:30 A.M. and the Indian States' Representatives in the afternoon, next Saturday 17 May, 1947, the purpose being, "To present to them the Plan which His Majesty's Government has now made for the transfer of power to the Indian hands." Because of the sudden change in the Plan it became necessary to issue a second communiqué for the meeting of the Indian leaders. Alan Campbell-Johnson in his *Mission with Mountbatten* states:

'Having scratched my head over the second communiqué, I went up with Mieville to see Mountbatten in his study to discuss the publicity difficulties and dangers before us. His hair was somewhat dishevelled, but he was still marvellously resilient. He told us that only a hunch on his part had saved him from disaster. Without that hunch, "Dicke Mountbatten", he said, "would have been finished and could have packed his bag. We would have looked complete fools with the Government at home, having led them up the garden to believe that Nehru would accept the Plan." He said that most of his staff, with natural caution, had been against his running over the Plan with Nehru, but by following his hunch rather than their advice he had probably saved the day.'

'I stressed that it was out of the question for us to put out any postponement announcement without ensuring full clearance and consistency with London. After some urgent exchanges it was agreed that the announcement should read as follows: "Owing to the imminence of the Parliamentary recess in London, it has been found necessary to postpone H.E. the Viceroy's meeting with the Indian Leaders announced to begin on Saturday 17th May, until Monday 2nd June."'

'The wording of this communiqué, coming so closely upon our Press party and within twenty-four hours of our firm announcement to the world of the earlier date, has caused me more anxiety than any Press statement I have issued in the past or am likely to issue in the future. So carefully built up falling to the ground and an unrivalled feast being provided for the hungry Press speculators.'

'The weakness of our position is that at a moment of crisis we have told the truth, but it is not the whole truth and nothing but the truth. No one in Delhi is likely to believe that London was the source of the postponement, and if they do, that in itself will only help to evoke old suspicions. Everyone knows that Nehru has been staying with the Viceroy, and from the strictly Public Relations point of view I believe it would have been preferable to base the postponement on the grounds of drafting detail. However, there was certainly no time to argue out the publicity refinements of the dilemma we are in. The essence of the matter is that we have put out with the utmost speed a firm decision no less firmly postponed, and have secured London's approval for it. Textual adornments involving delay are unacceptable.'

The crucial message which endorsed the Plan Menon was telegraphed to Lord Ismay still in London on the evening of 11 May, 1947. Some excerpts 'I had a long and satisfactory meeting with Nehru, Mieville, and VP Menon yesterday (the minutes are being sent to you) on the possibility of an early transfer of power on a Dominion Status basis...

'I am convinced that in order to have the best chance of obtaining our long- term object, the grant of Dominion Status must take place during 1947.'

'The instrument under which the transfer of power would take place would be the 1935 act with certain modifications. For instance, the Secretary of State, the India Office, and the special powers of the Governor-General and the Governors would disappear. One constitutional Governor-General could serve both parts of India. Governors would be appointed by him on the recommendation of the Central Executive.

On 12 May, 1947, Mieville telegraphed to Ismay:

'We are naturally a bit rattled by Nerhu's *volte face* yesterday and can only be thankful that we did not wait until meeting of leaders to find out his attitude. I cannot help thinking that his party must have got at him. The Viceroy is now wondering more and more whether we ought not to work on the lines of trying to demit power on Dominion Status basis at an early date with Jinnah being given adequate safeguards in the interim period. What do you think?'

In a top-secret meeting on 12 May, 1947, in Simla, Mountbatten said that whereas all the Indian parties seemed to have reasonable faith in the honesty and straightforwardness of himself and his staff, there appeared to be a unanimous phobia amongst them about any document issuing from

London. Therefore, **reframing of the Draft Announcement in a way to make it acceptable to Congress would have to be done by his own staff in India**.

Another momentous decision was taken when Mountbatten directed that the Plan should be redrafted on the basis of **no option for independence being given to Bengal or any other Province**. Mountbatten said that he had the previous evening further discussed with Nehru the Plan which he had put forward for the early demission of power to the interim government on a Dominion Status basis and further stated in quite a partisan manner that this Plan was really very similar to the alternative Plan with which he had previously decided to threaten Jinnah if he did not accept the Plan WE (more about Plan WE and Plan THEY later). Mountbatten further stated that it was apparent that control of the army was going to be the most difficult issue in the transfer of power on a Dominion Status basis. It was apparent that it was Congress' idea that they should have full control of the army except on very limited subjects, for which the joint defence council would be in control.

Plan 'WE' & Plan 'THEY'

In Simla Mountbatten was told by Nehru that it would not be possible for either Mountbatten or the British as a whole, to devise an acceptable solution for India. Furthermore, if the British did give a decision and it was regarded as an award, and if bloodshed followed, not only would the British have to take the blame but also Indo-British relations would deteriorate. Nehru had expressed the view that the Indians should take the blame. Nehru had often repeated that he would be prepared to afford all manner of safeguards and assurances to the Muslim League if power was handed over to the Interim Government. Mountbatten said that Nehru's Plan might be acceptable to Jinnah if all preparations including, choice of capitals were made before it was put up to him. Simla might be loaned to Pakistan as the seat of Government as a temporary measure. Lahore might become, with the existing machinery, the seat of the Western Punjab Provincial Government. East Punjab might be amalgamated temporarily with the United Provinces. The Government of Western Bengal would presumably be at Calcutta. Dacca and Chittagong were possibilities for the Capital of Eastern Bengal.

This plan was called planned THEY as it would be the Indians who would be responsible for carrying it through. The plan in the Draft Announcement was referred to as PLAN WE.

After Mountbatten's 'hunch' and Nehru's *volte face* the Draft Announcement was proposed to be amended as follows:

The revised plan's whole object was to leave the decision-making to the Indian people themselves who would regard it as an award of H.M.G. Through the agreement of the Indian leaders to it, it will be considered as an imposition of the British, who would get the blame for any subsequent bloodshed with a consequent worsening of the Indo-British relations. The draft announcement was called "Plan WE", because it would be H.M.G. who would be responsible for putting it into action and for the consequences.

The alternative was to make the Indians really and blatantly responsible for their own future. This was called "Plan THEY".'

Mountbatten in a telegram to Ismay on 13 May, 1947, records: '4) "Plan THEY" is steadily taking shape. It is a mixture of: -

(a) The alternative with which I said intended to threaten Jinnah (see my 20-S.C. and 21-S.C. of 8th May).

(b) Gandhi's opinion (see my 40-S.C. of 10th May).

(c) My Dominion Status proposals (see my 28-S.C. of 8th May and 54-S.C. of 11th May).

(d) Suggestions which have been put forward during the last few days by Pandit Nehru, who does not believe that it is possible for me or the British as a whole to devise a peaceful solution for India.

And (e) Plan "WE".'

The salient points of the amendments to the Plan were:

It would mean the early demission of power on the basis of the 1935 Act with dominion status to the Interim Central Government and to existing Provincial Governments and the construction of Pakistan on dominion status thereafter.

It would involve as a *sine qua non* the public declaration by Congress of a number of safeguards for the Muslim League. These would include undertakings:-

- to give every facility and assistance to those areas which wished up secede from the Union of India not only to go but to set themselves up independently,

- to assist with the splitting of the armed forces and not to interfere with the use of the armed forces in the seceding areas.

- to co-operate in such procedure, for example a referendum in the N.W.F.P. and the setting-up of boundary commissions, as was necessary to ascertain the will of the people and to demarcate the areas which wished to leave. In fact the whole procedure in Plan "WE' might be handed over to the Indians to carry themselves,

- not to use the Congress majority in the Interim Government against the Muslim League.

Mountbatten further records:

'Nehru is most convincingly genuine about these safeguards. He has said time and again that, once they were announced, Congress could not conceivably disregard them; if they did, there would be the most extreme repercussions not only on world public opinion but also on India. And he honestly says that the Congress leaders would be ready to give far more away to the League if left to themselves than if under British pressure.'

'The crux is, of course, to get this across Jinnah. HE has never given any indication that he would be ready to trust Congress for one moment. But if I can get him and Nehru together I might be able to convince him. In any case, "Plan THEY" remains the only alternative if Jinnah does not accept "Plan WE'. He can have his choice. I would not, even if Congress preferred it, allow them to have "Plan THEY" if Jinnah accepted "Plan WE".

Meanwhile Prime Minister Attlee was most confused about events in India and sent a strong note to Mountbatten on 14 May, 1947:

'We were under the impression that Nehru had more or less accepted the plan that you sent home. All that we have done is to try to clarify the presentation of the case. We have made no alterations in substance, except as regards the referendum in the NWFP, which was include at your suggestion to meet Nehru's objection to a General Election. I cannot, therefore, understand what Nehru means by saying that H.M.G. "seems to function in an ivory tower of their own, isolated from realities in India", and that the "things that emerge from London are so peculiar".'

'Cabinet Committee is meeting tomorrow to consider Menon plan and the general position. It is difficult for us here to evaluate the position. I think that it would be advisable for Ismay to return to India at once in order to inform you of the views of the Government and to know your mind on recent developments. It will be desirable for him or even yourself to return here to report, but on that point I shall be glad to have your mind.'

'In order to avoid any further bombshells, Mountbatten proposed now to see Jinnah and then Nehru again privately to clear the draft as far as possible with them.'

The momentous changes made by Mountbatten in the Partition Plan were:

'I leave it to you whether or not to circulate this to Cabinet Committee now, in view of possible subsequent changes. You will note that there is no reference to Dominion status in this draft. I am dealing with this in a separate telegram.'

'4) I have following comments to offer in explanation of changes incorporated in this draft.

(a) Introduction has been recast with a view to trying to meet viewpoints both of Congress and League. We should avoid saying as has been done in both of Congress and League. We should avoid saying as has been done in Cabinet Committee draft that arrangements must be made for transfer of power to more than one authority. Our procedure is intended to find out if such a step really proves to be necessary.

(b) I have omitted para. 5 of Cabinet Committee's draft. See (c) below.

(c) The issues as you will see from para 4 of my draft are limited to joining existing Constituent Assembly or joining together in a new Constituent Assembly. I have omitted choice to Provinces for standing out independently. In principle if choice is given to one Province to stand alone we shall not be able to prevent them, but I do not now like the idea of H.M.G. giving them that choice. One of Nehru's main criticisms was that we were encouraging the Balkanisation of India. I am seeing Surhawardy on Wednesday, May 14, and will tell him that I cannot make provision in the plan for Bengal remaining independent; but that there is nothing in the plan to prevent the Bengal Legislative Assembly passing a resolution for independence which I would treat on its merits.

(d) In deference to Nehru I have omitted giving any choice to Madras, Bombay, etc. now represented in Constituent Assembly.

(e) I have omitted all provision for election of representatives on one to quarter million ratio. This will lead to absurd results particularly in Bengal where 225 members between them will have to elect 241 representatives. This principle was devised mainly for the N.W.F.P. where there is considerable weightage for minorities. Since we propose to hold referendum in that province we can safely go back to original plan whereby members of Legislative Assemblies take the decisions. In Sylhet this will produce 19 Muslim votes as against 12 General which is more advantageous to Muslims than 8:5 under Cabinet Committee draft.

(f) I have revised the para. relating to the N.W.F.P. which as it now stands will be more acceptable to Nehru.

(g) Nehru took very strong exception to the proposed procedure for ascertaining the wishes of British

Baluchistan. I am in consultation with the External Affairs Department for devising a more democratic procedure, and hope to be able to include this in the final announcement.

(h) You will see from para. 13 of my draft that we have made no arrangements for fresh elections to the Constituent Assembly in Sind and the N.W.F.P. This may not be acceptable to Jinnah but I shall point out that once he has his Pakistan he can do what he likes about his Constituent Assembly.

(i) Nehru agrees to principle of paragraph 18 but seems to think that to give such public assurances to tribes would be dangerous. I think we must keep it in.

(j) Nehru intensely dislikes the para in the Cabinet Committee's draft relating to States. He feels that as drafted it will encourage disruptive tendencies with which I agree. We must preserve the position of the States but at the same time we cannot avoid giving a lead to the Princes.'

It is obvious that Nehru and Patel and indeed all of Congress were ecstatic in having the Partition Plan draft totally accepted as per their dictates.

The Simla Plot – A Post Mortem

Once in Simla, Mountbatten and Menon had a heart-to-heart talk. Menon told the Viceroy that Patel was indeed ready to accept Dominion Status, if power was transferred in two months. Menon himself says that: 'It was at Simla that, for the first time, I had an opportunity of explaining my point of view to the Viceroy in person.' But he suddenly stops three, and does not take the reader into his confidence any further. The minutes of the Viceroy's Staff meeting on 7 May, however, mention that Menon said that, 'if the Viceroy approached Sardar Patel on the subject, he would get a positive reply. Pandit Nehru would say the same.' He also quoted another high official, Sir Chandulal Trivedi, Governor of Orissa, as suggesting that the word 'Emperor' should be dropped from the title 'King-Emperor'.

It was at the same meeting that Menon expressed the view that it was constitutionally possible for a *British* Governor-General to be responsible for the two Dominions of India. He also said that the problems of setting up an administrative machinery for Pakistan in six months were not 'insuperable'. Mountbatten then ordered Menon to prepare a paper setting out the procedure whereby a form of Dominion be given to India by *January 1948*. The next day Nehru arrived.

In the course of discussions at the Staff meeting on 8 May, Nehru urged early transfer of power –

in *June 1947* – and said that 'the Congress-majority part of India would be able to take over power almost immediately.' At this, the Constitutional Adviser said that if Pakistan was not ready to receive power, Mountbatten could 'continue as Viceroy for Pakistan and Governor-General for the Union of India.'

Menon gives no account of discussions of 7 and 8 May, except that Nehru and Krishna Menon arrived on the 8th, and the Viceroy asked him to 'discuss my plan with Nehru and find out his reactions'. 'I had discussions with him on that and the next day… I gathered the impression that he was not averse to the proposed transfer of power on the basis of Dominion Status.' Menon then mentions the Staff Conference on 10 May, *when* Mountbatten told Nehru that Menon had been working on a scheme, and asked Menon to explain it. The farce continued, and Menon 'repeated much of what I had already discussed with Nehru.'

All this points to a Congress-Mountbatten understanding having already been reached *before* Mountbatten had his 'hunch'. This was as much a part of play- acting as Nehru's fury. The stage was set by V.P. Menon telling him about the Congress conditions. All that was now required was to settle the procedure and minor points of detail and to finalise and seal the deal after Nehru's assumption; they also considered the *modus operandi* and the tactics to be employed against Jinnah. Menon does not give the date, but apparently, he talked to Mountbatten soon after his arrival on the evening of the 6th; for the meeting on 7 May not only decided on the Demission plan to threaten Jinnah, but Mountbatten is also recorded as saying that if that plan was implemented, it would be 'most highly desirable' for India to get Dominion Status 'at least six months in advance of June 1948'. At the next day's meeting Nehru was demanding that the date be advanced further to June 1947, i.e., within two months; an Menon was suggesting that if Pakistan was not ready, Mountbatten could continue to be its Viceroy.

The dramatic turn of events – the 'hunch' of Mountbatten, the angry reaction of Nehru,the hurried preparation of a new plan – are nothing but a smoke-screen to disguise the conspiracy that was hatched at Simla. We hear almost nothing about the activities at Simla of Krishna Menon, who had been discussing the Commonwealth question with Mountbatten. There is no record of the Viceroy's discussions with either Nehru or Krishna Menon, although since the day he came to New Delhi, Mountbatten had made it a habit to record such discussions immediately after every interview. We find Mountbatten becoming lyrical about the advantages *to Britain* if India stayed in the Commonwealth. These included India filling in 'the whole framework of the world strategy' on Imperial defence; 'the greatest advantage to the prestige of the present British Government; and the enormous enhancement of British prestige', 'this factor alone was of overriding importance'. At the same meeting, on 9 May, Mountbatten said: 'if Dominion Status was granted to India before June 1948, the grant should take place during 1947.' Speaking of the difficulties of quickly transferring power on the basis, Mountbatten said that 'they could be overcome in the same way' as difficulties has been overcome 'during the war'.

The same day, 9 May, Patel, whom Menon says 'I was keeping informed of the developments in Simla', issued a press statement demanding that power be transferred to the Indian Government on the basis of Dominion Status. He also assured Menon that 'there would be no difficulty in the Congress accepting Dominion Status.'

The theory advanced by an Indian historian that the original plan with Ismay had been presented with the intention that it be rejected and pave the way for the acceptance of Dominion Status, is wide of the mark. It assumes cunning on the part of Mountbatten and innocence on the part of Nehru. Actually both were co-conspirators, and each was playing his part in a put-up act. Nehru's strong reaction was unnatural for he certainly knew the basis and the main features of the Plan. On 22 April Mountbatten had discussed it in 'every respect' with Krishna Menon, who could not have failed to report it to Nehru. The details of the plan were published by the Delhi *Hindustan Times* on 3 May, and by *The Hindu* even earlier, 'almost completely.' Mountbatten himself told a Staff meeting on 3 May that 'the only Indian leaders who had seen the *full draft of the plan* were Mr. Jinnah and Pandit Nehru.' How was it, then, that the plan was shown to one of the parties again?

Actually, Mieville had gone 'through the draft statement with him' and in the Staff meeting on 11 May, after Nehru's angry letter, Mieville, in Nehru's presence, 'made it absolutely clear that the draft he had showed Pandit Nehru was the full draft of the whole plan.' Nehru had then made two small points about the NWFP and Balochistan, and had raised no objection about 'the whole approach'. Nehru's later 'forceful' reaction was supposedly caused by the part giving the provinces the right to form unions or stand alone, rather than starting with a Union and then opting to secede, as he wanted. But this was the starting point of the plan, and he could not have missed it when he went through the draft with Mieville.

Nehru tried to justify his attitude by blaming Whitehall for changes in the original draft, but these had been changes of drafting and arrangements and not of substance, as a comparison between the two document would show. Ismay rightly said in his telegram of 6 May to Mountbatten that 'substance remains same but we think you will find present considerably improved.' Mountbatten himself recorded on 15 May that 'the new draft appeared better than ours.' Nehru was never able point out any drafting change to which he took exception: and Mieville, Ismay, and even Campbell-Johnson called Nehru's act a volte-face. Volte-face it was indeed: but that was part of the deal.

The most revealing document in *The Transfer of Power*, however, is Mountbatten's telegram to Ismay of 8 May, the day Nehru arrived. It said:

'1) Patel and Nehru have now themselves indicated through V.P. Menon a desire for a form of early Dominion Status...'

and asked Ismay to circulate papers about Menon's Plan to the India Committee of the Cabinet. The telegram went on to say:

'2) We shall spend the weekend working out details with Nehru and obtaining Patel's concurrence. A further telegram will be sent to you on Sunday.'

'3) If this comes off it will not only produce a sporting chance of the main Union of India remaining indefinitely in the Commonwealth, but will also get over the difficulty of Jinnah having already indicated Pakistan's insistence on not being kicked out of the Empire. It will also largely solve the problem of those Indian States which refuse to join a Constituent Assembly.'

'4) I know that at the time that you and Abell left it did not seem that this scheme could be pulled off but the situation has completely changed by Patel and Nehru coming forward themselves. This is the greatest opportunity ever offered to the Empire and we must not let administrative or other difficulties to stand in the way. I rely on you both to give this your full backing.'

The telegram was sent in the evening of the day Nehru arrived – one day *before* Patel's statement and two days before Mountbatten's 'hunch'. It confirms that a deal was made that day. Thus the weekend was spent in working out details about the bargain, and the manner in which it was to be implemented. During the weekend Mountbatten 'made real friends with Nehru.'

CHAPTER 8: FROM PARTITION PLAN TO ACCEPTANCE

Prior Acceptance of Partition Plan

The revised final draft was telegraphed to Ismay by Mountbatten on 13 May 1947 from Simla. The plan was placed before India and Burma Committee of the British Cabinet with P.M. in the chair. After due examination of the plan it was decided to resume consideration of the revised plan when the views and intentions of the Viceroy had been further elucidated. The following day Ismay informed Mountbatten that the situation in London was so confused that it was essential either. That a Minister or Ministers should proceed to India to discuss the situation first hand or alternatively.

Mountbatten would be asked to fly home. Naturally, Ismay had strongly advised against any ministers going to India as that would have would compounded the confusion and took upon himself to inform the P.M. that Mountbatten would be opposed to the idea. The P.M., therefore, decided to ask Mountbatten to proceed to London immediately. Ismay further informed Mountbatten that should he decide to come to London the time factor and transport arrangement

General Hastings Ismay, WSC, Lord Louis Mountbatten, President Roosevelt (winstonchurchill.hillsdale.edu)

would be the decision in London would be complete by 24 May 1947 which would leave the Viceroy sufficient time to get back to New Delhi well before the meeting with the Indian leaders on 2 June 1947. The Viceroy had left his personal aircraft the York with Ismay this was to be rushed back to New Delhi to pick up Mountbatten. Mountbatten returned to New Delhi from Simla on the 14 May 1947 and the first Indian leader he met was Liaquat. On hearing that Mountbatten was flying home Liaquat heaved a sigh of relief and said "That is the only solution. I know you would have to go. When I met Muslim editors yesterday they informed me that they were certain that the reason for the postponement of the meeting of leaders was to enable you to go home". Mountbatten then asked Liaquat whether the Muslim League was going to accept partition of the Punjab and Bengal. Liaquat replied "We shall never agree to it, but you may make us bow to the inevitable".

Mountbatten then read over to Liaquat the revised plan (as concocted in Simla). Poor Liaquat was hardly aware of the goings on in Simla and background of the revisions. Mountbatten let Liaquat take away a copy explaining it was his personal copy and relied on him to show it to nobody at all, though he could discuss it with Jinnah. Mountbatten then asked Liaquat if he would like to accompany Jinnah who was coming to see him later in the day. Liaquat thought it would be better if Mountbatten saw Jinnah alone. It is well known that almost all Muslim leaders were pretty nervous in Jinnah's presence. There is no record of Mountbatten meeting Jinnah on the same day and when the two met on 17 May Liaquat was present. Meanwhile VP Menon had drafted a "Heads of Agreement" to which it was hoped to obtain the signatures of the Indian leaders. In a staff meeting held of 16 May 1947 Mountbatten said that, at his meeting the previous day Jinnah and Liaquat had refused to sign the document (Actually, no record exists of this meeting so there is no way of knowing if Mountbatten was telling the truth). Mountbatten further stated that Jinnah and Liaquat had appeared absolutely to accept the plan but not being willing to sign it. Mountbatten had even drafted a letter which he expected Jinnah to sign.

This was quite audacious on the part of Mountbatten to assume that Jinnah would sign a letter drafted by someone else. The draft "Although you cannot expect me to agree to the Partition of the Punjab and Bengal, for the reasons which I have made public, if H.M.G. rule that this is a matter which must be decided by the Provinces themselves, I give you my personal assurance that I shall accept this rule and use my best endeavors to get the Muslim League to accept it peacefully. You have asked me for an assurance that I will not allow any propaganda or activities on the part of any Muslims under my control which would tend to stir up communal strife in any part of India. My reply is that I will gladly give this assurance on the understanding that a reciprocal assurance is being given by Congress."

In the same meeting VP Menon said that he had seen Nehru and Patel that morning. The Maherajah of Patiala was lunching with Patel that day. Nehru and Patel had accepted the position in respect of the 'Heads of Agreement' but they had pointed out that there would be trouble if the League rejected the plan or accepted it as an interim agreement. Mountbatten said that he had already cautiously tried out threatening Jinnah that, unless he met the requirements adequately, power

Nehru and Sardar Patel
(Livemint.com)

would be demitted to the Interim Government on a Dominion Status basis. Jinnah had taken this very calmly and said that he could not stop such a step in any event. Mountbatten said this abnormal reaction, which was typical of Jinnah was rather disturbing. If Jinnah saw himself betrayed, he might derive great satisfaction by going down to history **as a martyr for his cause, butchered by the British on the Congress alter.** The Heads of Agreement given below:

(1) We agree to the acceptance of the draft announcement (attached) to be made by the Governor-General on behalf of H.M.G., and after it has been made we agree to recommend its ratification by the organisations which we represent.

(2) In view of the need for stabilising the political situation in the country we strongly press H.M.G. for early transfer of power on a Dominion Status basis as an interim arrangement. This transfer should take effect as soon as the final decision is known according to the procedure laid down in the draft announcement.

(3) The basis of such transfer of power should be the Govt. on India Act, 1935, with modification.

(4) In the event of the decision being taken that there should be one Central authority in India, power should be transferred to the existing Central Government.

(5) In the event of the decision being that there should be two sovereign States in India xad of one, the Executive of each area should be responsible to its respective Constituent Assembly.

(6) The Governor-General should be common to both the States. We suggest that the present Governor-General should be re-appointed.

(7) The Governors of the Provinces should be appointed on the recommendation of the respective Central Governments.

(8) When the new act comes into operation, the Armed Forces in India should be divided between the two States. The unites will be allocated according to the territorial basis of recruitment and will be under the control of the respective Governments. In the case mixed unites, the distribution should be entrusted to a committee consisting of Field- Marshal Sir Claud Auchinleck and Chief of the General Staff of the two States under the supervision of a Council consisting of the Governor-General and the two Defence Ministers. This Council will automatically cease to exist as soon as the process of division is completed.

This was a shrewd move by Mountbatten to have got full assurance from both the Indian parties that they would abide by the decision of the British Government. The plan, of course, was that of the Congress. The League was hardly given any time to study it and comprehend its implications. It will be seen later this undertaking was to prove very detrimental to the League's interests.

Suhrawardy outplayed

Muhammad Ali Jinnah, Liaquat Ali Khan, and Jawaharlal Nehru with Lord Mountbatten during a meeting

(herald.dawn.com)

While rapid developments were taking place in New Delhi and Simla they seem to have prevailed a confused situation about the future of Bengal. On 14 May, 1947, Mountbatten met Suhrawardy in New Delhi on his return from Simla. Suhrawardy informed Mountbatten that as a result of Mountbatten's meeting with him earlier, Kiran Sankar Roy and Sarat Chandra Bose they had been discussing the possibility of retaining the unity of Bengal. Suhrawardy informed Mountbatten that he had made good progress and on the whole, he was hopeful about a positive result. Mountbatten however records, 'He did not mention to me, however, that the document which Bose and Roy had handed to him, but of which I fortunately had already procured a copy myself, contained in its opening clause the words that 'Bengal was to be a Socialist Republic'.

Mountbatten challenged Suhrawardy and told him that obviously if the term 'Socialist Republic' were to be adopted now it would debar their entry into the British Commonwealth, whatever the rest of India might decide to do, and that if they wished to turn to any big power, the only one that Mountbatten could think of if they insisted on calling it a Socialist Republic would be the U.S.S.R. Mountbatten went on to say that if Bengal wished to be independent, it would be quite enough for them to call themselves **just Bengal** and if necessary, describe themselves as a 'Free State.' When Bengal would draft its constitution, they could call themselves anything they liked but calling themselves Socialists would pre-judge the situation at that stage. Mountbatten drew Suhrawardy's attention to the recent statement by Patel on Dominion Status, and suggested to him that until the situation was cleared up it seemed to him the greatest mistake possible for Bengal to call themselves a Socialist Republic.

Mountbatten went on to tell Suhrawardy that in the most recent correspondence with the British Government the suggestion was that Provinces or parts of Provinces not in Group A (of Cabinet

Mission Plan) were going to be given the option of voting for Hindustan or Pakistan and not the option of remaining independent, but if of course, the Bengal Legislative Assembly were to pass a resolution asking for independence and gave it to Suhrawardy Mountbatten would examine the proposal for further consideration.

Mountbatten told Suhrawardy that if an agreement were to be reached by the Hindus and the Muslims in Bengal on a Coalition Government, he would urge the leaders of the Congress and the Muslim League High Commands to accept it, and knew that Gandhi might help. If this were done by 2 June, 1947, he would do his utmost to obtain the agreement of the leaders that the final announcement should contain no reference to the partition of Bengal.

Mountbatten warned Suhrawardy that Nehru was not in favour of an independent Bengal unless closely linked to Hindustan, as he felt that the partition would anyhow bring East Bengal into Hindustan in a few years.

Suhrawardy continued by referring to the question that, if the word 'Socialist Republic' were cut out and Bengal asked to remain within the British Commonwealth, whether Mountbatten would be prepared to support such a proposal. Mountbatten told him that his position remained the same that under no circumstances would he recommend to the British Government that Bengal should be allowed to come into the Commonwealth unless the bulk of India were to make a similar request.

Mountbatten urged the Governor of Bengal Sir Frederick Burrows to use all his influence on Suhrawardy, Sarat Bose and Kiran Roy not to use the phrase 'Socialist Republic' or anything like it until the Constituent Assembly has met later on because it would be the greatest mistake in the light of Patel's statement on Dominion Status, for Bengal to declare itself a Socialist Republic until the situation has been cleared up and until it can be definitely seen whether the Indian Union was going to remain within the British Empire, which then seemed to be a likely eventuality.

Meanwhile more or less simultaneously Sir Frederick Burrows, Governor of Bengal, was writing to Mountbatten stating that he believed that Suhrawardy had seen the Viceroy. He stated, 'No doubt he informed you fully regarding progress of his negotiation for a sovereign, independent, but united Bengal. As you know I myself feel strongly that formation of a Coalition Government now (Which will probably have to be on some such basis as is contemplated by Suhrawardy, Kiran Sankar Roy, and Sarat Bose), offers best prospects of a peaceful transfer of power in Bengal. Indeed, if Cabinet Plan of May 1946 is not accepted I should regard this as only hope for peaceful transition.

While Burrows realised that negotiations must be conducted primarily between party leaders, the governor felt he should be in a position to help if and when help was required. To do this he must be prepared to some extent to show his hand and this obviously involve giving his blessings to the principle of an independent Bengal. The tentative Suhrawardy-Sarat Bose-Kiran Sankar Roy agreement contemplated recognition of an independent Bengal with a right, after it had been set up, to link itself with any authority that would exist in India and also to stand aloof.

A danger which Burrows foresaw was that if agreement should be reached by Congress and League in Bengal on these lines, the Provincial Parties concerned may wish to proceed on these lines in preference to Cabinet Plan for a Union of India. This would raise a difficult problem and Burrows felt that in any case his support to present tentative arrangement should be without prejudice to possibility of acceptance of Cabinet's Union of India Plan. Burrows felt however he was doubtful if Suhrawardy and Congressmen with whom he was dealing would get agreement among themselves and their parties in Bengal and with their all-India leaders in time to place an agreed plan before the Viceroy for incorporation in the scheme approved for presentation to the Indian leaders on 2 June, 1947.

On 15 May, 1947, a day after meeting Mountbatten, Suhrawardy wrote to his Private Secretary, Sir Eric Mieville. He stated:

'I hardly think it necessary for me to reiterate that it will be a most colossal mistake to partition Bengal. If, however, the mistake has to be committed, then I would like to be clear on what steps His Excellency proposes to take. Please correct me where I am wrong, even on the basis of present knowledge. I am told that in the first instance a decision of the Legislature as it exists today will be taken on the question whether Bengal should go with Group A or B or be an independent state. I suppose I could carry the resolution regarding Group B or independence by a majority. But what would be the difference in essence? If I were to carry the independence resolution, would that mean that there will be no further steps at partition? This is the first question.'

At the end of the letter he states:

'As to the possibility of an agreement meanwhile, it appears to be remote. The Hindus want to browbeat me to accept a Socialist Republic. This demand cannot be made if it is decided to keep Bengal as one and allow Bengal to frame its own constitution. If I reject this, *as indeed I must*, Mr. Sarat Bose walks out, and Mr. Kiran Sankar Roy is too weak to fight the Hindu Mahasabha which has captured the imagination of the Hindus on the score of partition.'

'Keeping in view all these factors I think it will be distinctly unfair to partition Bengal and drive Muslim Bengal to the verge of ruin. How Muslim Bengal will react in terms of violence I do not know.

I hope there will be no outbreak for as long as there is life there is hope. But I must emphatically declare that it will be criminally unfair if Calcutta is taken out of Muslim zone, which comes very near it. On one side it touches the subdivision of Baraset, where the Muslims are in a majority. There is no natural dividing line either other than the River Hooghly between the Hindu zone and the Muslim zone and this leaves Calcutta in the Muslim zone. In Calcutta and the industrial areas the Hindu majority is largely due to influx of foreign Hindu labour which it would not be fair to count. Calcutta will long remain a bone of contention and I would earnestly request His Excellency to consider that if Calcutta cannot be given to the Muslim zone it should not also be given to the Hindu zone, and Calcutta and the industrial areas round about it should be made into a free international zone.'

With the benefit of hindsight, it can be stated that all Suhrawardy's eloquence was falling on deaf ears as the blueprint for the partition of India had already been drawn in the rarefied height of Simla in early May 1947.

Draft Announcement Antics

Very soon after the return of Nehru to New Delhi from Simla on 13 May, 1947, he was arranging for Krishna Menon to depart for London in anticipation of Mountbatten's visit to London to see the Prime Minister who had urgently summoned him to clarify the confusion surrounding the Partition Plan. In a secret and personal memorandum Nehru wrote to Mountbatten 'I am trying to arrange for Krishna Menon to leave for London as soon as possible. I understand that there is a BOAC plane going tomorrow. I do not know yet if accommodation in this plane will be available or not. Krishna Menon could consult our High Commissioner in London as well as the Secretary of State for India in regard to which proposal for some kind of an Ambassador for various countries in Europe with his headquarters in London. These discussions will enable him to present a more detailed and worked-out scheme which can be considered by the Cabinet here.' Why Menon was going to London coinciding his visit with that of Mountbatten is anybody's guess.

In the same letter Nehru suggested that in Sylhet there should be some provision for a referendum at some stage or other. Nehru thought it would be fair to all parties concerned and in view of the major change involved and the balance of population there it would be desirable to have a final verdict from the people concerned. Nehru also pointed out that a small change would be necessary in regard to a predominantly Hindu Rajput area in Sind. Mountbatten replied to Nehru's letter of the same day and acknowledged the changes to the draft plan as suggested by Nehru. Mountbatten promised to look into the point about a referendum of Sylhet. Subsequently, of course a referendum did take place in Sylhet as per suggestion of Nehru. As regards Nehru's point about Sind Mountbatten thought it was not a matter for mentioning in the main statement, since it would open the way for Muslim League claims in other parts, which Jinnah had already hinted at. Mountbatten thanked Nehru for informing him about the movements of Krishna Menon.

On 17 May, 1947, Muslim League gave its comments on the Draft Announcement as compiled by Jinnah. Some of the points raised:

- League had finally and definitely decided they could not accept the Cabinet Mission's Plan of May 16, 1946.

- League could not agree that the existing Constituent Assembly should be allowed to continue because in their opinion it was *ab-initio* invalid, League wished that two independent Constituent Assemblies should be established, one for Pakistan and the other for Hindustan; all power and authority should be transferred to the Pakistan and Hindustan Constituent Assemblies.

- League vehemently opposed the partition of Bengal and the Punjab. In their opinion it could not be justified historically, economically, geographically, politically or morally.

On the same day Nehru sent a note to Mountbatten giving his comments on the Draft Announcement. Some of the points raised:

- The Congress fully accepted the Cabinet Mission Scheme of May 16, 1946, and had acted in accordance with his provisions. (It may be incidentally recalled that it was the statement of Nehru in July 1946 rejecting the Cabinet Mission Plan which sparked off the Direct Action of the League resulting in the Calcutta debacle in August 1946).

- Apart from minor comments Congress accepted the Draft Announcement.

Mountbatten met both Jinnah and Liaquat on the same day that is 17 May in the evening. Mountbatten said that he intended to recommend to HMG that the Transfer of Power in India should take place as soon as possible – preferably by 1st October. He had informed the Prime Minister of Jinnah's expressed desire that Pakistan should remain within the British Commonwealth. Congress had now put forward a similar request. Mountbatten intended to go ahead and pass both requests to HMG. The question which now required clarification was whether Jinnah would refer Pakistan to have its own Governor-General or to share a common Governor-General with Hindustan. He asked for Jinnah's personal views.

Jinnah said that he could not commit himself on this subject straightaway; but he had been giving some thought to it and he felt that it would be better to have two Governors-General. Also there should, in his opinion, be a Representative of the Crown to be responsible for the division of the assets as between the two states. Jinnah said that he was extremely keen that Mountbatten should fill this post. He said that he had complete faith in Mountbatten, all of whose awards would be binding on him. Jinnah vehemently and repeatedly declared his desire that Mountbatten should stay on in India. Mountbatten replied that he was very honoured by Jinnah's remarks. However, he could not consider taking on a post such as the one Jinnah had suggested nor could he think of anybody else who would wish to do so. It would be an impossible position if the so-called 'arbitrator' was junior in rank to the Governors-General who would be King's representatives (Mountbatten was, of course, always eyeing the post of the Governor-General of both the countries).

Liaquat asked how if the two states wanted separate Governors-General it was proposed that all assets would be divided by 1ˢᵗ October. Mountbatten replied that in this case that the two Governors-General themselves would form an arbitration board. He went on to say that he was under extreme pressure from Congress who had stated that they would not continue in the Interim Government unless they were granted Dominion Status immediately after the announcement. Mountbatten felt that he might be able to hold the situation for a time but certainly not until the end of the year.

After further discussion Mountbatten suggested that Jinnah should send him a letter the following Monday (19ᵗʰ May) giving a full description of his suggestion of a supreme arbitrator and two Governors-General. However, he wished it to be quite clear that he would reserve his personal position unless it was clearly stated by Jinnah in this letter that, if his scheme was found by HMG to be impracticable, he would accept, as a less desirable alternative and as an Interim measure, the appointment of a common Governor-General between the two states. Jinnah at first expressed himself violently opposed to this suggestion but eventually, after prolonged discussion he said that he would think it over. He pointed out that, if HMG decided, contrary to his opinion, that his suggestion was unworkable, there would be no reason for him not to accept an alternative.

It was agreed that Jinnah should give this letter to Sir Eric Mieville on 19 May and that a copy of it would be sent to the Congress. Mountbatten pointed out that besides requiring the approval of HMG, Jinnah's suggestion would also require agreement by Congress. Liaquat stated that the name of the Muslim state to be set up would definitely be Pakistan. Jinnah explained the derivation of the word – P for Punjab; a for Afghan (i.e. Pathan or NWFP.); K for Kashmir; I for nothing because this letter was not in the word in Urdu; S for Sind and TAN for the last syllable of Baluchistan. Liaquat said the literal meaning of Pakistan was "pure land."

As to the explanation of the acronym it can be seen that it did not include Bengal which had more than half the population of this country; it included Kashmir which opted for India; and Afghanistan is not a part of Pakistan. Therefore, the word Pakistan appears to be most inappropriate. After due consultation with the parties a revised draft announcement was prepared and taken to London on 18 May, 1947. On 20 May Sir Eric Mieville on

(L to R): Jinnah, Baldev Singh, Frederick Pethick-Lawrence, 1st Baron Pethick-Lawrence, Nehru, Krishna Menon (npg.org.uk)

Mountbatten's instructions sent copies of this revised draft announcement to Nehru, Jinnah, Liaquat, and Baldev Singh. It is interesting to see an appendix to the announcement.

'Muslim majority districts of Punjab and Bengal according to 1941 census.

1. *The Punjab*

Lahore Division. Gujranwala, Gurdaspur, Lahore, Sheikhupura, Sialkot. *Rawalpindi Division.* Attock, Gujrat, Jhelum, Minawali, Rawalpindi, Shahpur. *Multan Division.* Dera Ghazi Khan, Jhang, Lyallpur, Montgomery, Multan, Muzaffargarh.'

'2. *Bengal. Chittagong Division.* Chittagong, Noakhali, Tippera.

Dacca Division. Bakarganj, Dacca, Faridpur, Mymensingh. *Presidency Division.* Jessore, Murshidabad, Nadia *Rajshahi Division.* Bogra, Dinajpur, Malda, Pabna, Rahshahi, Rangpur.'

It can be seen that many districts earmarked for Pakistan were ultimately excluded by Radcliff's boundary commission.

Burrows' Efforts to Keep Bengal Independent

On 17 May, 1947, the Secretary of State for India Lord Listowel circulated a memorandum of Draft Statement Policy for consideration on Mountbatten's arrival a revised version of the Viceroy's latest draft. Among other points noted:

'(a) The arguments for giving an option to remain united to Bengal are: -

i)   With or without Sylhet, Bengal is large enough to form an independent state.

ii)   In any event Bengal, if it does not adhere to Hindustan, will be in effect a separate state even though politically linked with North-Western Pakistan. To give the option in this case does not therefore open us to the charge of balkanisation.

iii) Partition would be most damaging to the inhabitants of Bengal owing to the economic consequences of separating a large part of the hinterland from Calcutta.'

It appears that at the highest level of the British Government there still prevailed some enlightened appreciation of the Bengal situation as compared to Mountbatten's anti-independent Bengal stance. Just before his departure for his final round of discussions with the British Cabinet Mountbatten wrote to Sir Frederick Burrows, Governor of Bengal.

'My talks with Nehru at Simla let me to believe that it is extremely unlikely that the Congress High Command will accept an independent Bengal or allow their followers to support such a proposal, as their view is that Bengal has no future except in Hindustan; but I do not mean by this meet I should wish Suhrawardy to abandon his efforts for unity.'

In the crucial meeting of the India and Burma Committee held on 19 May, 1947, chaired by Prime Minister Attlee in which Mountbatten was present Bengal was discussed. Mountbatten informed the meeting that the Bengal Governor was anxious that the Province should not be partitioned; Suhrawardy thought that it might be kept united on the basis of joint electorates and a Coalition Government. Jinnah considered that, with its Muslim majority, an independent Bengal would be a sort of subsidiary Pakistan and was therefore to agree to Suhrawardy's plan. Congress might also agree, but only on condition that Bengal did not form part of Pakistan and that special arrangements, which were unlikely to be acceptable to the Muslims, were made with the Central Government of Hindustan. They were opposed to Jinnah's proposal that Calcutta should become a free city as they believed that, without Calcutta, Eastern Bengal might well, with 2 or 3 years, rejoin western part of the Province. Mountbatten had informed the parties that if, before 2 June, 1947, they were able to reach some agreement between themselves as to the future of the Province, he would embody such an agreement in the statement.

On 19 May, 1947, Governor of Bengal Sir Frederick Burrows cabled to Mountbatten in London.

The gist of his cable was that it contained a memorandum by Congress and League on independent Bengal:

Burrows reported that the trend of discussions among the League and Congress leaders was satisfactory and there was agreement in which Sarat Bose agreed to drop the proposed name 'Socialist Republic of Bengal' in favour of 'The Free State of Bengal.'

Burrows was impressed by the urgency of an immediate agreement if the British Government was to avoid reference to a possibility of partition of Bengal in proposals to be laid before Indian Leaders on June 2nd and he had therefore discussed with Suhrawardy and Kiran Sankar Roy separately a new approach, namely, that their present attempts to settle the broad outlines of future constitution of Bengal and its links, if any, with rest of India as basis of a coalition should be reversed and that immediate steps be taken to form a coalition for Bengal at once, before content and text of Viceroy's paper of June 2nd are irrevocably settled, leaving these matters to be thrashed out in the coalition of the Bengal Constituent Assembly later. Burrows believed that when faced with formation of such a coalition in Bengal neither the high command of Congress could repudiate it and that there were advantages in setting out to frame a constitution for free state of Bengal untrammeled by conditions such as those set out in Sarat Bose's list of points. Suhrawardy agreed and said he thought he could persuade his party and Jinnah to accept this solution. Kiran Sankar Roy also gave Burrows his personal but very cordial agreement both as regards the line of action and to proposition that nothing else would avert bloodshed now or at all events after the British left. Kiran Sankar Roy was meeting representatives of his party and Sarat Bose that evening and would put the matter to them. Suhrawardy had made it plain to Burrows that success of proposal, from his point of view, depended entirely on his ability to assure his party that formation of a coalition then would avert any reference to partition of Bengal in statement of June 2nd.

As a result of the Governor's talks he had great hopes of forming a Coalition Ministry. If that could be assured in time he hopes it would be possible for H.M.G.

(i)   to omit any reference in statement to be made on June 2nd to possibility that Bengal may be partitioned and

(ii)   to omit any reference to ultimate or constitutional connections of future Bengal, tacitly leaving these to Bengal Constituent Assembly which Coalition Cabinet would get elected.

Mountbatten in his letter of 16 May, 1947, to Burrows had remarked that "Bengal is going to be a difficult case to fit into the new plan." Burrows hope that solution on lines described above may assist but in any case, he advocated it on its own merit and as a means, perhaps the only means, of averting grave disorders in Bengal. Burrows was not aware of form the statement of June 2nd may then take but if reference to Bengal could be restricted to something on the following lines, it would meet wishes of leaders he had consulted and avoid immediate risks of a conflagration. Formula he suggested was "In Bengal where two major parties have recently agreed to form a Coalition Ministry a separate Constituent Assembly will be elected to draft the future constitution.

Memorandum submitted by the League and Congress leaders

1. Bengal to be a free independent State. The Free State of Bengal will decide its relations with rest of India.

2. It is agreed that constitution of Bengal will provide for elections to Bengal Legislature on the basis of joint electorate with reservation of seats proportionate to population among Hindus and Moslems. (The seats as between Hindus and Scheduled Castes will be distributed among them in order to give to Scheduled Castes their existing proportion). The constituencies will be multiple constituencies and votes will be distributive and not cumulative. A candidate who gets majority of votes will be distributive and not cumulative. A candidate who gets majority of votes of his own community cast during elections 25% of votes of other communities so cast will be declared elected. If no candidate satisfies these conditions, that candidate who gets largest number of votes of his own community will be elected. The franchise should be as wide as possible and should ultimately be adult franchise. In the case of women the franchise would be restricted on property qualification basis as at present for next 10 years.

3. On announcement that proposal of Free State of Bengal has been accepted and that Bengal will not be partitioned, the present Bengal Ministry will be dissolved and a new Ministry brought into being consisting of an equal number of Moslems and Hindus (including Scheduled Caste Hindus) but excluding the Chief Minister. In this Ministry and Chief Minister will be a Moslem and Home Minister *a Hindu*.

4. Pending the final emergence of a Legislature and a Ministry under new constitution the Hindus (including the Scheduled Caste Hindus) and Moslems will have an equal share in Services including Military and Police. The Services will be manned by Bengalis.

5. A Constituent Assembly composed of 30 persons, 16 Moslems and 14 Hindus, will be elected by the Moslem and non-Moslem members of Legislature or by Moslem League and Congress respectively. Power will be transferred to this Constituent Assembly on or before June 1948. Alternatively, the persons already elected to the Constituent Assembly from Bengal Legislature will form the Constituent Assembly of Free State of Bengal.

It can be seen that Sir Frederick Burrows, the Governor of Bengal, made Herculean effort to keep Bengal united and independent. Jinnah and the League had given wholehearted support to the idea. Burrows had a very intimate and a close appreciation of the situation prevailing in Bengal from the British point of view. This was supported by London but all his efforts were rendered fruitless. It was the machinations of Patel, Nehru, and Gandhi that frustrated this magnificent initiative. Only history can tell whether the people of Bengal would have been better off within an independent Bengal or be partitioned and become parts of two states.

Mountbatten Triumphs in London

The Mountbattens left New Delhi on Sunday 18 May, 1947 for London. Mountbatten took with him V.P. Menon and Erskine Crum, his conference secretary. V.P., after all his efforts at Simla, was then in the ascendant and enjoyed Mountbatten's complete confidence. Mountbatten was overpowered by V.P.'s drafting skills and political flair and of course his connection with Patel. V.P.'s position as a member of the Viceroy staff was one of considerable delicacy, but his skill as a rapporteur and mediator was formidable.

Mountbatten had been at great pains to make that flight, one of the fastest India-to-England flights. He was traveling in his wartime York MW 102, which was especially flown back from London to take the Mountbattens to England. The York was especially fitted with long range tanks and was using double crews. They touched down only twice, at Mauripur (in Karachi) and Fayed (in Egypt) before reaching Northolt at 10:30 the following morning, in a little more than 24 flying hours.

The day Mountbatten reached London, he attended the India and Burma Committee meeting of the cabinet chaired by Prime Minister Attlee. At the Prime Minister's request, he informed the Committee of the latest developments in his discussions with Indian political leaders on his proposal for arranging for the transfer of power in India. We have already seen at length the changes Mountbatten had made to the draft that had already been approved by the cabinet earlier. Mountbatten's amended draft was accepted by the cabinet in totality. Let us see Mountbatten's own comments on the presentation of his case before the India and Burma committee. Modesty, not being one of his strong points, he states:

"And, all the way through, I said how lucky they were- you see, I made no apology at all. I turned them inside out, I gave them no apology, nor any explanations. I simply said we had to work fast and at this rate. I think I had complete control, the whole Cabinet just listened. Nobody argued with me at all.

I had as great control over the Cabinet as I had over the leaders in India at that time, and I had the most frightful, not so much conceit, but a complete and absolute belief that it all depended on me, and they had to do what I said or else...

So, I had no difficulty at all. I can remember not feeling the least bit worried. I had convinced myself that they were lucky that this had happened, and I was going to tell them how lucky they were. The point is I'd been given this job, and I knew that they thought it was very difficult to pull off. They had no option but to follow me, and Lord Ismay said to me, 'They're pretty hopping mad with you, they don't know what you're doing. I don't know that you expect me to do; you've played fast and loose with me, you've sent off on a wild-goose chase.' He was very angry with me when he saw me, and he said, 'You'll find it very difficult.'

'Pug,' I said, 'I'm not in the least worried. They're so lucky this has happened.' And I went in, and I remember his saying afterwards, 'Honestly, I've seen a few performances, but what you've done to the people over here beats anything you've done in India' I mean, they were bewildered!"

While Mountbatten's Congress-dictated revised Partition Plan was sailing smoothly through the British Cabinet he kept a constant liaison with the ubiquitous Krishna Menon who had arrived in London with the Congress brief. The fact that Mountbatten was getting a daily congress brief is amply evident from the following letter which Krishna Menon wrote to Mountbatten on 21 May, 1947, from India House Aldwych, London:

My dear Lord Mountbatten,

'I have now (since I saw you this morning) a letter from Panditji. It was unfortunate that it did not come to hand before I saw you. He refers in it to the possibility of seeing you again that night (the 17th May).'

'The letter to me deals with the question of immediate Dominion Status and his talks with you on the subject. I do not know whether this matter now appears in the draft. However, I should point out that the transfer of power as under Dominion Status is integral to finding a solution. Congress will not find it possible to agree to any arrangement which leaves this matter unsettled and prevents the Central front functioning even moderately well. I do not think they will agree to the plan of Deputy

Ministers. I have already said to you that they would agree to any reasonable proposals, including your veto on specified matter, undertakings not to do anything contrary to the partition agreements (if reached), agreement to refer to a body constituted by agreement (such as two judges and an umpire) to decide whether any issue comes under the reserved matters, and so on.'

'I rather think that it is felt there that you have not quite appreciated the strength of the opinion held in this matter. As I am anxious that there should be no misunderstanding, I am writing to you even though I have seen you this morning! If Mr. Jinnah wants a total separation, and that straight away, and if we agree to it for the sake of peace and dismember our country, we want to be rid of him, so far as the affairs of what is left to us of our country are concerned. I feel sure you will appreciate this, and also that it is not a matter of detail, but is fundamental.'

'I am always available, through India House, or through my personal secretary at Temple Bar 6426 or 6427.'

With kind regards,

Yours Sincerely,

Krishna

'I will set my mind to work on what you told me and I hope you will [give] consideration to the important matters of extra-territoriality I mentioned. There is also the question of the composition and functions of the Boundary Commissions. Once partition is unhappily decided Pakistan has its states, which are provinces, the transfer of central authority, which is limited, is in the same category as the partition of the armed forces, assets and liabilities. I should also have remembered to mention that the question of the settlement on Sterling balances with U.K. should be subject to a standstill arrangement and be part of the overall settlement with H.M.G. and not one by Liaquat as at present. I believe this matter will also be before you when you return!

V.K.K.'

Mountbatten having gotten the plan through the British Cabinet the only obstacle that still remained was to get it through the Parliament before the summer recess and here the cooperation of the conservative party was essential. Conservative Party meant Winston Churchill. Prime Minister

Attlee knew that without Churchill's full cooperation it would have been impossible to get the necessary legislations to grant independence to India. Attlee left the matter of getting Churchill's approval to Mountbatten. Churchill liked Mountbatten and was indeed the architect of his career. During the war Churchill had given two plum jobs to Dicke. The first was in 1943 when Mountbatten was made Chief of the Combined Operations where he was given command over military officers several ranks above him. After that in the closing stages of the war Mountbatten was made Supreme Commander of the Allied Forces in Southeast Asia.

When Mountbatten called on Churchill on 22 May, 1947, he found Churchill in bed. Mountbatten records: 'He handed me a copy of the letter that he had written to the Prime Minister, which is attached, and was extremely pleasant about what had been achieved in India in a short while.'

'He said that he hoped to get India matter dealt with on a by-party basis. If I could achieve Dominion Status for both Pakistan and Hindustan the whole country would be behind us, and the Conservative Party would help to rush the legislation through.

'Finally, he asked me to advise the Prime Minister to tell the other Dominions what was going on, so that they could get in touch with the prospective Indian Dominions and possibly help them to come in on a reasonable basis.'

'He z me to give Mr. Jinnah the following message: "This is a matter of life and death for Pakistan, if you do not accept this offer with both hands."'

'Finally he suggested that if I were appointed Governor General of Hindustan and Governor General of Pakistan, I might adopt the title "Moderator", which at one time had been suggested by the late President Roosevelt, instead of the title "Viceroy."'

Undoubtedly Mountbatten's performance was extraordinary. His was a double victory completely overwhelming the British Cabinet but also Winston Churchill.

Mountbatten & the Royal Family

During their triumphant visit to London end May 1947 Mountbatten and Edwina stayed at the Buckingham Palace. Apart from business they had a hectic social merry-go-round. Edwina recorded in her diary, 'So cold we are

Lord Mountbatten and Elizabeth (Future Queen of England)
(Cosmopolitan.com)

nearly dying of it and sitting in inadequate thin suits and a pathetic fur coat.' The days were packed for Edwina: 'Too strange being back so soon!' She met Lord Listowel the new Secretary of State for India. There were appointments with dressmakers and doctors. The Mountbattens dined with the King, the Queen, and the two princesses, and they went to see *Bless the Bride*. Nothing could be more appropriate. 'Saw Elizabeth re Philip', Dicke noted in his diary next day and, the day after, 'Philip and I talked re Lilibeth,' Princess Elizabeth was almost twenty-one, Dicke's nephew twenty-six, 'He has now got engaged to Lilibeth,' Edwina wrote happily in her diary.

The way Mountbatten promoted Prince Philip to marry Princess Elizabeth the future monarch of the United Kingdom is a fascinating tale. When Mountbatten's eldest sister, the deaf Alice, Princess Andrew of Greece, had given birth to a fourth daughter, Princess Sophie in 1914, he wrote crossly to his mother asking why Alice never had a boy. Mountbatten's wish for Alice to have a boy was fulfilled

Queen Elizabeth and Prince Philip's Wedding
(people.com)

in 1921. Philip was born in Corfu on 10 June while Mountbatten, his future Uncle 'Dicke' was falling in love with Edwina. Because of changes in the European royal families as a result of World War I Prince Philip's boyhood was a nomadic one and he found himself in succession in the hands of numerous of his far-flung family. This beguiling, bright, fair- haired boy who, if not quite abandoned by his parents, was destined to lead an unsettled life marked by long periods of separation from his father or mother, and most often both. He was loved by all, his treatment varying from firm with Victoria (Mountbatten's mother) to very free and easy in his German home at Hesse. The nearest thing to a home was grandmother Victoria's chambers at Kensington Palace. 'It was a sort of base, a place where I kept things,' Prince Philip said. 'She was very helpful and I liked her very much'. Asked if Victoria was a sort of second mother, Prince Philip replied emphatically, 'No. You see, it was a very large family and there were always plenty of relatives and places to visit. Dicke was very good at that time too. I used to see a lot of him, though he was away for a long time.'

Prince Philip lived with the Mountbattens for long stretches of time. Philip fitted in easily in the Mountbatten household particularly with Pamela and Patricia. 'Dicke took a great pride in his nephew' Edwina's biographer noted, 'who was to take the place of the son he would never have. During the holidays the placid and feminine Mountbatten nursery was much enlivened by the appearance of young master Philip, who, always a tease, imposed his will on Patricia, who soon became his willing slave and imitator.'

Of Prince Philip's upbringing in England, Mountbatten has said, 'We all rallied round but there is no doubt that my mother took the main burden. Andrea (Prince Andrew, Philip's father) was in no position to help, nor was his mother. Andrea was a charming and delightful person, but he lived abroad until he died in Monaco at the end of 1944-after the invasion (of Greece). He was a great Anglophile and wanted Prince Philip to be brought up as an English boy. When we asked him about his career and suggested the Navy, he liked the idea-but on no account the army.'

Prince Philip chatting with his Uncle,
Lord Mountbatten, 1948
(Tatler.com)

Mountbatten saw in Prince Philip all the characteristics he would have liked and expected in a son of his own. There was, from the start a wonderful compatibility and understanding between the 30-year-old Naval Officer and 9-year-old boy. For his part, Prince Philip admired his uncle greatly, but without sycophancy, and was more than ready to shape himself in Mountbatten's likeness. Mountbatten said, 'From early on I had no doubt that Prince Philip was abnormally intelligent. 'Prince Philip,' continued Mountbatten, 'is an absolute Mountbatten and not a bit Hanoverian, and his children have a degree of intelligence quite lacking in King George V, King George VI, or any of those people at all. Prince Charles, too is an absolute Mountbatten. The real intelligence in the royal family comes through my parents to Prince Philip and the children. 'The queen of course is a marvelous person. Her ministers are always surprised at how well informed she is. She is extremely sound-not brilliant- there was great worthiness in King George V and King George VI and even King Edward VII, but that old Hanoverian line was becoming dimmer and dimmer so that they could not even pass their exams.'

Mountbatten's shaping of Prince Philip the man, and his destiny, is always regarded highly in any estimate of Mountbatten's achievements. Some people think it was the greatest thing he ever did. Prince Philip showed early promise in school and passed out as a Naval Officer from Dartmouth winning the best cadet prize. During the visit of Princess Elizabeth and Margaret to Darmouth along with the royal entourage with King George VI and the Queen, Mountbatten was present in this select group acting in the capacity of ADC to the King. He was also anxious to see how his nephew was getting on. It was during this visit love seems to have blossomed. Mountbatten was always equally vague about the date of the birth of romance, and the decision to marry between Elizabeth and Philip. He would say that it was just something that grew. 'When you plant something,' he said, 'you don't keep lifting it to see how the roots are progressing.' However, Mountbatten could not even accept he was the gardener who did the planting. 'Of course, it was something that I had hoped for from quite an early time, when it was clear that Philip was going to settle here and his father said he wanted him to join the Navy.' But any sort of matchmaking is sheer nonsense.

Mountbatten was not content in just getting Prince Philip married to the heir to the throne but he made great effort to have the name of the royal house changed from House of Windsor to the House of Mountbatten. If Mountbatten's role so far as the match between Philip of Greece and the heir to the throne was passive, the question of his name and title was something close to his heart and genealogical enthusiasm. With the sense of family pride, always the mainspring of his energies and achievements, Mountbatten was determined that this surrogate son of his would carry on his name.

In a dinner party held in the Mountbattens' home on 25 January 1947 where King, Queen, Princess Elizabeth were present the engagement of Prince Philip and Princess Elizabeth was announced. In that very party among the subjects they discussed was Prince Philip's name and the process of naturalisation. It may be recalled till then Philip had a Greek nationality. The name, of course, would be Mountbatten. He would have a surname for the first time. Prince Philip acquired the British nationality on 28 February 1947. The date of the wedding was to be on 20 November 1947.

'When the suggested, and fairly obvious, name Mountbatten was first put to Prince Philip he was not, as he said, 'madly in favour'. By this time, 1947, his uncle was a world hero in war and peace, and Prince Philip has always attempted to guard his own individuality as strongly as his own achievements. He had no wish to be linked with 'a legend in his own time', no matter how much he loved and admired his uncle.'

'The debate – or even struggle – over the future name of the royal family was not yet over. When Mountbatten had accepted with seeming casualness the loss of his family's name Battenberg in 1917, and the assumption by the King of the name Windsor, he could have had no idea of the dynastic complexities and conflicts that lay just thirty years ahead. When Queen Elizabeth succeeded King George VI for the first two months she ruled as a Mountbatten and not as a Windsor at all.

The first setback came in April 1952 when the Queen commanded by Order in Council that she had taken the name Windsor for herself and her children. Some seven years later Mountbatten countered by reaching a compromise. Charles and Anne and the Queen's yet-to-be-born children (Prince Andrew and Prince Edward) were given the surname Mountbatten-Windsor. But the legal wording was so ambiguous that the Queen's wishes, claimed Mountbatten, were not clearly established until the marriage of Princess Anne on 14 November 1973, when, in the marriage register, she was described as Anne Mountbatten-Windsor.

Mountbatten seized on this as a great family vindication. Now the four children of this marriage and their descendants would bear the surname 'Mountbatten- Windsor', and 'surely this gives the satisfaction of publicly linking the two-family names in the Prince of Wales and his mother and their descendants.'

To have put his family name Mountbatten, which was acquired only in 1917 in the British Royal Family can be rated as one of Mountbatten's most extraordinary achievements.

Jinnah's Desperations

While Mountbatten having triumphantly got his plan through in London and was busy matchmaking his nephew, Prince Philip, with the future monarch of England, there were some ripples back in India. Jinnah dropped a carefully timed and placed bombshell. He demanded an eight-hundred-mile corridor 'to link West and East Pakistan which caused considerable consternation. Interviewed by Reuters as the British Cabinet was putting into final form its plans for transferring power to either a united or a divided India, Jinnah explained what a separate State of Pakistan, demanded by the Moslem League, would mean to India and the rest of the world.

Other points made by Jinnah were: Firstly, the Moslem League will demand a corridor through Hindustan to connect the two groups of Pakistan Provinces in North-Western and North-Eastern India. Secondly, the League will "fight every inch" against the partition of Bengal and the Punjab. Thirdly, a "really beneficial" relationship can be established between Pakistan and Britain. Fourthly, relations between Pakistan and Hindustan would be "friendly and reciprocal." Fifthly, the government of Pakistan would be "popular and representative." Sixthly, Pakistan would seek membership of the United Nations.

Jinnah said: "All the armed forces must be divided completely. I envisage an alliance, pact or treaty between Pakistan and Hindustan in the mutual interest of both and against any aggressive outsider."

Asked if he favoured a federation of Pakistan States even if there is to be a partition of the Punjab and Bengal, Jinnah answered: "The new clamour for a partition that has been started by a vocal section of Hindus in Bengal and by Sikhs in particular in the Punjab will have disastrous results if these two Provinces are partitioned, and the Sikhs in the Punjab will be the greatest sufferers. Caste Hindus will suffer most in Western Bengal and Eastern Punjab.

The basis of central administration of Pakistan, and that of the units to be set up, will be decided no doubt by a Pakistan Constituent Assembly. But a government of Pakistan can only be a popular, representative and democratic form of government. Its Parliament, and the Cabinet responsible to the Parliament, will both be finally responsible to the electorate, and the people in general, without any distinction of caste, creed or sect.

"As regards our attitude towards the Indian States, I make it clear once more that the policy of the Muslim League has been, and is, not to interfere with the Indian States with regard to their internal affairs."

"The foreign policy of Pakistan can only be for peace and friendly relations with all other nations and we shall certainly play our part in the membership of the United Nations."

Asked what his views were in regard to protection of the minorities in Pakistan territories, Jinnah answered: "There is only one answer – the minorities must be protected and safeguarded. The minorities in Pakistan will be the citizens of Pakistan and enjoy all the rights, privileges and obligations of citizenship without any distinction of caste, creed or sect, and I have no doubt in my mind that they will be treated justly and fairly.

"The government will run the administration and control legislative measures by its Parliament and the collective conscience of Parliament itself will be a guarantee that the minorities need not have any apprehension of any injustice being done to them."

The Congress Secretary gave a forceful rejoinder, 'Jinnah's demands will not merit a moment's scrutiny,' and the Secretary considered that they, 'are increasing under the illusion that the British can still help. The country, however, cannot be intimidated with such bullying tactics, and the demands for a corridor cannot be granted.'

Dawn, the League mouthpiece hit back at the Congress statement with a provocative leader under the heading 'Cranks All.' The key passage of which ran as follows; 'The demand for a corridor is not a new one. Quaid-e-Azam Jinnah has many times in the past raised that point which is so vital in the context of Pakistan. If Pakistan is to be real, solid, and strong, the creation of a corridor linking up its eastern and North Areas is an indispensable adjunct. Be that as it may, we have no doubt, however, that if Muslims can win Pakistan – and indeed they have already won it – they can just as well build a corridor somewhere for the linking up of the two segments of Pakistan.'

Undoubtedly, this was an absurd demand. The story was released by Reuters and Jinnah's secretary specially rang up foreign correspondents drawing their attention to it. Reuters was a well-chosen instrument for Jinnah to exert maximum pressure on London at this critical stage in Mountbatten's deliberations with the British Government, for through the exclusive use of this source Jinnah was ensuring for himself the greatest possible coverage in the British Press.

The following day Nehru gave an interview to the United Press of America. 'Mr. Jinnah's recent statement is completely unrealistic and indicates that he desires no settlement of any kind. The demand for a corridor is fantastic and absurd. 'We stand for a Union of India with the right to particular areas to opt out. We envisage no compulsion. If there is no proper settlement on this basis without further claims being advanced, then we shall proceed with making and implementing the constitution for the Union of India.'

Nehru wrote to Sir Eric Miéville that his attitude was hardening and that he was falling back on the alternative Demission Plan, in view of Jinnah's rejection of the main proposals of the Draft Announcement. Nehru would like the Interim Government to be treated immediately by convention as a Dominion Government. Jinnah would never commit himself. Nehru alleged that Jinnah accepted that what he got and went on asking for more. There could be no one-sided commitments.

While the Indian press was full of Jinnah's strident demands and Nehru's contemptuous rebuttals for the rest of the week, Gandhi was doing his bit to keep the political pot bubbling. At his daily prayer meetings he was loudly demanding a united India, and was calling on the British to impose the Cabinet mission plan, by force if need be – despite the fact that he had been largely responsible for persuading Congress to reject it a year before Alarmed by this, Sir John Colville, Bombay's governor who was acting Viceroy in Mountbatten's absence, saw Gandhi and managed to extract a promise from him that although he was unhappy with Plan Partition, he would not push his opposition to the point of actually sabotaging it.

Colville was even more alarmed by disturbing reports from Burrows in Bengal: communal tensions in Calcutta were now so great that violence seemed imminent. *The Times* correspondent, Eric Britter, told Campbell-Johnson that Muslims and Hindus had already taken up battle posts in the city: 'Houses and whole streets have become prepared positions, providing strong points and fields of fire.'

Bengal, and the British government's policy on Suhrawardy's demand for an independent state, was the only outstanding item left for Mountbatten to discuss with the India Committee by 28 May. Nehru solved the problem the day before, however, by announcing that Congress could only agree to Bengal remaining undivided if it stayed in the Union. This unequivocal statement not only removed the possibility of a third dominion, it also destroyed Jinnah's arguments against the partition of Bengal, and hence the Punjab, too. He had won the battle for Pakistan, but he would have to be satisfied with his moth- eaten version. Meanwhile in London Mountbatten was finalising the procedure that would be followed in regard to the proposed statement of policy. The India and Burma Committee having approved the Partition Plan Mountbatten proposed the following action.

At the conference of the Indian leaders which was to commence on 2 June, 1947, Mountbatten would pass round copies of the Plan and tell the leaders: -

(i)   That it had the approval of His Majesties Government and

(ii) That Mountbatten did not propose to accept any amendments on points of substance, unless they are agreed by all parties. In that event he would be prepared to submit them to HMG for their consideration.

(iii) Mountbatten would report the latest position about Bengal and, if both parties agreed to the proposals for partition being taken out of the announcement, this would be done.

(iv) If as Mountbatten hoped all parties accepted the arrangements set out in the announcement, he would inform the meeting that he intended to broadcast before the announcement and invite Jinnah and Nehru to broadcast after he had finished and call on their followers to cooperate in implementing the arrangements.

(v)   Later on, the same day the Viceroy would see the States' negotiating committee. The Indian leaders would wish to consult their working committees and Mountbatten thought they should be given twenty-four hours to do this. He would then inform HMG of the result of these discussions, and he hoped it would be possible to make the announcements public immediately.

It may be mentioned that in the deliberations of the India & Burma Committee of the British Cabinet it was decided that early autumn 1947 would be the date for independence. It will be seen later that the date 14th August, 1947, the date of independence was claimed by Mountbatten a date that he had pulled out of a hat.

Beginning of the End

Mountbatten returned to India on 31 May 1947. According to Lord Ismay, "A long flight with Mountbatten was an experience which I was careful not to repeat. The idea of a reasonable degree of comfort never entered his head. Speed was all that mattered".

More or less immediately after his return Mountbatten plunged into a series of meetings in preparation for the 2 June meeting with the Indian leaders. The very morning of his arrival he held staff meeting and it is interesting to note that one of the first item that was discussed was relating to Bengal. Governor Burrows was still persisting with his independent Bengal project. Mountbatten referred to a letter he had received from the governor who asked him to grant an interview to Suhrawardy, and stated both parties in Bengal were preparing to be attacked if there was a decision in favour of partition. Mountbatten asked his Principal Secretary Mieville to arrange for him to see Suhrawardy that afternoon. He went on to point out that HMG had declared themselves willing to an independent Bengal — in fact willing to agree to any solution for Bengal with which the leaders of the principal parties agreed. Mountbatten said, however, that Nehru had stated he would not agree to an independent Bengal. Therefore, the only profitable line of negotiation was to find out whether the leaders would agree to Bengal being given a status similar to that of an Indian State and being allowed to negotiate its own separate agreements with either side.

John Colville First Baron Clydesmuir
(Wikitree.com)

Sir John Colville who acted as the Viceroy during Mountbatten's absence stated that he considered that the future of Calcutta was the most difficult point of all. Mountbatten pointed out that HMG had decided that it would not be practicable to declare Calcutta a free city. They had also ruled that Dominion status would not be granted to Eastern Bengal. At the end of the discussion on Bengal Mountbatten directed his Principal Secretary to arrange for him to see Suhrawardy that day. Throughout the deliberations Mountbatten's anti independent Bengal stance was clearly evident. We have seen earlier that the British cabinet was fairly favourably disposed towards the idea of an independent Bengal. Mountbatten was only playing to the Congress tune.

In fact, Mountbatten met Suhrawardy the same afternoon. The interview was kept a secret and did not appear in the Court Circular and no minutes exist. Mountbatten records in his personal reports. 'It was essential, however, to find out the latest position about Bengal, so I arranged for Mieville to see Suhrawardy and bring him into me (so that the interview would not appear in the Court Circular). I was distressed to learn from Suhrawardy that Kiran Shankar Roy had been unable to persuade the Congress High Command to allow Bengal to vote for independence. Suhrawardy pleaded for Calcutta to be allowed to be a free city during the period of partition, since he felt that in this period communal bitterness would thus be relaxed and sufficient confidence might be re-established for the Congress eventually to decide to leave it a free city. He feared that nothing he could do would prevent riots and great damage in the City before partition. I sent V.P. Menon to see Patel to obtain his agreement to six months joint control of Calcutta. Patel's reply was very firm: "Not even for six hours!"

In fact, what Mountbatten told Suhrawardy was that the fate of United Independent Bengal was sealed. The same evening Suhrawardy wrote to Mountbatten's Principal Secretary reconciling himself to the partition of Bengal.

SECRET 6 CANNING ROAD,

[NEW DELHI]

31 May 1947

Dear Sir Eric,

I have had an interview with Mr. Jinnah. He asked me if I had seen H.E. and, may the Lord forgive me, I told him "no" as I did not want him to think H.E. had seen me. (Please show this to H.E.). He told me that if H.E. were to see me tomorrow, I should impress upon him the necessity for ascertaining the wishes of the people on the question of partition by utilising the electoral roll on the basis of 1941 census. *He says this is very important*, and he does not know what H.E. has brought back from London on this point. He says that getting the wishes of the present members of the Legislature would not be fair, as the opinion of the Scheduled Castes will not be expressed — and we must not let the Scheduled Castes down. He seemed to think that we could create sufficient atmosphere to maintain peace after the announcement. I hope the appeal of the Leaders, accepting though no agreeing or even deliberating, will be simultaneous with the announcement in the interests of peace. He insists that Calcutta should be a free city, otherwise it will always remain a bone of contention. I have made clear to him my views regarding the Commonwealth, and I have every hope — all in good time. For this reason, I am even reconciling myself to partition (if it is inevitable) and if zone A does not come within the Commonwealth. If it does, then, of course, the Congress can have no objection if independent Bengal also comes into the Commonwealth: if it does not and Bengal is independent, I shall have to work hard to get it in. I wonder if I am clear.

Yours sincerely,

H.S. SUHRAWARDY

Suhrawardy's letter was discussed in a staff meeting of the Viceroy the next day. Reference was made to a letter addressed to Mieville by Suhrawardy. The two points which Suhrawardy stressed were:

(a) The necessity for holding a referendum in Bengal, so that the true wishes of the Scheduled Castes could be ascertained, and

(b) the desirability of Calcutta being a free city, if only for a limited period. MENON said that Congress reaction against any suggestion of Calcutta becoming a free city was likely to be extremely strong. However, Congress might consider if it was only for a limited period and under a neutral authority, preferably the Governor General.

ABELL said that he considered that any changes in the Draft Announcement at that stage, to deal with either the opinions of the Scheduled Castes or special arrangements for Calcutta, would prejudice the change of Congress accepting the Plan as a whole.

THE VICEROY said that he entirely shared this viewpoint. The question of Calcutta could come up after the main meetings. If, however, he was attacked on this point or on the Scheduled Castes at these meetings, it was essential that he should be properly briefed to give the right replies.

The grand design of the Congress was about to take shape on 2 June, 1947. Before that strong words were flowing from some of the Indian leaders. Nehru and Patel, the two big Congressmen in the Interim Government had accepted partition on the understanding that by conceding Pakistan to Jinnah they will hear no more of him and eliminate his nuisance value or as Nehru had put it privately that by 'cutting of the head we will get rid of the headache.' Gandhi too was not short of words and had told his evening prayer meeting 'Let the whole nation be in flames: we will never concede one inch of Pakistan.' Strong words from the prophet of non-violence.

On the eve of the momentous meeting, the new Chinese Ambassador threw a cocktail party which brought all the Indian leaders and Mountbatten together socially. They were not slow to attack. Nehru insisted that the Congress representation at the meetings should include Kripalani, the new president of the Congress and Nehru said that if Mountbatten would not increase the numbers he would himself stand down in favour of Kripalani. Mountbatten then tackled Jinnah and Liaquat, who were most averse to the idea of allowing Kripalani in. Finally, however, a compromise was reached with Kripalani being added to the Congress team and Nishtar to the League.

Meanwhile, a confused state prevailed in Bengal with Governor Burrows reporting:

'As soon as it becomes clear that partition of Bengal is probable I should expect that the Suhrawardy Ministry will resign either of its own volition or by Jinnah's order and in that case I may find it impossible to get Muslim League here to participate in a Coalition. I should then have to contemplate relying on a Minority Ministry and I should not wish to do this till after meeting of Legislative Assembly.'

'If League acquiesces in the scheme offering possibility of partition, Suhrawardy should be asked at once to form Coalition Ministry to work scheme out from start in atmosphere of impartiality.'

'If he fails to form Coalition in reasonable time he must be asked to resign and if he refuses he must be dismissed. In either alternative Kiran Sankar Roy must be invited to form a Ministry *with* Muslim representatives if possible but otherwise without.'

'If League refuses to the work plan involving the possibility of partition Suhrawardy should be asked to resign and if he refuses he must be dismissed and Roy must be asked to form a Ministry.'

The Crucial Meeting of 2 June, 1947

The crucial meeting which decided the fate of India began at 10 a.m. on 2 June, 1947. It was a Monday morning and the Indian leaders were driven into the North Court of the Viceroy's House in their large American cars. Nehru, Patel, and Kripalani representing Congress; Jinnah, Liaquat, and Nishtar, the Muslim League; Baldev Singh, the Sikhs. Jinnah as he often did, kept everyone waiting, making his entrance a carefully-calculated ten minutes late. Then they were all shown into the Viceroy's study which was now duly

India Round Table Conference
(newsroom.ap.org)

transformed, its dark panels painted a pale green. It was quite a small study, with an informal almost intimate atmosphere. The painting of Lord Clive in the entrance hall looked down upon the gathering as if to mourn the passing away of the empire that he had founded. Mountbatten had had the oppressive, dark, wooden panelling painted a refreshing shade of green, to match the study he had discovered in Simla. The new feeling of light and air was somehow symbolic of the new hope surrounding the men who gathered in the room that morning. But for the moment, as Mountbatten reported: 'The atmosphere was tense, and I got the feeling that the less the leaders talked, the less the chance of friction and perhaps the ultimate breakdown of the meeting.'

Mountbatten and the seven leaders sat around the circular table, with Nehru on his right and Jinnah on his left. Sitting immediately behind the Viceroy were Ismay, Mieville, and Erskine Crum.

Mountbatten did his best to promote some friendly small talk, but it was clear that the atmosphere was electric. Mountbatten was anxious not to have any hold up of proceedings for this initial meeting. Photographic coverage was confined to Government of India man. This caused immense indignation among Indian and foreign photographers who immediately walked out and submitted a written protest to the Press Secretary Alan Campbell-Johnson. Mountbatten began the meeting by explaining that he had asked the minimum number of party leaders to come to the meeting so that it could be held in a friendly atmosphere around a small table. He said that, during the last 5 years, he had taken part in a number of momentous meetings at which the fate of the war had been decided; but he could not remember any meeting at which decisions had been taken which would have such a profound influence on world history as those which were to be taken at that meeting.

Before he had left for India in March 1947, he had been given no indication in London of the necessity for speed in formulating proposals for the transfer of power. He had been led to believe if his recommendation was submitted in time for legislation to be introduce by the beginning of 1948, that would be time enough. However, from the moment of his arrival a terrific sense of urgency had been impressed upon him by everybody to whom he had spoken. Mountbatten continued by saying that he had tried at first to obtain an agreement on the Cabinet Mission Plan. His Majesty's Government had set great store by that Plan. At different times all parties had agreed to it. He had, however, now had to report to His Majesty's Government the view of Jinnah and the Muslim League that they could not withdraw their rejection of the Cabinet Mission Plan and they felt that it could not be made to work. He had asked Jinnah whether, in this, he had reported him correctly. Jinnah signified assent.

Mountbatten said that gradually over the course of the last two and a half months he had began to see the degree of acceptance by the different parties of the various alternative plans. Jinnah had stated a claim for complete Pakistan. From discussion which he had had with Nehru and Patel on the other hand it was clear to him that the partition of India was fundamentally contrary to Congress principles. But the Congress had now accepted the principle that no area which contained a majority of Muslims should be coerced into joining the existing Constituent assembly. In doing so they had made it clear that they could only see their way to accepting the principle of partition so long as it was applied also to the non-Muslim majority areas which had been included in the Pakistan plan. Jinnah, on the other hand, had pointed out that he could never agree to the partition of provinces, which he considered fundamentally wrong. Thus he himself was faced with the position that Congress would not agree to the principle of the partition of India; while Jinnah who demanded the partition of India, would not agree to the principle of the partition of the provinces. Mountbatten explained that he had made it clear to HMG the impossibility of fully accepting the principles of one side and not of the other.

Mountbatten stated that during visit to London, he had attended a number of Cabinet Meetings. At these meetings he had tried to put forward what he believed to be the points of view of both parties on the different matters. Mountbatten had spoken to not only the British Government leaders but also to the Conservative Party leaders particularly Churchill. Mountbatten had shown particular concern for the Sikhs. He had repeatedly asked the Sikhs whether they desire the partition of the Punjab, as they were so spread over that any partition would necessarily divide their community. And the Sikhs had repeatedly replied that they favoured partition. Mountbatten then turned to the question of Calcutta. The League proposal for referendum was rejected by the British Government and there appeared to be no enthusiasm to keep the city either under joint control or as a free city. Other matters discussed in the meeting were the abolition of the India office, the transfer of contiguous areas, Dominion Status, the need for secrecy, Defence arrangement and treaties, the appointment of Governors-General etc.

Mountbatten pointed out that he had formulated the plan as a result of many talks with five of the seven Indian leaders present at that meeting. It had been changed to meet their wishes during the last few days before he had left for London. Copies of the Statement were distributed among Indian leaders. (This Statement was made by Attlee in the House of Common and by Earl of Listowel in the House of Lords on 3 June 1947). Mountbatten stated that he was gratified to feel that the five of the leaders present had supported the Statement. The Viceroy asked the leaders to take copies of the Statement to their Working Committees and discuss it with them that day. He asked them to let him know by midnight that night what their Working Committees thought of it. He did not intend to ask either side specifically to agree to the terms of the Statement, but requested assurances from both that they would do their best to have it worked out peacefully.

There followed an involved but good-humoured semantic argument about difference between agreement and acceptance of the plan. Although none of the leaders agreed with it in its entirety, they accepted the need to make the plan work. Nishtar rounded off this devious dialectics by pointing out that acceptance of the plan really implied agreement to make it work. Mountbatten cordially agreed, and from that moment knew that the essential battle was over.

Jinnah then embarked upon an elaborate explanation as to why he, could not take any decision himself. The plan would have to approved by the Muslim League Working Committee. Mountbatten wanted the reactions of the Congress and Muslim League Working Committees and the Sikhs by midnight. Kripalani and Baldev Singh agreed to send a letter that evening. Jinnah felt unable to report the opinions of his Working Committee in writing, but agreed to come and see the Viceroy and make a verbal report. This satisfied Mountbatten. Mountbatten secured the agreement of Nehru, Jinnah and Baldev Singh to follow him with broadcast to the people over All India Radio the following evening. Mountbatten said he would let them see his script in the morning. Patel who had remained silent all along, pointed out with a smile on his face, that the general rule was for the scripts of broadcast speeches to be submitted to the Member for Information (i.e., himself) before they were used. Jinnah without a smile retorted he would say in his broadcast what came from his heart. As planned beforehand Mountbatten had asked Jinnah to stay behind partly to counterbalance any Muslim League criticism that he was about to see Gandhi, in a separate interview, and partly to apply more personal persuasion and form a clearer judgment of the ultimate attitude Jinnah would likely to take. But Jinnah made no comment. He promised to give his views by midnight.

Mountbatten and Jinnah

Mountbatten despite his busy schedule on 2 June 1947 attended a gala reception in the evening for the veterans of the war in Burma. This was a military affair. Before the party broke up

Lord and Lady Mountbatten with Jinnah
(dailytimes.com.pk)

Mountbatten and Ismay left to tackle Jinnah who was to give his final acceptance to the Partition Plan. Jinnah was in one of his difficult moods. In the meeting Jinnah described the plan as 'scandalous' and said that he himself would support it and do his best to get the League Council to accept it. Why Jinnah found the plan 'scandalous' is not recorded. After a good deal of 'horse trading' the most that the Viceroy could squeeze out of him was an admission that Attlee might safely be advised that he could go ahead with his announcement about the plan in the House of Commons the following day. Why Jinnah finally accepted the Partition Plan after finding it scandalous is difficult to understand. Mountbatten has left a detailed account of his midnight rendezvous with Jinnah along with other assessments of the League leader. It is interesting reading and gives a pretty good idea of Mountbatten's opinion of Jinnah. This is recorded by Lapiere and Collins in their book *Mountbatten and Partition of India.*

'I can remember when Jinnah had got his Pakistan. When the British Government was prepared to let me put forward the plan of June 3, when ever the Sikhs had swallowed it, and Congress. This is what he'd been playing for, and he'd got it. And he said, "No."

Actually, what he said was, "I shall have to put it to the Muslim League Council."

I said, "I can give you until midnight. Or 8 a.m."

He said, "I can't get them here before a week."

I said, "Mr. Jinnah, if you think that I can hold the position for a week you must be crazy. you know this has been drawn up to the boiling point. A miracle has been achieved in that the Congress Party, for the first time, is prepared to accept this sacrifice of partition. But they are not going to be shown up. Having to wait for you to get your Muslim League to accept it tonight or tomorrow morning, it's out for good. And this is going to make a terrible mess and we aren't going to start again. you'll never again get the Congress Party to respond."

And we went on and on. And he said, "No, no, I must do this thing the logical, legal way, as is properly constituted. I am not the Muslim League."

I said, "Now, now Mr. Jinnah, come on. Don't tell me that. You can try and tell the world that. But please don't try and kid yourself that I don't know who's who and what's what in the Muslim League."

And then he said, "I must do this thing absolutely legally."

I said, "I'm going to tell you something. I can't allow you to throw away the solution you worked so hard to get. It's absolutely idiotic to refuse to say yes. The Congress has said yes. The Sikhs have said yes. Tomorrow at the meeting, I shall say I have received assurance from the Congress Party, with a few reservations, that I am sure I can satisfy and they have accepted. The Sikhs have accepted. And I had a very long, very friendly conversation with Mr. Jinnah last night, we went through every point and Mr. Jinnah feels this is an absolutely acceptable solution. Now, at this moment, I will turn to you and you will nod your head in agreement, and if you shake your head (to indicate disagreement) you will have lost the thing for good and as far as I am concerned, you can go to hell."

I didn't know whether he was going to shake his head or nod his head the next morning.

I said, "Finally, Mr. Jinnah has given me his personal assurance that he is in agreement with this plan," and I turned to him and he went like that (Mountbatten gave an imperceptible nod).

Now I can tell you that if he had shaken his head, the whole thing would have been in the bumble pot. To think that I had to say yes for this clot to get his own plan through, it shows you what one was up against. This was probably the most hair-raising moment of my entire life. I've never forgotten that moment, waiting to see if that clot was going to nod or shake his head. He had no expression on his face. he couldn't have made a smaller gesture and still accepted.

You can't make too much of that, that dramatic moment when this great clot was about to throw everything away and I don't even know why. I can't imagine. He was the Muslim League and what he said, they did. He knew he'd got the last dreg. He knew as far as I was concerned, "you're out whether I shall stay or not, you're out. No one's going to deal with you if you reject this. You'll just have to fight for it."

But isn't it fascinating that the whole thing should have depended on which way he was going to shake his head.

I have no worry about Jinnah being shown up for the bastard he was. You know he really was. I actually got on with him, because I can get on with anybody. He made not one single effort at all. The worse thing he did to me was that he kept on saying I mustn't go, that I must stay, that if I didn't stay they wouldn't get their assets transferred so that after the transfer of power I must stay out in over-all charge. When this was analysed by my staff and myself, we realised that we couldn't have two governors-general with a viceroy over them after independence. Quite clearly the only way we could do the thing was if I were Governor-General of both provinces just for the transfer, and that was accepted tacitly as the solution. My staff talked about it with his staff. And indeed we know that this came about because of the Indian side which first suggested that I should stay with them – and when they suggested that, which staggered me, that they were prepared to do it, then I said that I thought the solution would be if Jinnah wanted me to stay, then I must also stay as Governor-General of Pakistan.

It would have been absolute hell, living in two houses, it would be almost untenable, but I was prepared to try it. But he led us up the garden path. At the last moment this man – who obviously wanted to run Pakistan – instead of running it as the chief executive, i.e. the prime minister, decided to be the constitutional head of state who had no authority whatsoever under the Constitution.

When I discussed it with him I said, "You realise you've chosen the wrong thing. The man you want to be is the Prime Minister, he runs the country."

"Not in my Pakistan," he said, "there the Prime Minister will do what the Governor-General tells him."

So I said, "That's the whole reverse of the whole British concept of democracy."

"Nevertheless, that's the way I'm going to run Pakistan."

Then he said, "I'll accept you as Chairman of the Defence Council, a very important thing" – and he did until it finally broke down after the troubles. And he said, "I'll also accept the fact that you shouldn't feel that you can't accept the Indian invitation to be Governor-General of India. Please feel it would help us if you would, **because the only way to retain my influence with them is by remaining as Governor-General. After all they've got everything and we've got nothing.** We've got to get it out of them. Being Governor-General of Pakistan won't help you because we've got nothing to give, to transfer."

You see, I found it very difficult to believe that an educated man, a man of apparent goodwill, with great affection and admiration for the British, a man who'd shown me consideration, although of a rather cold sort, I found it rather difficult to believe that he would accept India becoming a second class power, and destroy everything, and produce what he himself had said would be an unviable Pakistan. I had hoped that he would say, "If you give me absolute and complete autonomy, if you limit the centre's interference to inter-dominion committees which will sit and elaborate a common defence policy, I might go along with keeping India together."

So it isn't surprising it was a one-man band, that I knew all the answers. It had to be a one-man band. Even a stenographer sitting in the room would have absolutely killed the effect. They never in their lives had been faced with a Viceroy all by himself. They'd never in their lives had to deal with day to day conversations and continuing dialogue that went on day after day after day. They were used to round table conferences, to endless great discussions. This was something none of them had ever come across before.

I produced quite a different result. People saw points and moved and spoke in a way they'd never done before. **I will at once confess that I failed with Jinnah**. But let me tell you this, nobody else would have been any more successful. I don't believe there was any more you could do with Jinnah. I must take the responsibility myself. And it was done at very high speed.'

Partition Plan Accepted

On the morning of 3 June 1947, reporting to London on the results of the first day, Mountbatten was far from giving the impression that the day had been a struggle.

'Jinnah saw me for an hour from 11 last night,' he reported, 'and I had letters during the night from Congress and the Sikhs. All three naturally emphasised points which they did not like, but their conclusions were generally favourable… Jinnah reiterated that he would support me personally and promised to do his utmost to get the plan accepted by the All-India Muslim League Council, which meets next Monday, but constitutionally they could not reply now on behalf of the Council.'

He summed up Jinnah's attitude by said: 'His delight was unconcealed.'

True, there was some trouble next morning. Congress had inserted two paragraphs in their letter of acceptance, one dealing with Dominion status and the other with the North West Frontier Province, which well-illustrated a bitter remark made by Jinnah about them: 'The trouble with the Hindus is that they always try to get seventeen annas for their rupee.' The first paragraph, reported the Viceroy, 'seemed to me so dangerous that it might well have wrecked the whole chance of agreement, since it was clear that Congress wanted HMG to give an assurance that rest of India wished to secede. V.P Menon, whose services in all these negotiations have been beyond price, rushed round to Patel and pointed out the HMG could never be expected to agree to such a proposal which negatives the whole principle of Dominion status, and urged him to drop it. I sent for Nehru half an hour before the meeting and told him the same thing. I told him that I did not even intend to mention at the meeting that this suggestion had been made. Both Patel and Nehru agreed to this course.'

In Kripalani's letter giving the Congress acceptance of the plan a paragraph had been inserted stating 'This will be without prejudice to the right of the Indian Constituent Assemblies to decide in due course whether or not the part of India in respect of which they have authority will remain within the British Commonwealth.'

It may be remembered that this was the sentence which Mountbatten thought in London might give trouble and which he had favoured omitting. Nehru began by saying he did not doubt the Viceroy's sincerity or that of His Majesty's Government, but that this sentence drew attention to the fact that Pakistan would be allowed to remain within the Commonwealth even if Hindustan wished to withdraw. Mountbatten pointed out that what the sentence really drew attention to was the fact that either side could withdraw whenever they liked. Nehru replied "But everybody knows that; why did you have to draw public attention to the fact that one side could stay in if the other side withdraws?"

Viceroy replied that this was done from motives of honesty. Nehru argued that His Majesty's Government could not be a party to allowing Pakistan to remain in the Empire if Hindustan wished eventually to withdraw. Mountbatten pointed out that His Majesty's Government did not run the Commonwealth; that all the States in it were free and equal partners; and that the only method open to him for getting Pakistan out would be either by persuading them to withdraw at the same time as Hindustan, or raising the matter at a Commonwealth conference and getting the other Dominions to agree to this course. Finally, Mountbatten told Nehru that he had no intention of raising such a controversial matter which would only infuriate Jinnah.

Congress tried a little sleight of hand over the North West Frontier Province by suggesting that the referendum which was to take place there under the terms of the Plan should not be simply to decide whether the population should become an independent State. The NWFP was still in the hands of the pro- Congress Muslims, whose leader, Khan Sahib, had begun propagating of idea of a separate Pakhtoonistan or Pathanistan. But he knew, and Congress knew, that the province could not exist independently; and once more the Mountbatten-Menon axis went into operation. 'V.P. Menon pointed out to Patel,' reported the Viceroy, 'and I pointed out to Nehru that since it was at Nehru's own request that I had dropped the original proposal to vote for Pakistan, Hindustan or independence (the basis of the **Dicky Bird Plan**) they could hardly expect me to reintroduce it at this stage. Nehru quite openly admitted that the NWFP could not possibly stand by itself, and it became clear to me that this was a device to free Khan Sahib's party from the odium [in a largely Muslim province] of being connected with Congress during the referendum period, since Nehru spoke about Khan Sahib wishing to join the Union of India at a subsequent stage. I told Nehru I had no intention of raising this at the meeting, and he accepted my ruling on this.'

Jinnah made a feint, too. He wanted a referendum for independence in Bengal, too for he believed that the Untouchables would vote with the Muslims rather than the Hindus; but the Viceroy talked him out of it.

The only delegate who might possibly have had something of genuine moment to say at the meeting other than the words, 'I agree' □ was Baldev Singh, the Sikh. For in the Plan the partition of the Punjab was implicit. Baldev Singh, who was never one of the most brilliant minds produced by his people, did not seem to realise what this was going to mean. The Sikhs were spread all over the Punjab. They had been there for generations. They owned and tilled the land. They had built the great systems of canals. Their shrines and places of pilgrimage were in western rather than eastern Punjab. It might have seemed likely that any far-seeing Sikh, realising the situation which would probably result from partition, would have cut his throat or gone to war rather than accept it. But then, as an Englishman later on bitterly remarked, 'is there any such thing as a far-seeing, Sikh?' Baldev Singh was acting under instructions from his committee, who were obviously as astigmatic as he was. But he kept largely silent during the all-important meeting, except to agree to the Plan that would cut the jugular vein of his people. 'Baldev Singh wanted the instructions to the Boundary Commission,' reported the Viceroy, coolly, 'included in the printed plan, and wished them to take Sikh interests more fully into consideration. I rejected this at the meeting and he accepted my ruling.'

He added: 'One of my difficulties had been to prevent the leaders from talking too much. For example, Liaquat started an attack on Gandhi in the second meeting which nearly wrecked the proceedings. When I think of the number of points over which the meeting could have been shipwrecked, I realise how miraculously lucky we have been.'

Mountbatten resumed the days proceedings on 3 June by duly reporting on Jinnah's visit to him last night and his acceptance of Jinnah's assurance and proposed action. Jinnah confirmed this by the appropriate silence and nod of the head. He then referred to the three Parties' grave objections to different specific parts in the Plan, and was grateful that these had been aired. But since he knew enough of the situation to realise that not one of the suggestions would be accepted by either of the other Parties, he did not propose to raise them at this meeting. He accordingly asked all the Leaders to signify their consent to this course, which they did; thus voluntarily but almost unwittingly settling of every substantial point of controversy.

After Mountbatten had pronounced that the Plan seemed to present as near to a hundred percent agreement as it was possible to get, Jinnah, Kripalani and Baldev Singh all added that they considered that the Viceroy had correctly interpreted and recorded their views. Mountbatten said the Plan would now be announced officially, and none of the Leaders raised any objection.

Confronted by the actual approach of independence □ or, perhaps in one or two cases, guilt-ridden by the vivi-section to which they were being a party □ the Indian leaders were actually too stunned to wreck anything now. The last phase of the second days' meeting was made particularly piquant by a gesture

— thought up by an Indian Civil Servant named John Christie □ to present them their freedom, with a document entitled *The Administrative Consequences of Partition.*

They all suddenly looked like goldfish out of water. 'I have given them copies of the paper to take away with them,' reported the Viceroy, and added: 'It was clear from their reactions at the meeting that none of the leaders present had even begun to think of the complications with which we are all going to be faced.' To which he appended the cheerful postscript: 'Perhaps this is lucky, since it will enable us to hold the initiative in Viceroy's House during the coming difficult period.'

CHAPTER 9: THE FALLOUT OF THE PARTITION DECLARATION

Mountbatten's Cryptic Radio Address

Undoubtedly, 3 June 1947 will go down in the history of the sub-continent as the most momentous day as on this very day the Partition Plan was accepted by all the contestants after years of bitterness and bickering. Not that acceptance of the Plan solved the monumental problems facing the sub-continent as we can assess in retrospect. Nevertheless, at the conclusion of the meeting of the leaders Jinnah declared stoutly that it would be his intention in Pakistan to observe no communal differences, and those who lived there regardless of creed, would-be fully-fledged citizens. This only proved to be an expression of a pious intention as we can see with the benefit of hindsight.

The rawest deal was to await the 625 odd Princely States of India. This aspect of the partition will be dealt with at length later. At four o'clock in the afternoon the members of the States negotiating Committee assembled in the Council Chamber to be briefed by Mountbatten of the most recent developments of the Partition Plan. Mountbatten was to give the Princes a preview of the official announcements and broadcasts that were to be made by him and the Indian leaders that evening. It was to be a most difficult and tense meeting as the Princes started realising gradually the fate that was awaiting them.

Mountbatten got off to a friendly and in formal start. He was certainly the master of the bluff. Round the big oval table were seated the cream of the Princely Counsellors. Their highnesses of Bhopal, Patiala, Dungarpur, Nawanagar and Bilaspur. Sir Ismail Mirza, Dewan of Hyderabad, Sir B.L. Mitter of Baroda, Sir Ramaswamil Mudaliar of Mysore, Kak of Kashmir, Srinivasan of Gwalior, Sir C.P. Ramaswami of Travancore, Sir V.T. Krishnamachere of Jaipur, Panikkar of Bikaner, Sir Sultan Ahmed, and D.K. Sen representing the Chamber of Princes.

It is interesting to note how many of the finest minds from British India were the Prime Ministers of the States. In 1947 most of these gentlemen were household words across the sub-continent. Many of them were front rank lawyers, which aided them in their approach to such constitutional conundrums as the lapse of Paramountcy. Their relationship to the Princes they served was very much like that of a barrister with a valuable brief.

Mountbatten knowing fully well what was in store for the Princes gave a skilful and persuasive explanation of the origin and purpose of the Partition Plan. He was subjected to some acute cross examination on its application to the Indian States. They were all particularly anxious to know whether it would be possible to arrange for Paramountcy to lapse before the actual transfer of Power in British India – the assumption being, of course, that the States would then be in a better position to bargain with successor governments. Mountbatten did his best to inject a sense of reality into the meeting. The creation of two new States would inevitably mean two strong central Governments which could not afford to delegate their powers instead of one weak one for the whole sub-continent which could. On the other hand, he felt that the acceptance of Dominion States by them both offered a measure of protection as well as compensation to those Princes who had stood so loyally by their alliances and friendship with Britain. Whatever decisions they reached, Mountbatten advised them to cast their minds forward ten years and to consider what the situation in India and the world was likely to be by them.

While the meeting with Princes was in progress, Mountbatten's Press Secretary Alan Campbell-Johnson was immersed in preparing releases, working out various deadlines and planning with All-India Radio world-wide transmission which included Britain and America. The concentration of Press and Radio interest on the events of 3 June 1947 was heavier than for any single development in Asia since the surrender of Japan. On the morning of 3 June 1947, the Dominion States secret had leaked into the Indian Press. Mountbatten was not unduly disturbed, and felt that the information might, indeed, serve to act as a shock absorber. However, there was the obvious risk of premature release of the announcement's actual text – a danger which in its turn had to be set against the likely dilemma arising from complete clogging of the entire Delhi Cabling System. To cope with the situation simultaneous releases of the Announcement were arranged through India's diplomatic representative in Western and Eastern Hemispheres.

When Mountbatten drove to the All-India Radio Station in his Vice-Regal Rolls a small crowd of Sadhus, distinctive in their bright caps of holy orange began shouting out slogans just as he was entering the building. No sooner had they started to demonstrate when they were scooped into the following police cars. The neatness of the operation made the assembled crowd, otherwise passively polite scream with laughter. These Sadhus had come from various parts of the country and had pitched their tents on the banks of the Jamuna, there to protest against the betrayal of Hindu life and custom which they were convinced any form of Partition must involve.

After a brief voice test, Mountbatten spoke with a slow deliberate diction, in contrast to the quick-fire delivery of his private conversation. Some extracts:

"A statement will be read to you tonight giving the final decision of His Majesty's Government as to the method by which power will be transferred from British to Indian hands".

"For more than a hundred years 400 million of you have lived together and this country has been administered as a single entity. This has resulted in unified communications, defence, postal services and currency; an absence of tariffs and customs barriers, and the basis for an integrated political economy. My great hope was that communal differences would not destroy all this".

"My first course, in all my discussions, was therefore to urge the political leaders to accept unreservedly the Cabinet Mission plan of 16 May 1946. In my opinion, that plan provides the best arrangement that can be devised to meet the interests of all the communities of India". Mountbatten was not really being sincere in this statement. Abundant evidence exists to this effect.

"But when the Muslim League demanded the partition of India, Congress used the same arguments for demanding in that event the partition of certain Provinces' Mountbatten's strong support for the Congress in this matter lead to the creation of truncated and moth eaten Pakistan which created a disequilibrium in the sub-continent leaving a legacy of strife and confontration for over half a century. 'For just as I feel there is an Indian consciousness which should transcend Punjabi and Bengali consciousness which has evoked a loyalty to their Province'. Mountbatten's actions certainly did not support this contention.

'It was necessary in order to ascertain the will of the people of the Punjab, Bengal and part of Assam to lay down boundaries between Muslim majority areas, but I want to make it clear that the ultimate boundaries will be settled by a Boundary Commission and will almost certainly not be identical with those which have been provisionally adopted.

Now the phrase in Mountbatten's radio address which is most critical is "almost certainly not be identical with those which have been provisionally adopted". It can be seen that Pakistan in Mountbatten's own words "will be made so unviable that in a few years they will be asking to join the India Union". Having already truncated Pakistan he was not satisfied. The Partition Plan accepted by all India leaders, Muslim majority districts in Bengal included Murshidabad, Nadia and Malda and the Punjab included the district Gurdaspur the only access to Jammu and Kashmir. It is intriguing why it was necessary to have a Boundary Commission even after only the bare bones was given to Pakistan. Not being satisfied with having given the bare bones, Mountbatten wanted to snatch even a few pieces of the bare bones by the clever ruse of the Boundary Commission – a Commission which Mountbatten could influence. More of that later.

"The solution to this dilemma, which I put forward, is that His Majesty's Government should transfer power now to one or two Governments of British India each having Dominion States as soon as the necessary arrangements can be made. This I hope will be within the next few months". The hurried scuttle making India the successor State and Pakistan the state that was seceding was to prove a disaster for Pakistan and was the well-conceived scheme of the Mountbatten – Congress axis.

Mountbatten ended his radio address with the pious hope "I have faith in the future of India and am proud to be with you all at this momentous time. May your decisions be wisely guided and may they be carried out in the peaceful and friendly spirit of the Gandhi-Jinnah appeal."

'Pakistan's in the Bag'

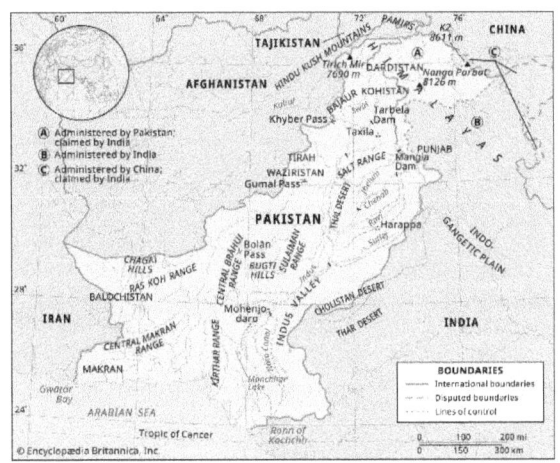

Map of Pakistan, 1947
(Britannica.com)

Mountbatten's address on the radio on 3 June 1947 was followed by an address by Nehru. It may be recalled that it was not the first time that Nehru had got the opportunity of a radio address on All-India Radio. On his joining the Interim Government Nehru had addressed India over AIR. There is no doubt that Nehru was certainly a scholar and an intellectual. His numerous publications bear adequate testimony to this. His speech was well thought out and can be rated as a historic statement. Some extracts:

'It is with no joy in my heart that I commend these proposals to you, though I have no doubt in my mind that this is the right course. For generations we have dreamt and struggled for a free and independent united India. The proposals to allow certain parts to secede, if they so will, is painful for any of us to contemplate. Nevertheless, I am convinced that our present decision is the right one even from the larger view point.'

'We are little men serving great causes but because the cause is great, something of that greatness falls upon us also.'

'I should like to express on this occasion my deep appreciation of the labours of the Viceroy, Lord Mountbatten, ever since his arrival here at a critical juncture in our history.' Naturally, this eulogy was quite understandable as we have already seen the Nehru-Mountbatten and all the Nehru - Edwina bond working effectively. Soon after Nehru's address followed Jinnah's speech on All-India Radio. It was for the first time that Jinnah had the opportunity of addressing the sub-continent over AIR. Some extracts:

'I am glad that I am afforded the opportunity to speak to you directly through this radio from Delhi. It is the first time, I believe that a non-official has been afforded an opportunity to address the people through the medium of this powerful instrument, direct to the people on political matters. I hope that in the future, I shall have greater facilities to enable me to voice my views and opinions, which will reach directly your life warm rather than in the cold print of newspapers.'

The high point of Mountbatten's power of persuasion and duplicity was that while he was leaving no stone unturned in his efforts to work against Pakistan he had managed to convince Jinnah of his impartiality. The writer actually finds it in comprehensible that a leader of Jinnah's stature should not have seen through Mountbatten's machinations. Jinnah in his radio address stated:

'But for us the plan has got to be very carefully examined in its pros and cons before a final decision can be taken. I must say that I feel that the Viceroy has battled against various forces very bravely - and the impression that he has left on my mind is that he was actuated by the highest sense of fairness and impartiality and it is up to us to make his task less difficult and help him, as far as lies in our power in order that he may fulfil his mission of the transfer of power to the people of India in a peaceful and orderly manner.'

The fact that Jinnah never had a negative word for Mountbatten is one of the greatest enigmas of the Jinnah-Mountbatten association. While Mountbatten had most degrading epithets imaginable for Jinnah, Jinnah had only praise for Mountbatten.

Mountbatten is on record for having described, Jinnah as 'the evil genius', 'a clot', 'shown up for the bastard he was', 'a psychopathic case', 'suffering from megalomania, in its worst form' etc.

With great skill Jinnah avoided a final declaration of intention while leaving an impression of acceptance. Perhaps the smoothest riddle was set in his words, 'It is for us to consider whether the Plan as presented to us by His Majesty's Government should be accepted by us as a compromise or a settlement. On this point I do not wish to prejudge.' Nehru's last words had been 'Jai Hind', Jinnah concluded with 'Pakistan Zindabad'. This he said in such a clipped voice that some startled listeners thought at first that Jinnah had thrown dignity to the winds and pronounced 'Pakistan's in the bag'!

Jinnah had only praise for Mountbatten. The fact is most historians have rated Jinnah as an honourable person – a man of high ethics and morality while Mountbatten's assessment by his official biographer, Philip Ziegler makes interesting reading.

'....like everything else about him, his faults were on the grandest scale. His vanity, though child-like, was monstrous, his ambition unbridled. The truth, in his hands, was swiftly converted from what it was to what it should have been. He sought to rewrite history with cavalier indifference to the facts to magnify his own achievements. There was a time when I became so enraged by what I began to feel was his determination to hoodwink me that I found it necessary to place on my desk a notice saying : REMEMBER, IN SPITE OF EVERYTHING, HE WAS A GREAT MAN.'

And the following picture which Ziegler draws of Mountbatten is even more distressing:

'Open diplomacy was, so far as possible, the order of the day .... yet openness did not exclude a degree of manipulation, even chicanery, which would have been inconceivable to either of his immediate predecessors. Mountbatten was well aware that certain of his advisers felt that his tactics sometimes verged on the unethical, but believed that sleight of hand was justifiable to achieve the greater good; the lie direct was to be avoided the lie circumstantial might be acceptable. Ian Scott, his Deputy Private Secretary, remembered the Viceroy looking up after proposing a certain course of action and catching the expression on his and Abell's faces: I know what you're thinking Wavell would never have done it. Well, I'm not Wavell, and I will.'

Jinnah's address was followed by a broadcast by the Sikh leader Baldev Singh. He made a generally conciliatory speech stating 'The plan that has now been announced steers a course obviously above the conflicting claims. It is not a compromise: I prefer to call it a settlement.'

A very strangely worded letter written by Krishna Menon to Mountbatten arrived the following day i.e. 4 June 1947.

VERY URGENT   17 YORK ROAD, NEW DELHI, 4

June 1947

STRICTLY PERSONAL

My dear Lord Mountbatten,

I do hope you feel that your efforts have been successful, and that the first bridge has been crossed.

(1) Gandhiji had a rather long talk with me yesterday. He is very disturbed. He has asked to speak to you about certain matters. Some of the difficulties could have been dealt with, without prejudice to whatever has been achieved if we had thought about it. It is important that he should be assured that the perils on which he is distressed is [are] in your mind. I think that much can be done to allay

his reasonable anxieties.

(2) It is rather pity that he will speak about them today before I have seen you and you have time to send for him again. But this cannot be helped and perhaps will have to be remedied in some other way.

(3) Jawaharlal also had talks with me about the "hereafter" and wants me to talk them over with you. They involve detail and important issues of principle which are vital to the furtherance of the success you have achieved. I hear matters are causing some anxiety.

I shall keep myself available and come over whenever required. Perhaps you will let me know some time today.

Yours sincerely,

KRISHNA

It is obvious from the above letter that Krishna Menon was meeting Mountbatten quite frequently. Although the Transfer of Power documents record practically every hour of the Viceroy's activities no minutes exist about Mountbatten's meeting with Krishna Menon. Obviously, Krishna Menon's hand was the guiding one and events and decisions were shaped by his dictates.

Mountbatten's Press Conference

On 4 June, 1947, Mountbatten gave a press conference in the Viceregal Council House. There were that morning some 300 representatives of the Indian and the World Press. Mountbatten spoke without notes or loss of words, expounding for some three quarters of an hour the political plan. Some of his arguments are questionable. Mountbatten said that the Cabinet Mission Plan was not an enforceable plan. It depended on the goodwill and mutual cooperation. He said that you could not make the Cabinet Mission Plan work anymore than you could make a horse drink after taking him down to the water. This is a debatable assertion as both the Congress and the Muslim League had initially accepted the Cabinet Mission Plan. Had the Mission been a bit more assertive then there was a good chance for the Plan to be accepted. When it came to determining the Muslim majority areas Mountbatten contended that from every point of view that the people of India should take it upon themselves to make up their own minds what they wanted to do for the future of their country. The next problem was how to produce the mechanism to ascertain the will of the people. Clearly, the adult franchise plebiscite would be the democratic idea. But such a process was utterly impracticable at that moment when they wanted a very quick answer and speed was one thing which everybody desired. The fact is that it was Mountbatten who was speeding things along which would ultimately lead to a disaster of monumental proportions.

Elections were held in 1946 and the Legislative Assembly appeared to him to be the right people to give a quick decision as to the wishes of the people. This was a very convenient strategy to give advantage to the Congress as will be seen when the performance of the Boundary Commission is examined. Mountbatten supported referendum in NWFP and Sylhet but not in Calcutta or for that matter in the whole of Bengal as demanded by the League. He was afraid that there was some chance of the verdict going in favour of the Muslim League so Mountbatten's excuses for plebiscite not being practicable is hardly tenable. Mountbatten promised the Boundary Commission would have representatives of all the parties so far as it was humanly possible there would be no interference or dictation by the British Government. If he could be of service in advancing impartial views and helping in this work he would not be afraid to do so. But he assured the Assembly that it was up to the Indian people to decide. In retrospect as we can see that this was hardly the case.

Mountbatten thought that the most interesting of all the developments was the speed with which all the leaders wanted an acceptable solution or settlement of the actual transfer of power. All the leaders were anxious to assume the full responsibility at the earliest possible moment, and Mountbatten was anxious to let them do so. Waiting would only mean that he should be responsible ultimately for law and order. Mountbatten stated all the leaders were anxious to assume their full responsibility at the earliest possible moment. He mentioned about the difficulty in handing over power in a hurry. One of the Governments was not even in being, nor was it certain it was coming into being. The other government would presumably take some time in framing their constitution because a constitution is a thing which should not be made in a hurry as it has to be there for all time.

Therefore, Mountbatten was faced with the first difficulty; was he to turn over to two Governments without a constitution? If not, was there any other constitution which can be possibly used. The Government of India Act 1935 provided the obvious answer. Some of the best brains had framed that Act. When the Secretary of State, Sir Samuel Hoare, was in the Witness Box of the Joint Select Committee, he answered up to 15,000 questions on this Act and he was able to answer everyone to the satisfaction of the questioner without having to alter the framework of the Act. That was a very remarkable achievement and that is the Act which will ultimately confer dominion status.

The British, Mountbatten continued would leave whenever they are told to leave. It maybe they shall all be out by the end of the year. It may be that it may be useful for some of the British to stay on. But the one thing Mountbatten thought would have been wrong to say that they were going to leave India in this mess and they were not going to give any help that would have been inexcusable. That meant the British would stay so long as they could be of use and when they are not wanted they would go exactly when they are asked to go. The facts are that despite Mountbatten's reassuring statements when all hell broke loose the British were totally helpless. The questions put to the Viceroy by the Press were numerous and varied. Many were of a trivial character. Among the points raised were three which were of special interest. The first was, what would happen if the Muslim League council rejected the plan? The second was, whether the basic determining factor in drawing the boundaries of the provinces would be the communal majority of the population, or whether other considerations such as property, economic viability, etc., would also be included in the terms of reference? The third related to the referendum in the North West Frontier Province.

The first, the Viceroy remarked, was a hypothetical question. As for the second, he pointed out that His Majesty's Government, least of all the present Labour Government, could hardly be expected to subscribe to a partition on the basis of landed property. With regard to the third question, the Viceroy explained that, compared to Bengal and the Punjab, the North-West Frontier Province Legislative Assembly had a heavier minority weightage viz., twelve seats out of fifty, although the minorities in that province only represented something like five per cent; that its referendum would be a perfectly straightforward one, and he proposed to depute for the purpose such British officers of the Indian Army, selected by himself, as could be relied upon to be completely impartial. As to why the voters had not been given the alternative to opt for independence, the Viceroy said it was a question of politics; if they could get the Congress and the Muslim League to agree, he too, would of course agree.

But the most important of the questions centred on paragraph 20 of the Statement, which concerned the immediate devolution of power on the basis of Dominion Status. In this connection the Viceroy explained that the British Commonwealth of Nations was a completely free association of peoples. Each State was completely independent, and, as far as he knew, they decided their own future. There was no power that he knew of to force them to stay in if they wanted to go out. People seemed to have some doubts about the term 'Dominion Status'. It was, he said, absolute independence in every possible way, with the sole exception that the member States were linked together voluntarily. In fact, they looked to one another for support, mutual trust and, in due course, affection. He was very closely cross-examined on the proposed referendum for North- west Frontier Province, which is still the focus of Congress attention, and there was also a prolonged inquisition about the status of the Indian Princes.

'May I draw your attention,' asked a correspondent in a voice registering self- satisfaction at the production of a teaser, 'to the Raja of Sarawak's example where he claimed to have the popular support and yet he was dethroned? Are you following two different principles in this instance?'

Back came the reply in a flash, 'Exactly the opposite is the case. He was not dethroned. He claimed that he had popular support to dethrone himself.

In other words, he meant, 'I have got the support of the people to take such action as I believe to be in their interests.'

Not only did he consult the legislative machinery, which was pretty primitive, but members of Parliament were sent out to decide whether the wishes of the people of Sarawak are that the Raja should abdicate in favour of a Governor, and they decided that that was wish of the people, and so he abdicated: He was not dethroned.'

Questioner: 'Is it not a fact that His Majesty's Government brought out the Raja of Sarawak and refused to countenance his re-installation?

Mountbatten: 'Most emphatically not. I personally took him back when I was in S.E.A.C. and put him on his throne.

Finally, Lord Mountbatten made it clear that the transfer would be in 1947 and not in June 1948.

He said, 'I think the transfer could be about the 15th of August.'

He appealed to the press to aim at one thing when putting out their news and their leading articles peaceful, quick and speedy settlement, which all of them so sincerely desired.

Gandhi's Reaction to the Partition Plan

The most startling piece of information provided at the conference was delivered casually, almost as if a passing thought, and was not even included in the excerpts telegraphed to London. 'How long will "His Excellency" stay as "His Excellency" and thereafter as Governor-General?' he was asked.

'That is a most embarrassing question,' he replied. 'I think the transfer could be about the 15th of August.' In mid-May he had told Jinnah that he proposed to recommend that the transfer of power should 'take place as soon as possible preferably by 1st October'. In one of his more picturesque accounts of the proceedings, Mountbatten claimed that the date came to him as by inspiration, the only reason for 15 August being the somewhat tenuous one that it was the anniversary of his appointment as Supreme Commander.

This is contradicted by his own retrospective dispatch in which he states that 15 August was agreed with the Indian leaders in the first days of June. No trace of such conversations is to be found in the copious records. Writing to Particia on 11 June, Mountbatten said that when "It can't be done! It can't be done!" When Nehru heard it, he is reported to have said, "I can't believe it!" 'At what moment or by whom this revelation was made to Nehru remains obscure. What at least is clear is that he and Jinnah had accepted that this or something close to it was to be the date before the news was broadcast to the world. In London Leslie Rowan, Attlee's Private Secretary, remarked that it would prove extremely difficult to get the legislation through on time. 'Accept Viceroy's proposal,' the Prime Minister minuted laconically.

Whatever the circumstances, the deed was done, and within a few days it had become accepted by everyone. The choice proved unfortunate for reasons that the Viceroy could hardly have predicted. 'The astrologers are being rather tiresome,' Mountbatten reported. 15 August was inauspicious for so significant an event. Whatever Nehru's private views of necromancy, he had no wish to offend public prejudice, yet to change the date would invite ridicule as well as cause inconvenience. Fortunately, midnight on 14 August would still be a suitable moment. The Constituent Assembly was summoned for late in the evening of 14 August. At the stroke of midnight it would take power. India would be free. Mountbatten had been worried that Gandhi might oppose the plan. He had immediately sent a message inviting Gandhi to come and see him at any time before the prayer meeting on 5 June 1947. He arrived at 6 with the prayer meeting due at 7 p.m.

Gandhi was indeed in a very upset mood and began by saying how unhappy he was. Mountbatten replied immediately that whilst he could quite understand and indeed shared his upset feelings at seeing the united India he had worked for all his life apparently destroyed by the new plan, he hoped to convince Gandhi that this plan was nevertheless the only possible course.

Mountbatten told Gandhi that although many newspapers had christened it 'The Mountbatten Plan', they should really have christened it 'The Gandhi Plan', since all the salient ingredients were suggested to Mountbatten by Gandhi. He enumerated these as follows:

(a) Gandhi advised Mountbatten to try and get the Cabinet Mission Plan or any other plan retaining the unity of India accepted by all the leaders provided it did not involve coercion or violence. He had bent every effort to follow the first part of his advice; but when no agreement could be reached Mountbatten had followed the second part of his advice and not insisted on a plan, which would involve coercion with its attendant risk of violence.

(b) Gandhi had advised Mountbatten to leave the choice of their own future to the Indian people. It was therefore Gandhi who gave Mountbatten the idea for letting the Provinces choose, and the method proposed seemed the simplest and fairest way to carrying out Gandhi's suggestion.

(c) Gandhi had told Mountbatten that the British should quit India and transfer power as soon as possible and not later than the end of 1947. Mountbatten told Gandhi that this had been the most difficult of all of his ideas to carry out, and Mountbatten was very proud to have found a solution.

(d) Mountbatten told Gandhi that he had understood that in his earlier days he had not been averse to dominion status. Gandhi was kind enough to say that this was indeed so, and that even during the war he had expressed himself as not being against it; and he later sent Mountbatten an extract from *Harijan* dated 16th December 1939, in which appeared the words: 'Similarly, I have said to a friend that if dominion status was offered, I should take it, and expect to carry India with me.'

Mountbatten subsequently reported this conversation to both Krishna Menon and V.P. Menon and asked them to work on similar lines in talking to Gandhi. Gandhi now felt that he had honestly tried to follow his advice, and that he had taken a far greater part in shaping the future of India than had at first sight appeared to him from the way the Plan was worded.

After meeting Mountbatten that evening Gandhi said in his prayer meeting 'The British government is not responsible for partition. The Viceroy has no hand in it. In fact he is as opposed to division as Congress itself. But if both of us, Hindus and Muslims, cannot agree on anything else, then the Viceroy is left with no choice.' It was, he added, on the basis of the plan that agreement could be reached. In fact, Gandhi had accepted partition, in principle, weeks ago but had been opposing it in public for tactical reasons. Abul Kalam Azad has left on record that soon after Gandhi's first meeting with Mountbatten on March 31, 'Patel was closeted with him [Gandhi] for over two hours. What happened during this meeting I [Abul Kalam Azad] do not know. But when I met Gandhiji again, I received the greatest shock of my life, for I found that he too changed. He was still not openly in favour of partition but he not longer spoke so vehemently against it. What surprised and shocked me even more was that he began to repeat the arguments which Sardar Patel had already used.'

The immediate effect of the announcement of the plan and its acceptance by the main political parties was to still controversy and bring about a semblance of calm. At last the great issues that had dominated the Indian political scene for decades and had aroused such strong passions were settled. Among Muslims there was a sense of fulfillment at having achieved Pakistan. It might be truncated – no one realised quite to what extent – but it would at least be their own, and they would be free to build a just social order. For the 40 million Muslims left in India there were fraternal feelings and deep solicitude. Both they and their more fortune brethren in Pakistan had known that they would inevitably be left behind in India; yet they had willingly and cheerfully rallied to the support of the movement for Pakistan, had made great sacrifices in its cause, and had earned the enmity of the Hindu majority in whose midst they would have to live. It was an astonishing phenomenon, only possible among a people possessed of a profound feeling of brotherhood.

The Hindus, on the other hand, felt that Pakistan had been extorted from them in the face of their opposition, and they were resolved to retrieve these lost territories. The All-India Congress Committee in its resolution accepting partition stated: 'Geography and the mountains that shape or come in the way of her final destiny. Economic circumstances and the insistent demands of international affairs make the unity of India still more necessary.' The Hindu Mahasabha was more frank, and said: 'India is one and indivisible and there will never be peace unless and until the separated areas are brought back into the Indian Union and made integral parts thereof.'

A still more dangerous trend was at work. Referring to the state of feeling among Congress leaders at the time of the passing of the All-India Congress Committee resolution, Abul Kalam Azad writes: 'All hearts were heavy at the idea of the partition. Hardly anyone could accept the resolution without mental reservations ……. What was worse was the kind of insidious communal propaganda which was gaining ground. It was openly said in certain circles that the Hindus in Pakistan need have no fear as they would be 45 million of Muslims in India and if there was any oppression of Hindus in Pakistan, the Muslims in India would have to bear the consequences. In the meeting of the All-India Committee the members from Sindh opposed the resolution vehemently. They were given all kinds of assurances. Though not on the public platform, in private discussion they were even told to some people that if they suffered any disability or indignity in Pakistan, India would retaliate on the Muslims in India.'

Problems of Partition

The time from June 3, 1947, when the partition plan was announced, to August 15, 1947, the date of the transfer of power to the two new Dominions – the Union of India and Pakistan – was seventy-two days in all. It took some days to sort out the major problems and to set up the machinery of partition; the effective period of work was just the two months stipulated by Sardar Patel. Within this period a host of problems had to be solved and innumerable administrative tasks had to be undertaken and completed. The problems were far more numerous and onerous for Pakistan than for the Dominion of India.

The Government of India in Delhi was going concern, which would continue to function much the same as before, except that it would cease to exercise jurisdiction over the areas which were to form Pakistan. The number of British and Muslim officials who might leave its service was not big enough to call for a major reorganisation. The diplomatic and trade missions that had been established abroad were taken over by the Union of India. The system of currency and banking, together with other economic and financial institutions, was operating on all-India basis and its control remained in the hands of the Government of India. The Indian of the subcontinent in a unified system of communications controlled from Delhi. Almost all the industrial installations and research institutions of the Government of India were situated in the territories of the Indian Union. Central government archives and records were in Delhi and the Imperial Library was in Calcutta. Army, Air force, and Navy headquarters were in Delhi, near the department of Defence. All ordnance factories and nearly all military store depots were located in the Indian Dominion. The reorganisation and division of the armed forces presented India with far fewer problems than Pakistan.

For Pakistan, by far the most important task was to devise an administrative machinery capable of performing all the functions of a modern government, and to establish this government in a new capital. Elections to a new Constituent Assembly had to be held and a new Federal Court had to be set up. Personnel, reference books, equipment had to be divided, and records and current files to be split up or duplicated. Arrangements for the separate collection of central government revenues had to be made to provide the financial resources for running the administration. Since partition was to take place in the middle of the fiscal year, which ran from April to March, there arose budgetary and accounting complications that had to be resolved. Then there were questions relating to currency and exchange. Pakistan had to have its own currency, but it was physically impossible to print new notes and mint new coins by August 15. Interim arrangements had to be made until Pakistan could set up its own currency authority with its own notes and coins. Trade and economic controls presented another set of problems. If India and Pakistan were immediately to embark on divergent policies, economic activity in both countries, might suffer injury. A proper trade agreement between the two countries would take time to prepare. Meanwhile, temporary agreements for the movement of commodities and for setting up tariffs and economic controls were necessary.

The share of each Dominion in the assets and liabilities of the undivided Government of India had to be determined. Different categories of assets had to be examined separately and divided on an equitable basis. For instance, the allocation of fixed assets, like railway and telegraph lines, could only be done on a territorial basis; military stores had to be divided on the basis of army units allocated to each Dominion. For the apportionment of assets, like cash balances and foreign exchange and the net liability of the government, a different formula was required. The provinces had yet to cast their vote for or against Pakistan. In particular, the referendum in the North-West Frontier Province and in Sylhet needed careful organisation and intensive political work. After the provinces had voted, the vitally important problem of the boundary between India and Pakistan would arise. In the two partitioned provinces, Bengal and the Punjab, new provincial governments would have to be organised. The relationship between the India states and the two Dominions had also to be determined. It was a task fraught with dangerous possibilities. These great changes had to find their constitutional formulation in parliamentary legislation and in adaptations of the Government of India Act, 1935, to provide the interim constitutions of the two new Dominions.

This brief and by no means complete outline of major problems is enough to show that partition and the transfer of power made the most strenuous demands on the energies of political leaders and officials. These varied problems had to be undertaken simultaneously, although logically some should have preceded others. In theory, the immense administrative tasks of dividing assets and liabilities, the civil services and the armed forces, should have followed the verdict of the provinces and the passage of parliamentary legislation, since only then would the issue of partition and the establishment of two new Dominions have been finally and formally decided. But this would have wasted precious time. After acceptance of the June 3 plan by Congress, the Muslim League, and the Sikhs, partition was foregone conclusion. Immediate steps were, therefore, taken to set up the administrative machinery of partition both in the central government and in the Punjab and Bengal. Every day, indeed every hour, counted. To emphasise the urgency, Mountbatten devised a tear-off calendar which showed in bold letters the number of days left to prepare for the transfer of power. Such a calendar was placed on the table of each officials dealing with the problems of partition. A prodigious amount of work was put through.

All exerted themselves to the utmost. Officers and staff worked, literally, day and night. It was a race against time, which seemed to be moving faster and faster every moment. A report or a statistical return which normally would have taken weeks to compile, had to be prepared in a day or two, and the staff of a whole office would work twenty-four hours or more at a stretch to get it ready in time. Then it was discussed with the other side, and, as often as not, revised. Immediate orders had to be issued for giving effect to the decision and a watch kept over its implementation. A delay in one field might upset the timetable in another interlinked field and slow down progress everywhere. The consequences of delay would be far more serious for Pakistan which would be so much the less equipped by August 15.

The Muslim League of the North-West Frontier Province had called off the civil disobedience movement on June 3 in response to Jinnah's broadcast that evening. It was in the obvious interest of the Muslim League that conditions in the province, before and during the referendum, should be peaceful. Abdul Qayyum Khan, the Pir of the Manki Sharif, and other leaders threw themselves heart and soul into the campaign for referendum. Muslim students from Aligarh University and other colleges played a notable part in carrying the message of Pakistan to every village. There was a danger that the Red Shirts might create disturbances. An agitation was being carried on by the Red Shirts to persuade people not to vote, and Mountbatten wrote to Gandhi that 'any action of this sort is likely to lead to the very violence you and I are anxious to avoid.' At the insistence of the Congress, the Government of the North-West Frontier Province, Sir Olaf Caroe, was replaced by Lt. General Sir Rob Lockhart. Under Referendum Commissioner, Brigadier J. B. Booth, forty British officers of the Indian army, with experience of the North-West Frontier Province, were put in charge of the referendum, and 50,000 troops were concentrated in the province to help the police keep order.

Administrative Consequences of Partition

In the press conference which Mountbatten gave on 4 June 1947 he had declared that partition of India would take place on 15 August 1947. He has already seen at length that the very short time allowed between the announcement and the actual partition would go to the benefit of the Congress. Most of the problems resulting from the brief time span allowed would have to be faced by Pakistan.

The administrative problems were monumental.

To get a preview of the colossal difficulties confronting the Indian leaders a meeting was held on 5 June 1947 with both the Congress and Muslim Leagues Leaders with Mountbatten in the chair. The meeting had before them a paper entitled 'The Administrative Consequences of Partition', copies of which had been handed to the Indian Leaders at the meeting on Tuesday, 3 June. Mountbatten emphasised that this paper was only a basis for discussion.

Paragraph 2 of this paper gave a list of matters on which a decision by agreement or, if necessary, by arbitration, would have to be reached. Mountbatten asked whether it was considered that these matters were correctly set out here. He pointed out that the list was not necessarily exclusive.

Nehru said that he did not understand the reference to a 'division of the staff, organisations and records of Central Civil Departments.' As he saw it, there was at present an Entity of India. Certain parts of India were being given the opportunity to secede from this Entity. The functions of the Government of India would continue. The seceding parts would have to build up their own Government.

Jinnah said that he and Pandit Nehru were starting off from completely different premises. It was not a question of secession, but of division.

Nehru said that he did not agree. It was a fundamental point that India, as such, would continue.

Concerning Nehru's misunderstanding of Paragraph 2, Mountbatten explained that it would be necessary for those members of staff of Central Civil Departments who lived in Pakistan to transfer to the Pakistan Service. Similarly, British officials would have to be divided between the two States. Back files would have to be copied. It was to be presumed that many of the laws at present in existence for India as a whole would be left in force in Pakistan until they were replaced. Copies of files appertaining to such matters would obviously have to be made available to the Pakistan Government.

Nehru asked how it was intended to carry on Government during period from the decision on Partition, which would probably take place towards the end of June, until the two new Dominion Governments were set up – a period of say six weeks. When the Partition decision was reached, a vital change would have taken place. The two new States would already then come into existence in embryo. When this happened, the whole nature of the Government of India would change. Some arrangements would then have to be made immediately, as certain members of the Interim Government would be interested in one State and some in the other. There would be a compete division of interest. It would become very difficult to carry on as at present. Arrangements would have to be made so that neither side would feel that the other was interfering in their business. The question definitely arose as to how the processes of Government could be carried on from then onwards.

Mountbatten said that this point had been stressed to him by the Congress Leaders before he had left for London. But now that the interim period before the transfer of power was to be so much shorter, the seriousness of the problem had diminished. He felt that this question should be considered separately at a later stage.

Paragraph 3 of the paper before the meeting read 'Similar decisions will be necessary as between parts of Provinces'. Pandit Nehru gave his opinion that the problem of the division of Provincial subjects was part of the main central problem. He did not agree that the Governors of the Provinces concerned should be solely responsible.

Jinnah said that there were many things to do. He wanted to try to understand which was the first. They could not all be done at once.

Mountbatten suggested that the first step should be to set up a Partition Committee. (It was subsequently provisionally decided to call this the 'Partition Tribunal') The Partition Tribunal would decide the order of priority with which to deal with the various other matters.

At first Jinnah took the line that no steps could be taken, not even with regard to setting up the Partition Tribunal, until the respective Constituent Assemblies were complete. Later, however, he agreed to the suggestion that the Partition Tribunal should be set up forthwith. He referred to the representatives appointed by either side to the Partition Tribunal as 'quasi-arbitrators'. He was, at first, in favour of only one member being nominated by each side, but later agreed to two; and that a third substitute should be nominated in case of sickness. Nehru also agreed with this. It was further agreed that the members of the Partition Tribunal should be the highest political leaders. Jinnah was violently opposed to there should be a fifth member of the Tribunal in the shape of a minority representative.

Jinnah gave his view that the Partition Tribunal should be the supreme and final authority. It should not be responsible to the present Interim Government. He visualised that present Government would continue to work only on a caretaker basis. Neither the present Executive nor the present Legislature could undertake and question of policy or planning.

Mountbatten said that the question of to whom that Partition Tribunal should be responsible was a very interesting constitutional point. In his opinion, it could be resolved by saying that in the first instance, it would be responsible to the Governor-General in Council, but that all its decisions should later be ratified by the two Governments after power had been transferred.

Nehru said that he disagreed that the functions of Government could be completely stopped during the interim period, as he had understood Jinnah to suggest. He further stated that he considered that the All-India Congress Committee and the All-India Muslim League Council should ratify the appointment of the members of the Partition Tribunal and of the Umpire.

Jinnah suggested that the decisions reached by the Partition Tribunal should be signed by the members thereof, who would afterwards be bound to see that their respective Constituent Assemblies ratified them.

The Viceroy pointed out that the existing Constituent Assembly could immediately ratify agreements on behalf of Hindustan. Pandit Nehru agreed that the Hindustan Constituent Assembly might want to have a say in the matter. He asked what would happen to the Partition Tribunal after Dominion status had come into operation. The general feeling of the meeting was that the two new Governments would then have to decide whether to continue the previous system, or whether to change it.

Mountbatten stated that His Majesty's Government had declared themselves averse to him acting as Umpire, empowered to give a final decision. He also was averse to this procedure. The Umpire would undoubtedly very soon become the subject of considerable odium. Without any disrespect to either party, he wished to point out that completely impartial decisions were very seldom welcomed by both sides. The Umpire should be somebody agreed to by both sides – somebody who was willing to give true and fair service. Mountbatten suggested that a man experienced in judiciary affairs would be most suitable. With this suggestion there was general agreement. Mountbatten said that he was prepared to enter the discussions if required by both sides, but not to give final decisions. All the Leaders at the meeting expressed their complete agreement that Mountbatten should not be the Umpire. Mountbatten asked them to send him a list of names in order of preference for those whom they suggested should be appointed to this position.

It was provisionally decided that the next highest Committee should be called the 'Steering Committee'.

LORD ISMAY put forward the suggestion that this intermediate body instead of being called 'Steering Committee', should be a Joint Secretariat.

Jinnah expressed himself in favour of his suggestion. He thought that a highly efficient secretariat would be sufficient. There was not, in his opinion, any question of the intermediate body talking preliminary decisions. Eventually, however, he appeared to give his consent to the formation of a

Steering Committee.

Nehru was opposed to the suggestion that a Joint Secretariat should take the place of the Steering Committee. He considered that the Partition Tribunal would be unable to cope with it s task unless there was a whole-time intermediate Committee immediately subordinate to it to undertake all functions except the final decision.

Liaquat suggested that the Steering Committee should consist of experts or officials.

Nehru said that he considered that reference to 'officials' or 'non-officials' was confusing. He agreed, however, that the Steering Committee should be composed of experts. It was, he suggested, up to the two sides to nominate anybody they wised to serve on this Committee.

LORD ISMAY suggested a further alternative – that the Steering Committee should consist of two political leaders as joint chairmen and, for its members, the chairmen of the sub-committees. The general feeling of the meeting was opposed to this suggestion although it was considered that the chairmen of the sub-committees might well be *ex officio* members of the Steering Committee.

Mountbatten said that he was inclined to agree with the Congress viewpoint that something more than a Joint Secretariat would be required. He felt that a Steering Committee of experts was the right solution. He suggested that the Steering Committee might consist of three members from each side, including perhaps a minority representative from each.

The meeting agreed that the Viceroy should give an account of the decisions reached, in the form of a written paper, at the Cabinet Meeting the following day.

Mountbatten asked whether both sides agreed that he should call, after the decision of Partition, for the resignation of the members of the Interim Government in order that the prospective leaders of the new Governments or Government might be free, without embarrassment, to select *their colleagues*. Jinnah emphasised that he did not consider himself responsible nor a party to anything which the Executive Council or the Governor-General in Council might decide.

The above proceedings give us some idea of the total confusion prevailing among the leaders in the prelude to partition.

CHAPTER 10: TWO GOVERNOR GENERALS

Two Governor Generals for the Price of One - I

Jawaharlal Nehru with Mohammed Ali Jinnah
(Newindianexpress.com)

It was the ubiquitous V.P. Menon who also noticed in the Draft Bill that 'the India Office appear to be assuming that His Excellency would be asked by both parties (Pakistan and India) to become Governor General of the two new Dominions. It appears that the India Office were expecting both Mr. Jinnah and Pandit Nehru to write letters asking the Viceroy to accept this post, and that it would be possible to quote these letters in Parliament'.

Menon gave it as his opinion that someone had better hurry and get the letter from Jinnah immediately, because he anticipated trouble. He was quite right. The question of who was to be Governor General of Pakistan was to cause Mountbatten one of his worst embarrassments in the whole business of the transfer of power.

It had all begun on 17 May 1947, the day before the Viceroy left for London with the new Menon-drafted Plan for the transfer of power. Nehru had, of course, seen this Plan, and, in accepting it in principle, he wrote to Mountbatten:

'We [Congress] agree to the proposal that during this interim period [of Dominion status] the Governor General of the two Dominions should be common to both States. For our part we should be happy if you would continue in this office and help us with your advice and experience'.

The idea appealed to Mountbatten tremendously. He got a good deal of pleasure out of contemplating the history books of the future in which he would be named, not only as the man who discovered how to give India independence, but also as the one who taught the two infant Dominions how to walk and talk. From a practical point of view, too, there were obvious advantages. The task the awesomely complicated task, of dividing India's assets between the two countries had already begun, and so had the quarrels. Two Indians of great talent – one, a Muslim, Chaudri Mohammed Ali, the other a Hindu, H.M. Patel, but both close friends – were in charge of the operation and they worked together in harmony and with understanding of each other's problems. But they were under constant fire from the politicians – Mohammed Ali for not getting enough, H.M. Patel for giving away too much. A joint Governor General could obviously do much to smooth the operation by impartial judgement and arbitration.

Mountbatten indicated to Nehru and Patel that he would accept their offer with great happiness, but he pointed out that it would be difficult for him to remain as Governor General of one Dominion only. He hoped to receive a similar invitation from the Muslim League.

That same day, he called Jinnah had Liaquat Ali Khan in to see him. taking the plan to London the following day, and that he intended to recommend that His Majesty's Government should grant both Pakistan and India their independence as soon as possible, preferably 1 October. (This was 17 May, remember. Mountbatten had not yet decided to rush independence forward even more quickly). The question which would require clarification was whether Mr. Jinnah would prefer Pakistan to have its own Governor General or share a common Governor General with India. He asked for Mr. Jinnah's personal view.

The moment Jinnah considered that he was being rushed, he became immediately suspicious; his instinct was to retire to his cave and roll a stone in front of the opening. He reacted in such a fashion now. He said he could not possibly commit himself on this subject straight away. Jogged by the Viceroy, he then admitted that he had given the matter some thought and that he felt it would be better to have two Governors General. He also felt that there should be a Representative of the Crown who would be responsible for the division of the assets between the two States. Jinnah indicated that he was very keen that Mountbatten should fill this post, for, he went on, with certain unction, 'I have complete faith in the impartiality of Your Excellency and all your awards would be binding. Moreover, I am extremely anxious that you should remain in India, for we have need of you'.

The Viceroy replied that he was honoured by Mr. Jinnah's remarks. However, he had not considered taking on such a post nor could he think of anyone else who would wish to do so. In any case, he pointed out, it would be an untenable position if a so-called 'Arbitrator' was junior in rank to the Governors General, who would be the King's representatives.

Jinnah promised that he would send the Viceroy a letter by the following Monday (19 May) with a full description of his proposal for a Supreme Arbitrator and two Governors Generals. 'But let it be clear' said the Viceroy, 'that I reserve my personal position until you, Mr. Jinnah, clearly state in your letter that if your scheme is found by H.M.G. to be impracticable, you will accept as a less desirable alternative and as an interim measure the appointment of one Governor General between the two

States'.

Jinnah bridled immediately. He refused to suggest any such thing. But Mountbatten was determined that he should not go away without some concession having been extracted, and he kept the discussion going until Jinnah finally decided first to think it over and, second, to deliver his letter on 19 May to Sir Eric Mieville, who would cable it to Mountbatten in London.

During the next week, Mieville visited Jinnah and Liaquat Ali Khan repeatedly and asked for the letter. He never obtained it. The Muslim League leader would never say that he was not going to write it, but he never wrote it either. In the end, the Jinnah idea of a Supreme Arbitrator was put verbally to representatives of the India Office by Mountbatten for an opinion, and, of course, they agreed with him that such a post would be unconstitutional and unworkable.

He came back from London to Delhi more determined than ever to persuade the Muslim League leader that he (the Viceroy) should become joint Governor General. It should surely have been obvious to him by this time that Jinnah, selfish, proud, jealous, was going to allow no such thing, but Mountbatten persisted. It had become for him a matter of pride, too; and it was also rapidly becoming a matter of wills.

The Viceroy at one point thought of calling in Sir Walter (now Lord) Monckton, who was in India as legal adviser to the Nizam of Hyderbad, and having him concoct a convincing case for the Viceroy's assumption of the twin positions. Ismay hurriedly replied that there was no need to call in an outsider. In a memorandum he wrote (on 8 June):

'We have considered that advantages of Hindustan and Pakistan having the same man as Governor General. We suggest that they are broadly as follows: i) You personally have earned the confidence and trust of both parties. This is by far the most important factor. ii) There will be an immediate number of standstill orders and although both dominions will become autonomous it will be essential for certain matters to be run on a unified basis until they can be separated.

A good example of this is the Army. In all these matters your personal assistance towards enabling an agreement to be reached would be of the utmost benefit. iii) If there were separate Governors General, one for each Dominion, they and their Governments would look at all problems purely from their won point of view. There would be nobody whatsoever in India as a whole capable of taking a completely impartial viewpoint. Incidentally, two Governors General would be more expensive than one. iv) Pakistan would stand to gain even more from your continued presence than would Hindustan, because they are the weaker party and because Hindustan at present has nine points of the law . . .'

It was not, however, quite so easy to see Mr. Jinnah. The old man was brooding in his cave. In desperation, Ismay and Sir Eric Mieville went to see Liaquat Ali Khan on 20 June.

'I told Mr. Liaquat Ali Khan,' Ismay reported later, 'that we had already received certain propositions for the Draft Bill and that the Bill might reach us on Monday or Tuesday next. Meanwhile, H.M.G. had asked us to consult the Indian leaders on the following points: (a) Was there to be a common Governor General to start with, and (b) What was to be the procedure for appointing Governors?

As regards (a) I reminded him of a conversation which I and Sir Eric Mieville had had with him some days ago. He said that he had not yet had the opportunity of talking it over with Mr. Jinnah. I pressed upon him the urgency of this matter and emphasised how impossible it would be to get any sort of continuity or any sort of orderly partition if each Dominion had a separate Governor General. He said he would consult Mr. Jinnah at the earliest possible moment.

Mohammad Ali Jinnah and Miss Fatima Jinnah (left) with Liaquat Ali Khan and Begum Rana Liaquat Ali Khan (right) in New Delhi, 1946
(dawn.com)

But of course, Liaquat Ali Khan knew that this was a subject upon which his chief preferred to keep his own counsel, and he was far too terrified of him to insist. Jinnah rarely took his subordinates into his confidence, and certainly did not allow them to influence his decisions. The hours ticked away until 23 June. On that day, the Viceroy sent for Jinnah. Mountbatten said that he was not raising it on personal grounds, but he must really ask whom he would wish to be the first Governor General of Pakistan.

The Viceroy pointed out that while he did stress the advantages of having, during the partition, period, a common Governor General for both Dominions, he must make it abundantly clear that he was not asking for the appointment for himself, and that it was an entirely free choice of the two Dominions concerned. He also explained that an early decision was required because it affected a clause in the Bill which was shortly to be laid before Parliament. Jinnah saw a perfect opportunity to change the subject and remarked that he trusted he would be able to see the Bill and be allowed to comment upon it.

Jinnah did not mistrust Mountbatten in June 1947, but wanted him to continue after August 15 in the capacity of a super Governor General appointed by the Crown, and with powers to arbitrate between the claims of the two Dominions. Only thus could the division of assets and liabilities be carried out in a just manner. But this was the last thing the Congress wanted. Their deal with Mountbatten for an early transfer of power was made in order to deny Pakistan a fair chance of establishing itself. The British government, having decided to end their rule in India were anxious to retain no responsibility for Indian affairs after August 15. Jinnah continued to press

Mohammad Ali Jinnah, Governor General of Pakistan with Lord Mountbatten, Governor General of India
(dailyo.in)

his proposal till the last, but it was not acceptable to the Congress or to the British government. That left only the proposal for a common Governor General that was incorporated into the Indian Independence Act.

Jinnah, who by temperament and life-long training had a constitutional bent of mind, could not see how a common constitutional Governor General faced with conflicting advice from two Dominion cabinets could discharge his responsibility properly. All he could do was try to persuade, but would have no power to resolve the unsettled problems of partition. A common Governor General for two independent governments with opposed interests was, to his mind, a constitutional absurdity.

Strong as the constitutional argument against a common Governor General was, there was an even stronger political aspect. The powerful propaganda machine of the Congress concentrated on the theme that Pakistan was nothing but a temporary secession of certain territories from India that would soon be reabsorbed. A common Head of State for India and Pakistan, who would inevitably be stationed most of the time in India, would strengthen this belief in India and Pakistan and throughout the world. What sort of independence have we got, the people of Pakistan might ask, when the Governor General of India is our Governor General, and the King of England is our King?

And this impression would be greatly reinforced when they saw that three out of four provincial

Governors were British, and that the Commanders-in-Chief of the Army, Navy and Air Force were also British, not to speak of a large number of other civil and military British officials whom Pakistan would have to employ for want of experienced administrators and military officers. Pakistan would have a severe ordeal to face in its earlier years. Only a strong faith in their destiny as an independent nation could sustain the people through the trials and tribulations ahead of them. There must, therefore, be a visible act of cleavage between India and Pakistan. If Jinnah himself became the Governor General of Pakistan, he would be a living symbol of Pakistan's independent status. Perhaps, Pakistan would lose some millions worth of assets which the good offices of Mountbatten might have secured for it but, in the struggle for survival that lay ahead, moral factors would count far more than material losses. Such were the considerations of Jinnah and his Ministers had to weigh.

As June wore on, and Jinnah deliberated over this matter, Mountbatten's impatience was daily mounting. He had set his heart on going down in history, not only as the Viceroy who had been instrumental in granting independence to India and Pakistan, but also as the great statesman who had helped and guided the two new Dominions in their first faltering steps as independent States. The Congress leaders from whom difficulty might have been expected in accepting a Britisher as the first Governor General of new India and given their warm assent; but here was this difficult man Jinnah, holding his own counsel, and putting off a decision from day to day. Was it not obvious to him that, without Mountbatten's help, Pakistan as the weaker party would have a raw deal at the hands of the Congress, who were in possession of almost all the assets of India? There were, no doubt, advantages for Pakistan in having an impartial chairman to preside over the processes of partition till their completion.

Mountbatten pointed them out to everyone he thought could influence Jinnah, and sent Ismay and Mieville two or three times to Jinnah, hoping that Jinnah would be persuaded. Ismay wrote:

'It was not until the end of June, that we learned that ... Jinnah had decided to nominate himself as Governor General, and to make Liaquat Ali Khan Prime Minister. In breaking the news to Mountbatten, Mr. Jinnah expressed the hope that it would make no difference to his acceptance of office as the first Governor General of India, or to his being Chairman of a Joint Defence Council of the two countries. This unexpected turn of events was a blow. We had all felt that the best hope of an orderly transfer of power, an equitable partition of assets, and the establishment of friendly relations between the two new Dominions would be for them to start off with the same Governor General.'

Mountbatten was wounded in his tenderest spot: his vanity was hurt and his pride affronted. He had lost face with the British government who had been led to believe that Mountbatten was acceptable to both Dominions as common Governor General. To make matters worse, he and his advisers totally misunderstood the motives behind Jinnah's decision. A meeting was called at Ismay's house on July 2, 'to devise a formula whereby His Excellency the Viceroy could remain Governor General of both Dominions and the same time satisfy Mr. Jinnah's vanity.'

After the plan of 3rd June had been accepted, the issue became clear. A week later Lord Moutbatten expressed to his staff the view that it was essential that the legislation to implement the plan should enable both India and Pakistan to have the same Governor General, at any rate to begin with. His own name should in no way be associated with this provision. After careful consideration he had come to the conclusion that he could not stay as Governor General of India alone, if Pakistan did not want the same Governor General. It would be fatal for Mr. Jinnah to know of this decision. The Viceroy's mind was running on the lines of having in the shape of a common Governor General, a supreme constitutional authority who could bridge and settle by mediation the conflicts and issues inevitably arising between the two Dominions. He spoke of keeping on his present staff if he stayed in that role; he had told Atlee that were he to remain as a constitutional Governor General he would require, not as big a staff as at present, but 'a team of high-level experts' to aid him in giving advice and guidance and acting as a mediator. He had also discussed the matter with Nehru, whose view had been that the Governor General after the transfer of power would be in a very different position from a normal Dominion Governor General; in the initial stages at least, his influence would count for a great deal, and he, Nehru, doubted whether the processes of partition would work satisfactorily unless Lord Mountbatten personally stayed on. V.P. Menon observed at this staff meeting that in regard to the States also an independent advisor and guide would be of the greatest benefit. Even Gandhi had said he would be willingly guided by the decisions of any committee of which Lord Ismay, for example, was Chairman.

One acute member of the Viceroy's staff said firmly that in his view the Governor General should not be Chairman of any Committee with executive or political authority after the transfer of power. (If this counsel had been followed, history might have told a different tale of the crises in India, and between India and Pakistan, in the ten months after 15th August 1947.) Lord Mountbatten agreed that it would be out of the question for him to take the chair at meetings of either side separately: but precedent had to be dismissed in these matters. If he personally was the only man holding office in both Dominions, it might well be possible for him to take the chair at meetings between them, without a vote and only to guide discussion.

The position therefore was this: the Viceroy, assuming that both Dominions invited him – and the draft Bill had meanwhile been drawn to provide that the existing Governor General of India, unless and until another appointment was made, should become forthwith Governor General of each of the two Dominions – was prepared to accept the office for an interim period, not as an arbitrator but as a mediator, and as non-executive chairman, if required, of joint Indo-Pakistan organs; on no account would he become Governor General of one Dominion alone. Pakistan, he felt, would gain the most from a joint Governor Generalship on those lines, since she was the weaker party in many respects, the more in need of an impartial figure at the top watching the process of partition. His staff agreed with him. On those assumptions Lord Mountbatten suggested to them that Viceregal Lodge, Simla, might be considered 'neutral territory'. Although most of his staff as joint Governor General would obviously have to be Indians and actions that would be greatly handicapped in the difficult negotiations that would fall to him if he did not have at least Lord Ismay and Sir Eric Mieville to help him.

Two Governor Generals for the Price of One – III

Mountbatten was desperately continuing his effort to become Governor General of both India and Pakistan. On 22 June 1947 Jinnah was invited to have a last look at the draft Independence Bill that was to be presented before the House of Commons in London. Mountbatten had told Jinnah that he had had a great tussle with His Majesty's Government, who had taken the line that it was entirely contrary to Parliamentary procedure for anyone outside the government to see a Bill before its presentation before the House of Commons. He had, however, fought hard and won, and Jinnah would be allowed to see the Bill. The Indian leaders met at the Viceroy's House and were given copies of the Bill. They were then shown into private rooms and with their legal adviser and allowed to study it for two hours. Chowdhuri Muhammed Ali in his *The Emergence of Pakistan* has recorded:

'I was made painfully aware of the intensity of Mountbatten's feeling when he one day burst into the room in the Viceroy's house where the Quaid-e-Azam was working on the Indian Independence Bill with Liaquat Ali Khan and me. He belabored the Quaid-e-Azam with arguments and appeals and bluster. He maintained that the proposal for a common Governor General was inspired by the highest motives and was in the best interests of Pakistan. Without him as common Governor General, Pakistan would put itself at the gravest disadvantage. It was with the greatest difficulty that he was securing for Pakistan what was due to her and, unless it was known that he would continue in this position even after partition, his power to help Pakistan would rapidly diminish. The responsibility for the immeasurable loss to Pakistan would rest on the shoulders of Jinnah. He threatened to make all this public and let the world judge. He was sure that the verdict of history would uphold him and go against Jinnah. He said again and again that he was most surprised that objection to his continuance as common Governor General should have come from Pakistan and not from the Congress. Jinnah bore this onslaught with great dignity and patience; he answered that in coming to this decision he had not been moved by any personal considerations but had objectively taken only the interests of his people into account. He assured Mountbatten that he fully trusted his sincerity and impartiality, and reiterated his proposal for making Mountbatten super Governor General. But his protestations of faith in Mountbatten did nothing to assuage the latter's wounded vanity.'

It is worth going through the Viceroy's personal report of 5 July 1947. Mountbatten gives an elaborate account of the whole episode of the appointment of the Governor General of Pakistan.

'It will be remembered that I reported to the Cabinet Committee that Nehru had put in writing a request to me to remain on as the Governor General of India. As Jinnah had consistently impressed on me the absolute need for me to remain until the process of partition was completed I managed (not without difficulty) to persuade Congress to agree that I must also be allowed to accept a similar offer from Pakistan so that I could impartially look after the interests of both dominions during the period of partition.'

'Before I went to London Jinnah said that although he thought two Governors General would be better than one, he asked me specially to stay on as a Super Governor General over the other two. From that day to this he has repeatedly impressed on myself and my staff the need for us all to stay and see the partition through fairly; and we have all consistently told him that this can only be satisfactorily done by myself as a common Governor General and that fortunately for him Congress had already agreed to this system.'

Mountbatten states that for three weeks he was trying to get an answer out of Jinnah and Jinnah had always put off an answer, and finally Jinnah said he could not let Mountbatten know until he had seen the Bill. After he had seen the Bill, he still did not wish to answer until he had consulted two of his leaders who were away at the two Referendums. However, Jinnah finally came 'to seek my advice as to what he should do'. He began by saying that he wished to have British Governors in every province of Pakistan except Sind which, since it would be under his personal observation in Karachi, could have a Muslim Governor. He pointed out that he had already agreed to the three heads of the Pakistan Defence Services being British; but remarked that the only way in which he could sell the idea of all these British high officials to the inhabitants of Pakistan would be if he himself became the Governor General.

Jinnah said he had been unwilling to take this step but had been urged to do so by three or four intimate friends and colleagues whom he had consulted. The Nawab of Bhopal was Jinnah's principal friend and adviser and had told Mountbatten three days previously that Jinnah had specially consulted him on this point, and that Bhopal had told him that he thought that he would be mad to reject the chance of having a common Governor General with a British team to see partition through till the 31st March 1948 (which has been taken as the end of the partition period), 'and as it is quite clear that Liaquat Ali Khan strongly shares this view, I am afraid that the only adviser that Jinnah listens to is Jinnah.' records Mountbatten.

'He is suffering from megalomania in its worst form for when I pointed out to him that if he went as a Constitutional Governor General his powers would be restricted but as Prime Minister he really could run Pakistan, he made no bones about the fact that his Prime Minister would do what he said. 'In my position it is I who will give the advice and others will act on it.'

Then Mountbatten conceived the idea of putting a clause in the Bill to have an officiating Governor General in Pakistan whenever the Governor General was not in the territories of that dominion. Mountbatten got this passed by Congress at their meeting about the Bill and then went in to see the Muslim League representatives at their corresponding meeting.

On seeing Mountbatten Jinnah attacked him on the question of sanctions against the Union of India if they failed to comply with awards of the Arbitral Tribunal and hand over to Pakistan their fair share of assets. For, as Jinnah pointed out, nearly all the common assets happened to be situated in the Union of India's territory. Mountbatten replied in the presence of Jinnah's partymen that the provision which had been devised to safeguard Pakistan's interests in partition had been the system of a common Governor General with a high class British staff whom both sides would trust to see fair play.

Mountbatten pointed out that the Congress had agreed to this system, had nominated Mountbatten, and he and his British staff were willing to serve until the end of the partition period on 31st March. Mountbatten said he quite appreciated that most of the partition work would go on in Delhi, and that Mountbatten would have very little time to spare for Karachi. Mountbatten had therefore got Congress to agree that an officiating Governor General should be appointed during those 7☐ months and that he should only visit Pakistan territory by mutual arrangement with its officiating Governor General.

Jinnah categorically refused to accept this. Mountbatten told him he could hardly believe it was Jinnah's intention to reject the only practicable means of safeguarding the division of the assets – and a means to which Congress had agreed – for the sake of having a substantive Governor General instead of an officiating Governor General until the 31st March in Karachi; for after that, Mountbatten pointed out that they would of course have their own Governor General.

Jinnah solemnly assured Mountbatten that he realised all the disadvantages of giving up the common Governor General, that his one ambition was that Mountbatten should stay as Viceroy or overall Governor General to see the partition through, but he was unable to accept any position other than that of Governor General of Pakistan on the 15th August. Jinnah curiously enough begged Mountbatten to remain as the Governor General of India since he said unless there was a steadying influence he was afraid of what the Congress Government might do to Pakistan.

Mountbatten asked Jinnah 'do you realise what this will cost you?' He said sadly 'It may cost me several crores of rupees in assets', to which Mountbatten replied somewhat acidly 'It may well cost you the whole of your assets and the future of Pakistan'. Mountbatten then got up and left the room.

Mountbatten finally states 'I am now in a complete quandary. I have always held the view that I should stay on with both sides or with neither of them. I never dreamt that both sides would ask me to stay with one side.'

'My own inclination is to go, for I have always felt and said that I considered it morally wrong to stay on with only one of the two sides. But unfortunately, I fear that I have unintentionally led Nehru and all the Congress leaders up the garden path and that they will never forgive me for allowing Jinnah once more to have his way. I therefore feel that this is a matter on which I require higher guidance, and have considered it essential to send Ismay home to seek it.'

As subsequent events prove this was merely a hypocritical statement as Mountbatten had always intended to stay on as the Governor General of India to see the grand Congress design through.

Mountbatten was so furious at Jinnah indicating to him that he wished to be the first Governor General of Pakistan that a Viceroy's Meeting was held at Lord Ismay's House at 9:45 p.m. on Wednesday, 2nd July, to consider the situation arising from Mr. Jinnah's declared wish to be Governor General of Pakistan from 15th August, 1947. Mountbatten was so obsessed with the matter that he had a brainstorming session with his staff. It is interesting to read the trend of the discussions which presently appears to say the least quiet hilarious. It was felt that the possible courses were as follows:

A.   To accede to Jinnah's request, and for Mountbatten to stay on as Governor General of India alone,

B.   To accede to Jinnah's request, and to ask Congress to nominate someone other than Mountbatten as Governor General of India, or

C.   To devise a formula whereby Mountbatten would be enabled to remain as Governor General of both Dominions, and at the same time to satisfy Jinnah's vanity.

ADVANTAGES AND DISADVANTAGES

COURSE A

Advantages

(i) The benefit of Mountbatten's help and advice would remain anyhow for the greater part of the present India.

(ii) British Officers and officials at least in that part would stay on.

Disadvantages

(i) Although Jinnah evidently hopes to get many senior British officers, including Lord Killearn as a Governor, it is doubtful whether they would come, and indeed whether any British officers or officials would agree to remain in Pakistan.

(ii) Pakistan would be likely to get less than their fair share of all-India assets.

(iii) It is probable that there would be Conservative opposition to the Bill, an there might be difficulty in getting it through before the end of the present Session.

(iv) Mountbatten would probably go on leave until 15th August and would have to stop being Chairman of the Partition Committee, the work of which would be seriously compromised. Even then, he, and the British as a whole, might get a reputation for partiality.

COURSE B

Advantages

(i) Mountbatten could remain as Chairman of the Partition Committee.

(ii) The British, and particularly Mountbatten and his Staff, would go 'on the crest of the wave' – particularly if suitable publicity was given to Jinnah's action. All accusation of partiality would be avoided.

Disadvantages

(i)   It is very doubtful that Congress would choose another Englishman. As a result, very few British officers or officials, including senior officers and probably Governors, would remain in either Dominion.

(ii) Pakistan would get nothing like their fair share of all India assets except in such matters as were fully settled before 15th August.

(iii) The Conservatives would probably bitterly oppose the Bill and there would be no chance of getting it through during the present Session.

COURSE C

Advantages   The advantages of Mountbatten staying on for a period as Governor General of both Dominions are too obvious to enumerate. They include, of course, a strictly fair partition; a flying start for both Dominions; the Bill would go through without any difficulty; and a large number of British officers and officials would stay on.

Disadvantages The main disadvantage is that Jinnah might try to be a 'Hitler' and take no notice of what Mountbatten said. This would lead to an exceedingly difficult situation.

Possible Variations of COURSE C

(a) The following suggestions were made for the name of the post which Mountbatten would hold:

Governor General for Partition Supreme Governor General Overall Governor General Viceroy

(b) The following suggestions were made for the name of the post which Jinnah (and probably and equivalent in India) would hold:

Governor General Designate Acting Governor General Lieutenant Governor General Deputy Governor General Head of State

President

Officer Administering the Government

The Suggestions in (a) and (b) are in the order in which they were most favoured.

(c) It is felt that any formula conferring such titles should be based on the necessity for a Governor General not to leave his Dominion except on special occasions with the permission of the King; and on the impossibility of his being in two places at the same time.

(d) It was felt that the appointment of a Governor General Designate might be made optional.

(e) It was emphasised that any formula devised in this behalf must be one which Congress would accept.

(f) It was felt that it would have to be made clear in such a formula that Mountbatten would stay only until 31st March.

Consequent amendments to the Bill would of course be necessitated. For example, the powers of the Governor General Designate in the absence from either Dominion of the Governor General would have to be made clear.

In retrospect we can see hardly any of the matters discussed were experienced in practice except Mountbatten's severe India. One can only conjecture what would have happened if Mountbatten was appointed Governor General of both India and Pakistan. Perhaps his grand design would have been more facilitated.

Janet Morgan in her *Edwina Mountbatten* says 'there was another worry. Mountbatten had believed that, after independence, he would be asked to stay on as Governor General of both India and Pakistan. The discussions over Dominion Status had strengthened this impression, although on this subject, admittedly, Jinnah had given nothing away. At the beginning of July he at last came clean. 'What I thought would happen funnily enough', Edwina told Patricia,' and which neither Daddy nor any of his staff EVER contemplated has occurred, and Mr. Jinnah himself wants to be Governor General of Pakistan (highly confidential of course)'. Some stratospheric appointment might be available for Dicky – Jinnah suggested that he became Chairman of the Joint Defence Committee – but that was all. Jinnah could not be moved. When Mountbatten explained that a Governor General's powers were minute, a Prime Minister's very great. Jinnah smugly replied: 'In my position it is I who will give the advice and others will act on it.'

India wanted Mountbatten, Pakistan did not. 'Serious Staff Meeting re future GG', Mountbatten wrote in his diary on 4 July. 'Worrying day'. That night, after a dinner for American Independence

Day, he discussed the matter with Edwina. 'It's a complete nightmare', she wrote, 'and having come out to do and succeeded in doing a completely *impartial* job one dreads the thought of him, thru' a series of unexpected and possibly unpredictable events, being finally thrown into the one camp and having to go over to one side.' She had long ago made up her mind that in August they should go home. The staff, with the exception of Brockman, believed that they should stay. Mountbatten decided to seek advice and on 7 July Ismay and Campbell-Johnson set off for London. 'All going round in circles', Edwina wrote in her diary that night, 'tempers short and heat intense.'

Now Mountbatten was in a quandary. Previously he had taken it for granted that he would stay as Governor General of both Dominions or of neither. He had told Patricia on 11 June that he was still waiting for Jinnah to invite him to take on the office – 'I won't stay unless he does – so it's once more touch and go if I'm here for several years or until 15th August. To remain as Governor General of India alone would, he felt, identify the supreme British authority in the area as the servant of one country and thus destroy Britain's reputation for impartiality as well as his own. 'He fears the loss of objective status will be a crippling handicap to his usefulness and may well dissipate the good will he has won from Hindu and Moslem alike,' recorded Campbell-Johnson. Yet the Indians still wanted his services, and to refuse them on the ground that Pakistan did not feel likewise would be to cause quite unmerited offence. What was more, his Muslim advisers assured him that Pakistan too would welcome his taking on the Governor Generalship of India. Jinnah confirmed that, even if he did take on the task in New Delhi, the Pakistanis would wish him to remain as Chairman of the Joint Defence Committee. Auchinleck went so far as to say that few British officers would be prepared to stay on if Mountbatten left. The Viceroy's distress and confusion of mind is shown in his letter of Patricia.

'Your poor old Daddy has finally and irretrievably 'boobed' and I've now landed myself in a position from which I cannot conceivably extricate myself with honour.

Either I accept to stay with the Dominion of India and be for ever accused of taking sides … or I let down the Congress leaders … Mummy feels I should preserve my reputation for impartiality and go on 15th August. The others feel I cannot let down Nehru and must stay. In both cases I'm in the wrong. In fact I've at last made a mess of things through over-confidence and over-tiredness. I'm just whacked and worn out and would really like to go.

I'm so depressed darling, because until this stupid mishandling of the Jinnah situation I'd done so well. It has certainly taken me down many pegs.'

CHAPTER 11: MOUNTBATTEN'S LOBBYING EFFORTS

Mountbatten's Desperate Lobbying

One may well ask the question why Mountbatten was so desperate to become the Governor General of both the dominions of India and Pakistan? It was stated both by the Congress leaders and Mountbatten that Pakistan was to be a temporary aberration soon to be rectified. It may be recalled that in the Governors' Conference held in New Delhi in April 1947 Mountbatten had told the assembly he was not going 'lightly to abandon hope for a united India.' He wanted the world to know the British had made every effort possible to keep India united. If Britain failed it was of utmost importance that the world know it was, 'Indian opinion rather than a British decision that made partition the choice.' He himself thought, he told the Governors, a future Pakistan was so inherently unviable that it should 'be given a chance to fail on its own demerits' so that later 'the Moslem League could revert to a unified India with honour.'

It will be seen later with ample and irrefutable evidence of Mountbatten's Herculean efforts to make Pakistan as 'unviable' as possible just being Governor General of one Dominion. What he would have done had he been Governor General of both Dominions one can only conjecture. Was it the Congress grand design to have Mountbatten as Governor General of both India and Pakistan so that he could fulfil his objective of 'revert to unified India with honour?'

In Mountbatten's effort to become Governor General of both the Dominions he even enlisted the aid of the American Ambassador in New Delhi Henry Grady. An extraordinary telegram was sent by Henry Grady to US Secretary of State George C. Marshall on 2 July 1947 reproduced below:

SECRET AMERICAN EMBASSY No. 475,

NEW DELHI

2 July 1947, 2 pm

Received: 2 July 1947, 7.22pm

In private conversation after lunch yesterday, Viceroy told me that during morning he had been going over draft of new India Act with Congress and League leaders (meeting separately) and that 'things had been going very well'. He said draft would be based on conception of continuing GOI [Governor of India] and establishment [of] Pakistan as a secession Govt. and indicated clearly, he would like [to] remain after August 15 as Governor-General – at least of India, preferably of both Dominions. He seemed to feel it was important that he continue head of even after separation of Pakistan area from rest of India. (MYTEL 459, June 27, re[garding] Nehru's request that Mountbatten remain as Governor-General both Dominions).

In this connection Viceroy expressed hope I could talk with Jinnah in near future since he felt it would help matters if Jinnah had some indication U.S. intended establish diplomatic relations with Pakistan. He said it might be possible for U.S. set up a diplomatic mission in Pakistan under a *Charge [d'affaires]* responsible to AMA [American Ambassador] in Delhi. On other hand he said he had told U.K. High Commissioner Shone that U.K. should send High Commissioner to Pakistan (MYTEL 454, June 27). I gathered Viceroy would like U.S. to make an early commitment to Jinnah re. some of diplomatic representation to Karachi as an aid to him in his negotiations with Jinnah. I hope the opportunity will come soon to talk informally with Jinnah. I shall get his views without, of course, making any commitment so far as our Govt. is concerned.

Please repeat to [U.S. Embassy in] London.

GRADY

It may be noticed in the telegram that even Nehru had requested Grady to use his good offices to ensure that Mountbatten remained Governor General of both Dominions. What business Nehru had to meddle in the appointment of Governor General is left to the imagination of the reader. Meanwhile, Mountbatten was pretending all along that if he could not become Governor General of both the Dominions, he would not accept the Governor Generalship of India alone. Pretence it certainly was, as his main objective having failed, he was prepared to settle for India alone. Was he going to abandon all the glitter, pomp and ceremony that went with being a Governor General? Congress had already offered him Governor Generalship on 17 May 1947 assuming that Muslim League would certainly make Mountbatten a similar offer. One can only have grudging admiration for Jinnah for defying mighty Mountbatten at least on the score of the appointment of Governor General. How it must have deflated Mountbatten's ego! Neither Jinnah nor Mountbatten had any doubt as to who had emerged victor from the manoeuvres and intrigues of the past few weeks.

The question then arose whether Mountbatten should stay on as the Governor General of India since the League had given a written confirmation of Jinnah's decision to assume the office of the Governor General of Pakistan. In this connection it is interesting to look at a secret note written by Edwina to Mountbatten on 5 July 1947. In fact, the writer, has not come across any other note written by Edwina in the Transfer of Power Documents.

Edwina writes:

3. 'There is another factor which worries me and that is that if Jinnah adopts the complete Hitler attitude, even if that attitude were to be for the destruction of Pakistan and remove the chance of getting the assets he so badly needs, you will find yourself placed in a very difficult position and might, as a constitutional Governor-General to Congress, possibly prove a liability more than an asset. I think this is most unlikely but it should be borne in mind.'

4. 'Finally there is the factor that if the Congress offer is accepted one will have both mentally and practically to be prepared to serve their interests completely, excepting in those cases where approval will have been received for your services to be used for the best interests of both communities in connection with taking the Chair at Meetings, etc. If Congress felt that you were accepting the offer with the intention of seeing that Pakistan got a square deal from Congress, I sincerely think they would decide they would sooner be served by someone else.'

'One thing that weighs heavily with me on this whole question and makes me consider that you have a real duty to Congress is the fact that you are in some ways I think in honour bound to them by having let them understand that you would remain here to give your support after the 15th August, and although this was only a verbal assurance and had important qualifications they would, I am certain, feel you had broken faith with them. This however will be cleared up presumably by your talk with them.'

EDWINA MOUNTBATTEN OF BURMA

Even Edwina showed a clear bias for the Congress. Regardless of losing Pakistan Mountbatten was determined to stay on in India as Governor General of India alone. He made a complete U-turn denying his earlier stance and started canvassing to remain Governor General of India. He had a plan to carry through which be could not abandon. What did it matter if Jinnah had spoilt the party! Although he had stated time and time again that be could not continue as Governor General of one Dominion only why did be now resort to furious lobbying to remain Governor General of India alone? He had to get the blessings of his masters in London. To achieve this he sent his Chief of Staff Lord Ismay and his Press Secretary Alan Campbell-Johnson to London on 5th July 1947. Ismay was to lobby with the top brass and Campbell-Johnson was to take care of the press.

Meanwhile Mountbatten on the same day wrote to Prime Minister Attlee. Relevent extracts.

PERSONAL/CONFIDENTIAL

THE VICEROY'S HOUSE, NEW DELHI

5 July 1947

My Dear Prime Minister,

I hope you will not mind my sending Pug Ismay home. But I have reached a dangerous *impasse*. As you know, it was Jinnah who always begged me to stay as Viceroy or overall Governor-General, or in some capacity over the two Dominions until partition was complete; and it was Congress who were unwilling that I should have anything to do with the League. It took me quite a bit of persuasion, when Nehru asked me to become the first Governor General of the Dominion of India, to get him and Patel to agree that I should also be allowed to act in the same capacity for Pakistan in order to retain my impartiality. ....

.... You can imagine therefore what a bombshell it was when he suddenly announced his intention of being the Governor-General of Pakistan himself.

I have always held, and frequently stated my view, that it would be morally indefensible for me to stay with one side alone after having dealt impartially and justly with both sides for so long. I still adhere to that view.

There is, however, another moral consideration, which is that, though Jinnah having misled us, we have quite unintentionally misled Congress. There is no doubt that from mid-May up to this moment it has never entered their minds that I would not stay with them. Further, if I now refuse, they will say that Jinnah has secured his last triumph over Congress and through me.

I feel that I must seek a decision from the King based, of course, on your advice. I hope also that you may feel it right to consult the Opposition. If it is your wish that I should be Governor General of the Dominion of India, at all events till partition is over in April, then I trust that you will be able to make that clear in the debate. If on the other hand it is your wish that I should refuse, I am of course prepared to take full responsibility on my own shoulders, since it would embarrass H.M. Government with the Government of the future Dominion of India if they were to refuse to allow an Englishman to accept the position of first Governor-General.

Yours very sincerely,

DICKE MOUNTBATTEN

Mountbatten's Lobbying Continues

It is quite extra ordinary that although all along both Mountbatten and his staff were vehemently opposed to Mountbatten continuing as Governor General of India alone suddenly everybody changed their minds and supported Mountbatten's bid to stay on as the Governor General of India. It did not take long for Mountbatten to convince his staff to retract their decision.

To justify his continuing on as Governor General of India Mountbatten convened a meeting of his staff on 7 April 1947 to discuss the issue. The Viceroy stated that one of the main reasons why Her Excellency had expressed an option opposed to the Governor General suggestion that he should remain as Governor-General of the Dominion of India was that his whole staff had, three or four weeks previously, agreed that it would be unthinkable for him to stay on with one Dominion only (*writer's comment* - because they were all convinced Mountbatten would be Governor General of both Dominions). He said that it had been a great surprise to him when his staff, with the exception of Captain Brockman, had unanimously advised him that he should stay on. He still felt that, if he did so, there was very real chance that he would be accused of acting dishonourably.

It is strange that Mountbatten's entire staffs were till the meeting opposed to his staying on as Governor General of India found all sorts of arguments in favour of his continuing. Mieville his Private Secretary found and illogical argument to substantiate his support for staying on. He suggested that the main reason why the staff had, three or four weeks previously, advised against Mountbatten remaining as Governor General of one Dominion only was because they felt it likely that, in such circumstances, his usefulness would in the main disappear after the transfer of power, and that he would not be able to take the Chair at the Partition Committee and at the Joint Defence Council. All that, however, was now completely changed because Jinnah's attitude. Mountbatten confirmed that Jinnah, at his interview two days' previously, had been at great pains to emphasise what a great help to Pakistan it would be if he stayed on in any capacity. Jinnah had also at that interview agreed to Mountbatten acting Chairman of the Joint Defence Council. Jinnah had stated that nobody would question Mountbatten's impartiality – such a thought would not enter the minds of member of the Muslim League. The arguments appear to be quite incomprehensible.

The main reason why most of the staff were prepared to stay on in India was simple. Who wanted to abandon the life of luxury of the Viceroy's establishment for the grim conditions then prevailing in England. From all the VIP status they would be reduced to a pretty spartan life full of drudgery. Ismay describes the conditions that he left behind in London 'The last two or three months in England had been particularly cheerless and uncomfortable. There had been an almost record snow-fall, followed by a prolonged frost, there was grave shortage of coal, and electric power was drastically restricted, food and clothing rationing were still in force and finally there had been a very rapid thaw, with much flooding.' Who wanted to return to these grim conditions leaving a life of luxury?

When the Cabinet discussed the question on 7 July, only Cripps emphasised that, by becoming the servant of one of the two countries he had previously ruled, he would damage his position and reputation. Everybody else felt that the balance of advantage was heavily in favour of his staying on: 'In the interests of the new Dominion of India, he ought to complete the work he had started with such distinction: if his services were lost at this stage, the whole policy embodied in the Indian Independence Bill might be endangered.' Ismay argued Mountbatten was very uncertain what decision he should take about his own future, and would welcome the advice of His Majesty's Government. He had not so far given a definite reply to the Congress invitation to accept the post of Governor General of India; on the other hand, he had been made aware of a general assumption on their part that he would not refuse. Mountbatten felt that, if he accepted the Congress invitation after being largely responsible for partition, he might be subsequently criticised for siding with Congress and for failing in impartiality during his period of office as Viceroy; he compared his position to that of the Governors of Bengal and the Punjab who had declined to consider taking office in one part of their existing Provinces, after partition. From his personal point of view, he would gladly return in August. As against these considerations the Viceroy felt that it would be wrong to leave his work only partly done out of considerations for his personal interests.

It will surely be noticed both Jenkins Governor of Punjab and Burrows Governor of Bengal declined to continue after 15 August as this was the most honourable course to follow.

After the Cabinet meeting, Ismay was dispatched to Chartwell to establish the views of Churchill and secured an equally emphatic endorsement of acceptance: 'Lord Mountbatten might be of great help to the Hindustan Government in the next year or so and in Mr. Churchill's opinion he ought not to withhold that aid.' Finally, the King was also recruited to urge his cousin to take on the job. Mountbatten was already more than half convinced that he both ought and wanted to become the first Governor General of an independent India. He required no further encouragement.

The fact that an active politician had been appointed as Governor-General of Pakistan caused considerable concern among many circles in England. Campbell-Johnson, giving a resume of his editorial interviews in London to Mountbatten, wrote:

'Lord Layton said that in his view Jinnah's decision would be widely regarded as selfish and ambitious act, and that it would involve a remarking down here with the British Press of his reputation, which was at its peak during his visit to England in December last.'

It was also pointed out that Jinnah was not eminently suitable for this post because of his known autocratic ways. Thus, *The Economist* commented on 19 July 1947.

'The constitutional theory of a Governor-General in a Dominion is that he represents the King and bears the same relation to the Ministers forming the Government as the King does to his Ministers in the United Kingdom. It is recognised that the rights of a Dominion include the right of recommending a person for appointment as Governor-General. But that the Governor- Generalship should be held by an active party politician who frankly states his intention of continuing his political leadership after assuming the office, is an innovation which radically alters the nature of the Dominion bond. The development is the more serious because Mr. Jinnah's rule gives promise of being a very thinly veiled dictatorship. His motive in demanding the office of the Governor-General is no doubt to obtain the position which belongs to it in the eyes of the Indian masses. The Viceroy as Governor-General has been hitherto, even though to a restricted degree in recent years, the supreme executive ruler and his Ministers have been simply the members of his Executive Council. By force of mental habit the man in the street will continue to think of the Governor-General as being more important than his Prime Minister.'

As shown before, it is difficult to see how Jinnah could have put forward any name other than his own for Governor-Generalship. *The Times* apreciated Jinnah's difficulties when it said: 'Yet those who will be called to rule Pakistan may hold that the relatively undeveloped qualities that make up much of its territory must be guided by a Governor-General capable of exercising the functions of higher control and co-ordination which formerly vested in Canning or Curzon.

The Congress circles were indignant for they suspected that Jinnah, as usual, had tried to put them in a highly embarrassing position for Jinnah had gone a step further than the framers of the 'Quit India' Resolution in asking for an indigenous Governor-General. He was accused of a breach of faith on the score that it had been agreed by both parties that for the transitional period Mountbatten should be Governor-General of both Dominions. Jinnah denied these charges vehemently in his first press conference on 13 July 1947 after it had been announced on 10 July 1947 that he was to become Governor-General of Pakistan. 'These reports are entirely devoid of any truth and I am surprised that even responsible men have been misrepresenting me and making false allegations against the League and myself.'

In the same press conference, he also put forward his own theory of Governor- Generalship. Since the Governor-General were nominated by the successor authorities, namely, the Congress and the League, 'the Governors-General are the chosen of the people and not, as it is ordinarily understood, appointed by the King ....' Rather a startling statement from a constitutional purist like Jinnah! When he was asked whether it was not a fact that the Governor-General held office during His Majesty's pleasure, Jinnah replied. 'It is purely a form, nothing but a form. The Governors-General are the chosen of the people and that is the reason why I have accepted this honour.'

CHAPTER 12: BEGINNING OF PARTITION

Implementation of the Partition Plan

We have already seen the genealogy of the partition of Bengal and the role of the *Bhadralok*. When Curzon partitioned Bengal in 1905, this elicited a storm of protest which forced the British Government to rescind his decision within six years. In 1947, Bengal was partitioned again. On this occasion, however, hardly a voice was raised in protest. Although strong movements were going on India for the partition of both Bengal and the Punjab there was no British initiative on this subject till the arrival of Mountbatten. In the series of meetings that Mountbatten held with Jinnah in early April Jinnah was forced to accept the partition of Bengal and the Punjab which was never a part of the conception of Pakistan. To quote Mountbatten describing his encounter with Jinnah, "You know, not only did this go on for hours, it went over several discussions. He simply was caught in his own trap. He finally gave up and said 'so you insist on giving me a moth-eaten Pakistan'." Mountbatten's forcing the partition of Bengal and the Punjab was merely a part of the Congress' design.

The Statement of the British Government on 3 June 1947 laid down that the provincial Legislative Assemblies of Bengal and the Punjab (excluding the European members) should meet in two parts, one representing the Muslim majority districts and the other the rest of the province. For the purpose of determining the population of the districts, the 1941 census figures should be taken as authoritative. The Muslim majority districts in those two provinces were as set out in the appendix to the Statement. The members of the two parts of the Legislative Assembly sitting separately would be empowered to vote whether or not the province should be partitioned. If a simple majority of either part decided in favour of partition, division would take place and arrangements would be made accordingly.

Before the question of partition was decided, it was desirable for the representatives of each part to know in advance which Constituent Assembly (India or Pakistan) the province as a whole would join in the event of the two parts deciding to remain united. Therefore, if any member of either part of the Legislative Assembly so demanded, a meeting should be held of all the members of the Legislative Assembly (other than Europeans) at which a decision would be taken on the issue.

In the event of partition being decided upon, each part of the Legislative Assembly would, on behalf of the areas represented by it, decide whether its constitution should be framed by the existing Constituent Assembly, or by a new and separate one.

The partition of Bengal and the Punjab according to Muslim majority districts and non-Muslim majority districts was a preliminary step of a purely temporary nature. As soon as a decision involving partition has been for either province, a Boundary Commission would be set up by the Governor General, the membership and terms of reference of which would be settled in consultation with those concerned. The Boundary Commission would be instructed to demarcate the boundaries of the two parts of the Punjab on the basis of ascertaining the contiguous majority areas of the Muslims and the non- Muslims. It would also be instructed to consider the other factors. Similar instruction would be given to the Bengal Boundary Commission. Until the report of a Boundary Commission has been put into effect, the Provision Boundaries indicated in the Appendix of the Statement would be used. We shall see the workings of the Boundary Commission in depth later and assess the monumental problems created by the words 'other factors'.

The Legislative Assembly of Sind (excluding the European members) would also at a special meeting take its own decision as to whether its constitution should be framed by the existing, or a new and separate Constituent Assembly. With regard to the North-West Frontier Province, it would be necessary, in view of its special position, to give it an opportunity of reconsidering its position in the event of the whole or any part of the Punjab declaring against joining the existing Constituent Assembly. A referendum would be made to the electors of the present Legislative Assembly to choose between the existing Constituents and a new and separate one. The Governor General was examining how best British Baluchistan, in view of its geographical situation, could be given a similar opportunity of reconsidering its position.

Though Assam was predominantly a non-Muslim province, the district of Sylhet, which was contiguous to Bengal, was predominantly Muslim. If it should be decided to partition Bengal, a referendum would be held in Sylhet district to decide whether the district should continue to form part of the Assam province or should be amalgamated with the new province of East Bengal. Should the referendum result in favour of amalgamation with East Bengal, a Boundary Commission, with terms of reference similar to those for the Punjab and Bengal, would be set up to demarcate the Muslim majority areas of Sylhet district. In any case the rest of the Assam province would continue to participate in the proceedings of the existing Constituent Assembly.

The June 3rd plan had laid down that the question whether or not India should be partitioned was a matter to be decided by the Indian people themselves. In Bengal the provincial Legislative Assembly met on 20 June and decided by 126 votes to ninety in favour of joining a new Constituent Assembly (i.e. not remaining United). The members from the non-Muslim majority areas of West Bengal then met and decided by fifty-eight votes to twenty-one that the province should be partitioned and that West Bengal should join the existing Indian Constituent Assembly; while the members from the Muslim majority areas of East Bengal met and decided by 106 votes to thirty-five that the province should not be partitioned and, by almost the same majority of votes, that East Bengal should join a new Constituent Assembly and that Sylhet should be amalgamated with the province.

The voting in Bengal passed off in a comparatively peaceful atmosphere, but in the Punjab there were demonstrations and communal disorders. The Punjab Legislative Assembly met, in fact, under a strong police guard. It decided by ninety-one votes to seventy-seven to join a new Constituent Assembly. The members from the Muslim majority areas of West Punjab then decided, by sixty-nine votes to twenty-seven, against the partition of the province; while the members from the non-Muslim majority areas of East Punjab decided, by fifty votes to twenty-two, that the province should be partitioned and that East Punjab should join the existing Indian Constituent Assembly.

The Sind Legislative Assembly met on 26 June and decided by thirty votes to twenty to join a new Constituent Assembly i.e. Pakistan.

There was some difficulty in setting the procedure for ascertaining the wishes of the people of Baluchistan. Nehru had suggested the possibility of sending a commission to meet the tribal *jirgas* and of holding a referendum in Quetta town. But the Chief Commissioner, Sir Geoffrey Prior, advised that such a course was not feasible. The Viceroy finally decided that the Shahi *jirga* and the non-official members of the Quetta Municipality should be summoned in order to decide the future of the province. The members of these bodies met and unanimously decided to join a new Constituent Assembly. The seven Hindu and Parsi members of the Quetta Municipality did not attend the meeting.

With regard to Sylhet, neither the Congress nor the Muslim League was confident as to the outcome of the proposed reference to the Assembly voters from that district. Liaqat Ali Khan, for instance, pointed out that while the Muslims formed 60.7 percent of the population, they formed only 54.27 of the total electoral rolls; he suggested that the number of Muslims votes should therefore be multiplied by a factor which would equate the voting strength of the Muslims with their population strength. The Congress, on the other hand, claimed that the voters in the Labour and in the Commerce and Trade constituencies of the district should be allowed to participate in the referendum. Ultimately, the referendum was confined to voters in the General, Muslim and Indian Christian constituencies. It was held early in July. A majority of the voters – 239,619 to 184,041 – were in favour of separation and joining East Bengal.

In the North-West Frontier Province, though the Muslim League campaign of civil disobedience had been withdrawn, the situation was still tense. Sir Olaf Caroe had been replaced as Governor by General Rob Lockhart. The referendum in the province was entrusted to British officers of the Indian Army with experience of the frontier, under a Referendum Commissioner, Brigadier J. B. Booth. The referendum in the North-West Frontier Province was held from 6 to 17 July 1947. Of the total electorate of 572,798 slightly over 50% took part 289,244 voting for and took 2,874 voting against joining a new Constituent Assembly. Thus, in effect East Bengal, West Punjab, Sind, Baluchistan and North West Frontier Province all voted for Pakistan.

The Genesis of Partition

In the aftermath of the Cripps Offer of 1942, which contained the seeds of Pakistan as it were, the British had set about determining the territories visualised by the Lahore Resolution of 1940 as forming independent Muslim States in the North-West and the North-East of India. The exercise got under way not long after Wavell had assumed the Viceroyalty of India on 20 October 1943. A process of investigation and evaluation for demarcating the notional areas of Pakistan was thus begun both in England and in India. In this 'Pakistan enquiry', V.P. Menon came to play a rather crucial role. As Reforms Commissioner, he had had a close association with both Wavell and Mountbatten. Throughout the early 1940's there was a sustained demand for Pakistan from the Muslims. These demands prompted Viceroy Wavell to state it was imperative that the British Government reach some 'definite conclusions on the Pakistan issue'. Wavell asked V.P. Menon to examine the issue and prepare a report. On 23 January 1946, Menon and a senior ICS B.N. Rau produced the required note under the caption: Note on Demarcation of 'Pakistan' Areas.

Menon's plan stated that Muslims in British India numbered approximately 79 million out of a total population of 296 million or about 27 percent. The total population of the Pakistan areas claimed by the Muslim League in the Western Zone was about 36 million out of which 22 million were Muslims and 14 million non-Muslims. In the Eastern Zone, out of a total population of about 70 million, about 34 million or 49 percent were non-Muslims. Menon contended that according to these statistics, the non-Muslims in both zones were 'a substantial minority'; they also formed a majority of population in certain 'blocks of territory' in each zone. If Muslims, on the basis of 27 percent of total population, he argued, could claim separation of certain areas, the non- Muslims – Hindus and Sikhs – who formed a much larger percentage of the population in 'blocks of territory' in those zones could not be included in Pakistan areas. He stipulated that two conditions had to be satisfied by protagonists of Pakistan, i.e.

'(1) Each Zone must form a continuous block of territory in which the Muslims predominate.

(2) The non-Muslim population in each Zone … should not be much more than 27 percent of the total population.'

Menon admitted, by obvious implication, that both the conditions, so presumptuously laid down by him, were satisfied, because in the Western Zone Pakistan was to consist of Sindh, the North-West Frontier Province, Baluchistan and the Lahore, Rawalpindi and Multan Divisions of the Punjab, and the Eastern Zone was to comprise Rajshahi, Dacca, and Chittagong Divisions of Bengal. The total population of non-Muslims in the Western Zone was a little over 26 percent – about 7 million out of a total population of 26 million. In Bengal there were 30 percent non-Muslims, i.e. 11 million out of a total population of 37 million. The discussion should have ended here, but Menon deviated from his own formula and conveniently adopted a district-wise partition, according to which he excluded Amritsar, sacred to the Sikhs, from Pakistan's Western Zone and Calcutta from the Eastern Zone because both the districts were largely non-Muslim. According to the district-wise device, Darjeeling and Jalpaiguri were excluded but Nadia, Murshidabad and Jessore remained in the Pakistan Zone. So far so good; but soon his axe was to fall on Gurdaspur which he lumped with Amritsar on the ground of their forming a 'compact block', while Wavell mentioned 'geographical reasons' for allotment of Gurdaspur to India.

The novel criterion laid down by Menon was not only illogical but perverse; it ignored the fact that many of the non-Muslim majority districts in the proposed partitioned Punjab had more than 27 percent Muslim population. So far Menon had demarcated the areas on the basis of *divisional* boundaries. But he excluded Amritsar District from Lahore Division on the ground that it had a Muslim population of about 44 percent and that it was 'particularly sacred to the Sikhs'. He did not stop here: The District of Gurdaspur was also included in the Indian Punjab. Surprisingly, in his note, he did not give the population figures of Gurdaspur, presumably as it had a Muslim majority population of 51.1 percent. Ingeniously, he lumped Amritsar and Gurdaspur together, giving their total population with an explanation that these two districts had been excluded from Pakistan in order, ostensibly, to meet the Sikh objections. But his stratagem could not substantially solve the Sikh problem as he himself admitted that 'a substantial minority [of Sikhs] would still be left in Pakistan'. In the Eastern Zone, Menon's plan was to exclude Calcutta. In fact, the inclusion of Gurdaspur in the

India Punjab was not for the sake of the Sikhs. The real cause, as he wrote later, was:

'It is possible that a predominantly Muslim State like Kashmir cannot be kept away from Pakistan for long and we may leave this matter to find its natural solution. Unlike Hyderabad, it does not lie in the bosom of Pakistan and it can claim an exit to India, especially if a portion of the Gurdaspur District goes to East Punjab.'

We are not sure if Wavell was privy to Menon's machinations but he did admit that Gurdaspur had a Muslim majority, citing 'geographical reasons' in favour of its inclusion in India. As for Amritsar, its inclusion in the Indian Punjab was justified on the ground of its being the holiest city of the Sikhs. But Wavell was not unmindfull of the inconsistencies involved in the plan and admitted that but for 'the special importance of Amritsar, demarcation in the Punjab could have been on divisional boundaries'.

He also realised that it was 'awkward' to place Gurdaspur in India as much of the Lahore District was irrigated with water from the Upper Bari Doab Canal with headworks in Gurdaspur. But the Viceroy as well as the others associated with the 'Pakistan enquiry' chose to keep quiet except for I.D. Scott, Deputy Private Secretary to the Viceroy, who controverted Menon's formula for demarcation of boundaries. He pointed out the fallacy of Menon's argument by detecting the fact that while calculating the population figures, Menon had failed to take into account the Muslim population of the tribal areas in the NWFP which, if included, would reduce the non-Muslim element in the Western Zone from 27% to 25%. He also noted that Menon had conveniently overlooked including Sylhet, a predominantly Muslim district, in the Eastern Zone, which would have reduced Menon's figures of the non-Muslim population in that zone from 30% to about 28%.

Menon had purposely omitted discussion of Sylhet in his note. When asked by Abell, he explained, rather unconvincingly, that they, Menon and Rau, had adopted 'the most convenient basis of demarcation' and had left out Sylhet, though a predominantly Muslim district, because without Sylhet, Assam would not be a viable province. Governor Akbar Hydari of Assam suggested that the amalgamation of Sylhet with Bengal 'should be conditional on small territorial adjustments to secure Assam's communications with Cachar.' Nehru suggested a referendum in Sylhet in view of 'the balance of population there…'. In the final 'Revised Draft Announcement', provision was made, for the first time, for a referendum in Sylhet as well as for demarcation of 'Muslim majority areas of Sylhet district and contiguous Muslim majority areas of adjoining districts…'.

The district-wise demarcation in the Western Zone and in Bengal was a well- thought-out manoeuvre. But for such demarcation, Assam would have been cut off completely from the rest of India. The exclusion of Jalpaiguri and Darjeeling from Pakistan and their inclusion in India was intended to 'provide Hindustan with a corridor to the non-Muslim areas of Assam'. As if Gurdaspur's inclusion in Eastern Punjab troubled Menon's conscience, he decided to include Dinajpur with a Muslim population of 50.2 percent in Eastern Pakistan admitting:

'Since we have excluded Gusdaspur from the western zone of Pakistan, we might well include Dinajpur in the eastern zone.'

The division of Bengal and Assam into Muslim and non-Muslim majority areas as envisaged by the Plan came in for some trenchant criticism from a few of Jinnah's correspondents. They controverted the rationale of grouping the Scheduled Castes and the tribes with the Hindus, and of including Darjeeling, Jalpaiguri, Goalpara, Chachar and Purnea in Hindustan. They contended that, given the chance, the Scheduled Castes would cast their lot with the Muslims. Besides, the tribes, as had already been pointed out by Yeats, Census Commissioner in 1941, could not be 'classified religiously'. They maintained that Goalpara and Cachar in Assam, and Purnea in Bihar, could be claimed by Pakistan on the basis of Muslim-majority population; also that a claim could be staked for Darjeeling, fairly endowed with mineral resources, as a recompense for the loss of mineral-rich areas to West Bengal.

These suggestions, however, were obviously rather belated inasmuch as both Bengal the Punjab Legislative Assemblies had already voted for partition on 20 and 23 June, respectively.

Jinnah and the Muslim League, to some extent, fell victims to the Lahore Resolution of 1940 which included a clause for the 'territorial adjustments'. It is true that Jinnah had conceded that Ambala and Jullundur Divisions in the Punjab and certain areas in Bengal might have to be given up – a fact also firmed by Aga Khan who informed Wavell that 'Jinnah was prepared to concede Amritsar and Ambala and almost all – except Calcutta'. But Jinnah had definitely not bargained for the plan which was ultimately prepared and drawn up by Menon and British officers, particularly Glancy, Jenkins and Abell, and which was based on the following considerations:

(i)   to make Pakistan as 'small and unattractive' as possible by reducing its area;

(ii) to cede Gurdaspur to Hindustan in order to provide access to the Jammu and Kashmir State; and

(iii) to provide Hindustan with a corridor to the non-Muslim areas of Assam.

CHAPTER 13: INTEGRATING THE PRINCELY STATES

Patel, VP Menon and the Princely States

Sardar Patel and VP Menon
(hindustantimes.com)

It will be recalled that in the meeting Mountbatten had with the Indian Leaders on 13 June 1947 issues of far reaching importance were raised. The main conclusions reached were as follows: - It was decided to set up a new department, called the 'States Department', to deal with matters of common concern, divided into two section ready for the partition of the country. It was agreed that there should be a meeting between the Indian leaders and representatives of the States (possibly the States Negotiating Committee) to consider the draft standstill formula and any other matters of common concern on a date to be decided, probably in July. It was further agreed that the residents should go on with the destruction of ephemeral records and documents, but that the Political Adviser should apply to Member for Education in the interim Government for the services of experts to assist in weeding out and sorting out the crown Representative's records. These records which contained information regarding the private lives of the rulers and the internal affairs of the States should be handed over, on the Transfer of Power, to the United Kingdom's High Commissioner.

This decision was followed by an important communication from Nehru to Mountbatten setting out his views with regard to the functions of the proposed new organisation. The communication was the subject of discussion at a meeting of the Viceroy's advisers, as a result of which VP Menon was charged with the task of preparing, in consultation with the Political Adviser, a note which should present definite proposals. VP produced a memorandum in which he suggested that the proposed department should function as a single organisation with two ministers, one from the Congress and the other from the Muslim League, and having two secretaries in charge, so that it could be divided into two on the partition of the country. This memorandum was approved by Mountbatten and duly circulated among the members of the Cabinet. Nehru, on behalf of the Congress, included the name of Patel (who was Member for Home and Information and Broadcasting in the interim Cabinet) as Minister, while Jinnah on behalf of the Muslim League suggested the name of Abdur Rab Nishtar.

A few days later, Patel sent for VP Menon and offered him the Secretaryship of the States Department. VP Menon told Patel that it was his intention to take all the leave he had earned and to retire from Government service after 15 August. Ever since 1917, he had been dealing with constitutional reforms. He had never expected that he would see freedom for India in his lifetime. Since that had materialised, his life's ambition was achieved. Further, he had been overworked and was feeling the strain. He had not taken a rest for may years. Patel told VP Menon that because of the abnormal situation in the country, people like himself should not think in terms of rest or retirement. He added that VP Menon had taken a prominent part in the transfer of power and that he should consider it his duty to work for the consolidation of freedom.

Since VP Menon was the Constitutional Adviser to Mountbatten and since the appointment was to take effect immediately, VP Menon was obliged to mention the matter to him. Mountbatten told VP Menon that he was proposing his appointment as Governor of one of the more important provinces. VP Menon said that from his conversations with Patel, he understood that he felt it to be in the interests of the country that he should remain for some time at least with the Government of India. Mountbatten advised VP Menon to accept Patel's offer and later on confirmed their conversation in a letter.

Following day, VP Menon called on Patel and showed him Mountbatten's letter and intimated his acceptance of his offer. VP Menon then had a long and frank conversation with him. VP Menon reminded him that ever since he had met him, for the first time on 21 August 1946, he had made it his purpose to consult him as far as possible on important developments in the constitutional field, and he particularly added that it had been his powerful support that had made possible the transfer of power. They had indeed got on well together, resolving occasional differences of opinion by mutual and amicable discussion. The position at that time was that though VP Menon consulted Patel, the final responsibility for whatever advice he gave to the Governor-General was his. Now that they were to work as Minister and Secretary, he was not quite sure how far they should hit it off together.

Patel replied that the question did not arise at all and that VP Menon should not think along those lines. When VP Menon said that there was a feeling that Congress leaders distrusted the permanent Services he replied that his fears were groundless. He added that, whatever might have been the attitude of politicians to the Services in the past, he was confident that in future everyone would play the game. For his own part, he would do everything possible to bring about a most cordial atmosphere between the Cabinet and the Services. And he kept his word.

VP Menon has recorded in his *The Integration of the Indian States* 'We then discussed the general situation in the country as a result of partition and the problem of the States in particular. VP Menon told Sardar that, under the Cabinet Mission plan, the States need not join either of the Constituent Assemblies, but that they could have particular arrangements with the Government of the Dominion to which they were geographically contiguous.

After the announcement of the partition, the rulers on our side of the border realised that they should strengthen the Indian Union and so were gradually coming into the Constituent Assembly. They were, however, very jealous about their sovereignty and I felt strongly that they should not be rubbed the wrong way. At the same time, the attitude of some of the rulers of the big States was disconcerting and Pakistan was playing with, the idea of getting some of the border States to cast in their lot with her. Sardar told me that the situation held dangerous potentialities and that if we did not handle it promptly and effectively, our hard-earned freedom might disappear through the States' door.'

Readers please note that although VP Menon was Reforms Commissioner in early June 1947 he was referring to independent India as 'the rulers on our side of the border.'

Patel next referred to the consequences of the lapse of paramountcy. VP Menon remarked that it was the greatest disservice the British had done them as well as the rulers. During the course of a century, the provinces and the States had been welded together. The edifice of central authority had rested on two pillars, one with foundations in the provinces and the other in the States. In all-India matters, co-operation and uniformity of policy so far as the States were concerned had been enforced through the residences. Important cantonments and military installations were located in the States. The Indian railway system spanned the territories of the States as well as the provinces and, in the interests of the safety and convenience of the travelling public, arrangements had been extended to the States whereby civil and criminal jurisdiction over railway lands had been handed over to the Crown Representatives. One of the provincial capitals was situated in a minor State. In posts and telegraphs, control of arms and ammunition, extradition and surrender of fugitives, control of opium and other narcotics, in the overall food policy, to mention only a few matters affecting all-India security and welfare, the machinery of the Political Department and the residencies had acted as a co-ordinating agency.

At the same time, VP Menon suggested to Patel that the British Government's decision to extinguish paramountcy might prove a not unmixed evil and that it was possible that good might yet come of it. The biggest advantage was that they would be writing on a clean slate, unhampered by treaties. VP Menon then told Patel that he was without any ready-made plan for the solution of the States' problems. In the meantime, they should be clear in their minds with regard at any rate to the procedure by which they should be tackled. The problems were altogether peculiar and in the unsettled state of things would sometimes demand quick decision. VP Menon deemed necessary, therefore, that the Prime Minister and the Cabinet should give a free hand to Patel in dealing with them. At its meeting held on 25 June the interim Cabinet accepted the proposal for the creation of the States Department and on 27 June a press *communiqué* was issued allotting the Department to Patel. VP Menon was named as the Secretary.

Enter Mountbatten to Influence Accession of States

VP Menon felt that with the disposition of some of rulers to cast in their lot with Pakistan, of a few others to assert their independence, and the keen desire of all to safeguard their sovereignty, some sort of organic bond should be forged between the Government of India and the States if the integrity of the country was to be preserved. The States which were geographically contiguous to India must be made to feel legally and morally that they were part of it. Some time back, in December 1942, VP Menon had drawn up a scheme for Viceroy Linlithgow in which he had suggested an interim federal government as a solution of the current political deadlock. VP Menon had made it clear that the federal scheme, as set out in the Government of India Act of 1935, was not a practical proposition during the war emergency. Its procedure for accession, which entailed protracted negotiations for the adjustment of treaty and fiscal rights, and the creation of the new legislature, which again involved difficult administrative arrangements, were far too complicated to be embarked upon at such a time.

VP Menon had suggested that the Government should ask the States to accede only on 'defence' and 'external affairs', without any other commitments. Since both the subjects were handled by the paramount power and not by the States, the rulers would not be losing any of the rights enjoyed by them. The existing Central Legislative Assembly and the Council of State could be enlarged to provide for the States' nominees, who would be appointed by the Governor-General from a panel of names suggested by the rulers. VP Menon saw that once this scheme (which would facilitate the unification of India's war effort) was implemented, a responsible government for the whole of India could be established at the centre and as such would attract all the principal political elements. The unity thus forged might heal India's internal dissension sufficiently to provide her leaders with a new outlook for the future constitution. Viceroy Linlithgow did not take any action on this suggestion. VP Menon felt that an analogous scheme should be tried now with regard to the States. To the two subjects of 'defence' and 'external affairs' they would add 'communications. The Cabinet Mission had suggested that these three subjects could be ceded to the Union Government by the States.

VP Menon approached Sardar and started giving him a brief outline of the plan which he had submitted to Lord Linlithgow. VP Menon pointed out the advantages if the States were to accede on three subjects. The basic unity of India would be achieved and, when the new constitution was framed, they could thrash out the necessary details concerning the relations between the centre and the States in due course. He explained to Sardar how the rulers could be brought in. 'Defence' was obviously a matter which no State could conduct by itself: 'external affairs' was a subject inextricably linked with 'defence' and, as the States had never handled it before, even the largest State could not hope to do so effectively: 'communications' was a means of maintaining the very life-lines of the country and without co-operation, the States could do nothing in this matter. VP Menon also pointed out that the communal flare-up in north India had made the non-Muslim rulers turn away from Pakistan and he suggested that they should use this development to their advantage. Provided that they did not demand any financial or other commitments, the rulers would not be unwilling to consider their proposal.

However, the time at their disposal was extremely short and if they planned for accession they should get it implemented before 15 August. Menon's most important consideration was the overall security of the country. If the rulers acceded on 'defence', the Government of India obtained right of entry into any State where internal stability was threatened. 'Defence' covered not only external aggression but internal security as well. Sardar was inclined to agree with Menon's proposal. VP Menon requested him to put it before Nehru and get his approval. To put down anything in writing at that stage was inadvisable as there was likelihood of leakage, and premature publicity would have been harmful to the plan.

Next day Sardar told VP Menon that Nehru agreed with the proposal 'if we could see it through.' It seemed to VP Menon from Sardar's remark that Nehru was probably sceptical about the success of the plan. Nor was Sardar himself over-optimistic. For one thing, he was doubtful whether they could get the accession policy implemented in the few weeks before 15 August; but, as Menon suggested to Sardar, the very shortness of time might work to their advantage. VP Menon proposed that the active co-operation of Mountbatten should be secured. Apart from his position, his grace and his gifts, his relationship to the Royal Family was bound to influence the rulers. Sardar whole-heartedly agreed and asked to approach him without delay. Here begins the real story of the accession of the States and Mountbatten's naked India bias.

Two days later, VP Menon met Mountbatten and mentioned to him his talk with Sardar and their tentative plan. VP Menon asked for his help in getting the States to accede on three subjects. VP Menon pointed out that they would not be losing anything in the result and suggested that it would be a great act of statesmanship on his part if he could bring it about. VP Menon felt that he was deeply touched by his remark that the wounds of partition might to some extent be healed by the States entering into relationship with the Government of India and that he would be earning the gratitude of generations of Indians if he could assist in achieving that basic unity of the country.

Mountbatten told VP Menon that he would think the matter over. VP Menon felt that he was seized momentarily by the fear that Mountbatten might be adversely influenced by some of his advisers. But to his joy, he accepted the plan. Mountbatten discussed the matter with Sardar. This frank talk enabled them to explain and understand each other's point of view. Nehru with the approval of the Cabinet, readily entrusted Mountbatten with the task of negotiating with the rulers on the question of accession and also with the task of dealing with Hyderabad.

Though the main policy was thus settled, VP Menon had not yet taken over charge of the States Department. He was fully occupied at the time with the Indian Independence Bill, the adaptation of the Government of India Act of 1935 for India and Pakistan and the administrative details connected with partition. They had on an average as many as seven or eight meetings a day, besides their own work in the Department, and later when the two-way exodus of populations started, the burden grew heavier. Meanwhile, Sir Conrad Corfield, the Political Adviser, had been pressing VP Menon to set up the States Department and was asking repeatedly for the agenda and other details of the forthcoming meeting of the rulers. Sardar and VP Menon finally held a meeting with him. His Department had circulated a preliminary draft of a Standstill Agreement between individual States and the two successor Governments.

The draft provided for the discontinuance of the payments of cash contributions and of the continuance of existing administrative arrangements in respect of such matters of common concern as were specified in the schedule. The schedule dealt mainly with matters in the economic field; it did not include even 'external affairs'. When VP Menon told Sir Conrad Corfield that the Government of India had decided on the policy of accession, he literally threw up his hands in surprise. He considered the policy of accession far too ambitious and recalled the tortuous and infructuous negotiations with the rulers between 1934 and 1939. VP Menon pointed out that those negotiations had been conducted in other circumstances by the Political Department but that now in the changed conditions they hoped to succeed. It was made clear to him that, while they would welcome every assistance from the Political Department, the ultimate responsibility of negotiating with the rulers would rest with the new States Department.

VP Menon assumed charge of the States Department on 5 July. On 3 July, he had met Sardar and suggested that the first thing to do when the States Department came into being was to allay any possible suspicions on the part of the rulers and that this could be done by means of a statement defining the attitude and policy of the Government of India towards the States. Sardar agreed that such a statement was necessary and he asked VP Menon to prepare one. This he gave on 4 July 1947.

Patel and Basketful of Princely Apples

V.P. Menon held a position of extraordinary influence in July 1947. While Secretary-designate of the States Department, and indeed after he assumed the Secretaryship on 5th July, he remained Constitutional Adviser to the Viceroy and was one of the latter's principal consultants on the drafting of the Indian Independence Bill, for weeks the subject of daily telegraphic exchanges between the Governor-General and the Secretary of State. Menon had earned the complete confidence both of Mountbatten and of Patel. Though his relations with Nehru were less intimate, he had been brought into close contact with the Prime Minister in the negotiations over the new plan for the transfer of power, and in that quarter likewise he was a valuable mediator. So closely did Menon work both with Mountbatten and Patel that it is difficult to be sure, from the records, in what sequence their key discussions occurred, or who originated ideas or actions in regard to the States at this time.

According to Mountbatten, the first time that he debated the States problem with Patel — and this must have been before the setting of the States Ministry, since he records that he did so because Menon had told him Patel was much more interested in the States than was the Prime Minister — Patel told him that he need not bother about the States because after the transfer of power the States peoples would rise, depose their Rulers and throw in their lot with the Congress. The Viceroy reminded him that the States had forces, trained and equipped by the British, ranging from a division in Hyderabad to personal bodyguards in small States, which would shoot down the rebels, and that the Princes were preparing themselves, on the advice of the Political Department, against any uprisings. A civil war would result, and India would lose far more than she would gain from a peaceful settlement. Patel asked what he meant. The Viceroy replied that the peaceful settlement he had in mind was to allow the Rulers to retain their titles, extra-territorial rights and personal property or Civil List, and in return they would join a Dominion — most of them India, a few, like Bahawalpur, Pakistan — only the three subjects of defence, external affairs and communications being reserved to the Central Government. Patel said he would think it over.

When he next came to see the Viceroy, having meanwhile talked with V.P. Menon — and here the two accounts converge — Patel said 'I am prepared to accept your offer provided that you give me a full basket of apples.' 'What do you mean?' asked Mountbatten. 'I'll buy a basket with 565 apples' — the computed number of States — 'but if there are even two or three apples missing the deal is off.' 'This,' said the Viceroy, 'I cannot completely accept, but I will do my best. If I give you a basket with, say, 560 apples will you buy it?' 'Well, I might,' replied Patel.

Menon assumed charge of the States Department on 5 July. On 3 July, he had met Patel and suggested that the first thing to do when the States Department came into being was to allay any possible suspicions on the part of the rulers and that this could be done by means of a statement defining the attitude and policy of the Government of India towards the States. Patel agreed that such a statement was necessary and he asked Menon to prepare one. This he gave on 4 July 1947.

Patel was well pleased with the statement. He was satisfied that it was concise and conciliatory in tone. With its issue by Sardar the next day, the States Department was formally inaugurated. The statement appealed to the rulers to accede on three subjects. It pointed out: 'The States have already accepted the basic principle that for defence, foreign affairs and communications they would come into the Indian Union. We ask no more of them than accession on these three subjects in which the common interests of the country are involved.'

The statement went on: 'This country with its institutions is the proud heritage of the people who inhabit it. It is an accident that some live in the States and some in British India, but all alike partake of its culture and character. We are all knit together by bonds of blood and feeling no less than of self-interest. None can segregate us into segments; no impassable barriers can be set up between us. I suggest that it is therefore better for us to make laws sitting together as friends than to make treaties as aliens. I invite my friends the rulers of States and their people to the councils of the Constituent Assembly in this spirit of friendliness and co-operation in a joint endeavour, inspired by common allegiance to our motherland for the common good of us all.'

The statement stressed that the Congress 'are no enemies of the Princely Order, but, on the other hand, wish them and their people under their aegis all prosperity, contentment and happiness. Nor would it be my policy to conduct the relations of the new department with the States in any manner which savours of the domination of one over the other; if there would be any domination, it would be that of our mutual interests and welfare.' The statement ended with the appeal: 'We are at a momentous stage in the history of India.

By common endeavour we can raise the country to a new greatness while lack of unity will expose us to fresh calamities. I hope the Indian States will bear in mind that the alternative to co-operation in the general interest is anarchy and chaos which will overwhelm great and small in a common ruin, if we are unable to act together in the minimum of common tasks.'

Two things are clear. First, the policy of pressing for accession before 15th August on the three subjects, without financial commitment, as the alternative to confronting the States with the choice between joining a Constituent Assembly whose outcome could not be foreseen, and attempting a precarious if not spurious independence, originated as a joint decision of the Viceroy and the Indian section of the Government (specifically, Patel with Nehru's assent). When V.P. Menon told Sir Conrad Corfield of the decision 'he literally threw up his hands in surprise'. He did not then know the part of Crown Representative himself was to play. Sir Conrad, when he did learn of Lord Mountbatten's intentions, warned him what he was agreeing to use his influence as representative of the paramount power to recommend to the rulers a bargain which could not be guaranteed after independence.

The Political Adviser also considered the policy of accession within six weeks far too ambitious. He was told on behalf of the States Department that they assumed the responsibility for negotiating with the Rulers, though they would welcome assistance from the Political Department. Nor was the policy of rushed accession agreed with the Pakistan section of the Government. It was conveyed through official channels to Sardar Abdur Rab Nishtar, the Muslim League Minister for States. He made no comment, but both privately to the Viceroy and publicly Jinnah proclaimed his objection to the accession plan and his intention to guarantee the independence of States adhering to Pakistan.

Secondly, Mountbatten's direct and personal assistance in securing accession was asked for by the Indian leaders, though the Viceroy certainly welcomed the request. They believed that his personality, prestige and Royal connection would be invaluable in dealing with the Princes. Besides, they had plenty of other things on their hands.

The broad policy having been decided upon, intensive discussion, sometimes highly contentious, was then applied to four necessary corollaries: the drafting of standstill agreements covering all non-acceded matters, the drafting of a standard instrument of accession, the construction of machinery for negotiation, and the amendment of the draft Indian Independence Bill. On negotiating mechanism, Lord Mountbatten, speaking to the Chamber of Princes as Crown representative on 25th July, announced the formation of a Negotiating Committee consisting of ten Rulers and twelve Ministers of Princely States. This apparatus had in fact been decided upon after heated political debate. The Congress leaders would have nothing of negotiation by the British Residents and Agents in the States. To send Indian Government representatives to all the States was impossible in terms of personnel, and would have been resisted by many Rulers, who certainly could not be forced to accept them. It was agreed that there must be direct negotiation in Delhi and through correspondence. The Negotiating Committee was not a plenipotentiary representative of individual States, but was guardian of the interests of States generally in drafting the Standstill Agreements and Instruments of Accession; its strength and prestige, however, carried immense weight with all the Rulers when they were asked to sign the documents that it had approved in common form.

Mountbatten Addresses the Princes

Mountbatten addressed The Chamber of Princes
(jammukashmirnow.com)

On 10 July, a number of rulers and States' ministers met at Patel's residence. The Maharajahs of Patiala and Gwalior, and Sir B.L. Mitter (Baroda), K.M. Panikkar (Bikaner) and Hari Sharma (Patiala) were present. Patel urged that the States which had joined the Constituent Assembly should forthwith accede to India on three subjects, and pointed out that such a course would enable them to have a direct voice in shaping the policies of the central Government. The States' delegation appreciated the logic of the suggestion, but emphasised that the matter required careful consideration and a cautious approach. It was decided to hold a series of informal discussions with the rulers and their advisers. Various suggestions were made relating to the functions of the States Department. It was suggested, among other things, that the Department should deal only with matters of policy; that so far as the States acceding to the Union were concerned, the Department should cease to function as soon as the Union constitution became operative and that in the meanwhile it should function in consultation with an advisory committee of Ministers from the States. It was this conference which influenced the Rulers in deciding in favour of joining the Indian Union.

The next day an agenda was issued for the conference of the rulers to be held on 25 July. It included: (1) Accession of the States on 'defence', 'external affairs' and 'communications'; (2) Standstill Agreement; (3) Advisory Council for the States Department; (4) Channels of correspondence and representation of central Government in the States.

As soon as the policy of accession had been decided upon, VP Menon communicated the decision to Akhtar Hussain, I.C.S., who was working in the Pakistan wing of the States Ministry. VP Menon asked him to inform Abdur Rab Nishtar, the League Minister for States, of the plan.

Jinnah objected to the policy of accession. He told Mountbatten that it was utterly wrong and he publicly announced that he would guarantee the independence of the States in Pakistan.

On 24 July Patel and Menon met another delegation of rulers and States' ministers which included the rulers of Patiala, Gwalior, Bikaner and Nawanagar. Among the ministers were Sir B.L. Mitter (Baroda), Sir A. Ramaswami Mudaliar (Mysore), C.S. Venkatachar, I.C.S. (Jodhpur) and K.M. Panikkar (Bikaner). This meeting was a crucial one for it showed that Congress was making head way with their plan. It was evident that quite a number of rulers had broken away from the leadership of the Nawab of Bhopal and were prepared to come in with the Indian union.

By this time Menon had produced a draft Instrument of accession, and revised the original draft of the Standstill Agreement prepared by the Political Department. These two drafts were circulated to the rulers at the special session of the Chamber of Princes on 25 July, when Mountbatten addressed that Chamber for the first and last time in his capacity as Crown Representative. The speech was made *ex tempore* and without any notes and was the apogee of persuasion with a tilt towards India. He advised the rulers to accede to the appropriate Dominion in regard to the three subjects of 'defence', external affairs', and 'communications.' He pointed out that 'defence' was a matter which a State could not conduct for itself; 'external affairs' was something that no State had dealt with before. The continuity of communications necessitated their accession on this subject also. Mountbatten said that accession on these three subjects left the rulers with all the practical independence that they could possibly use and made them free of those subjects which they could not possibly manage on their own. He assured them that their accession on these subjects would involve no financial liability and that in other matters there would be no encroachment on their sovereignty.

He made it clear that though the rulers were technically at liberty to link with either of the Dominions, there were certain geographical compulsions which could not be evaded. 'Out of something like 565 States, the vast majority are irretrievably linked geographically with the Dominion of India.' He stressed the urgency of the situation and said: 'If you are prepared to come, you must come before 15 August.' He concluded with the cogent appeal: 'You cannot run away from the Dominion Government which is your neighbour any more than you can run away from the subjects from whose welfare you are responsible.' Mountbatten then announced the personnel of the Negotiating Committee, consisting of ten rulers and twelve ministers, to consider in detail the items on the agenda. A number of questions were put to him by the rulers and ministers. His lucid replies helped to allay princely apprehensions and bring about an atmosphere of cordiality. Mountbatten was at his best in his partisanship for India. It is interesting to note that all the Princes present in the conference subsequently joined India.

The Negotiating Committee was split into two sub-committees, one to deal with the Instrument of accession and the other with the Standstill Agreement. These sub-committees held separate meetings daily at Bikaner House in Delhi. The deliberations were most businesslike. After six days and nights of hectic work, on 31 July the drafts were finalised. By the Instrument of accession, the States acceded to the Dominion of India on the three subjects of defence, external affairs and communications, their content being as defined in List 1 of Schedule VII to the Government of India Act of 1935, reproduced in a Schedule annexed to the Instrument. Accession did not imply any financial liability on the part of the acceding States. This Instrument was intended only for the rulers of fully empowered States, which numbered 140.

Besides these 140 States, there were *estates* and *talukas,* where the Crown exercised certain powers and jurisdiction, that were also counted as 'States'. These, numbering over 300, were situated in Kathiawar and Gujarat. Under the Attachment Scheme of 1943 some of these *estates* and *talukas* were tagged on to adjoining bigger States. But with the lapse of paramountcy, the Attachment Scheme came to an end. In any case, the rulers of these *estates* and *talukas* desired that they should be reverted to their former position and that the Government of India should administer their *estates* as was done by the Political Department before 1943. Another Instrument of Accession, suitable for their status and requirements, was prepared for these *estates* and *talukas*. This document, while preserving the form of accession, vested all the residuary powers and jurisdiction in the Central Government. Subsequently an ordinance termed the 'Extra Provincial Jurisdiction Ordinance' was promulgated for the exercise of the powers and jurisdiction acquired by the Government of India in these areas.

There were a number of intermediate rulers, higher in status than the *estates* and *talukas* and *estates-holders* of Kathiawar and Gujarat, who exercised wide but not quite full powers. These States, numbering over 70, were in Kathiawar, Central India and the Simla Hills. Menon devised still another Instrument of Accession for these States, the object of which was to ensure that the rulers did not exercise higher powers than they had prior to 15 August 1947. The rulers recognised that it was a fair condition that they could not expect to rise in status suddenly because of the lapse of paramountcy.

In all three cases, the Standstill Agreement was common. It laid down that all agreements and administrative arrangements as to matters of common concern specified in the schedule then existing between the Crown and the States should continue 'until new arrangements in this behalf' were made.

A meeting of the full Negotiating Committee was held at Bikaner House on 31 July. Twenty-five rulers and representatives of the States were present. The drafts of the Instrument of Accession and the Standstill Agreement as passed by the two sub-committees were approved. It was at this meeting that the question of setting up an Advisory Council was discussed. In his statement of 5 July Patel had said that he would explore the possibilities of associating with the administration of the new Department a Standing Committee representing both the States and British India. The ministers of the major States were anxious that a body of this kind should be brought into existence. Some of the rulers, like Maharajah Sir Sadul Singh of Bikaner and the Jam Saheb of Nawanagar, were not in favour of the idea. Finding that the rulers were not unanimous, the proposal was dropped.

While the Negotiating Committee was busy with its labours, the *Hindustan Times* managed to get hold of a copy of the draft Instrument of Accession and to publish it. When Menon met Patel that morning, he said: 'Menon, now that the *Hindustan Times* has published the Instrument of Accession, can I see a copy of it?'

Mountbatten in full throttle to herd the Princes into India

Mountbatten addressed the Chamber of Princes for the first and the last time on 25 July 1947. It was difficult assembly to address as the audience were like hereditary shepherds in the unenviable position of lost sheep. Thus, a certain Maharaja, absent from his State and from India at this critical moment, did not seem to appreciate the importance either of coming himself to the meeting or even or briefing his Dewan. For the Dewan had been sent no instructions whatever. "Surely", Mountbatten asked, "you must know your Ruler's mind, and can take a decision on his behalf?" "I do not know my Ruler's mind," the hapless Dewan replied, "and I cannot get a reply by cable." Mountbatten thereupon picked up a large round glass paper-weight which happened to be on the rostrum in front of him. "I will look into my crystal," he said, "and give you an answer." There followed ten seconds of dramatic pause when you could have heard a princely pin drop. "His Highness," Mountbatten solemnly announced, "asks you to sign the Instrument of Accession."

So accurately had he gauged the sentiment of this particular audience that everyone broke out into delighted laughter at this sally, which was clearly regarded as nearly combining the rebuke courteous with the advice timely. For on the whole it was probably wise to strike the humorous note as being the best method of penetrating what seemed to be quite a high proportion of thick skulls.

There was a colourful reception at Victory's House on 28 July 1947 in honour of over fifty Ruling Princes and a hundred of the States Representatives. The splendour of it only seemed to strengthen the sense of unreality and pathos surrounding the Princely order at that time. When unity of purpose was of overwhelming importance for them, they were to be seen uneasy and obsessed with their own problems of precedence, each anxiously watching what the other was doing — and, as a Dewan remarked of one of them, "wandering about like a letter without a stamp".

The Mountbatten-Patel-Menon trio were doing overtime in herding the Princes into the Indian Union. Those of their Highnesses who had not already signified their intention of signing the Instrument of Accession were duly shepherded by the A.D.C's one by one for a friendly talk with Mountbatten. He in his turn passed them on in the full view of the company to V.P., who conducted them across the room to see Patel. There were Maharajas three deep in a semi-circle watching this process. One veteran Prince was heard to remark, "who's H.E. gettging to work on now?" Craning forward to see, he added with relish, "There's no need for him to work on me. I'm signing tomorrow!" Overhead was the following exchange between an old Prince and a young one. The old Prince asked, "How are things in your State?" The young Prince replied, "We have been having trouble in one place (which he named), but we have reached a settlement now." "We have trouble everywhere," the old Prince exclaimed, "but I don't let it reach the stage of a settlement."

Elsewhere, Mountbatten enjoyed considerably more success in his efforts to fill Patel's basket with apples. For some of the rulers, appending their signature to the Instruction of Accession was a cruel tragedy. One Raja of Central India collapsed and died of a heart attack seconds after signing. The Rana of Dholpur told Mountbatten with tears in his eyes: 'This breaks an alliance between my ancestors and your King's ancestors which has existed since 1765.' The Gaekwar of Baroda, one of whose forebears had fed his British Resident diamond dust, collapsed weeping like a child in the arms of V.P. Menon on signing. One ruler of a tiny state hesitated for days before appending his signature because he still believed in the divine right of kings. The eight maharajas of the Punjab signed their Instrument together during a formal ceremony in the state banquet hall at Patiala where Sir Bhupinder Singh 'the Magnificent' had once lavished the most prodigious hospitality in India on his guests. This time, one participant recalled, 'the atmosphere was so lugubrious we might have been in a cremation.'

A handful of rulers continued to resist the blandishments of Mountbatten, V.P. Menon and Patel. One of Mountbatten's closest personal friends, the Nawab of Bhopal, bitterly claimed 'the rulers were being invited like the oysters, to attend the tea party with the Walrus and the Carpenter'. Udaipur tried to form a federation with a number of fellow princes whose states adjoined his. So, too, did Gwalior, the son of the man with a mania for electric trains. At the behest of his Prime Minister, the Maharajah of Travancore, a southern state with a seaport and rich uranium reserves, clamoured for independence.

The pressures to herd these last reluctant resisters into Patel's basket became intense as 15 August drew near. Where he had local Congress organisations, Patel ordered demonstrations and street agitation to force their hands. The Maharaja of Orissa was trapped in his palace by a mob which refused to let him leave until he'd signed. Travancore's forceful Prime Minister was stabbed in the face by a Congress demonstrator. Shaken, the Maharaja cabled Delhi his accession.

None of the accessions was quite as tempestuous as that of the young Maharaja of Jodhpur. Jodhpur had just ascended his throne on his father's death. He was given to a number of expensive hobbies like flying, women and conjuring tricks; none of them, he realised, likely to stir the sympathy of Congress's Socialists. Together with his colleague, the Maharaja of Jaisalmer, he arranged a secret meeting in Delhi with Jinnah to enquire of the Moslem leader what sort of reception they might expect if they took their primarily Hindu states into his dominion. Delighted at the thought of ripping two key princes away from his Congress rivals, Jinnah took a blank sheet of paper from his desk drawer and passed it to Jodhpur.

'Just write your conditions on his paper,' he said, 'and I'll sign it.'

The two men asked time to withdraw to their hotel to ponder them. There they found V.P. Menon waiting for them. Tipped off by one of his mysterious sources about their initiative which eventually could have drawn other states into Pakistan, Menon told Jodhpur the Viceroy wanted to see urgently at Viceroy's House.

Seating the prince in a waiting-room, Menon set off on a frantic search for Mountbatten. Finally locating the Viceroy, who had no idea what he'd done, in his bath, Menon begged him to come down and reason with the stubborn prince.

His recently deceased father, who'd been his friend for 26 years, would have been outraged by his behaviour, the Viceroy told the young ruler. It was folly to try to take the subjects of his Hindu state into Pakistan for purely selfish reasons. In return, he promised Jodhpur that he and Menon would persuade Patel to adopt as tolerant a view as possible towards his personal quirks. Mountbatten left Menon to get the impetuous young ruler's signature on a provisional agreement. When he'd gone, Jodhpur pulled a fountain pen made in his workshop out of his pocket. After signing the text, he unscrewed its cap and revealed a miniature .22 pistol which he pointed at Menon's head. I'm not giving in to your threats!' he shouted. Mountbatten, hearing the noise, returned and confiscated the pistol.

Three days later Menon delivered a final Instrument of Accession to the prince's palace. Glumly the prince signed. Then he decided to bury his past in a celebration with Menon as his unwilling guest. All afternoon he poured whisky down the poor civil servants throat. After that, Menon was forced to gulp draughts of champagne while the prince ordered a full-scale banquet of roast meats and game, an orchestra and a selection of dancing girls. For Menon, a prudish vegetarian, the evening was a nightmare. The worst, however, was still to come. Hurling his turban on the floor in a fit of rage because he thought the music was too loud, the drunken Jodhpur dismissed the girls and the band and announced he would fly Menon to Delhi in his private plane. He rocketed off the field, then twisted his violently ill passenger through every acrobatic stunt he could perform before landing him at Delhi airport. Green and retching, Menon half-crawled from the plane but in his shaking fingers was the document which would deliver one more apple into Patel's waiting basket.

Despite the vacillations of a last bunch of die-hards, the Viceroy would, by 15 August, be able to honour his contract with Patel. The basket of apples he would present him would be overflowing. Five princes whose states would be inside Pakistan rallied to Jinnah, Mountbatten and Menon had plucked all the rest, with just three exceptions. The exceptions, however, were major ones. Ignoring every effort to bring him into an agreement with India, the Nizam of Hyderabad strove in vain to force Great Britain to recognise his state as an independent dominion. From his palace the miserly ruler had not ceased a bitter plaint at being 'abandoned by his oldest ally', and seeing 'the bonds of long devotion' linking him to the King Emperor severed. Kashmir, too, continued in his refusal to align himself with either dominion. More about Hyderabad and Kashmir later. Junagadh also proved to be a thorn in the flesh of Mountbatten.

CHAPTER 14: ISSUES IN THE ACCESSION PROCESS
Accession Anomalies

On July 28, Mountbatten gave a reception for the princes which, V.P. Menon wrote, "was in the nature of a last-minute canvassing of voters near the polling booth. Those of the rulers who had not yet signified their intention of acceding were taken by the A.D.Cs. one by one for a friendly talk with Mountbatten. When he had finished with them, he passed them on to me in the full view of the company and I, in my turn, conducted them across the room to Sardar. This had a good psychological effect on the rulers who were present."

In short, Mountbatten did everything in his power to secure the accession of states to the Indian Dominion. By contrast, he did nothing for Pakistan, although as Crown Representative he owed an equal duty to both Dominions. But worse than that, in every disputed case of accession, he threw his weight in favour of India. The clearest and most indefensible example is the part he played in the occupation by Indian forces of the Muslim majority states of Jammu and Kashmir. A less well-known instance is provided by the states of Jodhpur and Jaisalmer where he intervened to prevent their accession to Pakistan.

Maharajah Hanwant Singh of Jodhpur continued to be intractable. Jinnah and the Muslim League leaders had a series of meetings with him. At the last of these interviews, Maharajah Hanwant Singh had taken the then Maharajkumar of Jaisalmer with him, because the Maharajah of Bikaner would not accompany him and he shrank from going alone. Theirs were the three States geographically contiguous to Pakistan. Jinnah signed a blank sheet of paper and gave it to Maharajah Hanwant Singh along with his own fountain pen, saying 'You can fill in all your conditions.' A discussion followed. The Maharajah was prepared to line up with Pakistan. He then turned to the Maharajkumar of Jaisalmer and asked him whether he would follow suit. The Maharajkumar said he would do so on one condition: If there was any trouble between the Hindus and Muslim, he would not side with the Muslims against the Hindus. This was a bombshell and took Maharajah Hanwant Singh completely by surprise. Sir Mohammad Zafrullah however made light of the whole affair and pressed Maharajah Hanwant Singh to sign the instrument. But the Maharajah now felt unable to take a decision. He suggested to Jinnah that he would go to Jodhpur and return the next day. The Maharajah remained at Jodhpur for three days. The atmosphere in the State was hostile to the idea that Jodhpur should cast its lot with Pakistan; the *Jagirdars* and nobles were decidedly opposed to it.

The Maharajah began to waver. When he returned to Delhi after three days Menon was informed that, unless he handled the Maharajah quickly, the chances were that he might accede to Pakistan. V.P. Menon went to the Hotel Imperial and told the Maharajah that Mountbatten wanted to see him. They then drove to Government House and V.P. Menon kept the Maharajah in the visitors' room while he went in and explained the situation to Mountbatten.

The Maharajah was then called in. Mountbatten made it clear that from a purely legal standpoint there was no objection to the ruler of Jodhpur acceding to Pakistan; but the Maharajah should, he stressed, consider seriously the consequences of his doing so, having regard to the fact that he himself was a Hindu; that his State was populated predominantly by Hindus and that the same applied to the States surrounding Jodhpur. In the light of these considerations, if the Maharajah were to accede to Pakistan, his action would be in conflict with the principle underlying the partition of India on the basis of Muslim and non-Muslim majority areas; and serious communal trouble inside the State would be the inevitable consequence of such affiliation.

The Maharajah started at once to ask for impossible concessions. Menon told him: 'If you want to sign on false hopes, I will agree to your demands,' adding that most of the demands could not be conceded. He then told Mountbatten that Jinnah had given him a blank paper in which he could put down all the concession he wanted. Menon urged him not to be swayed by promises. After a great deal of discussion, Menon gave him a letter conceding some of his demands. Thereafter he signed the Instrument of Accession. After a few minutes, Mountbatten went out of the room and the Maharajah whipped out a revolver, levelled it at Menon and said: 'I refuse to accept your dictation.'

Menon told him that he was making a very serious mistake if he thought that by killing him, or threatening to kill Menon, he could get the accession abrogated. 'don't indulge in juvenile theatricals,' Menon admonished him. Shortly after, Mountbatten returned and Menon told him what had happened. Mountbatten made light of the episode and turned it to jest. Presently the Maharajah returned to normal and they departed in company. After leaving him at his residence, Menon returned to office. The whole episode became a standing joke between Menon and the Maharajah.

But Mountbatten paid little heed to "the principle underlying the partition of India" when he accepted the accession of Kapurthala to the Indian Dominion. This state was ruled by a Sikh, but had a Muslim majority of 64 per cent and was contiguous to the Muslim majority area of West Punjab. Later, Radcliffe assigned these areas to India without any valid reason, but when Mountbatten accepted the accession of Kapurthala, he was not in possession of the Radcliffe award. Among the states that acceded to India were some – as, for example, Bhopal and Rampur – which were ruled by Muslim princes. Rampur had a high proportion of Muslims in the population. They rose against accession to India, but were suppressed by troops sent by the Government of India on the Nawab's appeal. General Tuker wrote:

"The Sirdar [Vallabhbhai Patel] was determined that no state, Muslim or otherwise, should secede from his Dominion, so before many hours had passed we received direct and urgent orders to send troops into Rampur. We sent the 6th Jat Regiment. In this case the insurgents were Muslim who wished to carve out their own destiny. Later on, we contrasted the speed in meeting the Nawab's request with the complete lack of being obliterated in the Hindu states of Alwar and Bharatpur."

By August 15, all the five hundred odd Hindu majority states had acceded to India except two – Hyderabad and Junagadh. One Muslim majority state – Kapurthala – had also acceded to India. The accession of other Muslim majority states, including Kashmir, was still undecided. The story of Junagadh, Hyderabad, and Kashmir will be related later.

In marked contrast to the spate of accession to the Indian Dominion, no state acceded to Pakistan before August 15, Ten states were contiguous to West Pakistan, had a Muslim majority in the population, and were ruled by Muslim princes. These were Bahawalpur, Khairpur, Kalat, Las Bela, Kharan, and Makran, and the four Frontier states, Dir, Swat, and Chitral. Bahawalpur had bigger resources in population and revenue than any of the other states, but even this state was too small to remain independent. Of its population of less than two million, 83 per cent were Muslims. Its prosperity depended upon the Sutlej Valley Project, which was essentially an extension of the irrigation system of West Punjab. That the economic interests of West Pakistan and Bahawalpur were closely allied was shown by the fact that Pakistan's counsel, Zafrullah Khan, represented Bahawalpur also before the Punjab Boundary Commission. The North-Western Railway, which linked the North West Frontier Province and West Punjab with Karachi, passed for a considerable portion of its length through Bahawalpur. If there were any serious threat to its security, internal or external, Bahawalpur would have to turn to Pakistan for protection.

These ties pointed inevitably to the accession of the state to Pakistan. Nevertheless, there was hesitation and delay caused by the desire of the Nawab and his Chief Minister, Mustaq Ahmad Gurmani, to "maintain a quasi- independent existence," and a strong negotiating position. On August 15, the Nawab assumed the title of Jalalat-ul-Malik A'la Hazrat Amir of Bahawalpur, which signified an independent status. At the same time, he decided to send representatives to the Pakistan

Constituent Assembly to take part in its deliberations and, in due course, to arrive at a satisfactory constitutional arrangement between the state and Pakistan. But events were moving too fast for these dilatory methods. In the second half of August, 1947, the Punjab authorities took vigorous measures to protect the non-Muslim minority, a fairly complete evacuation of Hindus and Sikhs from more than half the state had taken place by the end of September. On October 3, Bahawalpur acceded to Pakistan.

Khairpur state followed Bahawalpur. The Frontier states, Chitral, Swat, Dir, and Amb, also acceded to Pakistan during the next few months, leaving only the four Baluchistan states, Kalat, Kharan, Makran, and Las Bela undecided.

The Baluchistan states, although extensive in area, were sparsely populated and poorly developed. Their combined population was about half a million, and their financial resources meagre in the extreme. The Khan of Kalat wanted to stake a claim to independence. He employed an Englishman, Douglas Fell, as Foreign Minister. It was reported that Fell was negotiating with foreign companies for oil prospecting and was, possibly, seeking support through them. It was also alleged that the Khan's brother and uncle sought aid in Kabul. Negotiations for accession dragged on, although the Khan professed the highest veneration for Jinnah. Meanwhile, the rulers of Las Bela, Makran, and Kharan, over whom the Khan of Kalat claimed some sort of suzerainty, got restive and decided, early in March, 1948, to offer accession directly to Pakistan. The acceptance of their accession isolated Kalat, now entirely surrounded by Pakistan territory. Under these circumstances, the Khan saw the path of wisdom and acceded to Pakistan before the end of March, 1948.

'The Unkindest Cut'ter of All

In seven weeks, it was done, the frontiers decided A continent for better or worse divided. The next day he sailed for England, where he quickly forgot The case as a good lawyer must. Return he would not Afraid, as he told his Clerk, that he might be shot.

- W.H. Auden

There is poetic licence in Auden's poem as the job was done in five weeks and one day and Radcliffe travelled by air and not by sea. In June 1947 it was proposed that there should be an Arbitral Tribunal to deal with such matters as the sterling balances and two Boundary Commissions to define the borders between India and the Punjab and India and Bengal. The Earl of Listowel the Secretary of State on June 13, 1947 consulted the Lord Chancellor, Lord Jowitt, about a suitable person to act as Chairman of the Arbitral Tribunal. The Lord Chancellor replied that all the Lords of Appeal in Ordinary were ruled out on account of age. The job could prove a gruelling one in the hot Indian sun. He suggested Sir Cyril Radcliffe who had great legal abilities, the right personality and administrative experience. Listowel went to see Radcliffe at his home in Hampstead and told him what was needed. Radcliffe replied direct to Prime Minister Clement Attlee. The appointment was approved by the India Committee of the Cabinet, chaired by Attlee, and subsequently by the full Cabinet. Attlee, as an Old Haileyburian, would undoubtedly have known something about Radcliffe personally.

Cyril J. Radcliffe has remained an enigmatic character for most people. He spent only a few weeks in India but has left an indelible stamp on the sub- continent. Hardly anything is known about his life and character. Although he had a very eventful and distinguished career he never bothered to write his memoirs. If anything, he destroyed all his personal papers and as a result there is not sufficient material to write a full biography. Despite this, however, Edmund Heward after great deal of research has tried and come up with his *The Great and The Good - A Life of Lord Radcliffe.*

Radcliffe was a reserved and private man who did not court publicity. After his famous speech in the House of Lords in 1967 castigating the government about its decision not to build the new British Library on the Bloomsbury site he had a letter from David Frost asking for a television interview. This was refused. An invitation from Curtis Brown to write his memorials was also turned down. There is no portrait of him in the British National Portrait Gallery despite his achievements and public service.

Although a great lawyer the law was not sufficient to satisfy his intellectual appetite. His great achievements were in the service of the Sate. For nearly 40 years he served the State in many different capacities: as Director General of the Ministry of Information: as a Commissioner to divide India, and to make a new constitution for Cyprus: as Chairman of a Royal Commission to revise the tax laws: as Chairman of a committee to consider the monetary system and Chairman of a number of security inquiries. He was one of the greatest Chairman of committees of his day. Sir Norman Brook advised Sir Anthony Eden to reserve him for the most complex and demanding inquiries.

He had many interests in the educational and cultural world. He was chairman of the trustees of the British Museum, Vice Chairman of the Court of London University and Chairman of the Advisory Committee of the BBC. He was a collector of French Impressionist and other paintings and gave a

Pissarro to the National Gallery. He lectured on a variety of subjects from the law to Rudyard Kipling and was the Reith Lecturer for the BBC. He wrote and spoke in great style.

He failed in two projects near to his heart. He fought strenuously to build the new British Library on the Bloomsbury site but was defeated. His friend, Gulbenkian, wanted him to be the Chairman of a World-Wide Foundation for the Arts but failed to establish the trusts before his death. Radcliffe felt unable to undertake the trusts on the terms required by the Portuguese Government.

Radcliffe was not a politician. He liked to establish principles, e.g., for censorship or the tax laws and did not have the flexibility required by a politician. He hated the tax laws to be used for other purposes than taxation. He liked a problem to be circumscribed and disliked the use of metaphors. Lord Armstrong of Ilminster has written, "He cherished freedom and the liberal values, and order and the rule of law as conditions of freedom. He believed in the power of reason as determinant of human conduct and measured the foibles of men with an unsparing perceptiveness." He was at heart a romantic. Although outwardly formidable he was sensitive with a keen sense of humour and was held in warm affection by his family and close friends.

Cyril Radcliffe spent his life in the corridors of power. He once wrote "The English tradition is soundly based which sees in State power an agent for harmonising and reconciling conflicting loyalties, not a conqueror that supersedes them." He was a reconciler who used his power as the chairman of a committee to seek consensus and that there should be give and take except where an important principle was at stake. He believed that governments as well as the private citizen should behave morally. "There are certain rules of dealing between man and man, rules of fair conduct and good breeding, which are just as valid for the power of governments as they are for the court for law or in ordinary private life." He looked at public affairs as a moralist and not as a politician.

He was a man of middle height, 5'8□ ", and athletic build. He had the crinkly brown hair of all the Radcliffe which turned silvery with age brushed back from the forehead. He had a large square head; a firm chin and blue grey eyes behind thick spectacles. He had one of the finest brains of his generation, with quick apprehension, exceptional powers of concentration and prodigious memory. He gave the address at the Memorial Service of his friend, Sylvester Gates but kept no copy. Many asked for a copy so he set to and wrote it out exactly as given so that these requests could be met. Writing to John Sparrow he said, "I did not speak *ex tempore* in the sense that having thought much about what to say, I rely on the words coming out which one has made part of oneself. I think it more effective in relation to one's hearers to whom after all one is addressing oneself. But a number of people have asked for copies to read or circulate and I wrote down last week my idea of a version."

He had the gift of words both in speaking and writing. He spoke easily without hesitation and without notes and wrote elegantly without corrections. He had a fine touch in the choice of words and apt phrases. Dr. A.L. Rowse wrote "Spoke *ex tempore* without a note in perfect style. He could quote a whole paragraph of the philosopher Bradley, or the whole passage at the end of Balfour's Foundations of Belief ... And he wrote very well. Might have made a good writer." He was a master of invective but this was reserved for the folly of governments and not for individuals. His speech in the House of Lords castigating the Wilson government over its decision on the siting of the new British Library was devastating. He was an avid reader with a catholic taste and remembered what he had read. Many thought him formidable but he had a twinkling eye and a dry sense of humour. He was very ready to be amused and would tease his family and close friends.

Radcliffe was a quiet, fastidious and reserved man but quick to sympathise when sympathy was called for. He had friends in many different walks of life and preferred the conversation of his friends to the conviviality of clubs and colleges. Although a member of Brooks's he used the Club only for entertaining particular people. He was fond of tennis and golf and his Hampstead home, Squire's Mound, had a tennis court. He never took part in any field sports. He collected pictures (many impressionists), prints and china and had impeccable artistic taste. His eye was just right — the pictures in his house were hung low in each room, never high. He loved original characters such as Brendan Bracken and Calouste Gulbenkian. He put up with their vagaries and never quarrelled with them. Coming from a military family with a father and two brothers professional soldiers, he had many soldierly qualities, obedience to the call of duty, direct thinking and dislike of waffle. He had easy manners and was courteous to all but could not stand arrogance and pretentiousness.

CHAPTER 15: RADCLIFFE'S APPOINTMENT AND ACTIONS

Formidable Radcliffe

Cyril Radcliffe
(homegrown.co.in)

Undoubtedly Cyril Radcliffe's entire career was a very distinguished one. Cyril Radcliffe followed his father and two elder brothers to Haileybury. Haileybury is commonly associated with The East India Company but the only connection is with some of the early buildings. In 1805 The East India Company purchased the estate of Haileybury in Hertfordshire and built a school there to educate boys who wished to join the company. The architect for the new buildings was William Wilkins, the architect of The National Gallery in Trafalgar Square and of Downing College, Cambridge. After the India Mutiny in 1857 the British Government took over the Government of India and the school was closed. The buildings were empty for some time but eventually Mr. Stephen Austin and some local gentlemen bought the buildings and established a new school there. Haileybury college was opened on September 23, 1862.

Cyril Radcliffe entered Haileybury in March 1912 and left in February 1917. He was in Lawrence House and became a College Prefect. He was Head of School in 1916, played rugby football as a threequarter back and was Captain of the School Second Rugby XV in 1915 - 1916. He was brilliant academically and tended to be bored in his last two years at school. He owed much to the Headmaster, Mr. F.B. Malim, who went to Haileybury at the same time as Cyril Radcliffe in 1912. He had great gifts as a scholar, orator and administrator and was a fine teacher of the classics. Cyril Radcliffe had the benefit of individual teaching from him. He was called up for war service in 1917 and joined up on November 30, 1917. Owing to poor eyesight he was posted to the Labour Corps and commissioned as a Second Lieutenant in that Corps. The Oxford Roll of Service records that he was on active service in France in 1918 - 1919. Being in the Labour Corps must have been a thankless and unglamorous task, repairing roads and communications under the Royal Engineers, in discomfort. The writing of poems may have been his way of abstracting himself from the unpleasant present.

Cyril Radcliffe had obtained a classical scholarship at New College, Oxford, and on demobilisation he went up to Oxford and matriculated at New College in the Michaelmas term 1919. Immediately after the war New College, like other Colleges, was a mixture of ex-soldiers and boys straight from school. Maurice Bowra (later Sir Maurice Bowra, Warden of Wadham College, Oxford) one of Cyril Radcliffe's friends and contemporaries, had served as a gunner in the war. Bowra in his *Memories* wrote "Cyril Radcliffe commanded even at this time a perfect control of his sentences, never hesitated for a word, and knew exactly what sentiment to strike." Bowra said that they were all interested in general ideas and the fine arts but music did not mean much to them. Cyril Radcliffe was elected a Prize Fellow of All Souls College, Oxford, on coming down from New College in 1922. This involved taking an examination and being interviewed by the fellows. A Prize Fellowship lasts for seven years and on the expiration of that time he was appointed to £50 Fellowship which he retained until 1937. There was no condition of residence nor any teaching duties.

Cyril Radcliffe was appointed Eldon Law Scholar in 1923. The scholarship had been founded by Lord Eldon, the famous Lord Chancellor in the early 19th century and was awarded to "a Protestant of the Church of England who had obtained a first." Cyril Radcliffe was neither a believer or churchman but no doubt he had been confirmed while at Haileybury and would qualify as a member of the Church of England. His first was in Classics and not in Law but a first in any subject was sufficient. The trustees met annually in the Lord Chancellor's Room in the House of Lords to make the election. The scholarship was worth £100 a year and lasted for three years. With this behind him he was now ready to start his career at the Bar.

Cyril Radcliffe was admitted to the Inner Temple in March 1920 when he was still at Oxford. By 1930 Cyril Radcliffe's career was thriving. Cyril Radcliffe's earnings were 1930 - £3,045; 1931 - £5,097; 1932 - £6,287; 1933 - £6,945. This was before he took silk in 1935. In 1937 his fee books show an income of £17,584 and in 1938 - £19,334. 1939 closed on September 11, after eight months at £15,562. He must therefore have been earning around £20,000 when the war broke out. In 1946 fees amounted to £36,188 and in 1947 £19,693. This was the year that he was away in India dealing with the Partition. As he took no fee for this it must have cost him a large sum in lost earnings. In 1948 the fees were over £50,000. The highest brief recorded was £11,000. A ledger kept by his clerk shows that in the period from 1933 to 1949 he was instructed by over 420 different firms of solicitors with all the big London firms in the list. It is not surprising that his clerk, Thresher, ran a Rolls Royce and had a flat in the South of France.

At the outbreak of the Second World War, in September 1939, Cyril Radcliffe could be found filling sandbags in Regent's Park and the Mall. A friend in the Admiralty saw him at work in the Mall and thought his skills could be better employed in the Admiralty. An important event in Cyril Radcliffe's life occurred at this time as he was married to Antonia. At the beginning of 1940 Cyril Radcliffe moved from the Admiralty to the Ministry of Information to act as Assistant Controller News and Censorship. Sir John Reith (later Lord Reith), who was the Minister at the time wanted Cyril Radcliffe to take up an important post in the Ministry but Cyril Radcliffe felt that he was quite unsuited for it and unqualified. He felt that the Ministry of Information was the one department in which he could find no sort of interest. He could see, however, an intelligible service in Press Censorship. He insisted on staying in Press Censorship and was appointed Controller, News and Censorship in April 1940. Reith was right because in December 1940 under a new Ministry, Duff Cooper (later Lord Norwich) he was appointed Deputy Director General of the Ministry under Sir Walter Monckton as Director General. In December 1941 he became Director General.

In 1944 Cyril Radcliffe was appointed KBE for his services as Director General of the Ministry of Information. Civil servants had been surprised at Cyril Radcliffe's flair for administration and he was accepted in the Ministry "as one of the clearest brains in the building." Bruce Lockhart wrote in his diary on October 9, 1944: "Cyril is by far the best man in the Ministry of Information and has done a fine job. Apart from his deep-rooted prejudice against the Foreign Office which he hates and despises, he is a man of sterling honesty and high ideals. He is, in fact, the Ministry of Information and I do not see how it could function without him." At the end of the war Cyril Radcliffe was approached by the head of the civil service to remain in the civil service but this he refused to do. He was also approached by the Prime Minister, Mr. Clement Attlee, to become Chairman of the National Coal Board. The journalist, Francis Williams recalls a conversation he had with Cyril Radcliffe in 1945: "He had made such a success of being head of a great department and seemed to have enjoyed it so much that I asked him whether he had any thought of going into politics. He answered that his loyalty was to the law and that with the end of the war he felt that there would be more need than ever to restore and sustain the independent values of the law. It was to them that he intended to devote himself." This was the right decision as Radcliffe's mind was unsuited to the compromises required of a politician.

On July 7, 1945 there is an entry in Bruce Lockhart's diary: "Lunched today with Cyril and Antonia Cyril Radcliffe. Cyril was in rampant form and was delighted to be free again. Already he looks much better. Wise man that he is, he is taking three months full leave before he returns to the Bar in October. He goes to Devon in a day or two then to Ireland for August and September. He talked well and made very strong attacks on the PM. He has always been against him and has always refused to accept the theory that, but for Winston, we might have lost the war. But now he is not merely anti the great man theory, but regards the PM as a most dangerous menace to future peace. He also thinks his handling of the election (and for this he has words scathing enough) proves that the PM is hopelessly out of touch with realities. The fact that the P.M. took advice from a man like Beaverbrook was another Cyril Radcliffe nail in the PM's coffin."

By the second half of September 1945 Cyril Radcliffe was back in his chambers, 3 New Square, Lincoln's Inn, to resume his practice at the Bar. He practised at the bar for a further 3 years before becoming a law lord but less than two years later he was called on by the government to act as umpire on the Partition of India.

The Darker Side of Radcliffe

The commonly held perception of Cyril Radcliffe among writers on Indian independence is that he was a dutiful, brilliant, neutral umpire, summoned from the inner Temple by the forces of history to divide a nation on strictly impartial grounds. In fact, he was far from being an apolitical lawyer, having spent the war as Director-General of Ministry of Information under Brendan Bracken running government censorship and propaganda. One can imagine what this post must have meant in wartime Britain. He was in-charge of the entire propaganda machinery of the British government to counter the German propaganda onslaught. Joseph Paul Goebbels was Minister of propaganda for the German Third Reich under Adolf Hitler. He is generally accounted responsible for presenting a favourable image of the Nazi regime to the German people. His famous dictum that if a lie is repeated often enough then people tend to believe it is quoted frequently. The very fact that Radcliffe was pitted against Goebbels speaks for itself. For anyone to match Goebbels during wartime one had to be past master at duplicity and deceit.

Squit (his nick name) Radcliffe was the insider's insider - the ultimate Establishment figure who could be trusted to put the interests of the State before any other consideration. His philosophy is perhaps encapsulated in a quotation he once copied into his *Commonplace Book*: 'Free speech is all right as long as it does not interfere with the policy of the government. It's ironic that Radcliffe's World War II career should have begun filling sand bags in Regent's Park and the Mall. He was quickly spotted by friends who found an entrance for him in the Admiralty as Deputy Principal. Writing to a friend in November 1939 Radcliffe says, "This is my day off. This is a curious sensation. We work six days a week and even I who always come away first don't leave before 7.30 (it is because everybody in the

Admiralty does his work in such an extraordinary way and my great difficulty is to perceive what exactly the work is) ... Whether the Admiralty really wanted my assistance I have some doubts. I think they were told to get someone: but I am quite clear that they don't at present know what to do with me... I have four in my room. It is really run by a young man about 30 called Jarrett.

In so far as the Admiralty has an international lawyer, he is one: I think that my presence is really awkward and rather embarrassing for him. But he is very nice and friendly and copes with a mass of stuff he has to deal – most of it nonsense – extraordinarily well. I like him and find him very ready to help and patient." The young man, later Sir Clifford Jarrett, Permanent Secretary to the Admiralty, says that at the time they were concerned about the campaign of magnetic mine-laying in which the Germans were engaged. The government wanted to influence the neutrals against the Germans by propaganda arguing that the Germans were acting illegally under international laws. So, at the Admiralty Radcliffe found himself dealing with war propaganda right from the start. As we have seen Radcliffe's rise in the government was meteoric. Having started the war filling sand bags by December 1941 he was Director-General, Ministry of Information. Radcliffe joined the Admiralty in September 1939 and moved to Ministry of Information in the beginning of 1940.

In 1940 compulsory censorship was considered by the War Cabinet. Radcliffe was asked to draw up a scheme which envisaged compelling the Press to publish only official news, forbidding speculation and subjecting comment to compulsory scrutiny. Barrington-Ward, the editor of *Times* was consulted and thought that newspapers would be reduced to the status of Government propaganda organs and the public would be driven to listen to German radio. Barrington-Ward argued that in 1915, if there had been Press censorship the shells' scandal would not have been discovered. The Minister, Mr. Duff Cooper, opposed compulsory censorship on the grounds that it was administratively impossible. On June 9, 1940 the Chief of Naval Staff submitted a memorandum urging compulsory censorship as an uncontrolled Press plays an important part in assisting the enemy. The Government decided against.

Much against its wishes the Ministry of Information was compelled by the Home Office and the Foreign Office in March 1940 to assume responsibility for banning the export from Britain of undesirable publications. Published matter could only be sent by post and a permit had to be obtained. In May and June *The Daily Worker* and several small papers were banned for export. The banning was not popular amongst those affected. In September 1940 Radcliffe said: "I have always been against such a policy in respect of a publication which is legally produced in this country. The proper remedy, if any particular country objects to the circulation of such a paper within its own borders, is for it to impose an import ban." The Ministry of Information eventually succeeded in having the ban lifted in August 1943, nearly a year after *The Daily Worker* was allowed to resume publication in Britain.

Early in 1941 Duff Cooper, the Minister, was becoming very restive about the impotence of the Ministry. On May 21, 1941 Sir Walter Monckton and Radcliffe sent a joint memorandum to the Minister. They said that propaganda was vital to victory "Its raw material is news and information. But the Ministry of Information is so controlled by the government that it has no control over either of these. It can decide neither what to make public nor when to make nor what time or shape to give such information as is made public... The only function left to it is the purely administrative one of the distribution of government news, a task of the same order of importance as those assigned to the Post Office or the Stationery Office." The last sentence is a clear indication that the memorandum was drafted by Radcliffe. Both Monckton and Radcliffe thought that only if the Minister threatened to resign would he do any good. Duff Cooper was persuaded by Churchill to stay on but resigned shortly afterwards on July 20, 1941. Brendan Bracken was appointed Minister of Information replacing Duff Cooper. Radcliffe had better equation with Brendan Bracken than Duff Cooper. No sooner had Brendan Bracken joined the Ministry Radcliffe was appointed Director-General.

In April 1942 there were discussions in the Cabinet about the rationing of food. Radcliffe was always in favour of rationing when needed rather than reliance on appeals to the public. Radcliffe wrote a memorandum to the Minister. "There is already a good deal of suspicion that the government do not really believe in the possibilities of voluntary action and that they mean all along to resort to compulsion of after a show of appealing for voluntary effort... Further, the essence of this scheme is that rationing is a bogey which the individual will want to avoid. There is abundant evidence to the effect that this is a mistaken view of public reaction to rationing. Owing to the success of the food scheme, rationing is definitely popular since, in exchange for a certain amount of inconvenience, it has avoided the major inconvenience of many people getting nothing and is regarded as guaranteeing a fair share for all." Despite the difficulties at the end it was the skills of Bracken and Radcliffe which complemented each other. The Ministry's task was not only to give the public information about the war and how to cope with successive crises but also to give the government information about public opinion, reactions and behaviour and advise how best to unite and strengthen the people.

The best way to strengthen the war effort was to give the public as much and as frequent news as was compatible with security. The Ministry was determined not to become a Ministry of

Entertainment. There was to be no meddling by the Ministry in the expression of opinions. Morale was maintained by explanation and honesty and not by campaigns which often insulted the intelligence and courage of the ordinary man. One of Bracken's biographers wrote: "It was Radcliffe who masterminded the formidable task of streamlining the administration of the Ministry. He was a hard but just taskmaster... He had clear ideas on the role and function of a Ministry of Information in wartime and fought with inflexible determination, anyone who dared to disregard or override it. Yet he eschewed intrigue and stamped a certain high-minded quality on all he touched. The chameleon-like Bracken responded; it brought out the best side of him."

For his very distinguished service to the country Cyril Radcliffe was knighted in 1944. For the rest of the war the Ministry of Information was completely in Radcliffe's grip. As his colleague Robert Lockhart has recorded "He is, in fact, the Ministry of Information and I do not see how it can function without him." One would have imagined that Radcliffe would be a Conservative party supporter. Sir Robert Lockhart has recorded in his diary "Cyril informed me gleefully that during the election he plastered his house with Labour posters! He announced proudly that this had angered the other inhabitants of Elm Row. Cyril said he would welcome a Labour victory. Labour might do well to welcome Cyril to their ranks. He would make a first-class Lord Chancellor or Attorney-General and is far better in every way than Walter Monckton." So when Attlee selected Radcliffe as the Chairman of the Arbital Tribunal for partitioning India he was not appointing an apolitical person but a die-hard Labour supporter chosen to carry out the Labour mandate. As a postscript it may be added that Radcliffe was responsible for organising the campaign against Nehru's sister Vijaya Lakshmi Pandit when she travelled to the US, and for harassing P.G. Wodehouse when he made ill-judged broadcasts while in German captivity.

Who Appointed Radcliffe?

A statement was made in the House of Commons by Prime Minister Attlee on 3rd June 1947 giving an outline of the Partition Plan of India. The same statement was made in the House of Lords by Secretary of State the Earl of Listowel and was published in India at the same time. The statement envisaged "A Boundary Commission will be set up by the Governor-General, the membership and terms of reference of which will be settled in consultation with those concerned. It will be instructed to demarcate the boundaries of the two parts of the Punjab on the basis of ascertaining the contiguous majority areas of Muslims and non-Muslims. It will also be instructed to consider other factors. Similar instruction will be given to the Bengal Boundary Commission."

It is curious that in a meeting on 7 June 1947 held by Mountbatten with the Indian leaders to discuss the Administrative Consequences of Partition the question arose about the need of an "Arbitral Tribunal" which would be the final authority for matters not agreed by the bodies set up for Partition of the Provinces. The Arbitral Tribunal was a body distinct from the Boundary Commission envisaged by the Partition Plan.

The question now arises as to how Radcliffe's name came up for nomination as Chairman of the Boundary Commission. It is relevant to examine the circumstances that led to Radcliffe's appointment as a Chairman of both Boundary Commissions. A careful reading of the available material on the subject reveals that the leading part in securing Radcliffe's selections for that crucial position was played by Mountbatten himself, who had known him during the war.

After the meeting with Indian leaders on 7 June mentioned above. Mountbatten reported to the Secretary of State, Listowel the decision to set up an Arbitral Tribunal (Note: not Boundary Commission). Mountbatten gave advance warning that, though its composition was not yet settled, he might have to ask for a member of the Judicial Committee of the Privy Council as its Chairman, adding that "Men with previous experience of India, such as Jayakar and Beaumont would not be acceptable".

It is interesting to go through the letter of Listowel, Secretary of State addressed to Lord Chancellor Viscount Jowitt.

10 June 1947

Dear Lord Chancellor,

"I enclose a copy of a telegram I have just received from the Viceroy in which he says that it is contemplated that an arbitral tribunal may have to be set up in India to deal with matters arising out of the partition. You will see that the Viceroy says that he may have to ask for the services of a member of the Judicial Committee of the Privy Council as Chairman, and that men with previous experience of India would not be acceptable.

I am circulating this telegram to the India and Burma Committee, but I do not think we can do more at this stage than draw up a list of possible people, and, perhaps, take some soundings of those whom we think most suitable as to whether they would be available. You will see that the Viceroy refers to 6 months in the first instance as the term of service, but I feel convinced myself that any Chairman of such a tribunal will have work to do in India for at least 18 months if not for two years of possibly longer. It will be essential that he should be a person of the highest standing, but even though the Viceroy says that the tribunal will work in Simla in the hot weather, I should think that the person chosen ought not to be over 60 and preferably about 55. I doubt if we need limit ourselves to the Judicial Committee but we should need somebody of a recognised high status and at least that of High court Judge.

I am clear that any such appointment must be paid from Indian funds and I should be glad of your advice as to what emoluments you think should be offered. Probably the best course would be to give the same salary as is drawn here with substantial allowances for Indian conditions.

Would you please consider who there is who might be suitable for this work. I should be glad to discuss the matter with you if you would like to talk it over."

Listowel

From the above letter it can be seen that the British Government was not in any undue hurry to complete the partition process.

On 13 June 1947 the Lord Chancellor wrote to Listowel:

13 June 1947

"Dear Listowel,

I think I told you that on Wednesday I saw Cyril Radcliffe to sound him about his willingness to go out to India to fulfil the role which the Viceroy suggested. I read to him the telegram from the Viceroy: I did not read to him your letter to me: but I did warn him that he might have to stay very much longer than the six months indicated in the telegram.

He came to see me to-day, having thought the matter over in the meantime, to tell me that he was so impressed with the importance of the task that he was prepared to undertake it, subject to certain considerations which I will mention.

I want you to understand the position which he occupies at the Bar. I do not know what his precise income is, but I should think he is making at least £60,000 a year and could, without very much difficulty, make much more if it were worth his while. Further I want you to realise that in my considered judgement he has in a pre-eminent degree all the qualities that are needed for this great task which no one else has. And further, if he were to retire from the Bar definitely he has a strong inducement from the income tax point of view, for fees paid in respect of earnings at the Bar after retirement are exempt from both income tax and surtax. For instance, if he were to retire he could collect all his outstanding fees – probably about £50,000 – and not incur any obligation to pay tax thereon.

Yet the circumstances of this offer and the possibility that he would not be wanted for more than six months make it impossible for him to retire from the Bar, so that this income tax inducement does not apply in this case. You will therefore see, if he does go out, that so far as the money side of the matter is concerned he places us under an immense obligation to him. I do not think the amount of the salary which he is to receive matters very much: I should suggest £50,000 a year as this is the mark of the status he is to have. But what he does want may be summed up under the three heads – travel, accommodation and living allowances.

With regard to travel, arrangements must be made so that his wife and her boys can from time to time whenever possible come to visit him and the expense of this travel must be without cost to him. Secondly, he must be provided with suitable accommodation in India so that he and his wife and boys when they join him must be able to live in comfortable style without expense to him. Thirdly, living allowances must be paid to him.

These terms may seem considerable, but if you are asking a man in his position to undertake a job of this nature you must be prepared to do these things handsomely."

On 13 June 1947 Listowel replied to Mountbatten's telegram and informed him that he had approached the "Lord Chancellor about a possible Chairman. It seems that, apart from any other consideration, the members of the Judicial Committee of the Privy Council are all ruled out on account of age since 60 oughts, I think, to be regarded as an absolute maximum and 55 would probably be the optimum age. As you doubtless realise, the pressure upon High Court Judges at the moment is very heavy and the Lord Chancellor can hold out no hope of one being made available for your purpose. An approach is, however, being made to Sir sHewho would, I think, fill the bill admirably. Apart from his great legal abilities, he has just the right personality and acquired during the war administrative experience which would be likely to be of great assistance to him. Of course, he may well feel unable to leave the Bar, even temporarily, so soon after returning to it, however worthwhile your job can be made to appear, but there is just a possibility that he might be attracted by it.

I am also having the question of the manning of the Boundary Commissions, raised in your telegram No. 1364-S, looked into and the suggestion about U.N.O. taken up with the Foreign Office. Clearly, the handling of this Boundary Commission business is going to be of crucial importance. It seems as if the Sikhs may try to get back at the Boundary Commission stage some of the ground which they surrendered over the announcement of policy. It is to be hoped that the staking out of claims, as, for example, for the River Chenab line, in advance of the findings of the Boundary Commissions will not get out of hand since, once claims of this kind have been staked out, withdrawal is apt to prove difficult without loss of face."

As we shall see Mountbatten kept this information under the sleeve and did not disclose to the Indian leaders for the next ten days. It is also pertinent to note that in all the minutes and correspondence there is mention of both Boundary Commission and Arbitral Tribunal.

Radcliffe Appointed Chairman of Boundary Commissions

Radcliffe and his lines bled millions to
death in 1947
(freepresskashmir.news)

We continue our enquiry into the appointment of Radcliffe. In this connection it will be pertinent to see the minutes of Jinnah's interview with Mountbatten on 23 June 1947. We can see Mountbatten's own version of what was said:

"Mr. Jinnah said that he accepted the terms of reference that had been put up by the Congress Party and that he would have names of his nominees for both Boundary Commissions ready for submission to the Viceroy within the next day or two. He then said that he felt it would be impossible for both parties to agree upon the two Chairman and he therefore suggested that a distinguished member of the Bar from England might come out as an independent Chairman for both commission and that his decision should be final. He should, in fact, act as an Umpire. It was suggested that in view of the fact that the Arbitral Tribunal in Mr. Jinnah's opinion would not be functioning seriously for some time to come, whoever was appointed Chairman of that Tribunal (and the composition of the Tribunal has not yet been agreed to by Congress) might come out from England in the near future and act as Chairman of the two Boundary Commissions before taking over his duties with the Tribunal. He did not anticipate that the work of the Boundary Commission would last very long. The Viceroy told Mr. Jinnah, in confidence, that the man who had been suggested as Chairman of the Arbitral Tribunal was Sir Cyril Radcliffe. Mr. Jinnah, while saying that he would like a day or two to consider whether he thought Sir Cyril to be a suitable Chairman, knew of him and of the high reputation which he held at the Bar."

It is not quite clear who 'suggested' that whoever was appointed chairman of the Arbitral Tribunal could first act as Chairman of the two Boundary Commissions, but it seems that the suggestion was made by Mountbatten, basing it on Jinnah's view that the Arbitral Tribunal would not be functioning for some time to come. Be that as it may, two points are clear. First that Radcliffe's name was first brought into the conversation by Mountbatten, not by Jinnah, and that Listowel had recommended Radcliffe as Chairman of the Arbitral Tribunal only.

The question of the Boundary Commission was discussed in the meeting of the special committee of the Indian Cabinet on 26 June 1947. It may noted that Jinnah was not a member of the Indian Cabinet. In the meeting Mountbatten said that all parties had unanimously expressed the opinion that it was most desirable that the Boundary Commissions should finish their work by the 15th of August. If this was to be done, it would be necessary, he felt, to modify the previous decision that the Commissions should elect their own Chairman. In his view it would expedite work if the Partition Council could agree upon the names of two eminent men enjoying the confidence of both parties to serve as Chairman and having a casting vote. He had accordingly asked the Secretary of State if he could suggest suitable persons for appointment as Chairman and the latter had recommended Sir Cyril Radcliffe, a man of high integrity, legal reputation, and wide experience.

If it proved difficult to find any other person he would suggest that Sir Cyril might be considered for the Chairmanship of both Boundary Commissions. The advantage of such course would be that Sir Cyril Radcliffe would be enabled to adjust any slight loss one State might have to suffer in one particular area by compensating it in another and generally to see that justice was done uniformly to all claims. Further if, as was probable, the work of the Arbitral Tribunal would arise mostly after the 15th of August, it might be possible to retain Sir Cyril for that work also. The idea generally appealed to the members and they agreed to consider it further. Mountbatten for his part agreed to write formally to Patel and Liaquat asking them to consider the suitability of Sir Cyril Radcliffe and setting out details of his experience and the terms on which he might be invited to come to India. His fees would be debited to the general expenses of Partition. On 27 June 1947 Mountbatten wrote to Secretary of State, Listowel -

"I was very glad to hear of the possible appointment of Sir Cyril Radcliffe. I saw a certain amount of him when he was Director-General at the Ministry of Information during the war and formed a high opinion of him. I have put the matter in confidence to the Leaders and I hope to let you have a reply shortly to your telegram.

There is, as might be expected, some difficulty in finding a Chairman for the Boundary Commissions, for the setting up of which the Leaders have just agreed, and, as the Arbitral Tribunal will probably not have much to do in the early stages, Jinnah has suggested that Radcliffe, if he proves acceptable, might perhaps serve in the first instance as Chairman of both Boundary Commissions to sit only to settle disputes within the Commissions. This is so far a purely tentative proposal. If anything comes of it I will let you know by telegram."

Although in the minutes of Mountbatten's meeting with Jinnah it is not clear who suggested the name of Radcliffe in Mountbatten's letter to Listowel Mountbatten claimed that Jinnah suggested Radcliffe to be the Chairman of the Boundary Commission.

Mountbatten has also recorded in his personal report -

"We have reached a complete stalemate about the Arbitral Tribunal. Jinnah would like Radcliffe to be the Chairman; but Congress opposed this (apparently under the impression that he is a Conservative and therefore likely to favour the League!) and then put up the proposal that they should use the existing Federal Court. Jinnah said he could not possibly accept this. Judicious enquiry from the Chief Justice (who is staying with me in the house at present) has revealed that he chose his Muslim colleague Mr. Justice Fazl Ali for his non-communal outlook and fairmindedness; and presumably Jinnah would like to nominate a pro-League judge! In the meanwhile, Congress have stuck to their guns, and so has Jinnah, and I have now got a new headache in trying to get agreement about the personnel of the Arbitral Tribunal. Jinnah glibly remarked that until the Tribunal was set up, it would be for me to give the arbitrary decisions, but I made it abundantly clear that I have no intention of doing this."

The issue seems to have been resolved the same day as Mountbatten further records.

On the same day Mountbatten in his personal report wrote -

"The Boundary Commissions are now being set up, Congress and the League having each nominated two representatives to each Commission. The question of the Chairman has been causing a lot of trouble. At the first meeting of the Partition Council held to-day Jinnah's proposal was accepted by Congress, namely that Sir Cyril Radcliffe should be appointed as the Chairman of both

Boundary Commissions with a final casting vote, as this was settled before the 15th August. Meanwhile the Boundary Commissions would start work at once and only what is in dispute would be laid before the Chairman."

On 13 June it was decided:

i)   that each Boundary Commission should consist of an independent chairman and four other persons, of whom two should be nominated by Congress and two by the Muslim League;

ii)   that all these persons should, if possible, be of high judicial standing;

iii) that Congress would include a Sikh in the two persons nominated by them for the Punjab Boundary Commission...

And on 30 June the Viceroy was able to issue the following Announcement :

1)   There shall be two Boundary Commissions, one for Bengal and the other for the Punjab, consisting of the following [High Court judges]:-

Cyril Radcliffe Chairman... To be appointed later.

Members.... Mr. Justice Bijan Kuman Mukherjee) Nominees

Mr. Justice C.C. Biswas) of

Mr. Justice Abu Saleh) Congress

Mohammed Akram) Nominees... of the

Mr. Justice S.A. Rahman) Muslim League

For Punjab:-

Chairman... To be appointed later.

Members.... Mr. Justice Din Muhammad) Nominees... of the

Mr. Justice Muhammad Munir) Muslim League

Mr. Justice Mehr Chand Mahajan) Nominees... of

Mr. Justice Teja Singh) Congress

Note:- it is intended to appoint the same person as Chairman of both the Boundary Commissions.)

2)   The two Boundary Commissions shall be summoned to meet as early as possible by the Governors of the respective Provinces, and shall submit their reports at the earliest possible date.

3)   The terms of reference for the two Commissions shall be as follows:- For Bengal:-

The Boundary Commission is instructed to demarcate the boundaries of the two parts of Bengal on the basis of ascertaining the contiguous majority areas of Muslims and non-Muslims. In doing so, it will also take into account other factors.

In the event of the referendum in the District of Sylhet resulting in favour of amalgamation with Eastern Bengal, the Boundary Commission will also demarcate the Muslim majority areas of Sylhet District and the contiguous Muslim Majority areas of the adjoining districts of Assam.

For the Punjab:-

The Boundary Commission is instructed to demarcate the boundaries of the two parts of the Punjab on the basis of ascertaining the contiguous majority areas of Muslims and non-Muslims. In doing so it will also take into account other factors."

A close study of all the papers indicate that there was subtle manoeuvring of Mountbatten to appoint Cyril Radcliffe as a Chairman of both the Boundary Commissions and the Arbitral Tribunal.

Radcliffe's Ruminations

Radcliffe arrived at New Delhi Airport on Tuesday, July 8, 1947 and went straight to the Viceregal House where he spent the first two nights. A staff was assembled consisting of a Private Secretary from the Indian Political Service, Christopher Beaumont, one superintendent, five stenographers, five typists, one junior clerk and eight peons. An Assistant Secretary, Rao Saheb V.D. Ayer, a Hindu was appointed whose duties were purely secretarial. It was clear to Beaumont that Radcliffe and Mountbatten apparently did not much like each other. It was Edwina who kept the conversation going. After two days being briefed by Mountbatten, Radcliffe moved to a separate house on the Viceregal estate. From July 10 to 12 he was in Calcutta for preliminary talks with the Governor and other members of the Commissions there. On his return Mountbatten made a personal note: "Radcliffe came back with an optimistic report on the Bengal Boundary Commission in Calcutta. He thought that all the judges were of a higher calibre than he had expected and were fully determined to work as a team to a programmeme which would enable Radcliffe to give me a decision by August 12." In fact, the Judges never worked as a team. All four Judges took a rigidly communal view.

On July 14, Radcliffe flew to Lahore to visit the Punjab Boundary Commission. In Lahore he stayed at Falettis Hotel but the heat was overpowering. On the second day Beaumont arranged for them to move into the house of the Resident for the Punjab State who was away in Simla. This was an improvement and they had their meals at the Punjab Club where they had drinks and dined with many of the members. On occasions they dined with Sir Evan Jenkins, the Governor of the Punjab. Going on to Simla they stayed at the United Services Club. Mountbatten offered Radcliffe his private plane to enable him to view the terrain but unfortunately the flight had to be cancelled due to rain.

During his time in India Radcliffe visited Calcutta twice, once for two days in July and the second time for a week at the beginning of August. He stayed with the Resident, Col. Harvey, at Hastings House. He got on well with Col. Harvey and also with the Governor of Bengal, Sir Frederick Burrows. Sir Frederick was a splendid man, an ex-engine driver and CSM Grenadier Guards. During the August visit a friend took him to visit and old British Cemetery off Park Street, Calcutta and he recorded his impressions in a BBC broadcast on October 2, 1947. "The trees are very green and damp, and they droop appropriately: it is wet under foot, but anyway nowadays few people pass through the stucco lodges and iron gates that so much resemble the entrance to an eighteenth-century English gentleman's park. The monuments almost lower above you. You see the familiar English and Scottish names, and the familiar tributes to the mildness and benevolence of their owner's characters, but the obelisks, the pyramids, the temples that commemorate them, these indeed have an orient flavour. One could conclude that our countrymen in Calcutta in those earlier times went to their long rest in rather ornate style. "Man is a noble animal," Sir Thomas Browne has said, "splendid in ashes and pompous in the grave." Tried by this test the citizens of Calcutta were very noble animals indeed.

"What, then, do we know about them, these men and women who made a one- way passes from these islands to India: They died young in those days, as the inscriptions on the monuments show: in the twenty first year, the twenty second year, the, the twenty third year of his age. Or her age. You can hardly pass the monument 'to the memory of the Honourable Rose Aylmer' who, lovely, twenty years old and beloved by a poet, died of an illness brought on by that "mischievous and dangerous fruit the pineapple." At least her name Is in safe keeping.

Ah, what avails the sceptred race? Ah, what the form divine?

What every virtue, every grace? Rose Aylmer, all were thine.

"And now, that enormous pyramid – or was it an obelisk? I forget – to the right of Miss Aylmer's monument? That bespeaks the virtues and, in truth, the remarkable accomplishments of Sir William Jones, friend of Burke and Gibbon, a Judge of the High Court in Calcutta, and one of the first

Englishmen to become a master of Sanskrit learning. Sir William was not alone that India had to offer in literature, philosophy and the arts. The great Warren Hastings, who escaped the cemetery at Calcutta to endure seven years of impeachment in London, himself made translations from the Indian epics, studied Hindu Philosophy, and became as much an admirer of Persian Literature as any Mogul prince. Hastings in fact maintained that Persian ought to be studied in English universities as a companion classical language to Latin.

"I stayed for a week in August at the house which Hastings build himself as a country residence outside Calcutta. It is part of the town today, but the trees and the flowerbeds and the ornamental lakes are touchingly English in appearance. The house too recalls its owner. The rooms are well shaped and bare, with ceilings far higher than we use in England and long graceful windows. There are no doors in the rooms, so that any breeze that blows can blow right through the house. It is a ghostly old place at night with the muslin curtains blowing to and fro and the moonlight casting shadows through the trees. One room is haunted – or not haunted, according to your belief in ghost stories – by the ghost of Hastings, searching for some lost papers that were to prove his innocence before his accusers in London. I remain sceptical myself, for the great man did not number credulity among his virtues; and he would be credulous indeed who thought that any documents in the world could divert the eloquence of Burke and Sheridan. I like better to think of him at ease in his country house in that strange land as one historian has drawn his picture for us: 'he would take up a book of extracts from the Mahabharata and the lean disdainful face of the Governor-General would soften with emotion as he read of the old chivalrous heroes of the Hindus, of Arjun the charioteer and Prince Yudishthra who would not enter heaven unless his dog accompanied him.'"

Radcliffe lamented that so few people at home knew anything about the achievements of the British in India. He said that you would find in a few country houses aquatints by Daniell, Fraser and Salt. Zoffany alone among the great British artists wished to paint in India. "He was commissioned to paint a picture for the new Church at Calcutta, St. John. He chose as his subject 'The Last Supper,' and as his models the leading British citizens of the local community. Unfortunately, he selected a well-known auctioneer for the part of Judas Iscariot and Mr. Zoffany disappeared from Calcutta in a haze of vituperative libel actions."

Radcliffe emphasised the gifts that the British bought to India. "The gifts we brought were Roman" peace, order, justice and the fruits that these things bring. Men are apt to praise them the less the longer they enjoy them. Like the Romans, we built our roads, bridges and canals and we have marked the land as engineers if we have not improved it as architects. Like the Romans we brought and maintained a system of justice that we tried to make even-handed and a system of administration that we hoped was impartial. Of course, such gifts are not everything… It may be that the government of the people by another can never be the best government in the long run, since benevolence and fairness are no substitute for national inspiration. It may be that social democracy itself will prove no more finally satisfactory as a solution of the problem of human relations that the old imperial systems. I do not know, and I am not trying to suggest answers to these great questions."

In the Radcliffe family there are certain stories that have been handed down about his work in India. It is said that before 1947 he had acted as arbitrator about a mosque in Lahore and had greatly impressed his Indian clients by the results achieved. Again, he was said to have been told by the Judges on the Boundary Commissions that it was more than their lives were worth to make any concessions. He impressed on the Judges in the need for compromise but they could not risk it. Radcliffe destroyed all his notes and drafts in connection with the Boundary Commissions before he left India and brought no papers home. This followed his usual practice of destroying everything when no longer needed.

On his return home he clearly felt the need to discuss experience with a trusted friend, and invited Sir Robert Bruce Lockhart to lunch. Sir Robert was well known to him when Radcliffe was at the Ministry of Information. He gave me a very full account of his work on the Boundary Commissions… He found it quite impossible to persuade either side to make any modification of their views. His chief Moslem colleague told him quite frankly. 'It is not that I do not wish to make modifications, but I dare not. If I did my life would be in instant danger'… He found the conditions very trying as the summer was the hottest in India for 70 years."

The above ruminations may throw some light on Radcliffe's character.

CHAPTER 16: PUNJAB BOUNDARY DISPUTES AND DECISIONS

Congress Present Their Case

Punjab Pre-1947
(1947punjab.com)

To the Punjab Boundary Commission

'The partition of Punjab in mid-August 1947 was negotiated by the India National Congress, the Muslim League, representatives of the Sikhs and the various other minor religious and caste groups before the Punjab Boundary Commission. The deliberations served as the formal basis for the Radcliffe Award of 17 August (it was ready on 16 August), which demarcated the boundaries between India and Pakistan on the Punjab border. The Radcliffe Award, however, did not satisfy any of the major contestants, and has subsequently been criticised and even condemned by various disgruntled commentators. Especially in Pakistan the Award has been described as a conspiracy against it. This outcome should not be surprising, because the purpose of the Award was to divide and separate a people who had through the centuries learned to live together. In central Punjab especially, Hindus, Muslims and Sikhs were found to be living side by side in substantial numbers in various towns and villages. The main research source material are documents published in a four-volume compilation of official documents, *The Partition of the Punjab 1947*'.

While the Punjab Boundary Commission was in session, hectic political activities and initiatives relating to the question of partition were under way in the wider political arena. In the present study, the and happenings taking place outside are not included: only the proceedings of the Punjab Boundary Commission are presented and analysed. After a careful reading of the memorandums and statements submitted before the Boundary Commission by the various parties, it was decided that the distinct cluster of arguments put forth by the various actors should be identified. It is however the arguments espoused by the main contestants – the Congress Party, the Sikhs and the Muslim League (and in that order, because the cases were presented in the order) – which are dealt with in some detail. It is quite impossible to cover the whole range of arguments. The aim has been to select such arguments and examples which appear to be the most relevant. The arguments made in the memoranda and in the statements are more or less identical. Both have been used in the present investigation. The oral presentations, however, provide greater insight and clarifications and are therefore, referred to in most cases.

There were several different suggestions as to how the Boundary Commission should be constituted. It was finally agreed that the Commission would include an independent chairman and four other persons. Of these four, two were to be nominated by the congress (of which one was to be a Sikh) and two by the Muslim League. If possible, all the four nominated members were to be of high judicial standing. The Congress nominated Justice Mehr Chand Mahajan and Justice Teja Singh while the Muslim League nominated Justice Din Muhammad and Justice Muhammad Munir. Justice Mehr Chand Mahajan's proposal that Justice Din Muhammad, who was the senior most among them, should preside over the sessions of the commissions was adopted by the other members. On 27 June, it was agreed that Sir Cyril Radcliffe, a member of the Bar from England, should be the chairman of the commission. Radcliffe arrived in Delhi on 8 July. It is important to note that he had never been to India before. The proceedings of the Punjab Commission were held at Lahore for ten days between 21 July and 31 July 1947 (no proceedings were held on Sunday, the 27 of July) **but the Chairman did not attend any session. Arrangements were made to have the record of the proceedings flown to his office in Delhi for his perusal.**

The leading counsel who represented the main parties were Sir Muhammad Zafrullah Khan for the Muslim League, M. C. Setalvad for the Congress and Sardar Harnam Singh for the Sikhs (Sikh Assembly Party). Sir Zafrullah was assisted by Sahibzada Nawazish Ali, Sheikh Nisar Ahmad, Syed Muhammad Shah and Choudhuri Ali Akbar; Setalvad was assisted by Tek Chand, a former Judge of the Lahore High Court and Narotam Singh. In addition, the following counsels presented the cases of the minor communities or interests:

1) Bannerji, Secretary, Punjab Nationalist Christian Association.
2) Rai Bahadur Badri Dass, representing the Scheduled Castes.
3) Sardar Darbara Singh, representing the Mazhabi and Ramdasia Sikhs.
4) R. C. Soni, for Bikaner State
5) Dewan Bahadur S.P. Singha, on behalf of the Christians (Joint Christian Board).
6) C.E. Gibbon, representing the Anglo-Indian community.

7) Sheikh Bashir Ahmad, representing the Ahmadiyya community.

8) Salig Ram, representing the Scheduled Castes and Mazhabi Sikhs.

9) Sir Muhammad Zafrullah Khan, represented Bahawlpur State (also represented the Muslim League).

Although the major consideration in the demarcation of the boundaries was to be the contiguity of Muslim areas and of non-Muslim areas, the inclusion of 'other factors' in the Commission's terms of reference considerably historical, religious, geographical, social and economic aspects were brought into the discussions. That the Muslim-majority Rawalpindi Division should go to Pakistan and the non-Muslim majority Ambala Division should be allotted to India was not disputed by the parties concerned. On the other hand, conflicting claims were staked by both sides to parts and portions of Lahore, Multan and Jullundur divisions.

Terms of Reference

Setalvad opened his brief by emphasising that the terms of reference upon which the Boundary Commission was to ascertain the claims of the various parties appearing before it consisted of two sets of instructions. One, to demarcate boundaries according to the principle of contiguous majority areas and two, 'to consider other factors'. As regards other factors, these could not be ascertained in a general manner; these could differ from area to area and between parts of the boundary. Further, that there was 'no warrant for stating that '*other factors*' had a subsidiary place, nor any for stating that the '*other factors*' were such as might result in what was being termed as 'local deviations only'.

He remarked: *"It stands very much to reason that if it is a matter merely of ascertaining the contiguous majority areas, the work need not have been assigned to a Commission of this weight and importance, in that case a map could have been drawn by having the census figures on the one hand and any Deputy Commissioner could have drawn the line on the basis of contiguous majority area."*

1941 Census Figure Unreliable

The Congress' counsel contested the reliability of the 1941 census figures. According to the 1941 census there was an overall Muslim majority of 57.1 per cent in Punjab. Non-Muslims of which the bulk were Hindus and Sikhs, constituted 42.9 per cent. However, Census Commissioner Yeatts and another officer, Khan Bahadur Sheikh Fazal-i-Illahi, had suggested that political considerations made people greatly exaggerate their numbers in 1941. Fazal-i- Illahi called it a 'Census War'. It started as early as 1911 after separate electorates were introduced in 1909: each community exaggerating its numbers to secure more seats, which by 1941 turned into a complete farce.

Setavad argued that in 1931 the Congress had boycotted the census. According to Yeatts '1940-41 saw also political influences on the census but in the opposite direction, since whereas the difficulty in 1931 had been to defeat a boycott, the difficulty in 1941 was to defeat excess of zeal. However, the Congress' counsel admitted that the fault lay with both sides and it was not Muslims alone who had exaggerated their numbers.

Security

Setavad asserted that the Commission should take into consideration the rivers, the canal system built upon their water resources and the colonies developed by those irrigation systems. Together the rivers, canals and the colonies constituted the natural wealth of the province and were meant for the benefit of the whole of it. Moreover these formerly desert areas were developed mainly by the people of the eastern and central parts of the province. Sikhs and Hindus migrated in large numbers from these over-populated areas to the canal colonies. Through enormous sacrifices, hard work, perseverance and sheer stubbornness the Sikh Jats converted former deserts into the most productive areas of Punjab. Further, most of the land in Punjab, especially in the canal colonies, was owned by Jat peasant-proprietors and not by big landowners or capitalist farmers.

If the colonies in the Lyallpur-Sargodha and Montgomery districts of the Lower Bari Doab were awarded to West Punjab many of the Sikhs and Hindus would emigrate to India because anti-Hindu and Sikh riots in NWFP and northern Punjab had created great insecurity among them. Thus it was important to consider whether the demarcation of boundaries would not lead to their uprooting. On the other hand, Muslims who might leave from these areas which was being developed. In the absence of an obvious boundary such as a mountain range or a hill tract that could be used to demarcate international boundaries in Punjab, the best boundary would be a large river bed. The boundary should be one which could preserve peace between two states and prevent unnecessary conflict.

Economic Stability

Setalvad argued that if the notional basis of division of Punjab were to be accepted, the eastern part would receive only 26,442 acres of waste land as against 3,64,164 acres going to the western part: 4,85,862 acres of unclassed forests as against 11,44,000 being given to western Punjab, (Later, Setalvad corrected this figure, informing that it referred to the total area of unclassed forests, and therefore western Punjab's share would be 6,58,138 acres). Further that the most important were the Crown lands in the colony areas which yielded over a sixth of the total revenue of Punjab. In the colonies the temporarily leased and unallotted Crown lands made up 16,22,655 acres. Under the notional system they fell into western Punjab. 'The eastern part is clearly entitled to a substantial portion of these Crown lands. This substantial share can be awarded to the eastern part by so demarcating the boundaries as to include in them a substantial portion of the temporarily leased and unallotted Crown lands in the colony areas.'

It was claimed further that a non-Muslim majority was to be found in a contiguous belt extending over rural and urban parts of the Lyallpur colony. In the case of the Upper Bari Doab it was the same situation. The peasant was the tiller of the soil and thus tied to the land. Setalvad admitted that the cultivators were not only non-Muslims, but insisted that in the Lyallpur district and Upper Bari Doab colony non-Muslims were in majority in contiguous areas. He remarked 'also in an area extending right from the Gurdaspur district passing though Amritsar and extending to Lahore, known commonly as the Majha tract. All that tract is populated by a non-Muslim majority in whom all these economic interests are concerned. Further:

"If you find... the Muslim majority to be 5 to 7 per cent in a certain tract, but if you find in the landholders, who till the soil, a majority of non-Muslim peasant proprietors, the question for your consideration would be, putting it was a point by itself, whether in that area the economic factor would not override the population factor. The question will be whether you will give weight to excess of 5 to 7 per cent of the Muslim population or to the 60 or 65 per cent of the peasant-proprietors who are non-Muslims.

Presentations to Punjab Boundary Commission Continues

Setalvad continued his presentation before the Punjab Boundary Commission. Setalvad emphasised non-Muslims had deep cultural roots in Lahore. They had built colleges and libraries and also had outstanding economic interests in the district. Lahore district, although the 1941 census figures (disputed by Congress) showed a 60.62 per cent Muslim and 39.39 per cent non-Muslim population strength. Muslims paid only Rs. 5,81,235 as land revenue while non-Muslims paid Rs. 12,63,830. Moreover, Muslims owned only 5,11,867 acres while non-Muslims owned 11,50,450 acres. Thus, economic aspects of the division of Punjab must also be taken into consideration. As to Lahore:

"I will now take the city of Lahore. You will remember that so far as this city is concerned, the population ratio of Muslims and non-Muslims according to the census of 1941 is higher still; not 61 and 39 as in the district but 64 and 36. But… you will find that definitely a larger proportion of the land is in the hands of the non-Muslims… Another factor, which is an allied factor, is in regard to urban areas and also in some district's rural areas. Here again you will find that in certain areas which are Muslim majority areas, the position is that the trade, industry, and the factories and so on and so forth are almost entirely in the hands of non-Muslims."

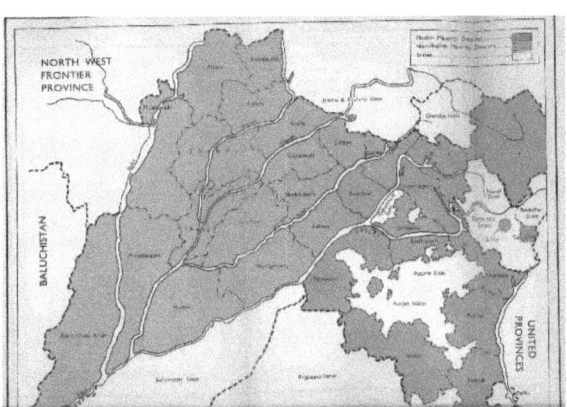

Districts of Punjab with Muslim (green) and non-Muslim (pink) majorities, as per 1941 census (1947punjab.com)

Another thing to consider would be the transport and road system. No division could be acceptable which cuts up the railway and the road transport into unworkable portions. Moreover, the facilities for repairs and maintenance of the railway line for the eastern part of Punjab require that the 'Moghalpura Workshops [Located on the outskirts of Lahore] should be available to the Eastern part in order that the railway in the part should be able to function.

Special Rights of the Sikh Community and Nankana Sahib

Commenting on the Sikh community, Setalvad emphasised that their rights in the province should be evaluated in terms of their historical services to Punjab. They were a martial race who had prior to British conquest been the ruling community in the province. Later after British annexation the Sikhs supplied large numbers of soldiers to the Indian army and contributed outstandingly to the development of the province. Accordingly, 'Efforts must be made by those who are demarcating the boundaries, as far as it is possible and consistent with other considerations and interests, to preserve the solidarity and culture of the Sikh community and its religious freedom. Muslim-Sikh history was one of antagonism between the two communities. Therefore, splitting up the Sikhs into two parts would be very wrong; they should be placed in eastern Punjab. More importantly, according to the notional principle Nankana Sahib, which was the birthplace of the founder of the Sikh faith, fell in West Punjab. This was unacceptable. Therefore, necessary adjustments should be made in the demarcation of boundaries so that Sikh history and culture were not split up into two separate states. Moreover, the Upper Bari Doab canal [which passes through the Majha tract] had been constructed by the British primarily to settle the disbanded soldiers, mainly Jats, of the defeated Sikh armies of 1849 to a livelihood based on agriculture. This area should therefore be given to East Punjab.

'Substantial area': Proper Unit for Demarcation of Contiguity

Regarding the question of demarcation of contiguous Muslim and non-Muslim areas, Setalvad argued that the term 'area' could not mean any infinitesimally small area, but must mean a substantial area. What constituted a break in the contiguity must also be a substantial area. As to the word 'contiguity', it meant, according to the Oxford Dictionary, in a literal sense: touching; in actual contract; next in space; meeting at a common point; bordering, and adjoining. In the loose sense it meant neighbouring; situated in close proximity though not in contact. However, it was only in the strict literal sense, that contiguity should be understood in the context of boundary demarcation. As for Ambala and Jullundur divisions (as well as in the smaller form of districts0 they were not only non-Muslim majority areas but also showed that economic interests and social and cultural factors were predominantly of non-Muslim character. However, the map of the Muslim League based on the smaller unit of a *tehsil* or less had tried to connect some areas together to present a Muslim majority contiguity in them. This was inadmissible.

Gurdaspur District

Coming to the crucial Gurdaspur district, Setalvad informed that it consisted of an area of 1,827 square miles. Up till 1921 it had a non-Muslim majority. In 1931, however, Muslims were reported to be in a majority of 15,534 while in 1941 that majority had been recorded as 26,435. Thus, according to the 1941 census figures there were 5,89,923 Muslims as against 5,63,588 non-Muslims and therefore on the basis of notional division it had been

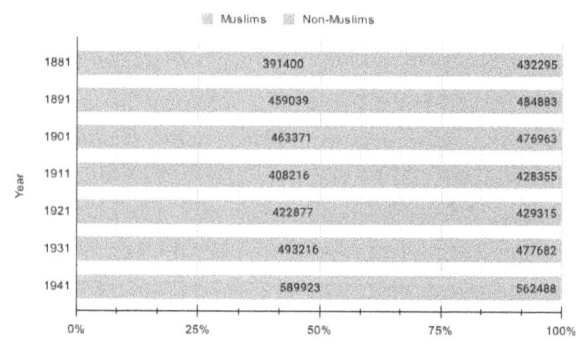

Population of Muslims and Non-Muslims in Gurdaspur District, 1891-1941 (1947punjab.com)

- 327

placed in western Punjab. As pointed out earlier, Congress did not accept the 1941 census as reliable.

Arguing further Setalvad said that the districts of Amritsar and Gurdaspur were united by very close trade relations. Amritsar was the clearing house for exports and imports of Gurdaspur. Further, the rail and road connection were such that it came up from Lahore to Amritsar and then went on to Gurdaspur and it linked Kangra Valley and district with Amritsar and Lahore. Therefore, Amritsar and Gurdaspur should be taken as one unit rather than be divided into two separate districts. They together formed a non-Muslim majority and therefore should be awarded to eastern Punjab. Another major consideration for placing Gurdaspur in the eastern part was its intimate relationship with Sikh history. Many famous Sikh shrines were located in it.

Gujranwala and Sialkot Districts

It was also argued that the Gujranwala district's importance for Sikhs should not be forgotten. It was here that Maharaja Ranjit Singh was born. As for Sialkot district, its north-eastern part was for centuries part of Jammu State. This part was populated by Dogras who had linguistic and cultural links with the Dogras of Kangra and Gurdaspur and with those of Jammu. Moreover, both in the Gujranwala and Sialkot districts non-Muslims owned more property and paid more revenue. Therefore, they should also go to eastern Punjab.

Extent of Area Claimed for Eastern Punjab

Proceeding on the assumption that partition of Punjab would involve massive population movement, the Congress memorandum claimed altogether the following areas for eastern Punjab:

1) The whole of Ambala division.

2) The whole of Jullundur division

3) The whole of Lahore division

4) Layallpur district.

5) Montgomery district.

6) Such other adjoining areas as may be necessary from considerations of canal and colony needs. Such a division of Punjab would consolidate some 34 lakh Sikhs out of their total population of 37,57,401 in East Punjab.

The Sikhs

Sardar Harnam Singh presented the case before the Punjab Boundary Commission on behalf of the Sikhs.

Terms of Reference

Agreeing with Setalvad's interpretation of the terms of reference, Sardar Harnam Singh chose to comment on the Muslim League's memorandum in order to show that the importance of 'other factor's was admitted by it even when its main stress was on contiguous Muslim and non-Muslim areas. Thus it had asserted that the boundary should be a workable and practicable one and should be capable of fulfilling the functions of a boundary between two neighbouring states. Further, 'It should not be a crazy line running backwards and forwards over the areas of several districts and in and out of every village…. Another point emphasised by the Muslim League was that there must be some rationalisation of the canal system: the headworks of an irrigation system should be in the same part as the canals emanating from it. Reasoning thus, it was pointed out, the Muslim League had claimed portions of the non-Muslim majority Pathankot *tehsil* because Madhopur waterworks are located there. However, if that were granted Muslims would be 45.4 per cent while non-Muslims would be 54.6 per cent of the population there. Similarly, like the Congress the Muslim League also laid great stress on economic stability. It even alleged that judicial notice be taken of the source of non- Muslim wealth: 'they say that the non-Muslim property has been purchased from the proceeds of money-lending which have gone into the coffers of the Hindus and Sikhs.

Transfer of 'Floating' Population and Rights of the Tillers

Harman Singh argued that the commission had to consider how the demarcation of boundaries would affect, on the one hand, the transfer of people from one part of Punjab to the other, and on the other hand, how the consolidation of the Sikh community could be realised in eastern Punjab. As to the question of transfer of people, the predicament of those who were rooted in the soil was different from those who followed a profession such as that a lawyer or doctor or the various other rootless menial classes would be easily be moved. In the Lahore district, out of the total paid land revenue of about 18 lakhs approximately 13 lakhs was paid by non-Muslims of which Sikhs alone paid 12 lakhs. Lahore was not an area of big landlordism. Here were to be found mostly peasant-proprietors, the majority of whom were Sikhs. It was virtually impossible to transfer people who were rooted in the soil. On the other hand, according to the 1931 census which included information on races, tribes and castes etc., in the Lahore district out of the total Muslim population of 1,49,29,896 some 46,95,957 consisted of fakirs, beggars, weavers, herdsmen, cobblers, *khumars* or potters, *musallis*, carpenters, oilmen, bards, barbers, blacksmiths, washermen, butchers and *mirasis*, people who are described in the settlement reports as landless people and menials. These were a 'floating people' and could therefore be transferred easily.

Moreover the question of 'one man, one vote' should apply only to the basis of legitimate government, not to the division of a country. Other factors such as relationship to the land, ownership of property and economic viability should be given proper consideration rather than just mere numbers. The Muslim League wanted the partition of India because it could not accept the principle of 'one man one vote', which it feared would place Muslims in a minority situation. However, it insisted that the division of Punjab should proceed purely on the basis of numerical strength. Thus it was exploiting an apparently democratic device to achieve an undemocratic political end.

No Unanimous Verdict of the Punjab Boundary Commission

Pre-partition Punjab province
(1947punjab.com)

As expected the Indian Members of the Boundary Commission were heavily influenced by the communities to which they belonged. Each member promoted the case of his own community and there was hardly any objectivity in their individual verdict. This left the field wide open for Radcliffe to exercise his discretion which he indeed did as we shall see later. Much before the meeting of the Punjab Boundary Commission severe communal disturbances had erupted in many places in the Punjab. This undoubtedly had a bearing in the decision-making process of the Boundary Commission. The four nominated members of the Punjab Boundary Commission could not reach a unanimous decision and therefore submitted separate reports. The verdicts of each member are summarised below:

Justice Din Muhammad

Din Muhammad described the Sikh demand for special rights as 'most ridiculous, most unjustifiable and most unreasoned.' The maps produced by the Hindu-Sikh side were declared misleading. He accepted numerical majority and contiguity as the main criteria for allocation of territory, but dismissed ownership of property as an invalid basis for such a claim. On the other hand, security and economic stability, including allocation of waterworks, were considered by him as important 'other factors'. However, in contrast to the Hindu-Sikh demand, he found the Muslim demand, 'to have been framed reasonably and moderately and not with a view to bargaining. It was properly related to the population factor.'

Justice Mhuammad Munir

According to Munir, the Sikh claim to special rights by virtue of their shrines had no direct force. Muslims also had shrines all over the Punjab. Nor was the stand on language a valid one because Lehnda was only a dialect of Punjabi. He also sought to refute that Muslim rulers had persecuted Sikhs and quoted instead several Sikh sources urging hatred and strife against Muslims. The claim to hard work and exclusive contribution to the development of the canal colonies by the Sikhs was also dismissed as wrong. Muslim peasants had also made equal contribution to development. In Lyallpur not only the Sikh Jats but also Muslim Arains had played a great role in development. The economic exploitation of Muslims by Hindus and Sikhs was the real reason for demanding a separate Muslim state. Therefore, invoking greater property ownership in Punjab could not be an admissible factor for the allocation of areas. Looking at the question of security, Munir opined that the Muslim League's proposal was the correct one. As the measure of contiguity only the *tehsil* could be employed fruitfully. Therefore '…the frontier between the two States should be that suggested by the Muslim League.' He assured the non- Muslims that they had nothing to fear in Pakistan because Islam treated all citizens alike.

Justice Teja Singh

Teja Singh laid great emphasis on the fears of the Sikhs to live under a Muslim communal government. While reiterating the Sikh counsel's version of the Muslim-Sikh animosity during the Mughal period he went on to discuss contemporaneous events in great detail. Commenting on the Muslim League agitation against the Unionist ministry. Justice Teja Singh asserted that it was not only violent but also proclaimed patently hostile slogans against non- Muslim such as:

Assey lengey Pakistan (We will take Pakistan)

*Jaise liya tha Hindustan (*the same way we took India).

According to Teja Singh, the authorities did not move a finger when the agitation was on, but when the Sikh and Hindu students took out a procession on 4 March 1947 they were *lathi-charged*. Troubles spread from Lahore to other parts of Punjab. There were serious communal riots in the districts of Campbellpur, Rawalpindi, Jhelum, Amritsar, Multan and later on in Gurgaon. In the rural areas of Rawalpindi, Jhelum and to a lesser extent in Multan districts, Sikhs were raided by Muslim mobs. Further:

'In some places the rioters numbered five to ten thousand, and almost the entire Sikh population including the old and infirm, women and children were either killed or burnt alive. A large number of people were forcibly converted, children were kidnapped and young women were abducted and openly raped.'

According to Teja Singh, although the Hindu and Sikh version placed the number of victims at a very high figure the official figures mentioned as follows:

	Killed or burnt alive	Injured
Rawalpindi district	2,263	397
Multan district	189	183

Official estimates were that property worth two million rupees was destroyed in Multan and one hundred million rupees in Rawalpindi district. 'It is alleged that the whole thing was organised.' Comparing the Muslim League's demand for the partitioning of India with the Sikh demand for the partitioning of Punjab, he observed:

'The Muslim League depended solely upon the fact that they (Muslims) formed the majority of the population of the provinces which they desired to be made into an independent state. The Sikhs, on the other hand, not being in majority in any district of the Punjab demanded that part of it in which the bulk of them lived and which they claimed to be their homeland, be separated from the rest of the province so that they might escape communal rule of the Muslims. They knew that unlike the Muslims they could not have a state of their own but they preferred to live in that part of the Punjab which would join the Indian Union rather than Pakistan. They never relied upon their numerical strength, but stressed that because of certain factors they occupied a special position in the province and were consequently entitled to a special consideration on that account.'

Teja Singh pointed out that the Ahmadiya community who supported the stand taken by the Muslim League and to which community Sir Muhammad Zafrullah Khan belonged had also stressed the necessary of preserving the solidarity of their community. Further, he reiterated that because many holy shrines and historical sites of the Sikhs were located in Lahore, Amritsar, Gurdaspur, Gujranwala and Sheikhupura districts they should go to eastern Punjab. In conclusion, he recommended a division of Punjab largely though not entirely followed the position of the Sikhs. He observed, 'I have not calculated the figures but I believe that it would raise the number of the Sikhs in the eastern Punjab to about 31 lakhs [the Congress and Sikh plans placed 34 lakhs in eastern Punjab] out of their total population of about 37 lakhs in the whole of the British Punjab.'

Justice Mehr Chand Mahajan

Acknowledging that contiguous Muslim and non-Muslim areas should be separated and allocated to Pakistan and India respectively. Mahajan observed that 'other factors' were left to be determined at the discretion of the Commission. He made this interesting observation:

'I am convinced that it is possible for an ingenious Muslim to make the whole Punjab a contiguous Muslim majority area by adopting a certain line and, similarly, it is possible for an ingenious non-Muslim to make the province of the Punjab right up to the River Jhelum a non-Muslim area by adopting another line. He may go up even to the city of Rawalpindi.'

Proceeding in a relatively neutral and independent vein, Mahajan rejected the Congress and Sikh suggestion that the Chenab river should be the frontier between India and Pakistan. He said:

'This suggestion would seriously prejudice the claim of the Muslim League on the basis of the population factor and would also clash with the main principle of partition as it would include within the Eastern Punjab a huge majority of Muslims residing in areas which are predominantly Muslim. There are no such factors in this area which can override the population factor.'

Regarding the Muslim League's suggestion to fix the border on the Sutlej river, Justice Mahajan found that it had been worked out on the basis of *tehsil* as the unit for demarcation of contiguous areas. It could easily be reserved and then non-Muslim parts of *tehsils* could be put together to create non-Muslim majority contiguous areas and this could extend well into western Punjab.

On the other hand, in the distribution of the two major canal systems and the colonies of Lyallpur and Montgomery, Mahajan sought to compensate both sides. Therefore while most of Lyallpur including substantial portions of the Sahidi Bar were to be awarded to western Punjab, Montgomery was to go to eastern Punjab. As regards Lahore, according to his scheme it went to India but Mahajan acknowledged the common claims of all communities and preferred an arrangement under which it could be made a 'free city' jointly supervised by India and Pakistan. On the other hand Nankana Sahib was to go to India.

He said in conclusion: 'In my view the frontier of India and Pakistan should be demarcated on the west of the Ravi and in the neighbourhood of that river, as strategically speaking this is the only workable frontier that can be laid down between these two states which are being divided on religious basis.'

CHAPTER 17: CONTROVERSY OVER BENGAL'S PARTITION

Prelude to Partition of Bengal

"Partition of Bengal along the Radcliffe Line"
(thedailystar.net)

Chronologically speaking 3 June 1947, the date of Mountbatten's partition plan, is assumed to be a dividing line. Before 3 June, politicians are known to have jockeyed to influence the terms of partition and the transfer of power. After 3 June, the bureaucrats are believed to have taken over to sort out the administrative technicalities. As a result of this, historians of partition, all of whom have been interested in the political rather than the administrative issues involved have tended to end their stories with the 3 June plan. Few have ventured beyond this date.

Yet the moment one crosses this Rubicon, the picture that emerges is much more complex. We shall see briefly the stages of the partition process from 3 June until 17 August 1947, when the Radcliffe Award was published. We now turn specifically at the making of the Boundary Commission Award for Bengal, which defined the borderline between West Bengal and East Pakistan. By attempting to analyse the various shifting and competing priorities of those immediately involved, it will be revealed how political concerns continued to play as much of a part in the drawing of this borderline as they had ever done at any stage of the partition saga.

The 3 June Statement

Before we begin to look at this process, it is worth recalling that certain significant political choices on the form that partition would take had been written into the 3 June Plan itself. Though apparently leaving the entire question of partition open, the Plan delimited the parameters within which a division could take place. According to the Plan, the Bengal Legislative Assembly was to divide itself into two parts, one consisting of the representative Muslim-majority districts and the other of the Hindu-majority districts. Each assembly was to meet separately to ascertain whether the majority of its members favoured partition. In the event that they did, they were to indicate whether they wished to attach their half of the province to India or to Pakistan. Accordingly, on 20 June 1947, these two provisionally partitioned units met to vote on the question of partition. The majority of representatives of the Hindu majority districts voted in favour of the partition of Bengal, while those of the Muslim majority districts voted against it. On the basis of this vote, it was taken that the will to partition had been sufficiently established. It was only after this vote that the Boundary Commission was set up to determine the real or final border between the two Bengals.

This procedure, though seemingly uncontentious, had some remarkable features. These become apparent if we consider the process by which the people's will to partition was assumed to have been established. Even if we disregard the fact that members of the voting Assemblies had been elected by a very limited segment of the population, and ignore altogether the more fundamental questions regarding the representativeness of elected representatives, there were significant flaws in the process that was chosen to ascertain their will. The vote that was taken to establish their will to partition had had been cast in an Assembly temporarily or notionally divided into two parts. Before the Boundary Commission had given its Award, there was no knowing to what extent these notional units would match the final shape of the two partitioned states. The partition vote was therefore necessarily an imperfect one. Many members of the notional West Bengal Assembly voted for partition without knowing for certain whether their constituencies would continue to be in West Bengal when the Award was finally made. For instance, members from Khulna, a Hindu-majority district that was included in the notional West Bengal, might conceivably have voted differently had they know that Khulna would eventually be awarded to Pakistan. Whether or not such foreknowledge would have made a difference to the final outcome – the majority in West Bengal assembly deciding in favour of partition – must remain a matter of conjecture. But it is significant that the procedure for establishing will on a question of such momentous importance was dealt with so summarily.

Yet if we think about it more closely, this is not as surprising as it seems. This entire proceeding was essentially tautological: the election was set up in such a way that its result could not possibly be any different. First the electorate (consisting of members of the assembly) was divided into two parts in such a way that in one-part partitionists were in the majority. Then it was decided on the basis of their majority vote in favour of partition that a majority will for partition had been adequately demonstrated. The procedure, though apparently careless, was in all likelihood deliberately designed to produce the specific result that it did: i.e. to prove the existence of a convincing majority in favour of the partition of Bengal. From Mountbatten's point of view, it was necessary to have such a result because the success of the entire partition plan hinged on the partition of Bengal (and Punjab). This was after all, the condition on which the Congress leadership had given its consent to the plan as a whole. In this sense, the whole exercise of voting was little more than window-dressing designed to create the impression that the representatives of the people of these two provinces had exercised their choice in favour of partition. It was certainly not designed to yield any surprises.

One other notable feature of these arrangements was that the two voting blocs were divided on territorial lines. This is significant because everyone agrees that the basis of the partition was to satisfy a communal demand for autonomy: that its purpose was to ensure, for those who demanded it, a communal right to self-determination. But from the very start of the process of implementing the partition, this principle had to be tempered by a host of other considerations, amongst which territorial questions were paramount. The two voting groups into which the Bengal Assembly was divided were composed of the representatives of territorial rather than communal units: Hindu-majority and Muslim-majority districts respectively. Hindu and Muslim members were not invited to meet separately to determine their collective communal will on what was in its primary form, a communal question. There is little doubt that the result of the voting (Hindus voting aye and Muslim nay) would have been the same. But it is interesting that the option of a communal vote was not raised by any of the parties concerned.

By this stage, therefore, the parties appear to have accepted that communal autonomy was to be realised by the creation of separate territorial sovereignties. There are subtle but significant differences between the notions of communal autonomy and territorial sovereignty. The first emphasises the rights of the people of a community to self-determination, rights which could in theory be achieved within a single state. The second stresses the bounded space within which a community is sovereign, and could be realised only by a territorial separation. This difference was, we may recall, also the essence of the difference between the Cabinet Mission's Plan A (which provided for a single loose federation with a greater degree of autonomy for its constituent, communally determined units) and its Plan B, which provided for a separate, sovereign (albeit truncated) Pakistan. It is also interesting that no one objected that the package being offered to the members for their approval was in fact the Cabinet Mission's Plan B – which had not been officially accepted by either of the two parties involved. What had been accepted by both parties, albeit grudgingly, was the Cabinet Mission Plan A.

Once again it was crucial to the success of Mountbatten's Plan that this little detail should pass unnoticed. To succeed in getting partition through by 15 August (or indeed to get it though at all), Mountbatten had to avoid running up against the requirement that his 3 June Plan be ratified by the All-India Committees of the Congress and the League. To side-step this eventually, he went along with the Congress Party's effort to pass his 3 June Plan off as a modified version of Plan A. In other words he proceeded as if the support of the political parties for his Plan had already been constitutionally obtained and that the leaders who signed on the dotted line on behalf of their parties actually had the authority to do so. This suggests that Mountbatten shared the fears of the Congress leaders who gave their assent to the Plan that their party was not behind them. Together they colluded to push through a partition that even their own committed followers might conceivably have rejected.

Once it had been thus decided that Bengal was to be divided into two separate states, the focus of attention shifted with extraordinary speed from the question of how communal autonomy could be realised to the issue of how much territory was to be made available to each state. The tension underlying the two issues was not always apparent but nevertheless emerged quite sharply, as we shall see, when the actual process of division began.

The Bengal Award was a Perverse Award

Joya Chatterji, the noted Indian writer has recorded in *Region & Partition*. But if it is recalled that Mountbatten had allowed the Congress leadership not only to determine the structure and composition of the Boundary Commission but also to draft their terms of reference, it is not entirely surprising to find that the Commission awarded, to such extent as it did, in the Congress party's favour.'

The main objectives of the Bengal award appear to be –

1. To allot as much territory as possible to West Bengal

2. To keep Calcutta in West Bengal

3. To keep the communication line both road and railway intact from Calcutta to Darjeeling.

4. To ensure that the district of Darjeeling and the State of Cooch Bihar did not become enclaves within East Bengal.

5. To ensure passage between Assam and the rest of India.

6. Not to disturb the Hooghly-Bhagirathi river system.

To achieve these objectives the partition line had already been preplanned and all the hearings of the Boundary Commission and the legal framework were totally ignored as will be evident when the award is studied in depth. Poor Radcliffe was the scapegoat and stenographer to Mountbatten and faithfully took down his dictation. The legal framework and guidelines relating to the partition of Bengal were as follows:

The 3 June Statement 1947 of the British Government as announced by Prime Minister Attlee in the Parliament stipulated - 'A Boundary Commission will be set up by the Governor General, the membership and terms of reference of which will be settled in consultation with those concerned. It will be instructed to demarcate the boundaries of the two parties of the Punjab on the basis of ascertaining the contiguous majority areas of Muslims and non-Muslims. It will also be instructed to consider other factors. Similar instructions will be given to the Bengal Boundary Commission. Until the report of a Boundary Commission has been put into effect, the provisional boundaries indicated in the Appendix will be used.'

On 30 June 1947 Mountbatten announced the following guidelines for Bengal Boundary Commission –

'The Boundary Commission is instructed to demarcate the boundaries of the two parts of Bengal on the basis of ascertaining the contiguous majority areas of Muslims and non-Muslims. In doing so, it will also consider other factors.'

The Indian Independent Act, 1947 promulgated on 18 July 1947 stipulated inter-alia –

'3.(I)(a) The Province of Bengal, as constituted under the Government of India Act, 1935 shall cease to exist; and

(b) There shall be constituted in lieu thereof two new Provinces, to be known respectively as East Bengal and West Bengal. . . . .

(3) The boundaries of the new Provinces aforesaid . . . . may be determined, whether before or after the appointed day, by the award of a boundary commission appointed or to be appointed by the Governor General in that behalf, but until the boundaries are so determined –

'(a) the Bengal Districts specified in the First Schedule to this Act, together with in the event mentioned in subsection (2) of this section the Assam District of Sylhet, shall be treated as the territories which are to be comprised in the new Province of East Bengal;'

(4) In this section, the expression "award" means, in relation to a boundary commission, the decision of the chairman of that commission contained in his report to the Governor General at the conclusion of the commission's proceedings.'

The points to note are that all the legal guidelines clearly stipulated the Muslim majority Districts which were contained as an Appendix to the 3 June Statement and as the Schedule to the Indian Independence Act. The Muslims majority Districts were as follows:

In the Chittagong Division, the districts of Chittagong, Noakhali and Tippera. In the Dacca Division, the districts of Bakarganj, Dacca, Faridpur and Mymensingh.

In the Presidency Division, the districts of Jessore, Murshidabad and Nadia.

In the Rajshahi Division, the districts of Bogra, Dinajpur, Malda, Pabna, Rajshahi and Rangpur.

It may be noted that the districts of Khulna and the Chittagong Hill Tracts were not included in East Bengal.

In an earlier installment we have already seen the communal demographic distribution of population in Bengal in 1947. The points to note were –

1) In Bengal the proportion of the Hindus had been steadily decreasing and on the other hand, that of Muslims was continually increasing from one census year to another. It was also clear that only within the last 100 years the Muslims had outnumbered the Hindus by a clear majority. If the difference went on multiplying at the given rate, a time would have come when the Muslims would have outnumbered the Hindus by 6,000 per every 10,000 of the population. Therefore, taking 1941 census figures as the basis for partition gave a clear disadvantage to the ever increasing population of the Muslims.

2) Even taking the census figures of 1941 as the basis both the 3 June Statement of British Government and the Indian Independence Act, 1947 had clearly indicated the Muslim majority districts which would form the basis of partition. Neither the Statement nor the Act envisaged allotting the Muslim majority districts or any part thereof to West Bengal.

The award which Radcliffe gave in Bengal transferred a large number of areas from the Muslim majority part to non-Muslim Bengal. The entire Muslim majority district of Murshidabad (population 1,640,530, Muslim majority 56.55%), about two-thirds of the Muslim majority district of Nadia (population 1,759,846, Muslim majority 61.26%) and two police stations, Bongaon (Muslim majority 56.4%) and Geighata (Muslim majority 61.5%) of the Muslim majority district of Jessore (Muslim majority 60.21%) were transferred to West Bengal apparently to keep Pakistan territory far away from the Bhagirathi Hooghly River on which the port of Calcutta was located. Radcliffe undoubtedly thought that Pakistan would obstruct the flow of water in this River or divert the smaller rivers such as Churni and Jalangi which flowed into the Bagirathi-Hooghly. It should here be noted that Murshidabad was situated on both sides of this River, while the western border of Nadia extended to the western side of the River and the western border of Jessore was only about twenty-five files from this River.

In addition, Radcliffe transferred to West Bengal about two-thirds of the Muslim majority district of Malda (population 1,232,618, Muslim majority 56.78%) and about on-half of the Muslim majority district of Dinjapur (population 1,926,833, Muslim majority 50.20%).

Defenders of Radcliffe would have us believe that his award was fair because he also transferred to East Bengal non-Muslim majority districts or parts of them. One of the districts transferred was Khulna and the other Chittagong Hill Tracts. In the case of Khulna (population 1,943,218) it should be noted that the non-Muslim majority there was nominal (50.64%) and of its three sub- divisions, the only one which had a mentionable non-Muslim majority was Khulna (Sadar) which was sandwiched between Muslim majority subdivisions of Satkhira on the west (Muslim majority 52%) and Bagherhat on the east (Muslim majority 54%). The other district of Chittagong Hill Tracts was very sparsely populated (total population 247,053) and 94.5% of its inhabitants were tribal people, Buddhists and animists. Besides, as Mountbatten himself wrote to the Secretary of State, the Governor of Bengal "had explained to me that the whole economic life of the people of the Hill Tracts depends upon East Bengal, that there are only one or two indifferent tracts through the jungle into Assam, and that it would be disastrous for the people themselves to be cut off from East Bengal . . ." The only other area which Radcliffe transferred to East Bengal comprised three Muslim majority and two non-Muslim majority police stations of the district of Jalpaiguri (Muslims 23.1%, Hindus 50.6% and Tribal people 25.6%).

Three points should particularly be noted about Radcliffe's award in Assam and Bengal. Radcliffe's boundary line gave East Bengal about 60% of the total population of the two undivided provinces but only about 40% of their areas. This is a very important consideration because, as noted earlier, Bengal was a very heavily populated province and, compared with West Bengal, East Bengal had very few natural resources and there were hardly any industries there. Two, one of the Muslim members of the Boundary Commission pointed out to Radcliffe that because he was allocating the sub-division of Basarat (Muslim majority 58%) to West Bengal for the benefit of Calcutta, he should allot to East Bengal Jalpaiguri and the catchment areas of the Teesta River in the interest of the river system of East Bengal but Radcliffe did not accept that argument. Finally, as well as known geographer A. Tayyeb has noted, "on the whole the boundary award in East Pakistan was more illogical and unsatisfactory than the award in West Pakistan. It followed no consistent criteria and unnecessarily produced a number of obtrusive salients."

Comparing the partition of Bengal by Radcliffe with its "notional" division, Hugh Tinker in his *Experiment with Freedom* has concluded:

... Murshidabad district, the centre of the old Muslim culture and tradition, was allotted to India. Other Muslim majority districts were divided and the allocation of Khulna ... was not adequate recompense. However, the Chittagong Hill Tracts were given to Pakistan ... Altogether West Bengal gained substantially over East Bengal under the award.

Curiously enough, adds Tinker, "this did not prevent a blaze of indignation from the Congress side over the allocation of the Chittagong Hill Tracts ...

Had Radcliffe followed the legal framework the following would have happened –

1. Calcutta would have been totally cut off from North Bengal.

2. Both Jalpaiguri and Cooch Bihar would have become enclaves in East Bengal and consequently would have had to accede to East Bengal.

3. East Bengal would have been deprived of Khulna and Chittagong Hill Tracts.

4. East Bengal would have had some control over the Hooghly and Bhagirathi river systems.

The Radcliffe's Bengal Award will remain forever as a travesty of justice.

CHAPTER 18: PUNJAB BOUNDARY DECISION

The Punjab Boundary Award

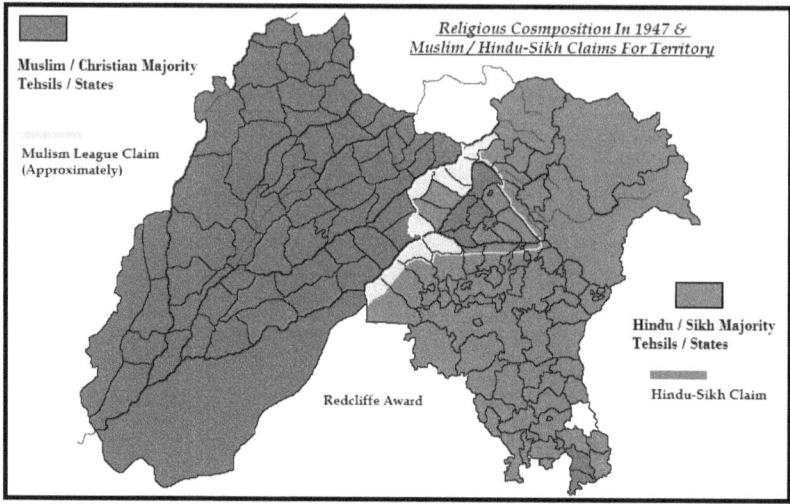

Partition of Punjab Boundary
(defence.pk)

The genesis of the Kashmir dispute lies in the Punjab Boundary Award. Ample evidence exists to substantiate the fact that Mountbatten intervened in the Radcliffe's Award in the Punjab. The award that Radcliffe gave in the Punjab lopped off a number of contiguous Muslim majority areas from Pakistan, but not a single non-Muslim majority area was taken away from India. If the justification for this decision is sought in the phrase, "other factors", it is very strange that other factors should have worked consistently in favour of India and against Pakistan. In Gurdaspur district, two contiguous Muslim majority *tahsils,* or sub-districts, Gurdaspur and Batala, wre given to India along with Pathankot *tahsil* to provide a link between India and the state of Jammu and Kashmir. The Muslim majority *tahsil,* Anjala, in the Amritsar district, was also handed over to India. In the Jullundur district, the Muslim majority *tahsils,* Nakodar and Jullundur, which lie in the angle of the Sutlej and Beas rivers, were assigned to India. The Muslim majority *tahsils,* Zira and Ferozepore, in the Ferozepore district, which were east of the Sutlej River, were also transferred to India. All of these Muslim majority areas were contiguous to West Punjab.

For some of these transfers of territory from Pakistan Radcliffe offered no explanation. He merely said that he was "conscious that there are legitimate criticisms to be made [of his award] as there are, I think, of any other line that might be chosen." But there were certain areas about which he felt it necessary to offer some sort of explanation. It is worth quoting his exact words:

'I have hesitated long over those not inconsiderable areas east of the Sutlej River and in the angle of the Beas and Sutlej Rivers in which Muslim majorities are found. But on the whole, I have come to the conclusion that it would be in the true interests of neither State to extend the territories of the

- 343

West Punjab to a strip on the far side of the Sutlej and that there are factors such as the disruption of railway communication and water systems that ought in this instance to displace the primary claims of contiguous majorities.'

However, Pakistani grievances with regard to the Punjab Boundary Award have real substance. The most bitter criticism is directed against the grant to India of those important areas in Gurdaspur and Ferozepore districts which had Muslim majorities and were contiguous to Pakistan.

Chaudhri Muhammad Ali in *The Emergence of Pakistan* explains how Pakistan suffered from the way in which Radcliffe divided the district of Gurdaspur:

'The district had four *tahsils* of which only one, Pathankot, had a non-Muslim majority; the other three, Gurdaspur, Batala, and Shakargarh, had Muslim majorities. The district as a whole had a bare Muslim majority, but that was largely because of the high percentage of Hindus in Pathankot *tahsil*. Gurdaspur district was contiguous to the state of Jammu and Kashmir. For the Indian Union, rail and road communication with the state was only possible through the plains of this district that was flanked by high mountains in Indian territory to the east. If Radcliffe had awarded India only the non-Muslim-majority *tahsil*, Pathankot, India would still not have gained access to Jammu and Kashmir, since the Muslim-majority *tahsils*, Batala and Gurdaspur, to the south would have blocked the way. By assigning these two Muslim majority *tahsils* also to India, Radcliffe provided India with a link to the state of Jammu and Kashmir and paved the way for the bitterest dispute between India and Pakistan.'

Indian maneuvers to deprive Pakistan of Gurdaspur also go back to the Cabinet Mission days. The initiators were two Hindus in key positions in the Government of India: the ubiquitous V.P. Menon, and Sir B.N. Rau, a former judge of the Bengal High Court and Prime Minister of Kashmir and at this time on special duty in the Governor-General's secretariat. In response to a request from the Viceroy's private secretary, Menon on 23 January 1946 forwarded his own and Rau's joint 'suggestions for demarcation of the Pakistan areas'. The part relating to Gurdaspur read:

'The Sikh objection in the Western Zone can be met, to some extent, by excluding the districts of Amritsar and Gurdaspur from 'Pakistan'. These two form a compact block, whose total population is a little over 2.5 millions, of which a little under 1.25 millions – i.e., a little under 50 per cent, are Muslims. This form of partition will cut across existing Divisional boundaries, but has the advantage of meeting the most serious of the Sikh objections, though not all of them; for, wherever the line may be drawn, there will still be some Sikhs left on the wrong side. If the existing Lahore, Rawalpindi, and Multan Divisions are included in 'Pakistan', the number of Punjab Sikhs in 'Pakistan' would be about

2.2 millions and in 'Hindustan' about 1.5 millions; with the exclusion of the districts of Amritsar and Gurdaspur, the corresponding figures would be 1.5 millions and 2.2 millions, so that the majority of them would now fall in 'Hindustan', although a substantial minority would still be left in 'Pakistan'. On the whole the best plan would be to exclude these two districts from the Western Zone...'

British officialdom in India as well as in the UK readily fell for the cunning argument that the recommendation would help pacify the Sikhs. The Sikhs were the favourite 'martial race' of the British; they had rendered valuable services during the Great Rebellion of 1857 and the two world wars and had always formed a valuable part of the Indian army. And they were the ones who were going to suffer the most as the result of partition. The Hindus got Hindustan and the Muslims Pakistan. The Sikhs dreamed of Sikhistan but instead their community was going to be cut into two parts. Anything that would alleviate their plight was welcome and it was hoped that the proposed concession might even soothe their fury to some extent and reduce the amount of communal bloodshed.

That Amritsar should go to India because it is the sacred city of the Sikhs was understandable, but the assertion that Gurdaspur was inseparable from Amritsar because the two of them formed a 'compact bloc' was farfetched. Nevertheless, it too, was swallowed.

On 29 January 1946 the Secretary of State for India, who was preparing to lead the Cabinet Mission to India, urgently telegraphed the Viceroy to let him have recommendations 'as regards definition of genuine Muslim areas if we are compelled to give a decision on this.

The Viceroy replied on 6 February 1746:

'In the Punjab the only Muslim-majority district that would not go into Pakistan under this demarcation is Gurdaspur (51% Muslim). Gurdaspur must go with Amritsar if the Sikhs must stay out of Pakistan. But for this special importance of Amritsar, demarcation in the Punjab could have been on division boundaries.'

When the Cabinet Mission interviewed Jinnah on 16 April 1946, he was told that 'agreement might perhaps be reached on a separate state of Pakistan consisting of, say, Sind, North-West Frontier Province, Baluchistan and the Muslim-majority districts of the Punjab except perhaps Gurdaspur.'

It is not surprising that Mountbatten, who was pre-disposed to favour India, should have accepted the existing official position with regard to Gurdaspur with alacrity. During his press conference on 4 June 1947 he declared without hesitation that the Boundary Commission was unlikely to 'throw' the whole of Gurdaspur district 'into the Muslim majority areas' because of population of that district was 50.4 per cent Muslim and 49.6 per cent non-Muslim.

In pressing this view upon Radcliffe, he was on strong ground – it was not his own opinion, it was a question already carefully considered and settled by the Governments of India and the United Kingdom.

Secretary of State Noel-Baker conceded in a note he sent to Prime Minister Attlee on 25 February 1949 that:

'There is some reason for thinking that Sir Cyril Radcliffe at the last moment altered his boundary award so as to assign to the E. Punjab a salient in the original demarcation of the W. Punjab boundary which included Gurdaspur. But we have no knowledge that this was done on the advice of Lord Mountbatten.'

In refuting the allegation that Mountbatten persuaded Radcliffe to divide Gurdaspur in such a manner that India would obtain a land route to Kashmir, Hodson writes that the Kashmir frontier 'was not in anybody's mind at the time'. But in fact it definitely was in the minds of three very important persons – V.P. Menon, Mountbatten and the Maharaja of Kashmir – all of them decidedly partial to India.

Menon prepared a brief for Mountbatten on 17 July 1947 for his talk with Abdur Rab Nishtar and wrote in it:

'Kashmir presents some difficulty. It is claimed by both the Dominions, and at the present moment my feeling is that the issue should not be forced by either party. It is possible that a predominantly Muslim State like Kashmir cannot be kept away from Pakistan for long and we may leave this matter to find its natural solution. Unlike Hyderabad, it does not lie in the bosom of Pakistan and it can claim an exit to India, especially if a portion of the Gurdaspur district goes to East Punjab.'

Mountbatten told the Nawab of Bhopal and the Maharaja of Indore, in an interview on 4 August 1947, that Kashmir 'was so placed geographically that it could join either Dominion, provided part of Gurdaspur were put into East Punjab by the Boundary Commission.'

The Maharaja's wish for a land link with India is mentioned in Mountbatten's Personal Report of 16 August: 'He [the Maharaja of Kashmir] now talks of holding a referendum to decide whether to join Pakistan or India, provided that the Boundary Commission give him land communications between Kashmir and India.'

Is it not possible that it was very much in Jawaharlal Nehru's mind as well?

Ziegler's defence that Mounbatten 'at the time was still engaged in trying to ensure that the Maharaja of Kashmir acceded to Pakistan' and could not, therefore, have been interested in providing

India with land communications with it, does not hold water when the two important items in Mountbatten's conversations with the Maharaja and Prime Minister Kak during his visit to Kashmir from 18 to 23 June 1947 are scrutinised. They have the appearance of a recommendation to join Pakistan.

Mountbatten Twists the Punjab Award

When Mountbatten was wheeling and dealing in the affairs of State relating to his Viceroyalty in India he was probably under the impression that his mendacity and duplicity would remain secret forever. Till the early 1980s the whole perception of events of 1947 in India depended largely on a few publications. The most popular and widely circulated books like *Mission with Mountbatten*-by Alan Campbell-Johnson, *The Great Divide*-by H.V. Hodson, *Freedom at Midnight*-by Collins & Lapierre, *Mountbatten a Biography*-by Philip Ziegler and countless other books were mostly commissioned by Mountbatten himself or by his family. Undoubtedly Mountbatten created history and made a remarkable effort to have it recorded as he desired it to be perceived. An entire book can be written on the efforts Mountbatten made to create a picture of himself as some kind of a legend without any blemish. In doing so he has left behind a trail of tell-tale evidences of black spots.

As recorded earlier historians owe a debt to Labour Prime Minister Harold Wilson who decided in 1966 to reduce the period for publications of secret official documents from 50 to 30 years. Had the law not been changed the documents relating to the most critical period in the Indo-British relations – namely the five years beginning with the Cripps Mission in March 1942 and ending with the transfer of power to India and Pakistan in August 1947 would not have been released till 1999. Therefore, all the books published before 1983 do not have the advantage of having access to the secret official documents and are to that extent unreliable.

A glaring case of a serious effort made by Mountbatten to conceal the facts relates to the case of Gurdaspur and Ferozepore. In the Punjab Boundary Award, we have already seen the episode of Gurdaspur let us now turn our attention to Ferozepore. On the 9 August 1947 (when it was expected the Awards would be sealed signed and delivered) Nehru wrote to Mountbatten –

'SECRET

Dear Lord Mountbatten,

Mr. A. N. Khosla, Chairman, Central Waterways, Irrigation and Navigation Commission, has sent me a note about the canal system in the Punjab. As he has been chiefly concerned with this system and knows all about it, I take it that his views have a certain value and importance. I am, therefore, sending this note to you. If you feel that this might be sent on to Sir Cyril Radcliffe, perhaps this might be done.

Yours sincerely,

Jawaharlal Nehru'

An extract from Khosla's note is given below:

'So far as the canal system in West Punjab is concerned, that serves exclusively the Pakistan area and, therefore, the question of joint control will not arise in their case; but the Upper Bari Doab canal which runs through Gurdaspur, Amritsar and Lahore districts will be irrigating areas both in east and west Punjab and even if Gurdaspur is given to East Punjab, it will still be doing irrigation in Lahore district in Lahore district, unless the whole of that district is given to East Punjab.

The next common system of canals is the Sutlej valley canals, taking the supplies from the joint waters of the Beas and the Sutlej. The first headworks of this system is at Ferozepore from which irrigation water is taken to Bikaner. The second headworks is at Sulaimanki, which is also in Ferozepore district. According to notional division both these headworks would fall in East Punjab. It, however, appears that Sir Radcliffe's mind may be working in the direction of giving Ferozepore and Zira tahsils having a small muslim majority east of the Sutlej to Pakistan in return for giving Gurdaspur and part of Lahore district to east Punjab. That will be disastrous from the point of view and view of East Punjab and Bikaner State from the irrigation point of view and disastrous to India as a whole from the strategic point of view, because the only line of defence, that is the Sutlej, will have been pierced by the bridge at Ferozepore and between this and Delhi there is no natural barrier. On the other hand, if Ferozepore and Sulaimanki remain in East Punjab according to the notional division and because they are Hindu majority areas, then the only point where the Sutlej could be crossed would be in Bahawalpur State adjoining Bikaner territory.

Both from the strategic and irrigation point of view it will be most dangerous to let Ferozepore go to Pakistan. Whatever may be the decision about area west of Sutlej, no area east of the Sutlej must on any account go to Pakistan.

The joint control of irrigation canals must on no account be accepted, even as a recommendation of the Boundary Commission – this aspect is outside the terms of their reference. Any acceptance, even in the remote way, of joint control of the irrigation system will kill all hope of irrigation development in the Punjab. Even the construction of the Bhakhra dam may be affected.

Similarly, no joint control of electricity must be accepted.'

The very fact that Nehru wrote to Mountbatten on what should have been a highly secret matter is itself an evidence that there must have been daily written and verbal contacts between the Congress leaders and Mountbatten on partition matters.

The following day Mountbatten wrote to Nehru;

Dear Mr. Nehru,

'Thank you for your secret letter of the 9th August about the irrigation system of the Punjab and the Boundary Commission's award.

I hope you will agree that it is most important that I should not do anything to prejudice the independence of the Boundary Commission, and that therefore, it would be wrong for me even to forward any memorandum, especially at this stage.'

Yours sincerely,

Mountbatten of Burma.

Ample evidence exists to testify that Mountbatten did influence Radcliffe on this matter. Let us examine the first is the following entry under 9 August in the diary of W.H.J. Christie, joint private secretary to the Viceroy:

'George [Abell] tells me HE is in a tired flap & is having to be strenuously dissuaded from asking Radcliffe to alter his award.'

The second is Hodson's statement that:

'At about the same time Lord Mountbatten had a private meeting with Sir Cyril Radcliffe to discuss the date on which the awards were to be announced…It took place in Lord Ismay's house on the viceregal estate in Delhi over an evening drink on or about 9 August.'

Given Mountbatten's state of mind as described by Christie, we leave it to the reader to judge whether, at the meeting with Radcliffe, he was content simply to discuss the timing of the disclosure of the awards and restrained himself from supporting the important request which had just been made by Nehru, who was not only his close personal friend, but was also the politician upon whose goodwill he depended the most for the success of his difficult mission in India.

Meanwhile, information had already leaked that most of Gurdaspur district and the tahsils of Ferozepore and Zira earlier assigned to Pakistan were being allotted to India.

Chowdhury Mohammad Ali has recorded in his *The Emergence of Pakistan* –

'On August 9, 1947, I went from Delhi to Karachi for a day to consult the Quaid-I-Azam and Liaquat Ali Khan about the Indian proposals for the treatment of the national debt. Before I left Karachi to return to Delhi, Liaquat Ali Khan told me that the Quaid-I-Azam had received very disturbing reports about the likely decision on the Punjab boundary, particularly in the Gurdaspur district. In the Amritsar and Jullundur districts contiguous Muslim majority areas were also in danger of being assigned to India. He asked me, on my return to Delhi, to see Lord Ismay and convey to him, from the Quaid-I-Azam, that if the boundary actually turned out to be what these reports foreshadowed, this would have a most serious impact on the relations between Pakistan and the United Kingdom, whose good faith and honour were involved in this question.

When I reached Delhi, I went straight from the airport to the Viceroy's house where Lord Ismay was working. I was told that Lord Ismay was closeted with Sir Cyril Radcliffe. I decided to wait until he was free. When, after about an hour, I saw him, I conveyed to him the Quaid-I-Azam's message. In reply Ismay professed complete ignorance of Radcliffe's ideas about the boundary and stated categorically that neither Mountbatten nor he himself had ever discussed the question with him. It was entirely for Radcliffe to decide; and no suggestion of any kind had been or would ever be made to him.

When I plied Ismay with details of what had been reported to us, he said he could not follow me. There was a map hanging in the room and I beckoned him to the map so that I could explain the position to him with its help. There was a pencil line drawn across the map of the Punjab. The line flowed the boundary that had been reported to the Quaid-I-Azam.

I said that it was unnecessary for me to explain further since the line already drawn on the map, indicated the boundary I had been talking about. Ismay turned pale and asked in confusion who had been fooling with his map. This line differed from the final boundary in only one respect – the Muslim majority *tahsils* of Ferozepore and Zira in the Ferozepore district were still on the side of Pakistan as in the sketch map.

It may be recalled that on 11 August 1947 Lord Ismay received a verbal message from Liaquat to the effect the Gurdaspur or a large portion of it, had been given to East Punjab by the Boundary Commission; that it was reported that this was a political decision and not a judicial one; and that, if it were true, it was a grave injustice which would amount to a breach of faith on the part of the British.

Since we now have the benefit of the *Transfer of Power* documents, it is most amusing to read the letter which Lord Ismay wrote to Liaquat. This letter only fortifies the perception that not only Mountbatten himself but his entire staff were involved in rigging the Boundary Award. Lord Ismay's letter is reproduced below:

'My Dear Mr. Liaquat,

I was dumbfounded to receive the private message which you have sent me through Mahommed Ali. As I understand it, the gist of the message is as follows:-

(1) Gurdaspur or a large portion of it has been given to East Punjab by the award of the Boundary Commission. The report is that this is a political decision, and not a judicial one:

(2) If this is so, it is a grave injustice which will amount to a breach of faith on the part of the British.

Before giving you my comments on these points, let me state the background as I see it.

(1) The Viceroy has from the outset made it absolutely clear that he himself must have nothing to do either with arbitration of any kind or with the Boundary Commissions.

(2) The Indian leaders themselves selected all the Boundary Commissions, drafted their terms of reference and undertook to implement the award, whatever it might be.

(3) The Viceroy has always been, and is determined to keep clear of the whole business. As I told you only last week, his reply to Sir Cyril Radcliffe's enquiry about the interpretation of a certain point in his terms of reference was that the Viceroy did not feel justified in even expressing a view.

Thus, I am at a loss to know what action you wish me to take on your message. In the first place, I am told that the final report of Sir Cyril Radcliffe is not yet ready, and therefore I do not know what grounds you have for saying that Gurdaspur *has been* allotted to the East Punjab.

Secondly, if this should be the case, you surely do not expect the Viceroy to suggest to Sir Cyril Radcliffe that he should make any alteration. Still less can I believe that you intend to imply that the Viceroy has influenced this award. I am well aware that some uniformed sections of public opinion imagine that the award will not be Sir Cyril Radcliffe's but the Viceroy's, but I never for one moment thought that you, who are completely in the know, should ever imagine that he could do such a thing.

Yours very sincerely,

Ismay'

With regard to Ferozepore district, Pakistanis point out that the Ferozepore Headworks, except for the Bikaner Canal, irrigated mostly Muslim-majority areas contiguous to Pakistani Punjab, and they allege that in fact the Muslim- majority *tahsils* of Ferozepore and Zira, contiguous to Pakistan, were at first allotted by Radcliffe to Pakistan and were made over to India as the result of a last-minute intervention by Mountbatten. The main evidence they rely upon is a letter and map which Abell, Private Secretary to the Viceroy, sent on 8 August to Abbott, Private Secretary to the Governor of the Punjab is reproduced.

According to the map the *tahsils* of Ferozepore and Zira formed a part of Pakistan but in Radcliffe's final award of 12 August they were included in India. It is important to note that while Abell had warned that some changes might have to be made in defining the village and *zilla* boundaries in Lahore district in the interest of greater accuracy, he had envisaged no change in the Ferozepore part of the award. Hodson in his *The Great Divide* has belittled the significance of Abbel's communication by stating that 'the exchange of information was entirely at private secretary level. Sir Cyril was aware that such correspondence was proceeding but did not see either the letter or the map. But this is not the way in which responsible members o f the India Civil Service discharged their duties. It is inconceivable that Beaumont should have acted in such an important matter without consulting Radcliffe and obtaining his precise instructions. Radcliffe proposed to announce the Punjab Award on 9 August, as we have already stated; the Award must have been almost ready on 8 August.'

At any rate, we have Radcliffe' own confirmation that the source of Abell's information was none other than Radcliffe himself, and that he did change his Award afterwards. Let us explain.

Sir Archibald Carter, Permanent Under-Secretary of State Commonwealth Relations Office, invited Radcliffe to his office on 9 August 1948 to assist in the formulation of an answer to a possible parliamentary question on the subject on 'influence' in demarcating the boundaries at the time of partition. Afterwards, Carter prepared a draft and forwarded it to Radcliffe for his comment and advice. The draft was amended by Radcliffe. The following versions shows the words excluded by Radcliffe in brackets and the words added by him in italics.

Sir George Abell's letter of the 8th August 1947, which has been made public by the Pakistan authorities, communicated to Sir Evan Jenkins, the then Governor of the Punjab, [a provisional] *the rough statement of a proposed* boundary between East and West Punjab. The information contained in it was derived from Sir Cyril Radcliffe, Chairman of the Boundary Commission, as the result of a very proper enquiry form Sir Evan Jenkins whether he could have advance information about the boundary so that the best dispositions might be made of military force and police.

The boundary indicated by this communication of the 8th August differed from that contained in [Sir Cyril's final] *the* award of the 13th August as *ultimately made by Sir Cyril in its treatment of an* [in respect of a small] area in the Ferozepore District. I understand from Sir Cyril that he found the treatment of this area a question of considerable difficulty and on this point he reached a final conclusion differing from that which he was disposed to adopt at [a slightly earlier stage] *the time when Sir George Abell asked him for advance information.*

Sir Cyril has informed me that his award of the 13th August was the result of his own unfettered judgment and that at no stage was any attempt [of any kind] made by the Governor General to influence his decision. That this is so I have no doubt at all. That Radcliffe had originally awarded the Ferozepore and Zira *tahsils* to Pakistan and later gave them to India is confirmed by Sir Evan Jenkins, Governor of the Punjab at the time of partition (from the footnote page 579 *Transfer of Power* Vol-XII):

Sir E. Jenkins, in a letter dated April 1948 to Lord Mountbatten in which he too discussed points of controversy which had arisen over the Punjab Award, described the two documents in question as follows: 'The enclosures were a schedule (I think typed) and a section of a printed map with a line drawn thereon, together showing a Boundary which included in Pakistan a sharp salient in the Ferozepore District. This salient enclosed the whole of the Ferozepore and Zira *tahsils*'. Jenkins also stated that: 'About the 10th or 11th August, when we were still expecting the award on 13th August at latest, I received a secra-phone message from Viceroy's House containing the words "Eliminate Salient"... The change caused some surprise, not because the Ferozepore sailent had been regarded as inevitable or even probable, but because it seemed odd that any advance information had been given by the Commission if the award was not substantially complete'.

On the question of whether or not Radcliffe changed the Ferozepore award under pressure from Mountbatten, we have already described the Indian representation forwarded to Mountbatten by Nehru on 9 August, and his meeting with Radcliffe in the evening of, or about, the same day.

Interestingly, an important Indian source not only concedes, but positively claims, that Radcliffe altered the Ferozepore award as the result of Mountbatten's intervention on India's behalf. This source is a book entitled *Reminiscences of an Engineer* written by Kanwar Sain, a canal engineer who was in the service of Bikaner state at the time of partition.

The book contains a chapter under the heading 'Mountbatten Alters Punjab Boundary (at Eleventh Hour)'. Sain relates that Sarup Singh, an Indian irrigation engineer, was told on the evening of 8 August that he should select his headquarters outside the three *tahsils* of Ferozepoire district – Ferozepore, Zira and Fazilka – because instructions had been received from the Governor of the Punjab that these *tahsils* were likely to be allocated to Pakistan. As this means the transfer to Pakistan of the Ferozepore Headworks and the head-reach of the Gang Canal which served Bikaner State, Sarup Singh reported the situation to Sain by special messenger. Sain received the message on the morning of 10 August and, accomplained by Sardar Panikkar, the Prime Minister of the State, saw the Maharaja of Bikaner on the same day. The Maharaja having placed his own plane at their disposal, Sain and Panikkar arrived in Delhi before the day was out and with some difficulty secured an interview with Mountbatten on the following morning.

At first Mountbatten's attitude was stern but:

I [Sain] picked up the courage to say to His Excellency, 'Our Master has asked us to convey that if the Ferozepore Headworks and the Gang Canal go to Pakistan, His Highness, in the interest of his subjects, would have not option left but to opt for Pakistan.' As I said this, I could see a change in the colour of the face of Lord Mountbatten. He said nothing and we left His Excellency's room.

In the evening, we heard on the radio that the announcement of the Radcliffe Award would be delayed by a few days. Sardar Panikkar and myself wondered whether this had something to do with our interview with His Excellency that morning. When the Award was announced on the night of 17 August, we were happy to find that the Ferozepore Headworks and the entire area on the left bank of the river in which Gang Canal was located, were left with India.

CHAPTER 19: CONTROVERSIES AROUND PARTITION DECISIONS

Mountbatten's Gerrymandering

The perception of Radcliffe and Mountbatten's role relating to the Boundary Award received a severe jolt by the revelations of Christopher Beaumont in February 1992. He was a retired circuit judge living in Yorkshire and was secretary to Sir Cyril Radcliffe, Chairman of the Boundary Commission, and as such he of course had access to all official papers and was present with Radcliffe at all meetings of the Commission. Although Beaumont did not keep a diary at the time, on returning to the U.K. he wrote down his own version of events. Realising , of course, that his document was of great historical importance, and inevitably controversial, he entrusted it to the care of the Warden of All Souls, Oxford. The document's importance was increased by the death in 1989 of Sir George Abell, Lord Mountbatten's private secretary. Christopher Beaumont then became the only person who knew the truth about the 1947 Partition of India, though he had confided to his close friend, Sir Penderel Moon, a well-known historian of India, and his brother-in-law, Sir Robin Latimer, what had happened.

In his first paragraph Christopher Beaumont requested that the contents of the documents should not be divulged until after his death, and then only to people approved by agreement between the Warden of All Souls and the Permanent Representative of the Foreign Office. But interviewed by Simon Scott Plummer for a long article published in *The Daily Telegraph* on February 24th 1992, Beaumont explained that he had been led to reconsider the question of publishing what he knew about the events of Partition on learning that his grandson had been given the Partition of India as a special subject for the History Tripos at Cambridge. This made him realise belatedly 'that the event had passed into history and that the time had come for the truth to be revealed'.

For these revelations Beaumont obtained the permission of the British foreign office.

Under the headline 'How Mountbatten bent the rules and the Indian border' Scott Plummer's account of the interview began with the statement: 'Earl Mountbatten manipulated in India's favour the findings of the (Boundary) Commission'. He then quoted Christopher Beaumont as saying that Radcliffe had yielded 'to what he thought was overwhelming political expediency' in agreeing, after he had decided the boundary, to the transfer of the Ferozepore and Zira sub-districts from Pakistan to India.

In his document Christopher Beaumont states that Sir Cyril Radcliffe was appointed Joint Chairman of the Boundary Commission on July 6th 1947, and that he was appointed private secretary to Radcliffe on July 8th. Rao Sahib V.D. Ayer, a Hindu, was appointed assistant secretary. Mountbatten, Nehru and Jinnah agreed that Radcliffe should complete his report on the boundary lines for Bengal and the Punjab by August 15th. 'Radcliffe objected, since it was clearly impossible to complete the task properly in one month and nine days. His objection was over-ruled. 'Mountbatten, Nehru and Jinnah must share the blame for this irresponsible decision' is Beaumont's comment.

Beaumont goes on to state that it was a serious mistake to appoint a Hindu (the same would have applied to a Muslim) to the post of assistant secretary to the Boundary Commission. In Beaumont's opinion an assistant secretary should have been sent out from the United Kingdom. He asserts that once the Hindu and the Muslim High Court judges, who were supposed to help Radcliffe draw up his plan, 'were discarded as useless, the only people who knew about the subsequent discussions were Radcliffe, Beaumont himself and Ayer.' Beaumont concludes this paragraph of his document by stating 'I have not the slightest doubt that Ayer kept Nehru and V.P. Menon informed of progress.'

Beaumont goes on to give evidence for this assertion based on the fact that Nehru voiced his concern to the Viceroy at the decision to give certain territories (he quotes the Chittagong Hill Tracts in East Bengal) to Pakistan. Nehru could not have known that unless Ayer had told him – and it was clearly a breach of confidence. Beaumont quotes John Christie, one of the assistant private secretaries to the Viceroy, as writing the following entry in his diary for August 11th; 'H.E. is having to be strenuously dissuaded from trying to persuade Radcliffe to alter his Punjab line'.

The most serious boundary alteration, however, concerned the tehsils of Ferozepore and Zira. A tehsil is an administrative area of some 400 square miles. Ferozepore was particularly important. This district included the canal headworks which largely controlled the irrigation system of the state of Bikaner. Radcliffe had allotted these two tehsils to Pakistan. Sir Evan Jenkins, Governor of the Punjab, had asked Sir George Abell to let him know the course of the Partition line, so that he could send troops to the areas in which violence might arise. Perfectly properly, Sir George Abell asked Christopher Beaumont for this information. Beaumont told him and sent him a map, which Abell passed on to Sir Evan Jenkins. This map was never destroyed and after Jenkins had left the Punjab in August in came into the hands of the new Pakistan government. Its discovery naturally gave rise to the suspicion that the original boundary line had been altered by Radcliffe. Christopher Beaumont is sure that the alteration was made 'under pressure from Mountbatten', who himself came under strong pressure from Nehru and also the Maharaja of Bikaner, whose state might have suffered if the canal headworks at Ferozepore had been controlled by Pakistan. The Maharaja was certainly friendly with

Nehru.

We have already seen how on 9 August 1947 Nehru had written to Mountbatten about the Ferozepore and Zira tehsils. Also on 10 August 1947 K.

M. Panikkar (Prime Minister of Bikaner) along with Engineer Kanwar Sain saw Mountbatten regarding the award of Ferozepore and Zira. In this document Christopher Beaumont tells how V.P. Menon, who played a key role in Indian politics at that time, had paid a midnight visit (the same day Mountbatten met Panikkar) to the Vice-Regal estate shortly after the boundary map had been sent to Jenkins. Menon asked if he could see Radcliffe, who was working there. Beaumont said he could not. Menon said Mountbatten had sent him, to which Beaumont replied that it made no difference.

'He departed with good grace' Beaumont said in his statement. 'I think he anticipated the rebuff. He was a very able and perceptive person'.

The next day Radcliffe told Beaumont that he had been invited to lunch with Mountbatten by Ismay. Radcliffe added that he had been asked not to bring his private secretary with him because there was not enough room at the table for an extra guest. 'Having lived for six months in the house occupied by Ismay I knew this to be untrue'. Beaumont statement said. 'But my suspicions were not aroused as they should have been. I was leaving India the next week, had many preoccupations and welcomed the chance to get on with my own affairs. This was the first time; however, Radcliffe and I had been separated at any sort of function. That evening the Punjab line was changed'.

Beaumont's judgement of this discreditable affair is as follows: 'So Mountbatten interfered and Radcliffe allowed himself to be overborne. Grave discredit to both'.

Beaumont says there were certain mitigating circumstances for this action. Mountbatten was overworked and tired and was doubtless told by Nehru and Menon that if Ferozepore went to Pakistan there would be war between the two states.

In Beaumont's view Radcliffe must have been persuaded by Lord Ismay and the Viceroy at the fatal lunch, from which he was excluded on flimsiest excuse, that if Ferozepore were given to Pakistan, despite its Muslim majority, civil war could follow. He points out that Radcliffe was largely ignorant of the India political situation – he had been there for only six weeks and had never visited the country before. He probably did not realise that Nehru and Menon were putting pressure on Mountbatten. Beaumont sums up this lamentable incident: 'He (Radcliffe) yielded, I think, to what he thought was overwhelming political expediency' and in his final sentence he says 'This episode reflects great discredit on Mountbatten and Nehru and less on Radcliffe'.

As one historian, Alistair Lamb, has put it, 'It was always improbable that the highly professional government of British India, even in its dying days, would leave matters of prime importance to amateurs like Radcliffe, who, although a distinguished jurist, had never been to India before he came to draw the partition line across Punjab and Bengal.' Lamb believes that the Radcliffe Commission was 'a device to load the onus of the details of partition on to the shoulders of a non-"Indian", so as to leave Mountbatten blameless of responsibility for unpopular decisions. . .Mountbatten hoped to be Governor- General of both India and Pakistan and this device would have made his task infinitely easier.'

Alan Campbell-Johnson Mountbatten's Press Secretary replied to Simon Scott Plummer's article in a letter to the *Daily Telegraph*. Campbell-Johnson stated that the Commission was 'a crucial and organic part of the inevitably improvised partition process', the fact remains that the boundary was secretly altered to the detriment of Pakistan. Campbell-Johnson blames 'the Punjab mafia', in which he includes Jenkins, Abell and Abbott, for the way the news of the alteration got out. Had Jenkins taken Abbott's advice and destroyed the map, it would not have fallen into the hands of the Pakistan Government. It did, however, and the Foreign Minister, Zafrullah Khan, later denounced the alteration to the Security Council of the United Nations. Beaumont, Back in England by then, visited Radcliffe in his chambers to ask him directly what had happened. 'He was very sheepish and never denied it. He didn't welcome my visit, said he was busy and shuffled me off.'

Mountbatten's Efforts to Conceal the Truth Fails

The disclosers of Christopher Beaumont created considerable stir in the U.K. and elsewhere. The major consequence was to cast doubt on the conclusions reached by Philip Ziegler in his official biography of Mountbatten published in 1985. In this work he rejects the suggestion that Sir Cyril Radcliffe, whom he describes as 'a man of monumental integrity and independence of mind', would have meekly allowed his recommendations to be altered. He concedes that at one point, under pressure from Nehru, Mountbatten might have contemplated asking Radcliffe to amend the awards, but that he was probably dissuaded by Lord Ismay to abandon such a move because of the risks it involved. Philip Ziegler adds 'He may have been guilty of indiscretion but not of the arrant folly as well as dishonesty of which his enemies accused him'.

In an interview with BBC in 1992, Philip Ziegler conceded that Mountbatten 'probably listened slightly more to the Indian than to the Muslim councilors. He then referred directly to the Boundary Commission, and the Ferozepore and Zira transfers, which he agreed 'were transferred from one side to the other rather late in the day'. He then himself posed the crucial question 'Was this transfer made by Radcliffe because it was more logical or under pressure from Mountbatten because he believed there was going to be an unholy row with the Maharaja concerned and that the whole settlement might break down if he didn't give way at this point?' Philip Ziegler continues 'There is some new evidence since I wrote my book that suggests that he (Mountbatten) may have been rather more involved with modifications to the line than had previously been accepted, but even so I don't think his primary concern was to help India against Pakistan . . . So, I think on the whole that his handling of negotiations up to the time of independence was pretty impartial and the Pakistanis don't have any right to say that he monstrously favoured the Indian cause, as they tend to do'.

It is clear that the transfer of the two tehsils was made on political rather than on economic or 'logical' grounds and Philip Ziegler's claim of the strict impartiality of the last Viceroy smacks of a wish to cling to lost cause, although to do this distinguished historian justice, he did later admit that his former 'nugget of doubt has become a boulder'.

According to the Noel-baker's report to the Prime Minister, Radcliffe had admitted that 'he showed the first draft of the proposed Award to the authorities in Delhi and that, on further consideration, he made the Award in terms which departed from the first draft'. By then Radcliffe had destroyed all his papers and notes relating to his work with the Boundary Commission. Mountbatten later criticised his work, informing Lapierre and Collins: 'I'll tell you something ghastly. The reasons behind his Awards weren't very deep- seated at all.'

Beaumont believes Radcliffe yielded 'to what he thought was overwhelming political expediency' and 'allowed himself to be overborne' by Mountbatten. When the affair came to light, Mountbatten made strenuous attempts to deny it and to shift the blame. He wrote to Ismay in London in February 1948: 'I am fairly satisfied that there can be no evidence in Jenkins' file to support any accusation that the Award was tampered with', hardly a ringing denunciation of the slander. He went on to ask his former Chief of Staff to get Abbel to 'explain the situation to Jenkins, Radcliffe, Abbott and Beaumont in case this subject is ever raised again'.

Abell and Beaumont, supported by Abell's junior, the Viceroy's Assistant Private Secretary, Ian Scott, considered that it would be best not to discuss what Mountbatten had done. 'We all agreed it was better for relations between the two countries for us not to spill the beans,' says Beaumont.

Although Sir Penderel Moon was informed of what had taken place, he agreed to 'skirt around it' in his history of British India.

When still in India, Mountbatten learned that the Pakistan Government was considering publishing Abell's map, letter and telegram, he contacted Ismay again in an attempt to distance himself from the controversy altogether: 'A reply will have to be published. The question is who should issue it. I am sure you will agree that it should not come from me.' Mountbatten was keen that either Attlee or Radcliffe should answer Zafrullah Khan's accusations. He went on to ask that Ismay, in further talks with Abell and Jenkins, should emphasise that 'the point that arises here was that Abell sent the letter concerned without *my* knowledge'.

He admitted that 'it may be hard to convince people that that was so. It will look to have been an odd procedure.' Considering that Abell had been his Principal Private Secretary, and specifically authorised by Mountbatten to keep Jenkins fully informed developments, this was no more than truth. Mountbatten's attempt to distance himself, and in effect to blame Abell, drew the private ire of those in the know, including Ian Scott. True to their 1948 commitment, however, they were reluctant to discuss exactly what happened Fortunately, a piece of *prima facie* evidence has survived, much against Mountbatten's wishes, which makes it quite clear what really took place.

Amongst Ismay's papers there is a copy of the letter Mountbatten sent him on 2 April 1948, once he realised that he was on the verge of being unmasked over Ferozepur and was attempting to co-ordinate the British response in such a way as to absolve him from any blame. The letter was ostensibly to 'remind' Ismay what they had both said to Radcliffe. Mountbatten asked him to burn the letter after reading it, but Ismay knew better than that, and instead added some highly instructive marginalia on Mountbatten's script.

'We felt that both sides would be equally dissatisfied [with the Award] and that instead of 15th August being celebrated as a day of national rejoicing they might well turn it into a day of mourning for the portions of territory they had lost,' Mountbatten 'reminded' his former Chief of Staff of the events of eight months earlier. Mountbatten then claimed that Abell had not informed him of the map sent to Jenkins 'because he said it was done on "staff level".' He added: 'If memory serves me right George [Abell] stressed that this was not the final award since Radcliffe had yet to balance the East and West Pakistan Awards.' There was certainly no mention of any such 'balancing' operation in the original letter Abell sent Jenkins; indeed, it seems to be the first occasion at which such a concept was introduced.

'About this time, I met Radcliffe with you at your house,' continued Mountbatten. 'The main object of this meeting was to discuss the date of the announcement of the Award. You will remember that I asked Radcliffe whether he could delay his final decision until after 15th August and you will also remember that he was quite firm and said that he could not delay it beyond the 13th at the very latest.' All this is well documented, but Mountbatten then wrote:

'So far as I remember I said to him that the Sikh attitude had become rather worse than we had anticipated, and that when he was balancing up the boundaries of East and West Pakistan I sincerely hoped that he would bear the Sikh problem in mind. . . . I think I went so far as to say that . . . I trusted that any generosity to Pakistan should be given more in Bengal than the Punjab since there was no Sikh problem in Bengal.'

Beside this statement Ismay penciled 'I do NOT remember this!' in the margin of Mountbatten's letter. Had Mountbatten's first worry really been the Sikhs – rather than the arsenal or Bikaner's concerns – he might have been expected to have taken more vigorous action himself. His real preoccupations are made clear in the next paragraph of his letter to Ismay.

In Mountbatten's own words:

'The conversation then turned to the irrigation canals and headworks and so far as I remember [Radcliffe] made some comment about having tried and failed to obtain agreement for joint inter-dominion working of the headworks and I think he remarked that the boundary was particularly difficult to adjust round about Ferozepur from this aspect, and I remarked that provided the overall east-west boundaries were scrupulously fair between the two dominions, it seemed to me that he could make any adjustments necessary for balancing out the boundaries in Bengal and the Punjab.'

Mountbatten then added:

'I must confess that I did not dictate a record' of the conversation, because it was 'of such a very "off the record" nature.'

Ismay replied on 11 April, making it clear that he could not agree with such a sanitised version of what had been said. 'My recollection of events is very different from yours,' he wrote. Had Ismay destroyed the 2nd of April letter, as requested, it would not be known that Mountbatten and Ismay ever did have a 'off the record' meeting with Radcliffe, during which, under the guise of 'balancing' the east and west Awards – which had nothing to do with Mountbatten anyhow – Radcliffe was asked to 'make any adjustments necessary' in the specific case of Ferozepur. Here is *prima facie* evidence both that Mountbatten brought pressure to bear on Radcliffe to alter the Awards in India's favour, and that he attempted to construct a 'line' for Ismay to take in order to conceal the fact.

Sinister Moves by Mountbatten

It may be recalled that in the last meeting of the Governors of the Provinces held in New Delhi on 15 April, 1947, over which Mountbatten presided, the minutes of the meeting state:

'His Excellency the Viceroy stressed that this was only one of the many plans which were at present being considered. He also emphasised that, if it was not possible to obtain a united India, it was of the utmost importance that, in the eyes of the world, it should be Indian opinion rather than a British decision which made the choice as to the future.

His Excellency the Viceroy gave his opinion that partition of India would be a most serious potential source of war.

Sir Conrad Corfield said that it was also surely true that, the earlier partition was carried out, if it had to be done, the greater was the chance of building up the machinery to organise an unified defence.

With this there was general agreement.

His Excellency the Viceroy pointed out that a quick decision would also give Pakistan a greater chance to fail on its demerits. The great problem was to reveal the limits of Pakistan so that the Muslim League could revert to an unified India with honour. Their Excellencies the Governors all agreed that the necessity for an early decision was paramount.'

Ample evidence exists to show the effort Mountbatten and the Congress leaders made to ensure 'to give Pakistan a chance to fail on its demerits'.

Congress leaders remained unreconciled to the partition of the country. On 2 June, the Congress President sent a letter to Mountbatten in which he said: "We believe as fully as ever in a united India… We earnestly trust that when present passions have subsided our problems will be viewed in their proper perspective and a willing union of all parts of India will result therefrom." About the same time the correspondent of *The Times* reported from New Delhi: "Congress will work to the present plan in the hope that it will ultimately lead to a restored union of India." On 15 June, in a secret letter, Jenkins informed Mountbatten what Congress leaders thought of the partition plan.

'It was a masterstroke by Patel, who, having pushed the Muslims into a corner (or into two corners) will be able to destroy them before very long. Patel's private conversation is reported to be menacing

– Barq who was a Minister in the Coalition Government told me he had heard him say that Hindustan could quickly make an end of its Muslim inhabitants if Pakistan did not behave.'

On 7 August when Jinnah left Delhi for Karachi he wished India well. In a press statement he then said: 'The past must be buried and let us start afresh as two independent sovereign states of Hindustan and Pakistan. I wish Hindustan prosperity and peace.'

Patel's reaction to Jinnah's message of good wishes of 7 August, which followed almost immediately, left no doubt about the Congress attitude to the emerging Muslim state. Jinnah got a bucket of water in his face in return from Sardar Patel who said in Delhi the following day:

'The poison has been removed from the body of India. We are now one and indivisible. You cannot divide the sea or the waters of the river. As for the Muslims, they have their roots, their sacred places and their centres here. I do not know what they can possibly do in Pakistan. It will not be long before they return to us.'

On 15 August the Congress President stated: "Let us henceforth bend all our energies to the unification of this land of ours." Towards the end of September, Patel declared at Amritsar: "I am quite certain that India's interest lies in getting all her men and women across the border and sending out all Muslims from East Punjab."

Jinnah, who had been showing signs of an unusual magnanimity, froze from that moment into his normal attitude of cold hatred and contempt for Congress. Nor was his temper improved when he read a statement from Kripalani, the Congress President, which he interpreted as inciting Hindus and Sikhs in Pakistan to practise non-cooperation with the new Dominion. Kripalani, was in fact, answering a query from a number of Congress Committees in Pakistan, which had asked whether they should fly the new Indian flag over their headquarters in Independence Day. He had told them to fly no flags and organise no demonstrations. 'This had nothing to do with the celebrations organised by the Pakistan Government,' he explained.

Jinnah and his followers, however, chose to believe otherwise. 'Let me tell Kripalani and other Hindu leaders that they are playing with fire,' declared Liaquat, in a tone as near to thunderous as that amiable man could get. 'If Hindu leaders like Kripalani succeed in inciting people, it would be foolish to expect that there will be no repercussions. No Government in the world can prevent such repercussions, no matter how undesirable they may be. Unless the Congress President and the Hindu leaders give up these dangerous preachings and join with us in restoring goodwill, and if they fail to stop acts of violence by their people, then God help both Pakistan and Hindustan.'

Jinnah told Mountbatten on 1 November, 1947 that it was quite clear that the Dominion of India was out to throttle and choke the Dominion of Pakistan at birth.

The Congress and the Sikh leaders were no doubt encouraged in their hostility to Pakistan by the statements of British Ministers. On 10 July, the Prime Minister revealed his thinking and voiced his expectations about the future of Pakistan in these words: "For myself, I earnestly hope that this severance may not endure, and that the two new Dominions which we now propose to set up may, in course of time, come together again…" Six days later, the Secretary of State stated: "It is greatly to be hoped that, when the disadvantages of separation have become apparent in the light of the experience, the two Dominions will freely decide to reunite in a single Indian Dominion…"

Mountbatten had his own ideas about how to divide the country and later to reunite the two Dominions. Mountbatten had advanced the date of the transfer of power several times, knowing full well that the earlier power was transferred the more difficult it would be for Pakistan to set up the required administrative machinery. At the same time, in the first instance, he was opposed to the proposal to partition the armed forces, and later when he agreed, he continued to delay their physical partition. On 20 June, 1947, Liaquat met Ismay and expressed his extreme dissatisfaction about this situation. Ismay replied that unless there was to be chaos, the Army must remain under a single administration. Liaquat replied that even if there had to be a single administration, by 15 August, 1947, Pakistan must not only have its own predominantly Muslim armed forces under its own commander-in-chief, the troops assigned to Pakistan must also be in its territory. Liaquat added that he and Jinnah were determined that unless by Independence Day Pakistan had its own Army "on the spot" and under its control, they would refuse to take over authority. Liaquat emphasised that the movement of troops "should be started at once and conducted as a war measure." It was only then that Ismay wrote to Mountbatten that he should instruct the Commander-in-Chief to put through the movement of troops "as a matter of the greatest urgency."

Rather surprisingly, the Secretary of State himself thought that India and Pakistan should have an agreed policy in the defence matters. He telegraphed to the Viceroy on 16 July:

'It has occurred to me that you might use ridiculous claims of Afghan Government to point out to Partition Council or perhaps to leaders individually how essential it is for India and Pakistan to have a unified defence policy. Nothing conduces to unity more than a common fear.

I cannot, for example, see how Pakistan Air Force, unless supported by Indian Air Force, could compete with anything but most trivial tribal incursion.'

Auchinleck the Commander-in-Chief and his staff tried to act impartially but the Government of India thwarted their efforts. In fact, to get the Supreme Commander out of the way, Patel accused him and his staff of being "all mentally pro-Pakistan." Instead of supporting Auchinleck, Mountbatten wrote to him on 26 September: "…my suggestion is that you should yourself write a letter to me as Chairman of the Joint Defence Council proposing the winding up of Supreme Headquarters as soon as the major units have been transferred to their respective Dominions…" Pursuant to this suggestion, in mid-October, in a memorandum to the Joint Defence Council, the Supreme Commander recommended the closing down of his Headquarters by 30 November, which recommendation was strongly opposed by Liaquat. But Mountbatten did not change his mind.

The Joint Defence Council remained in existence till 1 April 1948. But much to the disappointment of Mountbatten both Indian and Pakistani leaders did not agree to its extension beyond that date. Mountbatten revealed the reasons for his disappointment in a communication to the King:

'My original idea had been that the Council should continue in its existing form for at least another year – and I secretly hoped for ever… It was in my mind that its scope might indeed expand to cover financial and economic matters also, and eventually External Affairs and Coummunications, which would mean the 'virtual accession' of the two Dominions to one another on the same lines as the States.'

Parameters of Partition

Lt. General Sir Francis Tuker was the General Officer Commanding the Eastern Command with Headquarters in Calcutta. General Tuker who was known as a fairly neutral and moderate person has recorded in his *While Memory Serves* just before the partition in August 1947. "The most disheartening thing that appeared just now was the vindictive attitude of the majority of Hindus. In effect they said, 'Well, if the Muslims want Pakistan, let them damned well have it and with a vengeance. We will shear every possible inch off their territory so as to make it look silly and to ensure that it is not a viable country and, when they've got what's left, we'll ensure that it can't be work economically.' The Mahasabha therefore redoubled its effort and money poured into it which previously would have gone to the Congress Party. Swiftly the party turned from a thing of no significance into one of vital importance. Along with it grew the almost subterranean and highly dangerous R.S.S. Sangh, its militant body."

Tuker was certainly not only making his comment on contemporary events but also making an enlightened prophecy of shape of things come in the future. We can certainly consider his account to be credible as he had no axe to grind. A speech that Sardar Patel delivered in the Constituent Assembly in the November, 1949, fully bears out Tuker's impression. Although delivered more than two years after these events, it breathed a spirit of vengeance. In the course of this speech Patel said; "I agreed to partition as a last resort, when we should have lost all   Mr. Jinnah did not want a truncated Pakistan but he had to swallow it. I made a further condition that in two months' time power should be transferred."

The acceptance by Congress of partition was a tactical move, but the strategic goal - to rule over the entire subcontinent – remained unaltered. To ensure the success of this goal it was necessary that:

1. Hindustan or the Indian Union should be recognised as the only successor to the British Government in India; Pakistan would be treated as certain territories that had seceded.

2. The areas to be included in Pakistan should be as small as possible and confined to East Bengal, West Punjab, Sind and Baluchistan and should exclude North West Frontier Province. Pakistan should, if possible, be encircled strategically.

3. Pakistan should be subjected to the maximum handicaps by being denied time and resources – civil and military, manpower and material - to establish and consolidate itself.

4. Whatever could be done to make Pakistan unviable should be done (The Congress Leaders were convinced that Pakistan could not last for long; their aim and endeavour was to hasten the collapse of its economy).

5. The Indian States should be incorporated in the Indian Union.

Now one may ask how is it that the League Leaders were not aware of the Congress and Mountbatten's machinations. Chaudhuri Mohammad Ali an eye witness to events in 1947 and a close confidante of Jinnah has recorded in *The Emergence of Pakistan.*

'In the well-founded belief that political opponents of such long standing as the leaders of the Congress and the Muslim League would not exchange notes, he won the confidence of both by denouncing the one to the other. At the very time when he was wooing Congress leaders day and night, he was portraying them to Jinnah as unreasonable men whom it was exceedingly difficult to persuade into accepting and fair term. These words naturally found a sympathetic response in Jinnah's mind. It is not difficult to imagine the terms in which Mountbatten must have a described Jinnah to the Congress leaders; even his staff were told that a dinner engagement with Jinnah was put off by a day because "Mountbatten felt he could not sustain another session with him today." Nevertheless, the technique worked. Both the Congress and the Muslim League leaders felt that here was a man who had political and psychological insight, understood human character and motives, was frank enough to point out difficulties in the way, and made a sincere effort to remove them. In any case this voluble man of keen perception and quick understanding was a welcome contrast to his predecessor with his awkward silences and stony reticence."

The division of assets after the partition posed a serious problem. Even a pro- Indian book like *Freedom at Midnight* acknowledges the serious injustice done to Pakistan in this matter.

'The situation in Pakistan was far worse. The new nation was verging on chaos. Jinnah's missing croquet set had been located, but little else. Hundreds of railway carriages crammed with material destined for the new state disappeared, were stolen, or turned up at the wrong destination. In Karachi, the desks and chairs hadn't arrived. Government employees had to squat on the sidewalks in front of their offices, pecking out on their typewriters the official texts of the largest Moslem nation in the world. Inside, their seniors governed their new nation sitting on crates and boxes.

Muslim refugees gather in India to seek transport to Pakistan (bbc.com)

The economy was in a turmoil. Pakistan had warehouses bulging with hide, jute and cotton and no tanneries, factories or mills to process it. courseproduced a quarter of the sub-continent's tobacco but did not have a match factory in which to produce matches to light her smokers' cigarettes. The banking system was paralysed because the banks' Hindu managers and clerks had fled to India.

It was over her share of the goods of the old Indian Army, however, that Pakistan encountered Indian bad faith in a way that seemed tantamount to a deliberate effort to jeopardise her survival. Of the 170,000 tons of army stores Pakistan was allotted under the Partition Agreement, she would ultimately get 6000. Three hundred special trains had been assigned to carry her arms and ordnance. Three arrived. Opening them, a team of Pakistani officers discovered they contained 5000 pairs of shoes, 500 unserviceable rifles, a consignment of nurses' smocks, and a number of wooden crates stuffed with bricks and prophylactics.'

This trickery left bitter memories in Pakistan and a deep-seated conviction among many that their Indian neighbours were trying to strangle them in the cradle. They were not alone in that conviction.

Field-Marshal Sir Claude Auchinleck, who'd been asked to stay on to supervise the division of the armies' goods, informed the British Government, 'I have no hesitation whatsoever in affirming that the present Indian Cabinet is implacably determined to do all in its power to prevent the establishment of the Dominion of Pakistan.'

The division of assets between India and Pakistan in a matter of few days presented the most complex problem in history. There was absolutely no precedence to be followed as never before had anything even remotely like it had been attempted. Nowhere were there any guidelines, any revealing insights from the past to order what was going to be the biggest, the most complex divorce action in history. The responsibility for preparing the gigantic, unimaginably complicated property settlement accompanying the Indian divorce fell on the Partition Council. Needless to say Pakistan got the worst of everything. It was decided by the Partition Council that the movable assets in India's vast administrative machine should be divided 80% to India, 20% to Pakistan. All across India, government offices began to count up their chairs, tables, brooms and typewriters. Some of the resulting tabulations were particularly poignant. They showed, for example, that the entire physical resources of the Food and Agricultural Department of the most famine-haunted country on the globe consisted of 425 clerks' tables, 85 large tables, 85 officers' chairs, 850 ordinary chairs, 50 hat-pegs, 6 hat-pegs with mirrors, 130 bookshelves, 4 iron safes, 20 table lamps, 170 typewriters, 120 fans, 120 clocks, 110 bicycles, 600 inkstands, 3 staff cars, 2 sets of sofas and 40 chamber pots.

Arguments, even fights, broke out over the division of the goods. Departmental heads tried to hide their best typewriters or to substitute their broken desks and chairs for new ones assigned to their rival community. Some offices became *souks* with dignified men, joint secretaries in linen suits whose writ ran over hundreds of thousands of people, bargaining an inkpot against a water jar, an umbrella rack for a hat-peg, 125 pin cushions for a chamber pot. The arguments over the dishes, the silverware, the portraits in state residences were ferocious. One item however, escaped discussion. Wine cellars always went to India and Pakistan received a credit for what they contained. Some of the bitterest arguments came over the books in India's libraries. Sets of the *Encyclopaedia Britannica* were religiously divided up, alternate volumes to each dominion. Dictionaries were ripped in half with A to K going to India, the rest to Pakistan. Where only one copy of a book was available, the librarians were supposed to decide which dominion would have the greater natural interest in it.

CHAPTER 20: Early Departure, Lasting Damage

The Disaster of Early Transfer of Power

It is generally accepted that Philip Ziegler's official biography of Mountbatten is a reasonably fair account of his life. An extract from this book which we have already seen earlier reads:

"Open diplomacy was, so far as possible, the order of the day Yet openness did not exclude a *degree of manipulation, even chicanery,* which would have been inconceivable to either of his immediate predecessors. Mountbatten was well aware that certain of his advisers felt that his tactics sometimes verged on the unethical, but believed that *sleight of hand* was justifiable to achieve the greater good; *the lie direct was to be avoided the lie circumstantial might be acceptable.* Ian Scott, his Deputy Private Secretary, remembered the Viceroy looking up after proposing a certain course of action and catching the expression on his and Abell's faces: 'I know what you're thinking. Wavell would never have done it. Well, I'm not Wavell, and I will'." (Writer's italics)

Ziegler further goes on to conclude: "like everything else about him, his faults were on the grandest scale. His vanity, though child-like, was monstrous, his ambition unbridled. The truth, in his hands, was swiftly converted from what it was to what it should have been. He sought to rewrite history with cavalier indifference to the facts to magnify his own achievements. There was a time when I became so enraged by what I began to feel was his determination to hoodwink me that I found it necessary to place on my desk a notice saying: REMEMBER, IN SPITE OF EVERYTHING, HE WAS A GREAT MAN."

Why did Mountbatten choose 15 August 1947 for transfer of power.

We shall now examine why power was transferred in such a hurry when Mountbatten's mandate was to transfer power by 30 June 1948. What was gained by the early transfer and what was lost. The bringing forward of the date for establishing the two dominions of India and Pakistan from 30 June 1948 to 15 August 1947 posed formidable problems with inadequate time to solve them. We have already seen that the short time given for transfer of power was done at the behest of the Congress to allow minimum time to Pakistan to organise itself thereby ensuring its early demise.

The Congress blue print for the transfer of power as we have seen was made in early May 1947 in Simla where Nehru and Krishna Menon had an exclusive few days closeted with Mountbatten. One of the factors that was decided was the early transfer of power as a part of the Congress scheme.

Mountbatten, had, however, come to India with a mandate to transfer power by June 1948. The early transfer of power as we shall see not only favoured the Congress but had quite horrendous consequences not only during partition but having left a lasting wound in the sub-continental politics.

From May 1947 onwards we see in all the *Transfer of Power* documents a repeated urging by Mountbatten for the immediate transfer of power. In the meeting held in Simla on May 10, 1947 where Mountbatten, Nehru and VP Menon were present, Mountbatten said that he did not consider that the target for the end of the interim period should anyway be connected with June 1948. That had originally been the target due for transfer of power; and it was hoped to bring the transfer forward by almost a year. Nehru added conspiratorially that although he agreed with Mountbatten but to say that the date of June 1948, had been scrapped would certainly create suspicion.

It may be recalled at the very moment Mountbatten was meeting Nehru Ismay was in London with the partition plan that had been approved both by the League and the Congress. The Simla meeting appears to have been the turning point. The fact, that Nehru had deliberately back tracked on the already approved plan is quite evident from the telegram sent by Eric Mieville in Simla to Ismay in London on 12 May 1947.

"Strictly private for Ismay from Mieville. We are naturally a bit rattled by Nehru's *volte face* yesterday and can only be thankful that we did not wait until meeting of leaders to find out his attitude. **I cannot help thinking that his party must have got at him.** The Viceroy is now wondering more and more whether we ought not to work on the lines of trying to demit power on Dominion Status basis at an early date with Jinnah being given adequate safeguards in the interim period. What do you think?"

On the same day in a staff meeting Mountbatten said that he had the previous evening further discussed with Nehru the plan which he had put forward for the early demission of power to the Interim Government on a Dominion status basis. This plan was really very similar to the alternative plan which he had previously decided to threaten Jinnah if the latter did not accept Plan We (as opposed Plan They). Meanwhile, the Congress while reviewing the revised plan drafted in Simla in a secret memo to Mountbatten stated "What we are more interested in is the immediate transfer by convention so that

(Jawaharlal Nehru, left, and British Viceroy, Lord Louis Mountbatten)
(qz.com)

the present might be dealt with" . . . In fact, Mountbatten was summoned to London to clarify the revised plan (hatched in Simla) that he had sent to London over riding the partition plan which Ismay had taken for the approval of the British Cabinet. Mountbatten had no difficulty in persuading the British Government to agree to revised plan and an immediate transfer of power. In fact, the date 15 August 1947 for the transfer of power was agreed in London and as we shall see how Mountbatten lied about this matter after the 3 June 1947 announcement of the partition plan.

It is clearly stated in the minutes of the meeting held on 3 June 1947 with the Members of the Princely States "HIS EXCELLENCY explained that he had that day put before the Indian political leaders a proposal that power should be demitted on 15 August (this was, of course, a secret and the date should not be repeated). It meant that the leaders themselves would have to work night and day, but he felt that it was in their own interests not to delay."

In the press conference held on 4 June to explain the partition plan approved by the British Government and the Indian leaders the most startling piece of information provided at the conference was delivered casually, almost as if a passing thought, and was not even included in the excerpts telegraphed to London. 'How long will "His Excellency" stay as "His Excellency" and thereafter as Governor-General?' he was asked. 'That is a most embarrassing question,' he replied. 'I think the transfer could be about the 15th of August.'

In *Mountbatten and the Partition of India,* by Larry Collins & Dominique Lapierre, Mountbatten was asked – "Why did you go so fast in transferring power?" In view of what has been stated earlier Mountbatten lied – "Thus the date I chose came out of the blue. I chose it in reply to a question. I was determined to show I was master of the whole event. When they asked: had we set a date, I knew it had to be soon. I hadn't worked it out exactly then – I thought it had to be about August or September and I then went to the 15th of August. Why? Because it was the second anniversary of Japan's surrender. And I knew the thing was to have a date. And however much I consulted my staff, they would all give me different dates, later dates, and this ludicrously early date really put the cat among the canaries, frightened them all.

And they had to work. I'm quite certain that going slower would have meant that the breakdown would have occurred in Delhi. Now what would have happened? Under Section 93 I could have taken the whole of India under my own, personal direct rule. What a way to handle the country! And without that, the whole thing was breaking down. I am absolutely convinced and ready to stake everything on the fact that the time will come when it will be recognised that I couldn't have gone any slower. I only just held the position by going as fast as I did. The idea that my "reckless speed" caused all the bloodshed is absolute nonsense. I haven't the slightest doubt that any other course would have been a disaster. Read Lord Ismay. Ask any person who was out there with me. I just managed to hold out. That's one of things that's still not believed or understood.

Winston told me, "You killed two million Indians." First, the actual figures are not two million. Penderel Moon who is the editor of Wavel's papers gives in his book the estimate of 200,000. In fact the famine of 1943-44 killed two or three million who lacked proper British administration. And in fact, I let the Indians have five per cent of my military shipping to bring food to them. We saved many more lives by doing that than were lost in 1947.

The reason for speed was not to go and muck up Pakistan. It was because the thing was breaking up under my hands. The reason was that neither side would cooperate with each other. I could feel the damn thing simmering. It's like standing on the edge of a volcano and feeling the moment of explosion."

The reader can judge the startling absurdity of Mountbatten's statements for himself. Mountbatten dismisses the monumental cataclysm resulting from the hurried partition like chicken feed. The actual figure of casualty during partition from numerous sources is nearer 600,000. For Mountbatten a few hundred thousand killed here and there is of hardly any concern. Besides, the point he makes about the Bengal famine does not hold much water as it took place before his arrival and was certainly the responsibility of the British Government.

Mountbatten Ignores the Brewing Violence in the Punjab

The question whether the haste and hurry in bringing forward the date for partition of India was justified has been asked and answered by many writers since 600,000 lives were lost and 14 million people were involved in a painful and pitiful migration. Surely, this tragedy would rank as one of the worst in the entire history of the world. The only comparable event that comes to mind would be the Holocaust in Germany during World War-II. Could this catastrophe, measureless in its pain, have been avoided by fixing a later date which would have gained much needed time to prevent, or, at any rate to greatly mitigate, that disaster?

It has been suggested that in bringing forward the date to 15 August 1947 nobody could have foreseen the consequences. The fact that this assumption is totally erroneous is amply demonstrated by the numerous references available in the *Transfer of Power* documents. Evan Jenkins, the Governor of Punjab, gave clear and persistent warnings to Mountbatten about severe trouble that was fomenting in the Punjab.

On the 10 July 1947 Evan Jenkins wrote to Mountbatten giving an account of his interview with the militant Sikh leader Giani Kartar Singh. Some extracts - 'Proceeding, the Giani said that there must be an exchange of population on a large scale. Were the British ready to enforce this? He doubted if they were, and if no regard was paid to Sikh solidarity, a fight was inevitable. The British had said for years that they intended to protect the minorities, and what had happened now was a clear breach of faith by the British.

'I then reverted to the somewhat minatory remarks of the Giani about the attitude of the Sikhs should the new Governments be established on the basis of the "notional" boundary. I asked exactly what he meant by "other measures". The Giani replied that the Sikhs would be obliged to fight. I retorted that this would be very foolish and enquired how they expected to fight against trained troops. The Giani said in quite a matter of fact way that the Sikhs realised that they would be in a bad position and would have to fight on revolutionary lines — by murdering officials, cutting railway lines and telegraph lines, destroying canal headworks, and so on. I reiterated that this seemed to me a very foolish policy, to which the Giani retorted that if Britain were invaded, he had no doubt that my feelings would be much that same as his.

'I enquired when the fight would begin. The Giani said that protests would continue from now on. The Sikhs felt that it would be useless to wait for two or three years before taking violent action, and the execution of their plan would start with the departure of the British.'

Evan Jenkins wrote again on 13 July 1947 giving an elaborate report on the situation. By this time Jenkins had reconciled himself to the transfer of power by 15 August 1947. Jenkins now wished to get the boundary award at least one week before the date of transfer. As we shall see later this wish was not fulfilled with disastrous consequences.

We see once again a very detailed account of trouble brewing in the Punjab in the report of Evan Jenkins on 4 August 1947. It may be Summarised as follows:

There had been many criticisms of the Punjab Government's handling of the disturbances of 1947. During his visit to Lahore on 20th July Mountbatten had suggested that Jenkins should record them and add his comments.

The main criticisms were:-

i)   that while the British were able to crush without difficulty the disturbances of 1942, they failed to deal in the same way with the disturbances of 1947 (Congress – particularly Nehru and Patel).

ii)   that British officials had been callous and incompetent, and had taken the line that since the British were going, massacre, arson and looting were of no consequence (Congress – particularly Nehru and Patel).

iii)   that in the Punjab the worst districts had been those staffed by British officials – Indian officials had managed to maintain order (Congress – Nehru).

iv)   that Congress Governments had no difficulty in suppressing disturbances – the worst Province of all had been the Punjab, which was still "under British rule" (Congress – Nehru).

v)   that the fire services in the cities, particularly in Lahore and Amritsar, had been inefficient and useless (Congress)

vi)   that the Magistrates and Police had been both incompetent and partial, and that the Police had connived at and actually participated in murder, arson, and looting (Congress).

vii)   that Martial Law should have been declared at least in Lahore and possibly elsewhere (Congress).

Jenkins's reactions;

Attacks on the administration were not confined to the Congress Party the Muslim League were equally severe, though less precise except in their constant allegations of partiality against Jenkins.

There were two short answers to most of these criticisms.

In the first place, the critics had missed the significance of what was happening in the Punjab. Punjab was faced not with an ordinary exhibition of political or communal violence, but with a struggle between the communities for the power that the British were shortly to abandon. Normal standards could not be applied to this communal war of succession, which had subjected all sections of the population to unprecedented strains, had dissolved old loyalties and created new ones, and had produced many of the symptoms of a revolution.

Secondly, the critics were themselves participants in the events which they professed to deplore. During the disturbances Nehru, Patel, and Baldev Singh had visited various parts of the Punjab. They had done so nominally as Members of the Central Government, but in fact as communal leaders. To the best of Jenkins's belief not one of them made during these visits any contact of importance with any Muslim. Nehru was balanced and sensible; but Baldev Singh on at least two occasions went in for most violent communal publicity, and Patel's visit to Gurgaon was used to make it appear that Hindus in that district were the victims of Muslim aggression, whereas broadly the contrary was the case. Conversely when Liaquat Ali Khan or Ghazanfar Ali Khan visited the Punjab, they did so not to assist the administration, but to assist the Muslims. When a Hindu leader talked about "utter ruthlessness" or "martial law", he meant that he wanted as many Muslims as possible shot out of hand; Muslims were less fond of these terms, but all communities, Muslim, Hindu, and Sikh persisted in regarding themselves as blameless. Moreover, there was very little doubt that the disturbances had in some degree been organised and paid for by persons or bodies directly or indirectly under the control of the Muslim League, the Congress, and the Akali party. The evidence of this was to be found in the daily intelligence summaries, and in the solicitude with which prominent men – particularly among the Hindus – took up the cases of suspects belonging to their own community.

Criticisms which were based upon a genuine or studied misconception of the real situation, and which were made by people with an intense personal interest in the communal struggle could not be accepted at their face value. Jenkins continued;

Rioting had broken out in Lahore City on 4th March. The disturbances since that date had fallen into three main phrases:-

i)   *4th March to 20th March.* Rioting in Lahore, Amritsar, Multan, Rawalpindi, Jullundur and Sialkot Cities. Rural massacres of non- Muslims in Rawalpindi, Attock and Jhelum Districts of the Rawalpindi Division, and in Multan District, casualties very heavy, and much burning especially in Multan and Amritsar. Jenkins was able to report on 21st March that order had been restored everywhere.

ii)   *21st March to 9th May.* Minor incidents in many districts. Serious rioting and burning in Amritsar 11th – 13th April with some repercussions in Lahore. Trouble at Hodal, a small town in Gurgaon district, followed by the first outbreak along the Mewat in the same district.

iii) *10th May onwards.* The communal "war of succession". Incendiarism, stabbing, and bombing in Lahore and Amritsar. Serious incidents reported from various districts, particularly Gujranwala and Hoshiapur. Urban rioting almost unknown, and all activities in cities, including some organised raids, conducted on "cloak and dagger" basis. Village raiding begins, especially in Amritsar, Lahore, Ferozepore, Jullundur, and Hoshiarpur districts. Revival of disturbances in

Gurgaon with 140 villages burnt and very heavy casualties.

The first phase presented many of the features of normal communal disturbances of the past. The urban slaughter was without precedent (in Multan City about 130 non-Muslims were killed in three hours), and the wholesale burnings both urban and rural, and the rural massacres were new. But on the whole, the situation yielded to the usual treatment.

The second phase was used by the communities for preparations. It was relatively quiet, but there was much practicing with bombs, and ill-feeling never really died down in Lahore and Amritsar.

The third phase showed the real dimensions of the problem. The communities settled down to do the maximum amount of damage to one another while exposing the minimum expanse of surface to the troops and police. Mass terrorism of this kind offered no easy answer – troops and police could act, and sometimes acted decisively, against riotous mobs. They could do little against burning, stabbing and bombing by individuals. Nor could all the King's horses and all the King's men prevent – though they may be able to punish – conflict between communities interlocked in villages over wide areas of country. There were more reports by Jenkins giving a graphic picture of the break down of law and order in the Punjab. Surely these should have been enough to caution Mountbatten about the shape of forthcoming events.

Mountbatten Inactions Regarding Intelligence Reports

On 22 July 1947 the Partition Council met and decided to issue a joint declaration that all parties would respect the rights of the minorities. In retrospect we can see that not the slightest regard was given to this undertaking. The Partition Council meeting was chaired by Mountbatten and those present included Patel, Rajendra Prasad, Jinnah, Liaquat and Baldev Singh.

The deliberation of the Council may be Summarised as follows:

'Statement by the Partition Council. *Begins:* Now that the decision to set up two independent Dominions from the 15th August has been finally taken, the Members of the Partition Council, on behalf of the future Governments, declare that they are determined to establish peaceful conditions in which the processes of partition may be completed and the many urgent tasks of administration and economic reconstruction taken in hand.'

Both the Congress and the Muslim League had given assurances of fair and equitable treatment to the minorities after the transfer of power. The two future Governments re-affirmed these assurances. It was their intention to safeguard the legitimate interests of all citizens irrespective of religion, caste or sex. In the exercise of their normal civic rights all citizens would be regarded as equal and both the Governments would assure to all people within their territories the exercise of liberties such as freedom of speech, the right to form associations, the right to worship in their own way and the protection of their language and culture.

Both the Governments further undertook that there should be no discrimination against those who, before August 15th, may have been political opponents.

The guarantee of protection which both Governments gave to the citizens of their respective countries implied that in no circumstances would violence be tolerated in any form in either territory. The two Governments wished to emphasise that they were united in this determination.

To safeguard the peace in the Punjab during the period of change-over to the new conditions, both Governments had together agreed on the setting up a special military Command from the 1st August covering the civil districts of Sialkot, Gujranwala, Sheikhupura, Lyallpur, Montgomery, Lahore, Amritsar, Gurdaspur, Hoshiarpur, Jullundur, Ferozepore and Ludhiana. With their concurrence Major-General T.W. Rees was nominated as Military Commander for this purpose and Brigadier Digamber Singh (India) and Colonel Ayub Khan (Pakistan) were attached to Rees in an advisory capacity. After August 15th, Major-General Rees would control operationally the forces of both new States in these areas and would be responsible through the Supreme Commander and the Joint Defence Council to the two Governments.

The two Governments would not hesitate to set up a similar organisation in Bengal should they consider it necessary. Both Governments had pledged themselves to accept the awards of the Boundary Commissions, whatever these may be. The Boundary Commissions were already in session; if they were to discharge their duties satisfactorily, it was essential that they should not be hampered by public speeches or writings threatening boycott or direct action, or otherwise interfering with their work. Both Governments would take appropriate steps to secure this end; and, as soon as the awards were announced, both Governments would enforce them impartially and at once.

It is to be noted that very cleverly Mountbatten had taken undertaking from the leaders of India and Pakistan that they would accept the Boundary Commission Awards without question.

We now come to another episode of how Mountbatten was fully informed of the brewing trouble in the Punjab. In a meeting held on 5 August 1947 in which Mountbatten, Jinnah, Liaquat, Patel and

Captain Savage were present a full account was presented about the law and order situation in the Punjab. Captain Savage, who was Police Officer employed in the Punjab C.I.D. Control, said that he had been sent down by the Governor of the Punjab Evan Jenkins to make a personal report to the Viceroy. He explained that the C.I.D. Control coordinated investigation of disturbances cases, special interrogation, and intelligence from all sources.

Captain Savage related that one of the first instigators of disturbances to be arrested had been one Pritam Singh, an ex-member of the I.N.A. He had been roped in on 4th June, in possession of a wireless transmitter. This man was well known to the Punjab C.I.D. as he had been interrogated after arrest on his return to India some years previously from Chopra's Penang spy school. He had been one of the party to be landed in Southern India by submarine. Pritam Singh had made a long statement which involved Master Tara Singh in the production of bombs, and a Sikh plan to attack certain headworks. Captain Savage said that the next incident at which men had been arrested was an explosion in the Crown Talkies in Lahore. The main arrest in this incident was of Kuldip Singh, who had joined the R.S.S.S. in February 1947. He was a bomb maker and incendiarist and had done a lot of successful work. He was probably involved in six bomb-throwing cases and had specialised in train wrecking. He had been arrested on 30th July.

The next man to be arrested as a result of the statement made by Kuldip Singh and his friends of the Crown Talkies and Lyallpur derailing case was Goupal Rai Khosla, a clerk in the Secretariat at Lahore. This man had made a statement which involved Master Tara Singh very deeply. He had seen Tara Singh towards the end of July and had asked for Rs 700 outstanding for the purchase of rifles and for grenades already promised by Tara Singh. He had left one Ram Lal behind with Tara Singh who had got on very intimate terms with him. Ram Lal gave Goupal a note to take to Tara Singh. This contained information concerning trains and was somewhat cryptic. He had asked Tara Singh when he saw him what it was all about, and the reply had been that it referred to the Pakistan special trains carrying staff between Delhi and Karachi. Arrangements had been made to keep Tara Singh informed by wireless of the schedules of the trains.

Captain Savage went on to say that Master Tara Singh had stated that four or five young Sikhs were planning to blow up the Pakistan Special with remote control firing apparatus and after wrecking the Special, set it on fire, and shoot the occupants. Tara Singh had also said that Mr. Jinnah should be killed during the ceremonies at Karachi on 15 August.

Captain Savage said that independent and highly reliable sources confirmed Tara Singh's frame of mind as being completely one-track on the subject of revenge on Muslims. Tara Singh was collecting arms through Sikh Army officers and dumping them in States. The Raja of Faridkot had actually given help with transport and other moral and possibly material aid also. Tara Singh was reported to believe that the India and Pakistan Governments were sure to crash immediately.

George Abell gave his opinion that Master Tara Singh should most certainly be arrested.

Captain Savage said that such a step would certainly create trouble in the Central Punjab.

Patel said that he placed no reliance on statements made by arrested people, particularly ex-members of the I.N.A.

Captain Savage said that so far as one could be certain in these particular cases, those interrogated had been telling the truth. However, it was very difficult to produce concrete evidence against Tara Singh; but he could be detained under Section 3 of the Punjab Safety Act.

Liaquat stated that he had given directions for all the Pakistan special trains to take every possible precaution. A report had come through that a crowd had been collecting at one station and that there was danger of attack on a particular train. He had insisted that the train should go all the same but had strengthened its military escort and arranged for the Inspector General of Police to be informed. In his opinion, the Sikhs were likely to rise in any case on the announcement of the Boundary Commission's award.

Captain Savage gave his opinion that the Sikh Leaders had lost control of their people. However, Giani Kartar Singh was more hopeful that they would get through without major trouble.

Mountbatten, after further considering the matter, decided to recommend to the Governor of the Punjab that Master Tara Singh and the other ringleaders of this movement should be arrested at about the time of the Boundary Commission's award. He asked George Abell to draft a letter accordingly to Sir Evan Jenkins. George Abell wrote the following letter to the Governor of Punjab.

'4 August 1947 My Dear [Jenkins],

I heard Savage's story at breakfast and then passed it on to H.E. He was having a Partition Council this morning and decided at the end to keep back Jinnah, Liaquat and Patel and get Savage to tell them the story.

Savage told the story very well and it made a considerable impression. After some discussion it was agreed that it would be necessary to arrest Tara Singh and the more hot headed of the Sikhs. The only question was when this should be done. H.E. suggested that probably it would be best to do it at the same time as the announcement of the Boundary Commission's award. He pointed out that if it was done beforehand the trouble would probably spread and the announcement of an unfavourable award would make conditions even worse on 15 August than they will be if these men are arrested on 12th.

It was agreed that there would have to be a common policy in the matter and

H.E. said he would ask you to discuss the matter with Sir Chandulal Trivedi (Governor designates of East Punjab) and in due course with the premier East Punjab and the Premier (as soon as he is chosen) of the West Punjab.

It was recognised that you might wish for a little more time to consider the matter and possibly after your discussions to make other recommendations, but it was definitely the view of the meeting that

  a) the arrests should be made, and

  b) that they should not be made for a week or so. Yours sincerely,

  G.E.B. Abell'

In actual fact as we shall see no action whatsoever was taken with disastrous consequences as Mountbatten deliberately delayed the announcement of the Boundary Commission Awards.

Mountbatten deliberately delays announcement of Boundary Awards

We have already seen the serious communal disturbances that were prevailing all over Punjab from March 1947 onward. Evan Jenkins, Governor of the Punjab had repeatedly warned Mountbatten about the lurking danger of an impending disaster if proper precautions were not taken prior to partition. In fact, there was absolutely no case for rushing the transfer of power when there were clear indications that massacres would follow if prior arrangement for security and safety were not made. Since Jenkins was not able to influence Mountbatten in postponing the date of transfer of power he repeatedly urged that the Boundary Award should be in his hands at least a week before 15 August 1947 so that he could try to ensure that the transfer of power was orderly.

It appears from a reading of the *Transfer of Power* documents that at first Mountbatten had agreed on an early publication and announcement of the Boundary Award.

On 22 July 1947, writing to Radcliffe, Mountbatten said that he had a discussion at Lahore with the Punjab Partition Committee. Referring to the assurance he had given to that Committee that he would write to Radcliffe of the urgency of the earliest possible date for the Punjab Boundary Award, Mountbatten continued:

". . . It was emphasised (in the Punjab Partition Committee) that the risk of disorder would be greatly increased if the award had to be announced at the very last moment before the 15th August.

"2. I know that you fully appreciate this, but I promised that I would mention it again to you, and say that we should all be grateful for every extra day earlier that you could manage to get the award announced. I wonder if there is any chance of getting it out by the 10th?"

Replying the next day, Radcliffe said:

"I will certainly bear in mind that importance of the earliest possible date for the award . . . I do not think that I could manage the 10th. But I think that I can promise the 12th, and I will do the earlier day if I possibly can."

On 6 August 1947, Mountbatten wrote to Evan Jenkins, *inter alia*,

"I have not forgotten your request that you should be given advance warning of the nature of the Boundary Commission's award and I will try to secure this."

On 8 August 1947 Abell wrote to Abbott, Secretary to the Governor of the Punjab:

"I enclose a map showing roughly the boundary which Sir Cyril Radcliffe promised to demarcate in his award, and a note by Christopher Beaumont describing it. There will not be any great changes from this boundary, but it will have to be accurately defined with reference to village and zail boundaries in Lahore district.

"The award itself is expected within the next 48 hours, and I will let you know later about the probable time of announcement. Perhaps you would ring me up if H.E. the Governor has any views on this point?"

"No copy of this map, or of the note by Mr. Beaumont describing it, is on the file. In April 1948, in a telegram to Lord Ismay discussing points of controversy which had arisen over the Punjab Boundary Award, Lord Mountbatten made the following comment about Sir G. Abell's letter to Mr. Abbott: 'The point that arises here was that Abell sent the letter concerned without my knowledge. It may be hard to convince people that was so. It will look to have been an odd procedure.'

"Sir E. Jenkins, in a letter dated April 1948 to Lord Mountbatten in which he too discussed points of controversy which had arisen over the Punjab Award, described the two documents in question as follows: "The enclosures were a schedule (I think typed) and a section of a printed map with a line drawn thereon, together showing a Boundary which included in Pakistan a sharp salient in the Ferozepore District. This salient enclosed the whole of the Ferozepore and Zira Tahsils.' Jenkins also stated that: 'About the 10th or 11th August, when we were still expecting the award on 13th August, at latest, I received a secraphone message from Viceroy's House containing the words "Eliminate Salient" … The change caused some surprise, not because the Ferozepore salient had been regarded as inevitable or even probable, but because it seemed odd that any advance information had been given by the Commission if the award was not substantially complete'."

In his reply dated 9 August 1947, Abbott wrote:

"The Governor is taking law and order action on the preliminary information given. He trusts final version will be very precise and will be related as far as possible to existing administrative units and borders. To enable us to arrange publicity and administrative arrangements he would like document in official form 24 hours before it is released, e.g. if it could be flown U (sic) 10th evening, it could be released 11th evening in New Delhi."

The above correspondence shows a consensus of opinion between Evan Jenkins, the Punjab Partition Committee and Mountbatten that every day's delay in publication of the Punjab Award would greatly increase the risk of disorder in Punjab. With this consensus of opinion Radcliffe concurred, when he wrote: "I will certainly bear in mind the importance of the earliest possible date for the (Punjab) Award". And he added that he would try to have the Award ready on the 10th, if he could possibly do so. Radcliffe was better than his word, and the Punjab Award was ready on 9 August.

Departing from chronology, the following Note dated 11 August 1947 by Maj- Gen. D.C. Hawthorne, stated, *inter-alia*, (Gen. Hawthorne was Deputy Chief of General Staff)

"… The refugee problem mainly from East Punjab to West Punjab is becoming increasingly difficult and more and more of the population is on the move; naturally the Civil (sic) (authorities?) are demanding escorts from the Punjab Boundary Force to protect these defenceless refugees as they move and the Commander, Punjab Boarder Force is doing what he can."

Again, on 13 August 1947, Evan Jenkins wrote to Mountbatten, stating, *inter alia*,

"The Hindus are thoroughly terrified, and the Muslim movement from the East is balanced by similar movement of Hindus from the West. We seem to have for the moment scotched the Hindu-Sikh bombing conspiracy and the Hindus are more concerned to get out of Lahore safely than with anything else."

On 13 August 1947 a telephone message to the Viceroy's office from Gen. Messervy and Gen.

Rees stated, *inter alia*, ". . . Postponement of Boundary Commission's Award causing uncertainly." Finally, on 15 August 1947, in a Note prepared for the Joint Defence Council by the Commander-in-Chief Field Marshal Sir Claude Aunchinleck, on the situation in the Punjab Border Force area, he recorded his visit to Lahore on 14 August 1947 and observed:

"5. Border Commission: The delay in announcing the award of the Border Commission is having a most disturbing and harmful effect. It is realised of course that the announcement may add fresh fuel to the fire, but lacking the announcement, the wildest rumours are current, and are being spread by mischief makers of whom there is no lack."

On 14 August 1947, Mountbatten dispatched a telegram to Lord Listowell, the Secretary of State for India at 10.15 p.m., which stated, *inter alia*,

"2. I personally have scrupulously avoided all connection with Boundary Commissions, including interpretation of their terms of reference and putting before them the various points of view forwarded to me. *** 6. Radcliffe sent in the Bengal award on 12th August. This contained the allocation of Chittagong Hill Tracts to Pakistan and I was warned that there would be serious reactions amongst Congress leaders at this. *** 8. I have taken following actions:- (a) I have decided not to publish the awards myself; ..."

Mountbatten sent his "Personal Report No. 17" dated 16 August 1947 to Listowell, but it is too long to set out here. However, paragraphs 11, 12 and 13 are so important that they are set out below:

"11. It was on Tuesday, 12th August, that I was finally informed by Radcliffe that his awards would be ready by noon the following day, just too late for me to see before leaving for Karachi. For some time past, I and my staff had been considering the question of when and how this awards should be published. From the purely administrative point of view, there were considerable advantages in immediately publication so that the new boundaries could take effect from 15th August, and the officials of the right Dominion could be in their places to look after the districts which had been allotted to their side before that date. However, it had been obvious all along that the later we postponed publication, the less would the inevitable odium react upon the British.

"12. The matter came to a head at the Meeting which I held with members of my staff on the evening of the 12th. The Bengal award had by then been sent in but I had deliberately refrained from reading it. I was told however that it allotted the Chittagong Hill Tracts to Pakistan. My Reforms Commissioner,

V.P. Menon, was present at the meeting and was able to warn me of the disastrous effects that this was likely to have on the Congress leaders. He went so far as to say that Nehru and Patel were both certain to blow up, since they had only recently assured a delegation from the Chittagong Hill Tracts that there was no question of their being allotted to Pakistan. (V.P. Menon admitted that they had no authority for making such a statement).

"13. V.P. Menon went on to say that if the details of the award were given to them before the 15th he thought they might well refuse to attend the meeting of the Constituent Assembly which I was to address. If given to them later in the day he thought they would refuse to come to the State banquet and the evening party. In any case he said that unless the situation were handled with the utmost care, the Congress would blow up. I have never known V.P. Menon to mislead me, and I decided that somehow we must prevent the leaders from knowing the details of the award until after the 15th August; all our work and the hope of good Indo-British relations on the day of the transfer of power would risk being destroyed if we could not do this."

Early Partition was Senseless

In the nine months between August 1947 and the spring of the following year, between fourteen and sixteen million Hindus, Sikhs and Muslims were forced to leave their homes and flee to safety from blood-crazed mobs. In that same period over 600,000 of them were killed. But no, not just killed. If they were children, they were picked up by the feet and their heads smashed against the wall. If they were female children, they were raped. If they were girls, they were raped and then their breasts were chopped off. And if they were pregnant, they were disemboweled.

Partition displaced fifteen million people and killed more than a million (newyorker.com)

It was a period in India's history when India's women in Punjab and the United Provinces and Bihar were reminded of a useful hint handed down through harems and women's quarters from the time of the Moghuls – that the way to avoid pregnancy as a result of being raped is to struggle, always to struggle.

It was a time when trains were arriving in Lahore station packed with passengers, all of them dead, with messages scribbled on the sides of the carriages reading: 'A present from India'. So, of course, the Muslims sent back trainloads of butchered Sikhs and Hindus with the message: 'A present from Pakistan.' In a land, which, under Gandhi, had adopted as a national religion the cult of ahimsa and non-violence there took place murder, looting burning and raping such as the world has not seen since the days of Jenghis Khan. 'Freedom must not stink!' cried an Indian journalist in a famous pamphlet issued at the time. But all India stank – with the stench of countless thousands of dead bodies, with the stench of evil deeds, with the stench of fires.

India in 1947 was a bumper year for vultures. They had no need to look for rotting flesh for it was all around them, animal and human. One convoy of Sikhs and Hindus from West Punjab was 74 miles long, and the raiders who attacked it constantly en route did not need to watch for it: they could smell its coming, for it was riddled with cholera and other foul diseases. And such was its mood that, upon sighting a long Muslim convoy of refugees coming the other way, the able-bodied members of the Indian convoy set off to do some killing of their own.

If the Sikhs were sullen and vicious before independence, they became mad with rage after the announcement of the Boundary Awards on 17 August. It was worse than they had feared. Their lands, their canals, their homes in the rich and fertile West would all be within the boundaries of the hated Pakistan. They reacted in a monstrous reflex action, an ejaculation of berserk fury in which they cut down every Muslim in sight and vowed to kill them but not too quickly. Sikh leaders and Sikh princes joined in exhorting their unhappy followers to ever more extravagant excesses.

As seen earlier both sides had signed, on 20 July, at Mountbatten's behest, a declaration that they would respect the rights of minorities. But Mountbatten was right in suspecting that they did not know what they were signing. The Sikh policy was to exterminate the Muslims in their midst. The Muslims, with their eyes on the rich Sikh farmlands, were content to drive the Sikhs out and only massacre those who insisted on remaining. It is sad to have to admit that in their deliberate disobedience of their signed pledge they were encouraged by the British Governor of West Punjab, Sir Francis Mudie, who wrote to Mr. Jinnah on 5 September 1947:

'I am telling everyone that I don't care how the Sikhs get across the border; the great thing is to get rid of them as soon as possible.'

600,000 dead. 14,000,000 driven from their homes. 100,000 young girls kidnapped by both sides, forcibly converted or sold on the auction block.

In the light of what was achieved in giving India its freedom, the sacrifice was not so much, after all.

That, at least, is what supporters of Mountbatten would say. They make the point that while Mountbatten was Supreme Commander in South East Asia during the War he tried, while continuing to fight the Japanese, to do something for the victims of the great Bengal Famine. He assigned ten per cent of the holds of these ships, bringing supplies to the Fourteenth Army, to bring food for the Bengalis. Some members of the Government at home were furious when they heard about it.

'If Mountbatten can afford to assign ten per cent of his space to food for the natives,' they said, 'he can afford to do with less ships,' and they sent out an order to cut the 14th Army's convoys by ten per cent. In the event, even though Mountbatten got the cut restored, between three and four million people died in Bengal.

'If the Government could contemplate that number of dead with complacency,' say Mountbatten's advocates, 'why should they grumble about 600,000 dead to secure the establishment of a free and friendly India?'

No reasonable man will deny that Britain's decision to give India its freedom was a good one – taken not only because the Indian people could not be much longer kept under British control, but because the British people were no longer willing to keep them under their control. The decision of Prime Minister Clement Attlee to divest Britain of all control over India by June 1948 was a genuine expression of the British people's will even though some Tories, including Churchill, warned that it was too precipitate. There is no evidence that the Indians themselves – Hindus, Sikhs or Muslims – disbelieved Attlee's declaration. They accepted it was a genuine date limit for freedom.

Then why, after Mountbatten's arrival, did it have to be so drastically, shortened to a date ten months earlier?

It had to be, Mountbatten will say, because the situation was becoming beyond control. Conditions almost similar to war brewing. To leave the situation any longer as it was would have produced bloodshed and riot on a large scale.

The advisers of the Labour Government in Britain believed at the time, moreover, that if freedom did not come very quickly indeed, the Congress Party would break up and the Communists would take their place. With the subsequent knowledge we possessed today we know this to be a complete travesty of the facts. The stability and solidity of the Congress Party was never in danger. The Communists were never within a continent's distance of attaining power.

Which brings us to the point which seems to be important. 600,000 Indians died for Independence and 14,000,000 lost their homes. Men became brutes.

Then air over the Indo-Pakistan frontiers was soured for generations. Unnecessarily.

It need not have happened. It would not have happened had independence not been rushed through at such a desperate rate. Never has such a grave moment in the lives of 350,000,000 people been decided with such efficiency, such skill and charm, and without any real consideration of its profound consequences.

This is not to deny the magnitude of Mountbatten's achievement. As Noel Coward said: 'When the job's hopeless, they call in Dicke.' The Labour Government picked him for the job because they were, in the American phrase, stuck. He was sent into a fast job of salesmanship and painless surgery. It would be wrong to blame him for doing a distasteful job as fast as possible – especially as he believed that speed would save lives.

But when one considers how much goodwill there was behind Britain's wish to give India her freedom, what a stinking bog of unpreparedness, blunders, and appalling lack of planning separated the wish from the achievement.

Mistake after mistake

Wavell, whose plan would at least have kept India intact and unpartitioned, dismissed out of hand.

Jinnah's claim for separate rights for the Muslims accepted – but no attempt made to prepare for the consequences. No consideration of where Pakistan would be. No plans for dividing up the Army.

Agreement on partition secured – by a shuffling of the cards at Simla. But no realisation of the significance of the decision.

If the Labour Government was prepared to give united India its freedom by June 1948, how was it possible to promise a divided India freedom ten months earlier? The new date was admittedly an announcement with which to impress a Press conference – at which Mountbatten made it – but did not really expect it to create anything but chaos and the uttermost confusion – even if he could not have envisaged the killing and suffering which would stem from it?

Mistake after mistake, indeed.

Partition of India announced in May 1947, and no plans for dividing its Army until June, with only six weeks to go to the deadline.

Partition announced in May, but the Commission to decided the boundaries along which the two new States would be divided, not appointed until the end of June. Partition in May, and Independence in August, but a people desperate to know deliberately kept in ignorance of which country they belonged to until two days after Independence.

Works Cited

1. https://arynews.tv/lord-mountbatten-last-british-viceroy/

2. https://brownhistory.substack.com/p/nehru-and-edwina-an-unconventional

3. https://freepresskashmir.news/2022/08/18/tughlaqi-farmaan-protest-over-voting-rights-to-non-locals-in-jammu-order-set-on-fire/

4. https://herald.dawn.com/news/1153825

5. https://indianhistorycollective.com/vp-menon-and-the-birth-of-independent-india/

6. https://prepp.in/news/e-492-lord-mountbatten-1947-1948-viceroy-of-india-modern-india-history-notes

7. https://qz.com/india/1054815/impatient-to-return-to-the-uk-a-british-royal-rushed-through-partition-and-created-a-bloodbath

8. https://starofmysore.com/krishna-menon-alive-and-kicking/

9. https://thebetterindia.com/198487/v-p-menon-sardar-patel-history-jammu-kashmir-accession-india-unification/

10. https://www.dailyo.in/news/why-lord-mountbatten-called-jinnah-a-psychopathic-case-but-agreed-to-his-demand-for-pakistan-41080

11. https://www.jammukashmirnow.com/Encyc/2019/7/25/July-25-1947-When-Mountbatten-addressed-The-Chamber-of-Princes-to-choose-either-of-the-2-dominions-India-or-Pakistan-there-was-NO-THIRD-OPTION.html

12. https://www.neversuchinnocence.com/louis-mountbatten-partition-of-british-india

13. https://www.newyorker.com/magazine/2015/06/29/the-great-divide-books-dalrymple

14. https://www.opindia.com/2021/06/lord-mountbatten-plan-june-3-india-partition/

15. https://www.historiamag.com/partition-politics-prime-ministers-passion/

16. https://english.mathrubhumi.com/news/india/controversy-behind-nehru-letter-to-edwina-mountbatten-1.10169512

17. https://specialcollectionsuniversityofsouthampton.wordpress.com/tag/prince-louis-of-battenberg/

18. https://www.townandcountrymag.com/society/money-and-power/a36542121/lord-lady-mountbatten-biography-andrew-lownie-expert/

19. https://specialcollectionsuniversityofsouthampton.wordpress.com/2016/01/20/the-accession-of-king-edward-viii/

20. https://specialcollectionsuniversityofsouthampton.wordpress.com/tag/lord-louis-mountbatten

21. https://www.express.co.uk/news/royal/1761124/lord-mountbatten-king-charles-relationship-spt

22. https://www.andmeetings.com/blog/post/meetings-that-made-history-when-gandhi-met-lord-mountbatten

23. https://www.britannica.com/biography/Clement-Attlee

24. https://scroll.in/article/884176/patel-wanted-hyderabad-for-india-not-kashmir-but-junagadh-was-the-wild-card-that-changed-the-game

25. https://www.indianarrative.com/opinion-news/did-lord-mountbatten-have-blood-on-its-hands-by-preponing-partition-150234.html

26. https://www.bbc.com/news/world-asia-india-62422428

27. https://openthemagazine.com/lounge/books/vk-krishna-menon-the-man-behind-the-mystique/

28. https://www.dawn.com/news/1524311

29. https://www.firstpost.com/india/were-gandhi-and-jinnah-business-partners-in-south-africa-1147287.html

30. https://dailytimes.com.pk/463038/mr-jinnah-and-his-secret-battle-against-tuberculosis/

31. https://www.flickr.com/photos/pimu/30937602895/in/photostream/

32. https://indianhistorycollective.com/great-debates-nehru-vs-jinnah-1938/

33. https://www.nationalarchives.gov.uk/education/resources/indian-independence/map-possible-partition/

34. https://www.history.com/articles/mahatma-gandhi

35. https://picryl.com/media/gandhi-with-lord-and-lady-mountbatten-1947-6cfc77

36. https://www.governancenow.com/news/regular-story/when-gandhi-met-nehru-the-first-time-

37. https://www.ccw.ox.ac.uk/events/2025/ismay

38. https://winstonchurchill.hillsdale.edu/kiszely-hastings-ismay/

39. https://www.livemint.com/mint-lounge/ideas/nehru-sardar-patel-and-the-man-in-the-middle-111641410063815.html

40. https://www.npg.org.uk/collections/search/portrait/mw305790/Muhammad-Ali-Jinnah-Baldev-Singh-Frederick-William-Pethick-Lawrence-1st-Baron-Pethick-Lawrence-Jawaharlal-Nehru-Vengalil-Krishnan-Krishna-Menon

41. https://www.cosmopolitan.com/uk/reports/a34650302/lord-mountbatten-open-marriage/

42. https://people.com/queen-elizabeth-prince-philip-wedding-details-6740037

43. https://www.tatler.com/article/lord-mountbatten-relationship-prince-charles-death

44. https://www.wikitree.com/wiki/Colville-340#Photos

45. https://newsroom.ap.org/editorial-photos-videos/detail?itemid=0fbd8f0a7e2244d4b293d992e37517e8

46. https://theindosphere.com/history/british-shimla-summer-capital-india-1864/

47. https://medium.com/globetrotters/an-astonishing-personal-discovery-at-the-viceroy-lodge-in-shimla-india-9464475f6d09

48. https://www.bbc.com/news/world-south-asia-62467438

49. https://www.britannica.com/place/Pakistan

50. https://www.newindianexpress.com/magazine/voices/2018/May/13/one-mans-jinnah-is-another-mans-nehru-1813003.html

51. https://www.dawn.com/news/1362909

52. https://homegrown.co.in/homegrown-explore/cyril-radcliffes-story-the-man-who-drew-the-border-between-india-and-pakistan

53. https://1947punjab.com/

54. https://www.thedailystar.net/opinion/focus/news/partition-1947-partition-or-unity-bengal-1947-3095176

55. https://defence.pk/threads/partition-of-punjab.618061/

56. https://www.bbc.com/news/world-asia-india-66018688

57. https://www.theweek.in/news/india/2019/01/14/swamy-nehru-edwina-heritage.html